# Lovesick

*Lovesick* brings together an international collection of plays, from Britain, the US, Germany, France and Russia, depicting types of "homosexual" or same-sex love.

Most of these six *fin-de-siècle* plays are either previously unpublished in English or at all. Each comes enhanced with an editorial introduction and contextual documentation, including contemporary reviews, case histories and illustrations. The plays included are:

- *The Blackmailers*, a society comedy, by Oscar Wilde's associates John Gray and André Raffalovich
- *At Saint Judas's*, a symbolist one-act play of unrequited love, by Henry Blake Fuller
- *"Mistakes"*, a problem drama about social persecution, by Herbert Hirschberg
- *The Dangerous Precaution*, a poetic fable of cross-dressing, by Mikhail Kuzmin
- *The Gentleman of the Chrysanthemums*, a comedy of manners about the homosexual as celebrity, by Armory
- *Ania and Esther*, a lyrical drama of troubled adolescence, by Klaus Mann

The volume includes a substantial introduction by Laurence Senelick, providing a valuable historical overview of the ancestry of gay theatre and queer performance.

Making available a legacy of homosexual dramas of the past, *Lovesick* is a must-have volume for researchers and students of theatre history and lesbian and gay studies. It will also be of compelling interest to those within comparative literature, cultural studies, and sexology, as well as actors, directors and theatre-lovers.

**Laurence Senelick** is Fletcher Professor of Drama at Tufts University, and a member of the advisory board of the *Journal of the History of Sexuality*. His publications include *Gender in Performance* (1992)

Inquiries regarding performance, professional or amateur, should be addressed to:

Laurence Senelick
Department of Drama
Tufts University
Medford
MA 02155
USA

# Lovesick

*Modernist plays of same-sex love 1894–1925*

*Laurence Senelick*

London and New York

First published 1999 by Routledge
11 New Fetter Lane, London EC4P 4EE

Simultaneously published in the USA and Canada
by Routledge
29 West 35th Street, New York, NY 10001

Typeset in Veljovic by Keystroke, Jacaranda Lodge, Wolverhampton
Printed and bound in Great Britain by TJ International Ltd., Padstow, Cornwall

*British Library Cataloguing in Publication Data*
A catalogue record for this book is available from the British Library

*Library of Congress Cataloguing in Publication Data*
Lovesick : modernist plays of same-sex love, 1894–1925 / [compiled by]
    Laurence Senelick.
        p.   cm..
    Includes bibliographical references and index.
    ISBN 0-415-18556-4 (alk.  paper). — ISBN 0-415-18557-2 (alk. paper)
    1.  European drama—20th century—Translations into English.
    2.  American drama—20th century.   3.  Homosexuality—Drama.
    I. Senelick, Laurence.
    PN6112.L595     1998
    808.82'9353—dc21                              98-27240
                                                    CIP


ISBN 0–415–18556–4 (hbk)
ISBN 0–415–18557–2 (pbk)

This collection is dedicated to Giles Havergal, Robert David Macdonald and Philip Prowse, whose long and brilliant management of the Glasgow Citizens Theatre has been an inexhaustible inspiration.

# Contents

# List of plates

# Preface

This anthology has been germinating for a long time. For many years, I collected fugitive references to homosexuality in drama and the theatre, with the intention of some day working them into an extended study. It seemed as if most writing on the subject continually trotted out the same tired examples, repeating the same formulas, referring to a handful of much-anthologized plays. The period between Vanbrugh's *The Relapse* and Coward's *The Vortex* was *terra incognita* and writers seldom ventured beyond the safe confines of the English language.

Some of my research appeared in the entries I wrote for Wayne Dynes' *Encyclopedia of Homosexuality*, some was channelled into articles which appeared in periodicals as diverse as *The Journal of the History of Sexuality* and *Russian Review*. In the course of my research, I found that a better informed discussion was prevented by the inaccessibility of texts. The homosexual dramatic past had not so much been suppressed as rendered unavailable. I therefore set about collecting as many of these obscure and neglected scripts as I could.

In 1995 the organizers of the Queer Theatre Conference sponsored by the City University of New York suggested that I provide a staged recital of excerpts from these and other plays to explore the richness of the gay theatrical past. That garner was eclectic, ranging from Aristophanes and Kabuki to Restoration pornography and Yiddish theatre. The experience was exhilarating, for the audience's attentive enthusiasm showed just what a thirst there was for more evidence of a "queer" presence throughout cultural history. The importance of making more of these plays available for study and performance was borne in upon me.

This particular collection concentrates on the period from the mid-1890s to the mid-1920s when, it can be argued, a distinctive vision of the "homosexual" was promulgated in the public consciousness. Molds were cast from which later images of the sexual deviant would be produced. Therefore, in introducing these plays to a modern reader, I have provided a number of documents which either suggest a certain context for a particular drama, or describe the circumstances of the first performance.

Over the years a wide array of individuals has contributed to my knowledge and understanding, so thanks must be broadcast far and wide. In this case, I want particularly to thank Alisa Solomon and Framji Minwalla, who organized the Queer Theatre Conference, and the participants who acted in the staged readings. In the days before there was a Net to surf, Frau Ghesine Bottomley and her staff at the Bibliothek of the Wissenschaftskolleg zu Berlin found me all sorts of works that I had feared were *introuvable*. The staff of the Manuscript Division of the British Library was truly efficient in providing me with a photostatic copy of *The Blackmailers*, and the Directors of the Library have graciously allowed me to publish it. As usual, I am indebted to the holdings of the Harvard College Libraries, as wide as they are deep, and particularly to the staffs of the Harvard Theatre Collection and the Harvard Law Library.

Paul B. Franklin dug into the Fonds Rondel at the Bibliothèque de l'Arsenal to provide me with contemporary reviews of *Le Monsieur aux chrysanthèmes*. Dagmar and Roy Kift helped me in translating pre-World War I Berlin slang. James Nickoloff was a valuable preceptor about the psalms in Latin, Peter Reid aided with the Greek. Neil Bartlett's book *Who Was That Man?* provided me with more information about *The Blackmailers* than I had previously managed to winkle out; in his letters he shared his opinions about the play. Alan

Sinfield wrote a supportive evaluation of the proposal for this anthology which smoothed its way considerably. My graduate assistants past and present, including Denise Cole, Thomas Connolly, Mark Cosdon, Randy Kapelke and Jennifer Stiles, were very ingenious in tracking down leads and turning up obscure items. Michael McDowell regularly extricated me from altercations with my computer. At Routledge, Talia Rodgers warmly embraced the project from the outset; she and her assistants Sophie Powell and Jason Arthur have sped it along with remarkable dispatch.

# General Introduction

Dirty plays are always written by women or by effeminate men and always have been. There is, of course, a pathological reason for this, but the fact remains that the normal and healthy male is not especially interested in the eavesdropping of the servant's hall, and, although he may offend by bluntness and lack of taste, he is seldom downright nasty.

(Owen Davis, American playwright)[1]

## The enemy within

Max Nordau called it "degeneracy" (*Entartung*) at the turn of the last century. "Sexual anarchy" is how Elaine Showalter labels it at the turn of ours. John Fout declares that "the period beginning around 1890 is a 'new,' historically specific stage in the history of sexuality (concurrent with trends across the industrialized west)."[2] Millennial anxiety at that time was often manifested as a personality crisis, a psychic malaise affecting what would once have been called "the passions" or the "bump of amativeness." Its ganglia of complexes became known as Sex, a word hitherto used only as a synonym for gender. Controversies over divorce reform, disease prevention, female prostitution, and the regulation of public and private behavior were aired not only in scientific works but in popular journalism. Jurisprudence was teamed with forensics, clinical practice, and eugenics in classifying newly discovered or identified variations and anomalies in human behaviour. An ancillary criminological discipline, anthropometry, even claimed to be able to measure physically the quantum of vice or perversion in an individual.

The taxonomy of sexual deviance at the *fin-de-siècle* might bear the motto "Know Your Enemy," since these new types were viewed as a threat to society, disturbing fissures

symptomatic of an imminent crackup. Two of the most extreme specimens subjected to the microscope were the "hysterical woman," defined by Charcot's studies at the Salpêtrière hospital in Paris, and the male "homosexual" or "urning" (both neologisms) classified by alienists and lawyers. They differed from more familiar social misfits such as alcoholics and morphine addicts in that their deviancy was not necessarily defined by actions, environmentally or hereditarily determined, but by what was held to be their essential nature. Hysterical women and their counterparts, effeminated men, were thought to be driven by uninhibited desire, the product of biologically grounded flaws in their moral character that led them to prostitution, debauchery and other anti-social activities. Since their abnormality was congenital, they might be identified by any number of behavioural traits and outward manifestations, even when they were not engaged in specifically hysterical or homosexual activity.

Such pseudo-biological analyses of social behavior found a receptive audience among the middle-class, many of whom were prudish and apprehensive about the discordant trends of modern urban society, and its growing demands for women's rights and sexual tolerance. If the mannish woman and the womanish man could be explained scientifically as teratological phenomena, freaks of nature, as readily identifiable in their marginality as Siamese twins or dog-faced boys, they could easily be marginalized. In George Mosse's succinct phrase, "The concept of homosexuality had become absolute, the antithesis of respectability."[3]

Just as "degeneracy" was sounded as a leitmotif in the social sciences, it turned up as both form and content in the Arts. Critics who shared Nordau's censoriousness bemoaned the "degenerescence" of literature,

1

observable in the disintegration of form and the taste for minor modes and short formats, but more especially in the choice of "decadent" subject matter. Literature seized on the concerns of science, but in a subservient way. Owing to the slow rate of cultural seepage, art of any given period tends to recapitulate the prevailing ideologies, and so, as Jean-Paul Aron has wryly noted, it was "at the very moment when psychopathology is underlining the amphibology of the word *perverse*, referring concurrently to perversion, that is, to a morbid process, and to perversity, that is, to turpitude, that writers lift the veil from homosexuality."[4] Literature ratified, perpetrated and coarsened the clinical and legal models with which it had been supplied, transmitting to its public the negative images it inherited from medicine and jurisprudence.

## Keeping degenerates off-stage

*Fin-de-siècle* drama was even slower than the other arts in featuring the newly defined types of hysterical woman and homosexual man. This is all the more curious since the drama of ideas and the *pièce à thèse* or problem play seem ready-made means of publicizing the on-going debates of political and scientific circles. Moreover, as Simon Williams points out, "the plays of the Naturalist and Symbolist schools, which compose the 'Modernist' wave of the European theater, established the stage as a platform upon which the fallacies of conventional morality could be exposed."[5] However, there were built-in reasons why these schools were slow to take up the challenge of portraying the sexual degenerate.

Naturalistic drama, following Émile Zola's recipe, proclaimed an exemplary and reformative agenda; therefore, individual case studies of the neurasthenic would have to be examined within a medico-legal context or, at least, against the background of the criminal code. The difficulty is that naturalism's emphasis on hereditary or environmental factors made its heroes unique rather than representative. Zola's Thérèse Raquin or Gerhart Hauptmann's Rose Bernd are not so much types as dossiers, and Strindberg's Lady Julie is the product of his highly idiosyncratic and

pseudo-scientific concept of the *demi-femme*. They cannot be sufficiently generalized to promote social reform. Symbolism, on the other hand, with its emphasis on mortality as the central fact of human existence, was not interested in specific psychologies. The characters of symbolist drama are deliberately vague and easily abstracted from a specific milieu. Consequently, neither style of drama elected to deal with these new types of sexual deviant formulated by science and the law.[6]

Another important cause of this lacuna is theatrical censorship. The public nature of the theater limited it as a forum. In Great Britain, the Lord Chamberlain's Office effectively prevented any realistic or outspoken depiction of matters sexual from appearing on stage. Official government censorship in Germany and Russia had a like effect. In France, the police exercised control over plays deemed injurious to public morality and responded arbitrarily to the calls of puritanical legislators to shut down this or that display. Bernard Shaw could explicate the economic bases of prostitution in *Mrs Warren's Profession* (1893; published in 1898 and performed in 1902) and Eugène Brieux could warn of venereal contagion in *Les Avariés* (*Damaged Goods*, 1901, published and performed in 1902). Yet when they found managements courageous enough to produce their plays, the authorities stepped in and closed them down. Such bans could be skirted by organizing private performances, but in essence the stage was barred from joining contemporary debates on reform, except through glancing and allusive means.

Moreover, the medical and legal debates swirling around homosexuality were themselves so confused and contradictory that they tripped up inexperienced playwrights eager to put the issue before a theatre audience. August Adolf Friedrich's five-act play *In the Appropriate Case* (*In eigner Sache*, 1904) is the most egregious example. It begins promisingly enough with the irony of a hero who is both an intelligent member of parliament sitting on a subcommittee arguing law reform and a tutor with sadistic sexual longings for his 15-year-old pupil. Recognizing his condition as pathological, Dr Auer is undergoing hypnotic treatment to cure it; he also intends to marry the boy's sister Else as his only salvation. In so doing, he alienates his confidant, a newspaper editor in love with Else, who plants defamatory leaders in his paper. Auer plans to sue him but is visited by blackmailers who threaten to lay false evidence against him if he doesn't buy their silence. (Note that he has so far done nothing illegal.) Meanwhile he has had a weird interview with his pupil, the beloved Ernst, in which he punctuates outbursts of passionate affection with insulting invective, calling the naively trusting youth a "cruddy kid" (*Mistbube*).

Auer is equally open with his fiancée, laying out his emotional problems in prolix speeches, describing it as a sickness and refusing to excuse it as part of a cult of beauty or natural feeling. When he tries to break with her, she staunchly declares her insistence on the marriage, willing to follow him "to the madhouse, to the criminal court." The last act takes place in the committee room as the delegates debate the legal paragraph which imposes a prison sentence on homosexual acts. Auer defends its abolition "in the appropriate case," but when news of Else's suicide arrives, he gives up, asks only for a "righteous verdict" and dares not decide whether homosexuality is "a crime, a madness or high culture."[7]

No wonder Friedrich's readers were puzzled as to the play's intent, and it was never produced. Sinking under the weight of clinical and legal arguments, the dramatist is as befuddled as his unhappy protagonist, who comes across as the least persuasive champion of homosexual rights. Despite some well-paced dialogue, any rational discussion is defeated by the awkward mixture of speechifying, operatic behaviour and incredible coincidences. It would take a dramatist with the polemical expertise of Shaw or Brieux to bring it off, and the subject, unfortunately, did not engage their interest.[8]

Hedged round by the strongest taboos and obfuscated by pseudo-scientific jargon, homosexuality could not be exposed to the gaze of the general public. Recalling the prevalent attitude at the time of Oscar Wilde's trials in 1895, a French commentator on homosexuality remarks that "it would have seemed absolutely inconceivable, and public modesty at the time would not have tolerated an author choosing to describe such aberrations or analyze the psychological process *openly*. I emphasize the last word, it is essential."[9] Consequently, when

homosexuality does make it on to the stage, it is smuggled there in heavy camouflage.

Melodrama, the most popular genre on the nineteenth-century stage, proved to be an effective conveyance of the contraband. Melodrama has always been resourceful in adapting the latest in technology and invention to its uses. Dion Boucicault's employment of a daguerreotype camera as proxy for the Eye of God in identifying a murderer in *The Octoroon* (1859) is simply one among many exploitations of "progress" – railways, steamships, telegraphs and telephones – to serve the climaxes and denouements of sensational melodrama. Similar use was made of newly prominent professions and social types: the detective, the remittance man, the upmarket courtesan, the career diplomat, the prospector, and the self-made financier take stage almost as soon as their existence impinges on public consciousness. Thus melodrama acts as a kind of preceptor, familiarizing audiences with new phenomena while simultaneously, as a vehicle for moral propaganda, assigning these neoterisms benign or malign qualities. Through typology the unfamiliar is pigeonholed and labeled, and the public is indoctrinated into the proper attitude to take.

So when homosexuality, as the *fin-de-siècle* defined it, does make its stage debut, it is rife with melodramatic devices and closely associated with blackmail.

## *Exploiting exploitation*

Like melodrama, blackmail was perfected in the nineteenth century. Although the word itself is a good old Tudor term, the special sense "to extort money under threat of revealing a discreditable secret" does not appear before the 1890s.[10] (The French equivalent, *chantage*, had become current earlier in the century, transferred from underworld cant by the Parisian detective Vidocq; it was also borrowed by the Germans to replace the slang *Erpressung*, particularly in sexual contexts.) Both the word "blackmail" and the concept of extortion supplanted the earlier "delation," the act of informing against subjects or citizens to the government. The invention of a new word indicates that this kind of impeachment had shifted from state service to private enterprise. But before private blackmail can be effective or profitable, there has to be a modicum of social mobility with its accompanying standards of etiquette and morality. The victimized individual must be at risk of losing reputation, position, or influence in the eyes of his peers. An accusation of low birth, for instance, could be injurious only in a society that demands pedigree above all, and only for someone seeking to move in a higher sphere than that of his origins.

Social position or the perception of social position teetered insecurely on paper foundations. The Victorian blackmailer's prime weapon, the purloined letter, makes frequent appearances as the mislaid missives of the well-made play. *A Scrap of Paper* (*Les pattes de mouche*), Sardou's comedy of 1860, could well be the title of any number of plays, the scrap proliferating into sheaves of tell-tale correspondence on which the happiness of the heroes hinged. Rare was the society intrigue whose unravelling did not depend on the recovery of a perfidious note. It suggests a genre to be called "stationery drama."

Blackmail's continued viability as a plot-motor at the turn of the century can be seen in two adventures of Sherlock Holmes, "A Scandal in Bohemia" which dates from 1892 and the more scabrous "Charles Augustus Milverton" of 1904. Unlike fiction, however, which treated mainly of women blackmailed for adultery or for having a "past," the first detailed accounts of blackmail in police memoirs concern male homosexuality. Even in France where homosexual acts were not illegal *per se*, every government from Napoleon I to the Third Republic used homosexuality as grounds for political delation.[11] In private life, blackmail was a thriving and lucrative industry. Inspector Canler of the Sûreté enumerated "fear of scandal, fear of infamy, disgrace at depravity divulged" as sufficient motives for paying up. He pointed out that few men would be so frivolous as to go to the police and confess that they were vile wretches in order to denounce someone else as a viler wretch.[12] Wherever legislation did criminalize sexual relations between males, the victim of extortion was in greater jeopardy. The infamous §175 of the imperial penal code in Germany (1871) and the Labouchère amendment in Great Britain (1885) which imposed prison sentences on offenders became known as blackmailers' charters and

incidentally helped to define the popular notion of homosexuality.

Between 1899 and 1923, the yearbook of the German *Wissenschaftlich-humanitäres Komitee* (Scientific-humanitarian Committee), which militated for the abolition of §175, republished scores of newspaper accounts of blackmail cases, many of which ended in the suicide or imprisonment of the victim. An early article by Ludwig Frey on the *Rupfertum* or fleecing of urnings drew a lurid picture of proletarian criminals haunting public toilets at dusk to lure the "contrary-sexualist" to his doom.[13] A cartoon entitled "The Blackmailers" (*Die Erpresser*) published in 1905 shows a group of villainous-looking hoodlums gathered around a pamphlet, one saying, "Now I asks yez! They wanna drop Paragiraffe 175 from da penal code! Den how's da middle classes s'posed to make a livin'?"[14]

The German popular press stressed the victimization of the homosexual, whereas French illustrated newspapers laid the blame at the homosexual's own door. Their cartoons promoted an unsavoury stereotype of a symbiotic relationship: a depraved old gentleman, so jaded in his appetites that he sought forbidden fruit, puts himself at the mercy of an effeminate youth of the lower classes, who proffers the apple of Sodom. There is often a middle-man as well, an older ruffian who steps in to make the threats, but his sexuality is left in the dark.

This typology emphasized the generation gap between the players in this squalid triangle, suggesting that same-sex love was a "refinement" of worn-out voluptuaries. This was, after all, the period of Yvette Guilbert's popular music-hall song "Les Vieux Messieurs," a witty vilification of dirty old men, and Maurice Donnay's ballad "Eros vanné" in which the god of homosexual men and women was depicted as debilitated, one-eyed and crippled.

But, by insisting on the cash transaction, homosexual relations as prostitution and blackmail rather than love, the typology also emphasized the ways in which homosexuality crosses class lines. Syphilis had already intruded into the nineteenth-century consciousness as no respecter of persons, violating the middle-class family through its father's and son's traffic with women of the lower orders. Homosexuality went even farther in that direction. It was, declared a correspondent to a scientific journal in 1904, "the *only* vice which suppresses castes. The respectable man and the ruffian are equals – and talk to one another naturally, live together despite differences in upbringing. This vice achieves what charity cannot, equality among people. That should be strange and unnerving enough." Social critics who wanted to reduce sympathy for the victim of a hustler's blackmail might thus construe it as a symbol of the unsettling Masonic compact among homosexuals.

## First steps on stage

Under these circumstances, it should not be surprising that the earliest plays to foreground same-sex relationships regularly fall back on blackmail as a central plot device, although national tastes and characteristics determine how it is employed. German plays, such as Dilsner's *Jasmine Blossoms* or Hirschberg's *"Mistakes"*, have as their primary purpose law reform, and, drawing their arguments directly from the propaganda of Magnus Hirschfeld and his humanitarian committee,[15] serve primarily as didactic plays. They straightforwardly portray the homosexual as a worthy individual whose life is destroyed by a concatenation of unscrupulous blackmailers, unyielding courts, and uncomprehending wives and relatives. Although the style is baldly naturalistic, the implacability of these forces ranged against the homosexual is very much in the tradition of *Schicksalstragödie*, that peculiarly German form of tragedy in which a blindly raging Fate rides roughshod over its helpless victims. The sensational domestic catastrophes in the plays of Sudermann and Hauptmann draw on this tradition and provide the models for Dilsner, Hirschberg and other pioneers of plays about same-sex love. The German playwrights construct lay figures, made up of one part reformist propaganda, one part pseudo-scientific notions of homosexual essentialism. Morally accident-prone, inevitably suicidal, these born victims initiate a pattern which will be repeated *ad nauseum* in the stage depiction of the sensitive homosexual.

As its title makes clear, *The Blackmailers* (1894) by John Gray and Marc-André Raffalovich is entirely concerned with the matter. These intimates of Oscar Wilde,

however, internalize the issue by making their blackmailers the homosexuals. The complicity of an older, more experienced man with a promising youth trails vestiges of classic ideals of pederasty; here, however, the older man is an unconscionable scoundrel and the youth an equally amoral egoist. Because they believe that society has victimized them through its codes and sanctions, they victimize it in turn. Despite a few purple passages, the play is carried on in the bantering tone of a drawing-room comedy and the suicidal ending is averted by the anti-hero's cynical adoption of a life of crime. No wonder critics of the time were outraged by the play's rejection of conventional morality and confused by its seeming lack of a sympathetic focus. The authors, almost unwittingly, invested the strongest bond of affection in the two scoundrels. By hints and allusions, they suggested that, beyond both men being predators, they share an emotional affinity.

Another internalization of homosexual blackmail occurs in the American Henry Blake Fuller's *At Saint Judas's* (1896). Unlike society in the German plays, where it is a ponderous weight oppressing the homosexual victim, and unlike society in *The Blackmailers*, where it is a set of stuffy conventions to be flouted and exploited, society plays almost no part in Fuller's chamber drama. Borrowing heavily from Maeterinck's symbolist pieces, Fuller experiments with a psychological conflict between two officers. From boyhood they have been closely bound by emotional attachments which copy but do not overstep traditions of adhesive friendship endorsed by the Victorians. To put it more simply, they are loving friends whose manliness appears to be untainted by any sexual desire. One of these men, however, does covertly adore his friend with a love surpassing the love of women, and riven by jealousy at his friend's betrothal to an heiress, uses the blackmailer's ploy of anonymous letters to blacken his friend's reputation and break off the engagement. The strategy fails. As the wedding ceremony proceeds offstage, the best man confesses his plotting and his adoration to the horrified groom. The outcome is the bloody death of the best man, though whether by murder or suicide is left unclear.

In its passionate intensity and its symbolic

use of music and figurative shadows, *At Saint Judas's* is not meant to be taken realistically. It has to be judged as a dramatic poem, the outpouring of a closetted personality. It is typical of Fuller's own unresolved feelings that he cannot decide whether he shares the lover's devotion or the friend's revulsion. The title and the image of the Fall of Lucifer at the play's end would suggest that the best man's treachery is the point, but there may be irony in it as well. Certain indications in the stage directions imply that the dead man's love was the "best and brightest of all."

## *Where is love?*

Unaware of the existence of Fuller's play, the German critic Hanns Fuchs complained in 1902, "The ideal homosexual drama, which depicts the conflicts in the soul itself and their influence on the homosexual's actions and conception of life has not yet been written."[16] He recommended that dramatists devote their energies to analyzing the soul of a homosexual genius such as Franz Grillparzer or Michelangelo. There were a number of German plays which delved into the past to explore, at a safe distance, the sentimental affinities of certain historical figures such as Frederick the Great and the emperor Hadrian; one such comedy drew on Shakespearean devices to show James I of England deceived when he becomes infatuated with a youth who turns out to be a girl in disguise.[17]

On the other hand, there are sporadic manifestations, mostly in German drama, of loves that don't exactly fear to speak their names but don't know what names to call themselves. Otto Ernst's popular four-act comedy *Jugend von heute* (*The Youth of Today*, 1898) sets such a conundrum for the audience. Given the rarity of such manifestations in nineteenth-century drama, a plot summary may be called for.

Hermann Kröger, a young bacteriologist, has just published his doctoral dissertation and is returning home to his kindly, adoring parents in a small harbour town in North Germany. He brings with him his closest friend Erich Gossler, a coldly rude, supercilious dandy; under his influence Hermann has adopted a nihilist outlook, renounces research and any kind of work, and scorns the affections of family and friends. In the course of the play, as we

would expect, Hermann's eyes are opened to Erich's malign influence; he eventually repudiates him and returns to work and the arms of his childhood sweetheart.

Although Erich is the serpent in the petty-bourgeois Eden, he is portrayed with a good deal of ambivalence. He is described on his first entrance as:

> *elegant, dressed somewhat foppishly, slender, pale sallow complexion, dark eyes, dark blond moustache and goatee, carefully curled hair, yellow gloves, narrow white hands with very long nails, on the right hand a ring with a big ruby, really "high-class", aristocratically blasé demeanour. His politeness is of the kind which keeps distinctly aloof and tries to remain unbending.*[18]

His fastidiousness, misogyny and total apathy, in short, his pose as Nietzschean Superman, are soon revealed to be driven by his possessive love of Hermann, whom he wants to keep away from the world. When Hermann appears to be drawn back to his former life, Erich, threatening to break off their relationship, exercises a Svengali-like power over him.

> ERICH *(Looking into Hermann's eyes)* So that's to be the end result of all those nights when we stirred up wild and forceful thoughts. Perhaps you remember that you wanted to learn to be free, free of everything that might control you. That you wanted to go with me into the great isolation of those who are reckless – and now that sonnyboy is caught up in mother's apron-strings again, he cries: I didn't mean it. It feels better *here!*
> HERMANN   But dear friend –
> ERICH   *(Slower and slower and with the sharpest emphasis)* Perhaps you remember the corner in which we often sat and found a resting-place in one another's eyes. Do you remember?
> HERMANN   *(Elegiacally)* Yes.
>
> (pp. 69–70)

This is essentially a love scene, and yet when the men are challenged by Hermann's sweetheart or his mother to explain why they insist on being together, Hermann spouts his sub-Nietzschean credo and Erich withdraws into an affronted fit of pique.

In the last act, there is a remarkably original denouement. The scales fallen from his eyes, Hermann is now engaged to his sweetheart and determined to apply himself to scientific research in his hometown; amid the rejoicing of the assembled family, Erich unexpectedly returns. "I want to make you a declaration of love", he says to Clara the fiancée, "but my love does not concern you."

ERICH  (Still outwardly calm) – – – I love – that nitwit over there. (Indicating Hermann over his shoulder)

CLARA  (Gently) Really? Well, he –

ERICH  (Harsh) I love him more than you do!

CLARA  That'll be the day!

ERICH  Yes. You love him because he is a brilliant and strong and magnificent fellow –

HERMANN  (Embarrassed) But Gossler – !

ERICH  (Coldly) Be still! – – I love him, because I hate him.

(p. 134)

Erich goes on to explain that he was so convinced of the worthlessness of mankind that he was bowled over by Hermann's creativity and value to society, of which he himself is incapable.

ERICH  And when two such men become friends – there is a struggle – first a covert, skulking one – then an open brutal one, which means: I or you. I wanted to humiliate, subjugate, annihilate him – and if I had succeeded, I would have been entirely alone. Therefore I hoped, I longed in silence for him to rise up and crush me some day; I cursed in silence his modesty; for it was like a religious passion in me that the saviour of the mirthful dead should come, the hero of that deed which is not folly! (He has worked himself into a state of great excitement but shakes it off and adopts a brighter tone.) He never crushed me; he only conquered me. He blasted me like a wholesome storm and pressed my wrist so that I had welts for three days. Since this breakup I have really loved him for the first time. I can hold out no longer and will go to Berlin today.

(pp. 186–7)

The upshot of this sado-masochistic, mystically messianic declaration is that for two days every year Hermann will come for a visit:

on the first our hearts will flare up and each will seek to descry what he can do for the other's love. On the second day – for hearts cannot always keep a-flame – we will talk – for instance about Berlioz – or about liquid ammonia, it's all the same: anyway we'll start arguing, we'll get fed up with one another and relearn that we cannot behave to one another like royal siblings because too much water has gone under the bridge. Then I'll bring him to the railway station, buy him a rose or a couple of oranges and put him in the carriage. And for the rest of the year I'll live off the yearning. . . . I would like to sit in our corner tonight – you know the one – and think of you. Farewell.

(pp. 188–9)

The seeming villain has become the victim. A character originally set up to be the troubler of paradise turns out to be the one bereft of family happiness, sacrificing his own love for that of his beloved. There's a tinge of the last act of *The Merchant of Venice*, with Antonio, willing to give his life for his adored Bassanio, left alone as the happy couples pair off. Perhaps Fuller's overwrought heroes should have come up with a similar *modus vivendi*.

Erich's effusions cannot be written off as typical Biedermeier *Schwärmerei*, a reversion to the unbridled comradely hysterics of the *Sturm und Drang* movement; it ought to be seen as part of a continuum of German homoeroticism which called itself by other names for two centuries. One curious hint at latter-day homosexuality comes from Erich's fondness for hanging out in low sailors' dives, the only place, he claims, where real life can be experienced. With Erich, one has the beginnings of a fully-rounded homosexual character, one whose passional nature cannot be explained away by psychiatric formulas but whose happiness cannot be consummated within the stage conventions of the day.

One has to look to Russia to find a dramatic treatment of same-sex love that is free of recrimination. This may be because homosexual blackmail was relatively uncommon there and abundant testimony exists to the tolerance of the common people to homosexual acts, in the belief that they were special pastimes of the gentry. The leading art movements of the so-called Silver Age were infused with playful homoeroticism. In his *jeux d'esprit*, Mikhail Kuzmin is careful to set his scenarios in the legendary past – early Christian Egypt, the Middle Ages, eighteenth-century Venice – and creates pastiches of bygone dramatic styles – the miracle play, the *opéra comique*, the *fiabba*, the pastoral. This escapism frees him from both the need to make social commentary and the predictable reversals of melodramatic structure. As in *The Dangerous Precaution* (1907), he can create an ideal untouched by sordid reality. The male lovers of Kuzmin's divertissements are princes, pages, shepherds and masquers, heavily disguised ideals of any objective correlatives in Russian life.

## Sisters under the skin

Less subject to legal persecution and less distinct in the popular imagination, lesbians were largely subsumed under the categories "hysterical women," "emancipated women" or "*femmes fatales*" when they made rare appearances on the dramatic stage. Since the guild of dramatists in all countries was primarily a male preserve, the lesbian was bound to be viewed from the outside as a piquant addition to the erotic menu or as a somewhat absurd, somewhat sinister rival.

The sapphic subculture in *fin-de-siècle* Paris was well enough publicized for certain types of mannish females to show up in revues and comic sketches. Such is the "Importunate Androgyne" in Maurice Donnay's shadow play *Ailleurs* (*Elsewhere*), produced at the Chat Noir cabaret in 1891. "With its little hat, its little collar, its English tie, its man's shirt, its tailored jacket, and its umbrella-shaped fur dress," wearied of flesh-and-blood mistresses, it makes its declaration to a statue of Venus. Prior to this entrance, "the Lesbians" have been shown on the shadow screen as "voluptuous naked women, embracing like lovers in Dante," "women who indulge in blameworthy tribadiddling . . . there are great ladies, there are even crowned heads, these loves being reputed so rare, literary and aristocratic. True, their numbers also include young ladies from the Moulin-Rouge. . . . "[19] Such depictions mingle mild scorn with softcore pornography.

To titillate audiences with a portrayal of lesbian love less abstract than coloured sihouettes on a screen, one had to retreat to the realm of mythology. At a time when love relations between women were being described in a rather favorable light in a number of French novels and stories, the Paris Opéra mounted a lavish production of Xavier Leroux's sub-Wagnerian opera *Astarté* (15 February 1901) to considerable acclaim. Composed to a libretto by Louis de Gramont, it somehow conflated the legend of Hercules and Omphale with lubricities out of Flaubert's *Salammbô* (not to mention *Thaïs*, *Hérodïade* and a whole gallery of such exotica). Disguised in women's clothes, Hercules sets out to deal a crushing blow to the bloody and shamelessly sapphic cult of Astarté by killing her high priestess Omphale, Queen of Lydia. For no reason other than plot requirements, they fall in love, and the unholy rite is performed in their presence. The Parisian public particularly enjoyed this scene when Hercules in drag, narcotized by an opiate drink, settles in to watch the orgiastic dance of the cult's votaries. "Then, beneath a diffused rosy light, there begins a scene of general love, which does not seem, truth to tell, to be consecrated to the single-minded 'normal animal love' Verlaine speaks of, but which, by the harmonious arrangement of groups and colours, offers one of the most beautiful of spectacles."[20] In a climactic delirium the priestesses sink fast asleep in one another's arms. Shaken out of his torpor, Hercules moves towards Omphale and the stage is plunged into darkness, the audience's imagination free to roam as it will.

It is traditional that Omphale's lovers be sacrificed to the goddess, and Hercules willingly submits. At this point, the maid Iole arrives with a gift from Hercules' wife Deianira, the shirt of the centaur Nessus, which is said to have the power to restore "normal" love. Omphale becomes infatuated with Iole, and offers to release Hercules from his vows. As soon as he dons the shirt, he goes up in flames, along with temple and palace. The last scene shows Omphale, Iole and the local women erecting a new altar to Astarté on the Isle of Lesbos. Although this was the first time that lesbian love had been portrayed so graphically on a public stage, the message of the libretto is ambivalent, to put it mildly. Astarté's cult in Lydia has been extirpated, as Hercules intended, but it is reconstituted elsewhere, and the love of the two leading women comprises a happy ending.

Representations of modern life, on the other hand, formulated a more negative portrait of the predatory lesbian, poaching on masculine preserves. August Strindberg's marital difficulties and his paranoid belief that his wife was carrying on an affair with her best woman friend led him to portray lesbians in his fiction and memoirs (*Le Plaidoyer d'un fou*) as home-wreckers. In his plays, however, he was less outspoken and only hints at sexual irregularity in his satirical portraits of emancipated women. The exception is his comedy *Comrades* (*Kamraterna*, 1886) which originally bore the less ironic title *Marauders* (*Marodörer*) and had a happy ending, the estranged wife returning submissively to her husband; the final version is more embittered, tinged with bile emitted from Strindberg's personal life.

Set in an artist's studio in Paris, a bohemian milieu hospitable to eccentric behavior, the play demonstrates how an expatriate painter's wife becomes his rival by usurping male privileges without surrendering female prerogatives. Embracing the mendacious claims of an alcoholic divorcee, she becomes "one of those women with close-cropped hair!" The rift between husband and wife is engineered by a "cross between man and woman," a woman named Abel (perhaps based on Sarah Bernhardt's friend the lesbian artist Louise Abbéma). She describes herself as "a defective, a misfit of some sort. For I enjoyed watching you two, until the envy of the misfit set me afire." To the husband, she is simply "an interesting and amusing comrade who happened to be dressed as a woman. You never gave me the impression of belonging to the other sex; and love, you see, can and should exist only between individuals of opposite sexes."[21] Ultimately, Strindberg is more tolerant of the misfit than of the true woman; at the play's end even Abel walks out on the wife, appalled by her innately feminine lack of scruples.

It was Frank Wedekind who heavy-handedly attempted to reinterpret the lesbian as one of nature's disinherited, as her brothers had already appeared in German drama. The hopeless Countess Geschwitz (accent on the first syllable) in his Lulu plays, *Der Erdgeist* (*Earth Spirit*, 1893, published 1895) and *Die Büchse der Pandora* (*Pandora's Box*, 1901, published 1904) is the one important lesbian character in prewar German drama. Contrasted with Lulu's "natural" heartlessness and amorality, the countess is a freakish obsessive, so besotted with Lulu that she allows herself to be imprisoned, infected with cholera and eventually butchered for her beloved's sake. In a preface written some years later, Wedekind pointed to her as "the central tragic character of this play."

> However the curse of unnaturalness alone would not have led me to choose it as the subject of a work of drama. Rather, I did it because I find this destiny, as we encounter it in our culture today, has not yet received tragic treatment. I was impulsively inspired to keep the powerful human tragedy of an extraordinarily great, but totally fruitless psychic struggle from being doomed to derision and to introduce it to the sympathy and compassion of all who are not surprised by it.[22]

The Countess Geschwitz is a female version of the doomed heroes of Dilsner and Hirschberg: driven by her innate passions and bereft of any reciprocity in her relationships, her destiny is bound to be unhappy. Wedekind's character-drawing seems based less on observation than on literary conceits. "Fruitlessness" was a standard indictment of homosexuality by religious sects, and the countess's "selfless love" derives, at best, from some of the abject confessions that appeared in medical journals but ran counter to the more liberated statements coming out of the women's emancipation movement.[23] Wedekind's compassion is not for an oppressed minority but for a martyr to *Schicksalstragödie*.

Later dramatists may have been as fanciful as Wedekind in their creation of sapphic types, but, unlike him, they withheld their imaginative sympathies: the lesbians who appear in Hermann Sudermann's *Die Freundin* (*The Lady Friend*, 1913–14) and Edouard Bourdet's *La Prisonnière* (*The Captive*, 1926) are dangerous species of the genus decadent. In Sudermann's play, the *femme* is literally *fatale*: two men die on account of her machinations and she escapes stoning thanks only to a fast car. She embodies the modern evil, pronounced by the doctor/*raisonneur* in the last scene to be "the individual's cult of self, the ego made absolute, which turns divine, human and in this case nature's laws topsy-turvy."[24]

9

Bourdet's play, nicknamed "L'Arlesbienne", managed to become a commercial hit on two continents in part because the woman who exercises an unwholesome influence over the hero's wife never appears on stage. Another cause of its success was noted by André Gide. Rereading *The Captive* in 1931, he pointed out "its indirect flattery of the public's most vulgar instincts. It gives the impression that the greatest happiness is to be achieved only in coitus." He observed that the play's basic dilemma, a couple's inability to achieve sexual compatibility, let alone bliss, was essentially a problem for marriage counselors. Homosexuality had nothing to do with it.[25]

## The fall and rise of the stage homosexual

"Have patience," wrote the womanizing hack Willy, "at the rate we're going, one day we'll see on stage . . . a little male 'Captive' . . . kissed on the mouth by . . . a dangerous siren in an undershirt. And provincial notaries will come and applaud it, flanked by their ladies and their young ladies, while the orchestra will play pianissimo Lecoq's tune 'No women! No women!'"[26] This cynical prediction of seeing male endearments on stage had already come to pass at the Vieux-Colombier in 1904, when André Gide's Biblical drama *Saül* was put on with some success. At one point, the eminent actor-manager Jacques Copeau in the role of King Saul was seen to blush with jealousy and ill-repressed passion behind an arras, while his son Jonathan embraced the bare torso of David, "the adorable *Daoud*," as the play orientalizes his name, in the glow of bluish spotlight. Gide's literary reputation and the Biblical source reduced the shock quotient nearly to nil, and conferred an aura of respectability on what would on a lesser stage have been scandalous.

However, this was an exceptional occurrence, for by 1910 same-sex love vanished from the boards entirely, and it would require World War I to efface memories of the scandals that accomplished this disappearance. The trials of Oscar Wilde put paid to any attempts to naturalize the homosexual in the English theatre for almost two decades. On the Continent, Wilde's persecution and conviction were diagnosed as symptomatic, in the French mind, of the

double standard in the sex life of perfidious Albion; in the German mind, they became, in Sander Gilman's words, "part of the litmus test between the right, which condemned him as representative of the decay of the British, and the left, which saw the persecution of homosexuality as a sign of the inherent hypocrisy of German society."[27]

However, homegrown scandals soon aborted the development of the homosexual character on the Continental stage as well. Hanns Fuchs's complaint that no true homosexual drama existed had been made the same year in which German society was reeling from the expulsion from Capri of the munitions manufacturer Alfred Krupp, a close friend of Kaiser Wilhelm II, on account of sodomitical activities. 1906, when Hirschberg's apologetic play *"Mistakes"* was published, saw the first "outing" of Prince Philipp zu Eulenberg and Count Kuno Moltke, also intimates of the Kaiser. The ensuing court case, along with the trial of Prince Bernhard von Bülow, the chancellor of Germany, coated the Wilhelmine court with mud. These affairs made German production of any play on a homosexual theme an implicit act of *lèse-majesté*.[28]

In France, the increasing prominence and toleration of sexual deviants in the worlds of art and high society was mirrored in Armory's drawing-room comedy *The Gentleman of the Chrysanthemums* (1908). No longer is the homosexual an outcast clinging to the fringes of the *beau monde*: an etiolated dandy, he has become its ruler and arbiter. Armory's is a remarkably modern play in some respects, especially in the innuendo-filled badinage and the three-dimensional portrayal of a central character allowed to voice his own justifications. Perhaps it is most strikingly up-to-date in its awareness of the significance of the media celebrity in modern society, often a homosexual whose private life is indulged so long as it is not blatantly in evidence. In this play, blackmail still hovers offstage, but it is regarded purely as a nuisance to be bought off. This Gallic lightness in portraying a homosexual protagonist is poles apart from the *Weltzschmerz* and *Tendenz* that permeate the German plays.

Two years after *The Gentleman of the Chrysanthemums* was successfully performed at a public theatre, the voluntary exile of the dilettante poet Baron Jacques d'Adelswärd

Fersen, arrested for photographing naked schoolboys, produced a revulsion against such types in Parisian society. Even Robert de Montesquiou, a model for Proust's Baron de Charlus, renounced his acquaintance with Fersen, and a journalist insisted, "If there is any one vice or illness that revolts the French mind and French health, it is surely, to call a spade a spade, homosexuality."[29] The aesthete, previously a butt for satire or admiration, was now criminalized, a subject to be treated exclusively by police inspectors and psychiatrists. "It is ghastly," Proust wrote to Paul Morand. "Vice has become an exact science."[30]

The return of the homosexual to the stage was aided by a general abandonment of the grandiose heroics and moral systems that had accompanied the War. After a generation of young men had been mowed down owing to the boneheaded machismo of their elders and when a generation of young women had had to take on unaccustomed griefs and responsibilities, the decadent postures of the *fin de siècle* offered attractive models for rebellion. With an exasperation that sounds familiar to us in the 1990s, moralists and journalists railed against the growing conspicuousness of male effeminacy. In *Le Journal de Nice*, Clément Vautel complained, "Faggotry (*le tataïsme*) is spreading so rapidly that the sex to which we owe our mother will soon be fully eclipsed by that to which so many of our contemporaries owe their auntie." And in his novel *La Fortune et le Jeu*, Charles Derennes observed that "nowadays any young man who will not take on the airs of a pederast will appear, in modern society, as quite unpresentable."[31]

A younger generation was growing up, cynical of its elders' value systems and feeling estranged from any pre-existing traditions. As it began to reappear in German drama, same-sex love was conflated with the problems of adolescence consuming the new generation. Wedekind had been prescient in this, for in his 1906 panorama of agonized puberty, *Frühlings Erwachen* (*The Awakening of Spring*), male homoeroticism makes a brief appearance as one more vignette in the spectrum of hormonal anxieties. The Wilhelmine censor had insisted on the omission of this scene from the first production.

Censorship in the Weimar Republic was laxer. Edward II and Oscar Wilde were made

the focus of plays by Bertolt Brecht (1924) and Carl Sternheim (1925), respectively. The Eros Theatre (1921–24) was founded by a group of amateurs to spread the gospel of male–male love, chiefly in private performances; it even toured to the Czech National Theatre in Prague with Marlowe's *Edward II* and to the Schouwberg in Rotterdam with a three-act drama *Mustn't* by a Frau Schepper-Becker.[32] Nevertheless, most homosexual plays on the Weimar German stage were chronicles of troubled youth. Expressionist drama used crises of sexual identity as metaphors for rebellion, morbidity and confusion, most graphically in Arnolt Bronnen's *Vatermord* (*Parricide*, 1922) Brecht's *Baal* (1922) and *Im Dickicht der Städte* (*Lost in the Urban Jungle*, 1923), and Ferdinand Bruckner's *Krankheit der Jugend* (*Growing Pains*, 1926).[33] They culminate in Christa Winsloe's *Gestern und Heute* (*Yesterday and Today*, 1930), known more familiarly from its film version as *Mädchen in Uniform* (*Girls in Uniform*). There the contrast between a dreamy schoolgirl's sentimental attachment to her instructress and the Prussian inflexibility of the headmistress is as loud a political statement as it is a plea for sexual liberation.

Set within the context of these dramas of pubescent and post-pubescent longing, Klaus Mann's *Ania and Esther* seems less outlandish. Throughout his precocious career, Mann insisted that his was a lost generation, unstable in its beliefs, rootless and defenceless. The love of individual for individual, regardless of gender, was one of the few guarantees of authenticity, but was usually blighted by conventional morality or the crass pressures of everyday life. Not that Mann is a social protest writer in the tradition of German tendentiousness: he is a belated Romantic, whose homosexuality is a badge of artistic distinction and hypersensitivity. A good deal of his play is torn raw from his own life and that of his close circle; this proximity to the material generates a certain amount of obscurity, but also a deep sincerity. Just as Fuller's characters share their author's homosexual panic, so Mann's partake of his own febrile and neurotic craving for affection. It was the play's candour, as well as the *frisson* of seeing the author and his friends play themselves, that brought it success, while it also provoked the predictable jeremiads.

By the 1920s European boulevard drama and revue had naturalized the fairy (*tante*) as a figure of fun. Even the London stage, still governed by the ferule of the Lord Chamberlain, could offer drawing-room comedies such as Somerset Maugham's *Our Betters* (1915, produced 1917) and Frederick Lonsdale's *Spring Cleaning* (1925), in which waspish, maidenly gentlemen serve the same sort of function as witty commentators that fantasticals do in Jacobean drama. *L'Homme qui joue du banjo* (*The Banjo Player*), a three-act comedy which opened at the Théâtre Michel, Paris, on 23 September 1926 featured a powdered and made-up character, his lace handkerchief up his sleeve, habituating a gay bar called "The Hairy Spider." He turns out to be a professional queer, who finds male prostitution more remunerative than hard work, since he has six children to feed. Stories were told of young actors who made the "*tapette*" or pansy their line of business and achieved great success. Typically, when Edouard Bourdet returned to treat homosexuality in the early 1930s, he dropped the dire mood of his *Captive*. *La Fleur des pois* (*The Upper Crust*, 1932) was a light-hearted romantic comedy, in which effete social butterflies with names like La Moufette, Toto and Metekian (the Armenian/Jew as sexual exotic) gossip over gay affairs and put the moves on their underlings. It was an updating of *The Gentleman of the Chrysanthemums*, but now the homosexual, instead of being the odd man in was practically *l'homme moyen sensuel*.

Each of the plays in this anthology offers an archetype that will recur in numerous guises throughout twentieth-century drama. *At Saint Judas's* and "*Mistakes*" present variants on the victim of passion, in one case, a devoted friend who cannot survive lack of reciprocal love, in the other, a respectable man who commits suicide when his furtive sex life is about to be made public. *The Blackmailers* and *The Gentleman of the Chrysanthemums* both feature the effete dilettante as subversive, in one case, by working underhand and on the fringes to prey on society, in the other, by imposing his perverse tastes on society. *Ania and Esther* is suffused with adolescent *Angst* over sexual identity and a sense of estrangement from "normal life." Only the carefree gaiety of *The Dangerous Precaution*, with its insouciant gender-juggling, offers an untroubled view of same-sex love. The modernist theatre preferred its homosexuals unhappy or unscrupulous or, preferably, both.

## Notes

1 O. Davis, *I'd Like to Do It Again*, New York, Farrar and Rinehart, 1931, pp. 64–5.

2 M. Nordau, *Degeneration*, New York, D. Appleton, 1895; E. Showalter, *Sexual Anarchy, Gender and Culture at the Fin de Siècle*, New York, Viking, 1990; J. C. Fout, "Sexual politics in Wilhelmine Germany: the male gender crisis, moral purity, and homophobia," *Journal of the History of Sexuality*, 1992, vol. 2, p. 389.

3 G. L. Mosse, *Nationalism and Sexuality: Respectability and Abnormal Sexuality in Modern Europe*, New York, Howard Fertig, 1985, p. 37.

4 J.-P. Aron and R. Kempf, "Triumphs and tribulations of the homosexual discourse," in G. Stambolian and E. Marks (eds), *Homosexualities and French Literature: Cultural Contexts/Critical Texts*, Ithaca, NY, Cornell University Press, 1979, p. 151.

5 S. Williams, "Theatre and degeneration: subversion and sexuality," in J. E. Chamberlain and S. L. Gilman (eds), *Degeneration, the Dark Side of Progress*, New York, Columbia University Press, 1985, p. 249.

6 However, an argument can be made that many of the female characters of Ibsen, Strindberg, Przybyshewski, Artsybashev and others fit the "hysterical" pattern.

7 A. A. Friedrich, *In eigner Sache (Drama)*, Strassburg, Josef Singer, 1904. Numa Prætorius discusses it in the *Jahrbuch für sexuelle Zwischenstufen*, 1905, vol. 2, pp. 871–3.

8 One of Shaw's few extended comments on homosexuality appears in a letter to the Editor of *Truth*, concerning the Cleveland Street scandal of 1889, in which he deplores the jail sentence pronounced on the proprietor of the *North London Press* for publishing the name of one of the aristocratic habitués of a male brothel. He characteristically attacks social hypocrisy while pleading tolerance for actions between adult males. B. Shaw, *Collected Letters 1874–1897*, ed. D. H. Laurence, London, Max Reinhardt, 1965, pp. 230–2.

9 F. Poché, *L'Amour qui n'ose pas dire son nom*, Paris, Bernard Grasset, 1927, p. 15. Unless otherwise noted, all translations throughout this book are my own.

10 R. W. Burchfield (ed.), *A Supplement to the Oxford English Dictionary*, Oxford, Clarendon Press, 1987, s.v. "blackmail."

11 According to Léo Taxil, quoted in W. Johansson, "Blackmail," in W. Dynes (ed.), *Encyclopedia of Homosexuality*, New York, Garland, 1990, vol. 1, pp. 150–52. Studies of homosexual blackmail are abundant; for works more or less contemporary with the plays in this volume, see F. Carlier, *La Prostitution antiphysique*, Paris, 1887 (repr. Paris, Le Sycomore, 1981); E. Burchard, *Erpresser-Prostitution*, Berlin, Kampf-Verlag, 1905; and H. Ostwald, *Männliche Prostitution*, Leipzig, Emil Müller,1905.

12 J. Brenner (ed.), *Mémoires de Canler, ancient chef du Service du sûreté*, Paris, Mercure de France, 1968, pp. 316–39.

13 L. Frey, "Zu Characteristik des Rupfertums," *Jahrbuch für sexuelle Zwischenstufen*, 1899, vol. 1, pp. 79–96. Also see H.-G. Stümke, *Homosexuelle in Deutschland: eine politische Geschichte*, Munich, C. H. Beck, 1989, pp. 25–8.

14 "Nu frag' ick eenen! Den Parajraph 175 wollen se raushaben aus'm Strafjesetz! Ja, wovon soll der Mittelstand dann existieren?" *Lustige Blätter*, 1 Feb. 1905.

15 Magnus Hirschfeld himself makes a unique comic appearance in drama in Rudolf Presber's cabaret sketch "Eine Vorstellung mit Hindernissen" ("A Performance under Difficulties"), in which the Prologue to Goethe's *Faust*, played at a "Little Theatre," is constantly interrupted by special interests in the audience. At one point, a police inspector objects to the phrase "fraternal spheres" used in relation to heaven, whereupon a "Dr Magnus Rehfeld," sitting on the first-row aisle, interposes, "I should like to say something about the Inspector's exception. It is to the homosexual interest that there be no doubt that Goethe too, as proven by these lines positioned so conspicuously at the beginning of the tragedy . . . " He is interrupted and seconded by a "Gentleman with a soprano voice" who suggests that Goethe's conversations with Eckermann are also evidence. The men are shouted down by protestors shouting out the names of Goethe's female loves. R. Presber, *Theater: ein Bündel Satiren*, Berlin, Concordia, 1909, pp. 117–18. It sounds remarkably like the current controversy over Goethe's sexuality.

16 H. Fuchs, "Die Homosexualität im Drama der Gegenwart und der Zukunft," *Die Kritik*, 1 August 1902, p. 513.

17 These plays include P. Heyse, *Hadrian* (1865, about Hadrian and Antinous); F. Rückert, *Saul und David* (1843, about David and Jonathan); H. A. Schaufert, *Schach dem König* (1869, about James I).

18 O. Ernst, *Jugend von heute*, Leipzig, L. Staackmann, n.d., p. 12.

19 M. Donnay, *Elsewhere*, in L. Senelick (ed. and trans.), *Cabaret Performance: Europe 1890–1920*, New York, Performing Arts Journal Press, 1989, pp. 34–5.

20 P. de Bréville, "*Astarté*," *Mercure de France*, April 1901, vol. 38, p. 231, quoted in C. van Casselaer, *Lot's Wife. Lesbian Paris, 1890–1914*, Liverpool, Janus Press, 1986, p. 77. Also see Pierre Lalo's review in *Le Temps*, which complained of the excessive sensuousness of the music and the stage picture, and the account by Numa Prætorius, 'Reine Belletristik', *Jahrbuch für sexuelle Zwischenstufen*, 1901, vol. 3, pp. 439–41. Several articles on the designs and the staging appeared in *L'Art du Théâtre*, Mar. 1901.

21 A. Strindberg, *Seven Plays*, trans. A. Paulson, New York, Bantam Books, 1960, pp. 166–7.

22 F. Wedekind, *Gesammelte Werke*, Munich, G. Müller, 1920–24, vol. 3, p. 102. Many of Wedekind's early critics, including his first biographer Arthur Kutscher, point out that the preface was written after his trial and conviction for *lèse-majesté* and seek to dismiss this statement as a blind to deflect censorship; but there seems no strong reason other than heterosexism to discount the Countess Geschwitz's centrality to the plays. *Der Erdgeist* was performed privately in 1898, publicly in 1902. *Die Büchse der Pandora* was played privately in 1904 but not publicly until December 1918, by which time theatrical censorship was no longer effective in northern Germany. The role of the Countess was played by such *grandes dames* of the German stage as Hermine Körner and Adele Sandrock, but it may

have been most effective when interpreted by an acknowledged lesbian like Leontine Sagan (Frankfurt, 1920). See G. Seehaus, *Frank Wedekind und das Theater*, Munich, Laokoön, 1964, pp. 430–1; and M. Schäfer, "Theater, Theater!" in M. Bollé (ed.), *Eldorado: Homosexuelle Frauen und Männer in Berlin, 1850–1950*, Berlin, Frölich and Kaufmann, 1984, pp. 180–2.

23 The kind of documentation of lesbianism to which Wedekind might have had access can be found in I. Kokula, *Weibliche Homosexualität um 1900 im zeitgenössichen Dokumenten*, Munich, Frauenoffensive, 1981.

24 H. Sudermann, *Dramatische Werke*, Stuttgart and Berlin, J. G. Cotta'sche Buchhandlung Nachfolger, 1923, vol. 5, p. 300.

25 A. Gide, 1 Nov. 1931, *Journal (1923–1931)*, Paris, Americ-Edit, n.d., pp. 388–9. *The Captive* had a forerunner in Catulle Mendès's *Protectrices* and a later epigone in Roger Martin du Gard's *Taciturne* (1931). However, the definitive French image of the doomed lesbian appears in the film *Club des femmes*.

26 Willy, *Le Troisième sexe*, Paris, Paris-Edition, 1927, p. 250.

27 S. L. Gilman, *Disease and Representation: Images of Illness from Madness to AIDS*, Ithaca, NY, Cornell Univeristy Press, 1988, p. 159.

28 In a lengthy narrative transcript of the Eulenberg trial, Marc-André Raffalovich remarked that Wilde's fall seemed paltry (*mesquine*) compared with Eulenberg's (Raffalovich, "Chronique de l'unisexualité," *Archives de l'anthropologie criminelle*, 1909, vol. 24, p. 359). The best account in English is J. D. Steakley, "Iconography of a scandal: political cartoons and the Eulenberg affair," *Studies in Visual Commuication*, 1983, vol. 9, pp. 20–51; see also E. Ebermayer, "Glanz und Gloria verblasst: der Fall Fürst Philipp zu Eulenberg-Hertefeld," *Der Neue Pitaval*, 1967, vol. 14, p. 115–64.

29 E. Charles in *La Grande Revue*, July 1910. In Fersen's autobiographical novel *Lord Lyllian* (1905), its persecuted and disillusioned hero, unlike the author, commits suicide instead of going abroad, which indicates how requisite this fate had become for the homosexual in fiction.

30 Quoted in M. Delbourg-Delphis, *Masculin singulier*, Paris, Hachette, 1985, p. 162. Perhaps this is why Proust claimed that he was himself obliged to "dissect" homosexuality in *Sodome et Gomorrhe* and report his conclusions "with the good faith of a chemist." See L. de Robert, *Comment débuta Marcel Proust: lettres inédites*, Paris, Nouvelle Revue Française, 1969, pp. 64, 66.

31 Quoted in Willy, op. cit., pp. 246–7.

32 Willy, op. cit., p. 248.

33 Bruckner also carried on the tradition of the law-reform play in *Die Verbrecher* (*The Criminals*, 1928).

# The Blackmailers

*A play in four acts*
*by*
*John Gray and Marc-André Raffalovich*

(1894)

*The Blackmailers* is published for the first time from the typescript submitted to the Lord Chamberlain's Office and held in the Manuscript Division of the British Library. It is published with the permission of the British Library.

# Introduction

It is not surprising that the first *fin-de-siècle* play to present a modern homoerotic relationship in a reasonably overt manner is entitled *The Blackmailers* (1894). What is unusual is that the title characters are both members of high society and the deviants as well. The surprise grows on learning that the equation of homosexuality and extortion is made not by some bulwark of entrenched morality, but by John Gray (1866–1934) and Marc-André Raffalovich (1864–1934).

Gray, who occasionally signed himself "Dorian," was an irresistibly good-looking young man of working-class origins, whom Oscar Wilde befriended and launched into literature. Wilde defrayed the costs of Gray's first book of "decadent" poems, *Silverpoints* (1893), and introduced him into society. The manuscript poem "Passing the love of women" was thought to be his, and critics once mistakenly attributed to Gray a pedophilic story "The Priest and the Acolyte" that was cited in evidence at Wilde's trials. Although he gravitated to the *bon ton*, Gray was by no means a snob or an exhibitionist, and when *The Star* identified him as the hero of *The Picture of Dorian Gray*, he threatened to sue for libel, the case being settled out of court.[1]

Raffalovich, a rich French dilettante of Russian-Jewish parentage and flamboyant manners, saw himself as a rival of Wilde. Perhaps because of his European background, his finely crafted verse, five volumes of which had appeared by 1896, was far more emotionally outspoken than most English homophilic poetry. Wilde himself was bemused by Raffalovich's militant openness and, with a tinge of anti-Semitism, cattily remarked that Raffalovich had come to London to found a salon and succeeded in opening a saloon. (It might be mentioned that Raffalovich was definitely *not* good-looking.) He wooed Gray away from Wilde's circle, now increasingly dominated by Lord Alfred Douglas, and it has been suggested that Gray and Raffalovich began playwriting to emulate the more famous poet's recent success as a dramatist. Most of their efforts were realized in private theatricals.[2]

Raffalovich was sufficiently proud of their dramatic efforts to rent the West Theatre in the Albert Hall on 17 April 1894 to present two one-act plays, *Sour Grapes*, a masque in rhymed couplets by Gray and *Black Sheep*, a

*Plate 1* Oscar Wilde and Lord Alfred Douglas, 1893. The master–acolyte relationship between Wilde and Douglas served, in some degree, as a model for that between Claud and Hal in *The Blackmailers* (although, ironically, Douglas was more sexually experienced than the older man). (Laurence Senelick Collection.)

17

*Plate 2* W.L. Abingdon who created the role of the master criminal Claud in the only performance of *The Blackmailers*. Photograph by Alfred Ellis, from *The Theatre*, Nov. 1896. (Laurence Senelick Collection.)

pastoral pantomime with spoken prologue and epilogue by Raffalovich. The choice of genres remarkably forecasts Mikhail Kuzmin's *divertissements*, but the evening opened with a more Shavian squib, the "Dynamiter's piece," a rhymed monologue spoken by "Etienne Rozenwaltoff," a Franco-Polish anarchist who admits that he kills for fun; his terror is directed at a "fine young fellow" sporting a white carnation.[3] Offered to an invited audience, these fanciful pieces by their very titles reveal an eagerness to tease, which becomes open provocation in *The Blackmailers*.

*The Blackmailers* received a single matinee performance at the Prince of Wales Theatre on 7 June 1894. Although the only extant copy of the play exhibits no blue-pencilling by the Lord Chamberlain's Office, the authors complained that the play as performed was "a mangled and mutilated version of the first four acts . . . scene after scene ruined by cuts, omissions, impoverishment and slipshod" rehearsals.[4] What the authors lamented can be glimpsed by the one example of an altered

speech we can trace. In the licensed typescript, the final curtain line is given to a secondary character, Mr. Dangar Felbert, who says of the protagonist, as he disposes of a glass of poison, "Do you think it would have been better if he had taken it?" This verbose sentence with its conditional tense ends the play on a querulous and uncertain note, a further demolition of the moral pretences of the Dangar–Felbert clan. The actors apparently found this too feeble a curtain speech, and, as quoted by one critic, the last line performed was given to the protagonist's mother who exclaimed bluntly "Oh, why didn't he kill himself!"[5]

The performance also undermined the play's novelty in another way. The leading roles were cast from actors associated with the Adelphi Theatre, London's favorite home of melodrama. The critical part of the blackguard Claud was bestowed on Irish-born William L. Abingdon (1859–1918), the Adelphi's favorite villain who had made "his reputation for depicting the acme of scoundrelism."[6] To Abingdon's credit, it should be pointed out that he contributed his services to the reforming repertory of the Independent Theatre, and in 1891 had played both Dr. Rank in *A Doll's House* and the homicidal lover in Zola's *Thérèse Raquin*, a play regarded by the critics as "squalid and repulsive." In other words, recognizing Abingdon, the audience would immediately tag Claud as a bad sort, eminently hissable.

Similarly, the role of his chief victim Mrs. Bond-Hinton was taken by Olga Brandon (1865–1906), an Australian actress of Russian descent, a tall, graceful woman with large dark-brown eyes, famous as an "emotional actress" who wholeheartedly identified with her characters. Her skill was so great that the more discriminating were disappointed when she joined the Adelphi company to play melodrama heroines. Her entrance on stage would therefore alert the spectator to the fact that she would be made to suffer painfully over the course of the evening, and that one's sympathies should be invested in her character.

Nevertheless, whatever mangling the script underwent and whatever subtleties were occluded by the casting, the basic story remained.

Claud Price, an urbane and resourceful scoundrel of 31, is blackmailing a married woman in high society who had once been his mistress; he is also cultivating a contempt for the world in Hyacinth Halford Dangar, a 24-year-old scapegrace who amuses him. Hal (Hyacinth is an ancestral name, which only Claud uses) has already been practicing extortion on his college chums for some time and with some success. When he is exposed and rebuked by a family council and faced with exile to New Zealand, Hal briefly contemplates suicide, but a note from Claud arrives, inviting the disciple to join him in Paris. "I don't want to triumph without you, my pupil, soon to be my equal. Come. We understand each other now, and the World."

The *Times*, which found the play "sordid and repulsive," described Hal as a "foolish youth" and Claud's influence over him as "sinister"; it noted that their "game appears to be perfectly well understood by the society in which they move, and which, nevertheless, tolerates them."[7] The critics' opprobrium was reserved for the poor stagecraft and the "Ibsenite" final curtain, which left the cads unpunished. One can only assume that the perversion factor had also been elided in performance.

The dialogue portrays Claud as a drawing-room Svengali, his "soothing voice" uttering "long hypnotic speeches"; a young lady tells him, "The sound of your voice makes simply the old gurgling impression upon me, putting my senses to sleep." *The Blackmailers* was written at the same time as Svengali, George Du Maurier's striking depiction of the degenerate Jew as mesmerist, was taking hold of the popular imagination. The nexus of Jew, artist and sexual outsider was not unfamiliar, and, given Raffalovich's antecedents, might have triggered an unconscious shock of recognition.

Claud, his origins obscure, comes across as a tuppence-colored version of the romantic criminal, a loner who seeks a kindred spirit and finally finds him in the promising ephebe he molds into his weapon against society. The English playwright Neil Bartlett perceptively equates the pair with Vautrin and Lucien de Rubempré in Balzac's *Les Illusions perdues* and *Les Splendeurs et misères des courtisanes*.[8] The avowed intention of Gray and Raffalovich was to "trace the makings and downward career of a scoundrel," and Claud Price was seen by the critics as a "loathly object, played with due artistic loathsomeness,"[9] but it is clear that,

like Balzac, the English authors had more fellow feeling for their scoundrels than for their respectable characters. Balzac's picaresque couple are not so well-matched: Lucien returns Vautrin's affection only on the level of filial gratitude, whereas Hal sets out to emulate his mentor's criminality and outdoes him in callousness (Prince Hal to Claud's Falstaff? The endurance of this kind of relationship as a homosexual trope is shown by its recent revival in Gus Van Sant's film *My Own Private Idaho*). Claud combines Vautrin's Olympian contempt for society with Svengali's skulking caddishness, but his own peculiar integrity prevents him from taking £2,000 to release Hal from his clutches.

The disciple, on the other hand, does betray his preceptor for money; Hal's rebellion against society is motivated less by love than by hatred of his family, a grotesque cartoon of an upper middle-class clan – the pillars of society are caricatured as domineering matrons, dotards and mannish spinsters. In the confrontation scene of Act IV, Hal, *"apparently self-satisfied, a flower in his buttonhole,"* is allowed to rail at length against his mother, condemning her for sapping his father's authority and then "when we were older, and you needed his authority as a weapon against us, you called us unnatural because we despised him." Gray's biographer Jerusha McCormack suggests that this accusation has "the trenchancy of actual experience."[10] Indeed, in the typescript, the authors have expanded the speech with another full page of monologue, making it the longest utterance in the play. The symbiosis between Claud and Hal is made out to be more adhesive and more dynamic than the claims of the traditional family.

*The Blackmailers'* open-ended finale best reveals where the authors' sympathies lie. They had reinvented a hackneyed intrigue of society melodrama, the happily-married woman threatened by revelation by past indiscretion, and a hackneyed villain, the former lover turned blackmailer. The critics applied conventional moral standards to the plot, detested the villain, and wondered at the conclusion. They overlooked or undervalued both the novelty of the homophilic relationship between the worldly-wise older man and the apt disciple, and the irony of turning deviants – usually the target of blackmail – into perpetrators, who use extortion as a weapon against an unsympathetic society.

Elements in *The Blackmailers* bear a strong resemblance to similar plot points in *An Ideal Husband*, particularly the attempts of Lady Chiltern to keep her son protected from the influence of the dangerous Lord Goring (who turns out to be his father). A homoerotic (and in this case incestuous) element lurks in Wilde's play; and in a letter to Duncan Grant (2 June 1902), Lytton Strachey was not too fanciful in describing Goring as a "wicked Lord . . . who has made up his mind to bugger one of the other guests – a handsome young man of twenty."

Gray and Raffalovich, however, were copying not only Wilde's literary mannerisms but his personal habits as well. We know from Pierre Louÿs that Gray had felt suicidal when he was pre-empted in Wilde's attentions by Douglas, and that Raffalovich "denounced Wilde's intimacy with Douglas as vain and debauched."[11] Ellen Moers credits "Wilde's homosexuality" with the "division of the *genus* dandy into two classes, the old and the young. . . . With the Lord Gorings and the Lord Henry Woottons, cynical, domineering, intellectual, essentially aristocratic, Wilde tried to identify himself. They are the Brummels of his world. Toward the Dorian Grays, the beautiful Narcissus boys, his attitude was distantly adoring and fearful."[12] Moers overlooks the Greek pederastic model for this pairing, but it is certainly true that Wilde's contemporaries also pictured the homosexual relationship not as a union of equal coevals, but as the unequal and hence unnatural coupling of older man and youth. Wilde's association with Douglas certainly provided the model for the couple Esmé Amaranth and Lord Reggie Hastings in Robert Hichins's satirical novel *The Green Carnation* which appeared the following September. Are Claud and Hal a scurrilous transposition of Oscar and Bosie into a nefarious twosome? If so, none of the critics got the point.

After all, Gray and Raffalovich were accustomed to pitching their literary works at coterie audiences, and groups with special interests made a point of attending performances that spoke to their tastes and concerns. In March 1892, the Press has remarked on Wilde and a phalanx of ephebes in green carnations amid the brilliant audience at the Royalty Theatre, come to see Gray's translation of Théodore de Banville's *The Kiss* performed by the Independent Theatre.[13] A claque of floral gentlemen was also conspicuous on the opening night of Wilde's *Lady Windermere's Fan* in February 1893. The Prince of Wales was a high-class playhouse, which since its opening in 1884 had become known for such musical comedies as *A Gaiety Girl* (1893). Its audience was moneyed and fashionable; a contingent of artistic and homosexual acquaintances would probably have convened to see a one-shot performance of a work by Gray and Raffalovich. Such a group may well have heard of Wilde's 1893 love letter to Lord Alfred Douglas beginning "My dear Hyacinth", copies of which were going the rounds, and may have gossiped about the blackmail levied against the celebrity.

Certainly the in-crowd at the Prince of Wales Theatre, used to reading between the lines, could easily break the code of *The Blackmailers*. What kind of code? The first scene between Hal and Claud constitutes a cipher aimed at such cognoscenti. They speak of gathering apples in an Edenic past and, on a fishing excursion:

> PRICE  I think you were the only fish I caught that day. *(This with intensity)* You didn't like dogs, I remember.
>
> HAL  Ah, but I have a lovely poodle now.

The poodle, like the allusion to a new Marguerite at Covent Garden where they wish they had a box, may be a recondite Faustian reference; but more likely it is a clue to the predilections of London sophisticates. Claud, who has described himself as a "lonely man; so lonely" confesses that "I don't feel so much alone since we have met. I have been a lonely man. *(He pats Hyacinth's head very lightly once or twice.)* . . . When I met you you were on the verge of loneliness. No one understood you." Here the isolation of the romantic outlaw is diluted by a kind of self-pity which rings in the note of "all the sad young men." Raffalovich in a later article on "uranists" declared, "A man with this vice *withdraws* from himself, from the human community. . . . He leads a life apart, in a confined corner, in a brotherhood which recognizes one another by voice, by eye staring straight ahead, by that singsong tone they all affect."[14] "Loneliness", therefore, is a codeword for sexual deviance, just as "stupidity" is made a codeword for heterosexuality in a line spoken by Claud to Hal, which the authors cut: "You are unfolding yourself, freeing yourself from all the trammels of stupidity."

More ambiguous snatches of dialogue lend themselves to interpretation. Hal soliloquizes, "Only think of having to keep a watch over your face, your gestures, to be acting before one's nearest. Oh! that must be exciting, delightful, that must be knowing that one lives." Ostensibly, this relates to the victims of blackmail but can be read as the homosexual's creed, the double game constantly played to avoid detection. In Act II, the ambiguity grows even stronger when Claud backs Hal into a psychological corner:

> PRICE  You know what you are, Hyacinth, don't you?
>
> HAL  What am I? What do you mean?
>
> PRICE  You know the name by which this sort of transaction usually goes – even among the unprejudiced?
>
> HAL  No . . . *(Under Price's look he falters)*. Yes.
>
> PRICE  And it is?
>
> HAL  Spare me? Spare me! Claud!

After this hysterical crescendo, Claud Price's line "Blackmail" is almost anticlimactic; since the coterie audience would readily have had "sodomy" on its lips.

A year after *The Blackmailers* enjoyed its unique performance, the trials of Oscar Wilde would make even such an encoded and sublimated presentation impossible. Jeffrey Weeks calls the trials "labelling processes of a most explicit kind, drawing a clear line between acceptable and abhorrent behaviour,"[15] creating as never before a public image of the "homosexual" (a word that did not appear in English in print until 1897). As soon as the new type had become identified and defined, it was excluded from the dramatic gallery because of its "unspeakable" aspects.

Raffalovich, who confessed himself a congenital homosexual, lost no time in attacking with special animus the decadence he had once flaunted. His chapter on "L'Affaire Oscar Wilde" in *Uranisme et Unisexualité* (1896), the most comprehensive volume on the subject written in England to that date (characteristically published in French in a series on criminology), is unmerciful to his downed rival. As a prolific writer on "unisexuality" in European scientific journals, Raffalovich made the argument that "uranistes" were like anyone else and could play a valuable part in society once they "renounce sexual sensualities, and devote themselves to a celibacy which will not be sterile."[16] In his view, homosexual celibacy would be the equivalent of heterosexual marriage, and this appears to be the nature of his union with Gray. The two poets lived together first in London, then in Edinburgh, in a menage that was probably more comradely than passionate. Gray converted to Roman Catholicism in 1890; Raffalovich was to follow suit six years later. After Gray took holy orders, they both dedicated their lives to expiating the sins of their youth.

## *Notes*

1  For a minor figure, Gray has inspired a remarkable number of biographies, all of which give short shrift to his dramatic efforts. See B. Sewell (ed.), *Two Friends: John Gray and André Raffalovich*, Aylesworth, St Albert's Press, 1963; B. Sewell, *Footnote to the Nineties*, London, Cecil and Amelia Woolf, 1968; G. A. Cevasco, *John Gray*, Boston, Twayne, 1982; B. Sewell, *In the Dorian Mode: A Life of John Gray*, Padstow, Tabb House, 1983; and J. H. McCormack, *John Gray, Poet, Dandy and Priest*, Hanover, NH, Brandeis University Press, 1991. Also to be consulted are B. Reade (ed.), *Sexual Heretics: Male Homosexuality in English Literature from 1850 to 1900*, London, Routledge and Kegan Paul, 1970, pp. 31–5; and R. Croft-Cooke, *Feasting with Panthers: A New Consideration of Some Late Victorian Writers*, New York, Holt, Rinehart and Winston, 1967, pp. 208–26.

2  A couple of privately printed duologues *A Northern Aspect* and *The Ambush of Young Days* (1895) survive. Probably performed at a Raffalovich party, they are attempts at epigrammatic society comedy in the Wilde mode.

3  McCormack, op. cit., p. 153.

4  "The Blackmailers," *Theatre* (1 July 1894): 37–8. See Documents.

5  That Hal does not take poison may be an oblique reference to John Todhunter's *The Black Cat*, produced at the Opera

Comique the previous year, whose cast included a malevolent character named Cyril Vane, clearly based on Wilde. One of the central characters takes poison. William Archer, who had noted how a little while earlier, the play would have been attacked as "putrescent Ibsenism," also pointed out that "poison seemed out of place" in such a play. W. Archer, *The Theatrical 'World' of 1893*, London, Walter Scott, 1894, pp. 281–4; *The Theatrical 'World' of 1894*, London, Walter Scott, 1895, p. 94.

6  E. Reid and H. Compton (eds), *The Dramatic Peerage 1892*, London, Raithby, Lawrence and Co., 1892, pp. 3–4.

7  See Documents.

8  N. Bartlett, *Who Was That Man? A Present for Mr. Oscar Wilde*, London, Serpent's Tail, 1988, p. 123. That Raffalovich was familiar with Balzac's characters is proven by his reference to them in his article, "Chronique de l'unisexualité," *Archives de l'anthropologie criminelle*, 1909, vol. 24, p. 359.

9  *Theatre*, pp. 37–8.

10  McCormack, op. cit., p. 13. She claims to have examined a manuscript of the last act in the Gray papers at the National Library of Scotland, but the Keeper of Manuscripts there has assured me that no such thing exists.

11  R. Ellmann, *Oscar Wilde*, New York, Alfred R. Knopf, 1989, pp. 391–2.

12  E. Moers, *The Dandy Brummel to Beerbohm*, New York, Viking Press, 1960, pp. 306.

13  "Mr. Oscar Wilde and a suite of young gentlemen, all wearing the vivid dyed carnation which has superseded the lily and the sunflower," *The Star* (5 Mar. 1892).

14  A. Raffalovich, 'Les groupes uranistes à Paris et à Berlin,', *Archives de l'anthropologie criminelle*, 1904, vol. 19, p. 926.

15  J. Weeks, *Sex, Politics and Society: The Regulation of Sexuality since 1800*, London, Longman, 1985, p. 103. Also see his "Movements of affirmation: sexual meanings and homosexual identities," in K. Peiss and C. Simmons, (eds), *Passion and Power: Sexuality in History*, Philadelphia, Temple University Press, 1989, pp. 70–86.

16  A. Raffalovich, "A propos du syndicat des uranistes," *Archives de l'anthropologie criminelle*, 1905, vol. 20, p. 285.

# The Blackmailers

A play in four acts

*John Gray*
*and*
*Marc-André Raffalovich*

First produced at the Criterion Theatre, London, June 1st, 1894[1]

## Characters

ADMIRAL SIR FELBERT DANGAR, 68 years old

MR DANGAR FELBERT, 48 years old

EDWARD BOND HINTON, 45 years old

GUY JOSCELYN, 22 years old

CLAUD PRICE, 31 years old

HYACINTH HALFORD DANGAR, 24 years old

LADY FELBERT, 70 years old

THE HON. MISS ALCYRA FELBERT, 35 years old

MRS DANGAR, 48 years old

MRS TAUNTON (Mrs. Dangar's daughter), 27 years old

VIOLET BOND-HINTON, 27 years old

SUSAN (Mrs. Dangar's parlour-maid)

CAMILLA BOND-HINTON, 30 years old

TWO MEN-SERVANTS

## Act I: "Camilla"

SCENE: *a smoking-room at the Bond-Hintons' house. They have just given a dinner-party of six: Themselves,* MRS. DANGAR, MISS BOND-HINTON, CLAUD PRICE. HAL DANGAR *was asked, but failed; and a man, a neighbour, was called in in his place.* BOND-HINTON *and* PRICE *come into the smoking-room.*

BOND-HINTON   . . . so make yourself comfortable for a few minutes. . . .

PRICE   All right, old chap.

BOND-HINTON   It's no use letting him stay, he's too far gone: have a cigar, you know where to find them – oh, I see they're out. I'll talk to him for a minute or two and then send him home. I'm very sorry my wife asked him.

PRICE   Yes, he's not good for much. I might just write that letter now; it'll save time.

BOND-HINTON   Certainly, certainly; it'll save time.

(BOND-HINTON *goes out.* PRICE *sits down at the writing-table, writes a line; stops, thinks, looks at the fireplace. Gets up and removes the photograph of* MRS. BOND-HINTON'*s little girl from the place it usually occupies, on top of the clock.*)

PRICE   The signal agreed upon between us. I must see you alone whatever happens. (*He returns to the writing-table. A* SERVANT *comes in with coffee.*)

SERVANT   Coffee, sir? (PRICE *takes no notice.*) Take coffee, sir?

PRICE   Set it down.

SERVANT   Take cognac, sir?

PRICE   (*Still abstracted*) Set it down.

(*The* SERVANT *goes to the fireplace and puts the photograph back in its place.* PRICE *has been writing in thoughtful snatches. He is deeply absorbed and after the servant has gone out of the room repeats*):

. . . set it down . . . set it down . . . ah!

(*He rapidly finishes his letter, and seals it. He hesitates as to which pocket to put it in. As a sudden afterthought he tears off the piece of blotting paper and puts that in his pocket too. Goes to one of the little tables, chooses a cigar, bites off the end and spits it to the far end of the room. Puts a piece of sugar in a cup of coffee and thus observes that the photograph has been replaced on the clock. Takes it off again. At last composes himself comfortably in a certain chair when he hears the voice of* BOND-HINTON *returning.*)

(*Enter* BOND-HINTON)

BOND-HINTON   Price! Price! You must take the beast home.

PRICE   Must I?

BOND-HINTON   *(Excited)* Just that minute I was away, he finished the claret, and now I doubt if he can stand.

PRICE   *(Caressingly)* Don't get excited.

BOND-HINTON   It's only just round the corner, the second house on the right. Come on, make haste, while there's no one about.

*(They go out. Enter* CAMILLA. *She starts when she sees the moved photograph, the signal. She is very anxious. She looks at the photograph, sighs, and puts it back in its place.)*

CAMILLA   *(Murmurs)* I don't want to see him. *(She comes to* PRICE's *chair and sits down in it, leaning her cheek against the leather back.)* I don't want to see him.

*(Enter* VIOLET, *dragging* MRS. DANGAR. CAMILLA *stands up with a guilty start.)*

VIOLET   It's all right, Mrs. Dangar, Aunt Camilla is here smoking her cigarette.

MRS. DANGAR   Are you ill, Camilla? You looked so pale when you left us . . . and I was anxious about you at dinner. Are you ill? Violet tells me you often find your way here after dinner, so we came down to look for you. I confess I should not choose this atmosphere myself. There is always something unpleasant to me in a man's room. *(VIOLET laughs.)* I grant it is quiet, you can't hear the noise of the street. But the drawing-room is pleasanter.

CAMILLA   *(Very tired)* Much pleasanter.

VIOLET   This is more comfortable. When I am married I shall make my husband's smoking-room my boudoir.

CAMILLA   Why?

VIOLET   So much cheaper! I don't intend to marry a rich man; only one room to furnish instead of two and twice as much to spend on making that one comfortable.

CAMILLA   You make one laugh, Violet.

MRS. DANGAR   I wish I had the bringing-up of Violet. My daughter was so sensible at such an early age that I never had the pleasure of training her. She always knew more than anyone else. Her husband, who has more prospects than income, says that her business capacity is such that he dreads the day when he will come into his fortune. He says that when they have four thousand a year she will still cater for him as if he were on board wages. As it is she does not allow him to dine out too often. Dinner at home is so much cheaper.

CAMILLA   A wonderful woman. She has an ideal: cost-price.

VIOLET   Money is not happiness.

MRS. DANGAR   Don't fall in love, Violet. *(A pause.* VIOLET *expects* CAMILLA *to break it.* VIOLET *says):*

VIOLET   What a pity Hal could not dine. I have only seen him twice since his return.

CAMILLA   So have I, and neither time here. I saw him one morning *(To* MRS. DANGAR*)* at your house, and once in the Park.

MRS. DANGAR   You saw by his note that he was prevented at the last moment. *(Business)*[2] It has taken him a long time to realise what it means to work – and now he does not quite know when to begin and when to leave off. Of course any new profession is hard to learn; yet my boy is very clever, much cleverer than his sensible sister.

VIOLET   And yet he is not selfish. I have been told by his friends that circumstance when he was sent down was the beginning of his popularity at Oxford; and we know at what price a boy buys popularity.

CAMILLA   He is too popular.

MRS. DANGAR   Hal's generosity is spontaneous.

VIOLET   I am sure.

CAMILLA   I believe he is as single-hearted as kindhearted.

MRS. DANGAR   His poor father's character has been modified in Hal to his advantage. I see in the son the same rush, the same impulse which in the father I knew well was counter-balanced by unscrupulous calculation as the other side of his character.

VIOLET   Hal would have been so much nicer. Mr. Craven could never make up his mind between talking to me and eating his dinner. And being undecided he tried to do both at once.

MRS. DANGAR   Good-natured of him to come at a moment's notice, was it not, Camilla? I like him because of his dear mother, who was so eccentric at cards, so remarkable in her dress. He is a good-natured man is he not, Camilla?

CAMILLA   *(Absent-minded)* Yes . . . yes.

MRS. DANGAR   I dined at his house the other

day and he showed me his beautiful things. Have you seen his collection of Chinese china, Camilla?

CAMILLA   Yes . . . yes.

(MRS. DANGAR *looks at her impatiently*.)

VIOLET   I met Lady Fairvil in Berkeley Square this morning. Dear old Hero was with her. He knew me at once.

MRS. DANGAR   You did not speak to either of them, I suppose?

VIOLET   Could I cut her because she ran away with my cousin?

MRS. DANGAR   It is as disgraceful for a woman to run away . . .

VIOLET   From a brute?

MRS. DANGAR   From a brute as for a soldier to run away from his countrie's enemies.

VIOLET   Oh!

CAMILLA   Lady Fairvil is not a woman one can know; and if you meet her again in Berkeley Square, or anywhere else, you must not talk to Hero.

VIOLET   I assure you she tried to avoid me.

CAMILLA   I should be astonished if Emily Fairvil in spite of her abominable conduct did not remember what was due to you.

MRS. DANGAR   That is right, Camilla, spoken with your sound sense. You have never allowed an objectionable *woman* in your entourage. And when you were younger that required some character.

(A pause)

VIOLET   Aunt Camilla has not explained to us why she was not smoking her cigarette when we came in. Your maid tells me that of late you have been so much in this room that your hair has smelt of smoke. It made me laugh because of that one occasion I went to the Tivoli and could not unsmoke myself afterwards. I must have some of that smoke about me still.

CAMILLA   (*Angrily*) I am sending my maid away; she has become impertinent.

MRS. DANGAR   Send away Mary after all these years! – What will Cissie do when she is here for her holidays? Why Cissie will never forgive you, Camilla.

CAMILLA   Forgive! What a word! My Cissie does not know what it means to have to forgive, my dear Mrs. Dangar.

VIOLET   Aunt Camilla, you are so devoted to Cissie that sometimes I almost wish I were

a child – and I did not like my childhood. My mother did not spoil me as you spoil Cissie sometimes when you are sitting with us and are absent-minded (which you never used to be when she was at home). I think you are wondering whether Cissie has been good and knows her lessons, and not run in the sun without a hat.

(CAMILLA *is silent; but her eyes become sad and tender*. MRS. DANGAR *watches her*.)

MRS. DANGAR   Shall we go back to the drawing-room, Camilla?

CAMILLA   Yes . . . yes . . .

SERVANT   Mr. Halford Dangar!

(Enter HAL. *He goes over to* CAMILLA *and says*):

HAL   I am so sorry. I am so ill. I was detained. I will tell you all about it afterwards. You will be sympathetic, dear Mrs. Bond-Hinton and cheer me up. I require cheering up. (*He laughs*.)

CAMILLA   We missed you, my dear Hal.

MRS. DANGAR   How are you, my child?

HAL   So well, mother, I think work agrees with me. There's nothing like doing something after all.

(MRS. DANGAR *looks pleased*.)

CAMILLA   You have cured him. He was ill when he came a minute ago.

(VIOLET *laughs and pretends to feel his pulse*.)

MRS. DANGAR   Ill?

HAL   Nonsense, mother, they are making fun of me, don't you see? Dear mother does not take very kindly to jokes about her darling boy. That's why she took me away from school because she did not like my nickname. I've had such a day. I won't tell you about the business part of it because that would be tedious, and as I am trying to model myself on Mr. Bond-Hinton who never talks to you (*To* CAMILLA) of business, and yet he has so many companies to look after.

CAMILLA   But you have dined, Hal?

HAL   Dined? An excellent dinner! I should think so. (VIOLET *laughs*.) Of course I just snatched something whilst I talked business with a man. No, I am not at all hungry. Oh! I do take care of myself. My mother need not be anxious. And then I had such a jolly lunch, with Harry Scarsbrook and he became so cheery, oh! so cheery. (HAL *laughs heartily.*)

VIOLET   I should not be cheery if I had a stepbrother like his . . . depend upon it, Harry Scarsbrook's cheeriness is counted, and if he is not careful that stepbrother of his will work mischief between Harry and his father.

HAL   Oh! how melodramatic, Violet. This is real life, we have bothers, but no secrets, dislikes but no hates, spites but no revenge. I wonder sometimes whether people who lived in other days, in times when things happened, found life more exciting. What would you give for a secret? Only think of having to keep a watch over your face, your gestures, to be acting before one's nearest. Oh! that must be exciting, delightful, that must be knowing that one lives . . .

MRS. DANGAR   Camilla, shall we go back to the drawing-room?

(CAMILLA *gets up.*)

HAL   I want to smoke. I need a cigarette.
VIOLET   And I have to talk to him.

(MRS. DANGAR, *displeased, gets up.* VIOLET *and* HAL *laugh. He is showing her a letter.* CAMILLA *moves towards the door with an air of relief.* MRS. DANGAR *stops her.*)

MRS. DANGAR   This is the best opportunity, Camilla. I want to speak to you.
CAMILLA   Now? Here?
MRS. DANGAR   Yes, whilst these silly children are not listening, and before Edward comes. In the drawing-room Violet would keep her ears open, and I can't leave her here lest that man should return with his cautious voice and apologetic manner, and persecute Violet.
CAMILLA   I am sure that Mr. Price does not persecute Violet.
HAL   (*To* VIOLET) I have brought you the new puzzle. The Maze, or how to bring Queen Eleanor into the bower of Fair Rosamund. Queen Eleanor is the mustard coloured globule, and Fair Rosamund the white pellet. I am sure they would do one good to take after some tiring scene or before going to the ball.

VIOLET   Faithful to your passion for mysterious globules in your waistcoat pocket.
HAL   I wish you would give me some smelling salts for my birthday. I feel so faint sometimes.
CAMILLA   (*To* MRS. DANGAR) It is only that I am not very well. The season is a tiring time. Indeed I made up my mind not to go to that fancy dress ball this evening at the Cosways.
VIOLET   Mr. Price is going to the Cosways with Uncle Edward. They are to be dressed exactly alike, but how I don't know. Do you know, Aunt Camilla?
CAMILLA   How should I?
MRS. DANGAR   I do not care for idle gossip, Camilla, and I have lived my life without confidences, without violent intimacies, but there are moments in our lives when we are bound, some of us, to offer sympathy, and some of us accept it. You are still young enough to need help, and quite old enough not to reject it. That poor boy of mine, my Hyacinth, is alarmingly prompt in shrinking from all that is serious, but you, Camilla, are not a widow's spoilt darling.
CAMILLA   I am convinced of your kindness, but it is quite beyond me to guess the drift of your words. I may be fagged, but what is that?
MRS. DANGAR   Camilla, Camilla.
HAL   Mother is giving it to Mrs. Bond-Hinton. I wonder what about. Are you not curious, Violet? I am always so horridly curious.
VIOLET   Things have not gone well this evening. Mrs. Dangar was wondering why you had not come and if you were in any mischief. Bobby Craven was inarticulate before we left. Aunt Camilla told most of her best anecdotes so quickly that we never quite knew which one we were laughing at. Uncle Edward and that Mr. Price talked about the city and about people we don't know and are not likely to know.
HAL   What is he like, Mr. Price? City? Is he rich? Is he young?
VIOLET   He is the sort of looking man who asks to be introduced to one's chaperone and who speaks to a girl about the weather in so soft and soothing a voice that one's father becomes inquisitive.
HAL   You girls are always so spiteful and

such bad judges of men. Tell me some more about him.

MRS. DANGAR   One's family first and then one's other duties. There is some sort of resentment between you and Edward. He has been a good husband in his way, Camilla. He has always respected your home and your self-respect. He may have deceived you – our husbands don't call it deceiving when they are not found out, but you cannot complain. You are a practical happy woman of the world and you adore your Cissie.

CAMILLA   I don't complain, Mrs. Dangar. But if I choose to complain, I should have much to say. Edward may have been what you call a good husband but he has always counted on my forgiveness, on my anger, on my indifference. It is a dangerous game for a husband to play. As my Cissie grows older I love her more I am more anxious for her but she is less of a refuge for me. Then she is approaching that captious, critical, observant age . . .

MRS. DANGAR   Is that why you sent her to school?

(CAMILLA *flushes with anger.*)

HAL   (VIOLET *and he have been talking of* PRICE *all the time.*) *Is* he rich?

VIOLET   Looks rich, and prosperous, but overacts the part.

HAL   Lucky fellow.

VIOLET   Here he is. I don't like him.

(MRS. BOND-HINTON *looks up anxiously and is relieved to find her husband alone. He crosses to* HAL *and shakes hands.*)

MRS. DANGAR   (*Who has been talking earnestly to* CAMILLA) A dangerous game, my dear.

CAMILLA   (*With affected disdain*) Dangerous?

BOND-HINTON   "Dangerous" did I hear? (*Crossing to* MRS. DANGAR *and* CAMILLA. MRS. DANGAR *laughs.*)

MRS. DANGAR   Yes very.

CAMILLA   Has Mr. Price gone?

BOND-HINTON   He has gone home with Craven.

CAMILLA   With Mr. Craven?

BOND-HINTON   Yes. Bobbie was taken queer rather suddenly.

HAL   The old complaint I suppose? . . . Mumps.

BOND-HINTON   The old complaint.

VIOLET   He was sickening for it at dinner.

MRS. DANGAR   Violet! Violet!

CAMILLA   He was sickening *with* it . . . Forgive me.

BOND-HINTON   Well Hal, what's your news.

CAMILLA   Blow him up, Edward, the scapegrace.

BOND-HINTON   I suppose he had something more amusing to do.

(VIOLET *laughs.*)

HAL   I assure you –

MRS. DANGAR   Poor boy, he was detained by business.

HAL   How cruel you are Mrs. Bond-Hinton.

CAMILLA   Do you think so? Better wait till you have had experience of my cruelty. Edward, do you wish I were going with you to the Cosways?

BOND-HINTON   No, my love, it's wiser of you not to go; especially as it would bore you.

VIOLET   I wish I were going.

BOND-HINTON   Oh! Oh!

CAMILLA   I've arranged, Edward, to call to-morrow on your friend Mrs. Finchley.

BOND-HINTON   Mrs. Finchley? Oh, I'm afraid she's out of town.

MRS. DANGAR   A good thing.

(CAMILLA *turns to* MRS. DANGAR *to hear what she can about Mrs. Finchley.* VIOLET *is amusing herself balancing a paper-knife.*)

BOND-HINTON   Well, my boy, did you do good business in New York?

HAL   No, I can't say that I did. (*Getting confused.* BOND-HINTON *is amused at his confusion.*) You see, I've not very much experience; I'm not very old – you see –

BOND-HINTON   (*With sudden bonhomie*) Did you have a good time?

HAL   (*Grasping his hand*) Yes, yes. I had a good time. But oh, the crossing. Will you believe me I hardly know what an Atlantic steamer is like. I didn't even see the sea. I would rather starve in England than cross the Atlantic again for a fortune.

VIOLET   Didn't you like the Americans, Hal?

HAL   Yes, but in future they'll have to come to me. Ill I knew I should be; and I thought I was brave about it. But day after day, the terror of it. I've no more conceit about my courage. I did not know such suffering existed. I started in ignorance. And when I stepped on the steamer to return I was too idiotic to know what I was doing. If I could have thought about it I should have settled in America.

BOND-HINTON   Weren't you well at all the whole time?

HAL   Not for an hour. But I had a good time. Three months of wild bliss.

BOND-HINTON   *That's* all right.

HAL   I thank you for all you have done for me, but for nothing more than this, in spite of the sea. I am always more grateful for a pleasure than a service.

BOND-HINTON   That's very candid.

*(HAL is confused.)*

CAMILLA   *(To* MRS. DANGAR*)* Poor Mrs. Dove is always opening her mouth, and forgetting what she means to say; and then, not to look foolish, she says something spiteful. *(Laughing)* Why, the other day . . . *(Breaks off on hearing* PRICE's *voice)*

*(Enter* PRICE. VIOLET *looks up crossly,* HAL *with interest and curiosity.)*

PRICE   I am sorry to have deprived myself of your company so long.

CAMILLA   We are sorry, Mr. Price.

PRICE   *(To* MRS. DANGAR*)* Do I see your little boy Hyacinth, Mrs. Dangar?

MRS. DANGAR   He is grown up, Mr. Price.

PRICE   As I see.

MRS. DANGAR   And no one ever calls him Hyacinth. He left it off, when his hair was first cut.

PRICE   A most beautiful name, Hyacinth, I see in it all the fancy and romance of a young mother's imagination.

MRS. DANGAR   He is called so because he had an ancestor called Hyacinth d'Anguerre, who came into the family by marriage with a daughter of Lord Rutstoke of Rutstoke, who supported the Duke of Albany in his attempts for the crown of Scotland. The family have chosen to preserve the name.

*(PRICE observes* HAL *critically.)*

PRICE   Then Hyacinth *(Correcting himself)*, your son is of Scottish descent?

MRS. DANGAR   We are English. *(*CAMILLA

joins. PRICE *remains.)* Camilla, I want you and Edward to dine with me one day next week. Is there anyone you would like me to ask?

CAMILLA   Oh no. It is a pleasure to me to meet other people than my own friends.

*(PRICE has been observing* HYACINTH.*)*

MRS. DANGAR   Would Wednesday or Thursday suit you?

CAMILLA   Either day for me. I will ask Edward and let you know.

*(VIOLET, HYACINTH and BOND-HINTON in a group over the puzzle.)*

HAL   Violet is going to give me some smelling salts for my birthday.

VIOLET   Am I?

BOND-HINTON   Ah, Hal, with your puzzles and capsules and smelling salts. What a happy life yours must be!

HAL   So it is.

PRICE   What a fortunate boy, your son, Mrs. Dangar! How I envy him! How I should like to be like him and have people care for me. I wonder if he knows how well off he is? I wonder if he appreciates what it is to have a devoted mother. Ah! the disinterested love of a woman!

*(CAMILLA pretends not to be listening, she walks over to her husband.)*

PRICE   I am such a lonely man; so lonely.

CAMILLA   Ah! dear, you're not going?

BOND-HINTON   Yes, just off; presently.

CAMILLA   Cissie will be home for her holidays in a fortnight.

BOND-HINTON   So soon?

CAMILLA   Then I shall long for us to get away. *(Retreats and talks inaudibly)*

HAL   *(To* VIOLET, *with the air of someone who knows he is being looked at)* Guy Joscelyn was saying to me this evening . . .

VIOLET   *(Excited)* Guy!

HAL   Yes he made me late this evening. That is the real truth. We are both of us pretty near broke.

VIOLET   It's only because the boy is unhappy. If he had what he wanted he would not be extravagant. But how could you have seen him this evening?

HAL   Why, he comes to see me most days at least for a week and then I don't see him

for a year. Guy's way . . . always
exaggerating.

VIOLET   Your way you mean. But you can't
have been detained by Guy as his train left
Paddington at 5.37 this afternoon and at
that time my father saw you in a hansom
in Exeter Street with a most rascally
looking foreigner.

HAL   (*Shortly*) It isn't true. (*He laughs.*) I owe
him money. (*He sighs.*) Ah! you would be
miserable, Violet, if you hadn't any money.

VIOLET   I shouldn't want other people's.

(HAL *crosses to his mother and* PRICE. VIOLET
*follows shortly.*)

HAL   Mother, did you tell me you wanted
me to make calls with you to-morrow?

MRS. DANGAR   I did, my dear. Why?

HAL   I had an idea, that was all.

VIOLET   That is a rare event.

(HAL *turns away towards* PRICE *who takes his
opportunity.*)

PRICE   You don't remember me, I suppose.
. . . Claud Price.

HAL   Claud Price; of course. But how you've
altered!

(*They move away.*)

PRICE   So you are little Hyacinth Dangar. It
is funny; the sight of you brings back
memories I had thought quite lost.

HAL   Memories? I hope nothing
disagreeable.

PRICE   (*Laughing*) No. Think of our apple
gathering expeditions.

HAL   Pleasanter for you than for me. I had
the trouble and you had the spoils but
somehow, I didn't mind it. It was fun and I
did get an apple now and then.

PRICE   Great days. We are not contented
with apples now.

HAL   No, it isn't apples now.

PRICE   And that day when I took you fishing
to bait the hooks for me; and you fell in the
river.

HAL   Hey! by Jove yes. You fished me out.

PRICE   I think you were the only fish (*This
with intention*) I caught that day. You didn't
like dogs, I remember.

HAL   Ah, but I have a lovely poodle now.

VIOLET   Mrs. Dangar wants to speak to you,
Hal.

(*He goes.*)

PRICE   Are you going to the Cosways' ball,
Miss Bond-Hinton?

VIOLET   No. I am not allowed. (*She goes up to*
BOND-HINTON)

(PRICE *soon joins* MRS. DANGAR *and her son.*)

VIOLET   Dear Uncle Edward. (*Leading him
away*) Dear Uncle Edward, you are so kind,
so good.

BOND-HINTON   Yes?

VIOLET   You have so many opportunities. If
you get a chance, would you mind saying a
good word for Guy?

BOND-HINTON   Isn't it getting on? Say a
good word to whom?

VIOLET   To mother. She thinks so much of
what you think.

BOND-HINTON   Indeed I will. (*To* MRS.
DANGAR) Good-night, Mrs. Dangar. I must
apologise for leaving you.

MRS. DANGAR   Good-night, Edward.

PRICE   (*To* HAL) Will you come round to my
place and have a drink?

MRS. DANGAR   (*To* HAL) I want you to take
me back.

PRICE   Pardon me, Mrs. Dangar. (*To* HAL)
Perhaps you would come to tea to-morrow
afternoon.

HAL   With pleasure.

MRS. DANGAR   Don't forget, Hal, what you
have to do.

HAL   Oh yes, of course.

MRS. DANGAR   I am sure Mr. Price would
not ask you to break a long engagement.
(*To* PRICE.) My son is too young to neglect
social duties.

PRICE   Quite so, Mrs. Dangar.

BOND-HINTON   Good-night, Violet, good-
night Hal, good-night, dear.

(BOND-HINTON *and* PRICE *leave. As they leave*
PRICE *says to* BOND-HINTON *aside*):

PRICE   Here is the letter. If you see Mrs. K.
this evening you can tell her confidently
she has heard the last of him.

BOND-HINTON   Come up with me. (*Exit*)

VIOLET   What an ill-mannered man! He is
no loss.

MRS. DANGAR   We must be going back, dear.

HAL   I will go back with you.

MRS. DANGAR   Violet and I will go together.
Good-night, Camilla.

VIOLET   Good-night, Hal. Good-night, Aunt Camilla.

(MRS. DANGAR *and* VIOLET *leave.*)

HAL   Who is Mr. Price, Mrs. Bond-Hinton?

CAMILLA   A friend of Edward's. But you knew him.

HAL   A child doesn't know who people are. Where does he live?

CAMILLA   In Park Street.

(*Long silence*)

HAL   You don't ask me about New York, Mrs. Bond-Hinton.

CAMILLA   I don't know what to ask you. I don't know anything about it. If I thought you had left all your difficulties behind I might feel some interest.

HAL   Don't mention them. I'm worse off than ever.

CAMILLA   Are you?

(HAL *goes over to the fireplace and takes the photo of* CISSIE, CAMILLA *watches him.*)

CAMILLA   (*Drily*) Put that back where it was when you've looked at it.

(*He does so crossly.*)

HAL   May I smoke?

CAMILLA   Most certainly.

HAL   Will you?

CAMILLA   No thank you. I have not acquired the habit.

(*Long silence.* HAL *takes up a book on chair L.U., sits down and reads it. Enter* PRICE *L.U.* PRICE *does not see* HAL *and goes up to* CAMILLA *familiarly, insolently.*)

PRICE   So you waited for me, Camilla my girl? That's right. I thought you would.

CAMILLA   I thought you would return to say good-night, Mr. Price.

PRICE   Eh? What's the matter. (*Gesture of* MRS. BOND-HINTON *to let him know Hal is in the room.*) If you are put out with me, no sulks you know . . . (*And he bends over her, lifting up her chin.* HAL *shuts his book loudly,* PRICE *alters his attitude*) If I have displeased you, you will be generous enough to forgive me. (*Said with exaggerated civility*)

HAL   No. Mrs. Bond-Hinton is cross with me.

CAMILLA   (*Last pretence of civility; smiling*) Not at all.

PRICE   Do you ride to-morrow, Mrs. Bond-Hinton?

CAMILLA   No.

PRICE   At any rate we shall see you to-morrow at Mrs. Clough's. (*No answer*) As smart as ever. (*No answer*)

HAL   I am afraid I shall not get my pardon to-day. (*No answer.* PRICE *moves away.* HAL *goes to take an effusive farewell.* PRICE *taking him angrily by the arm.*) But, but . . .

PRICE   (*Roughly*) Come away! Come away, I'll tell you all about it. Good-night, Mrs. Bond-Hinton.

HAL   Good-night Mrs. Bond-Hinton.

(*No answer.* PRICE *takes* HAL*'s arm and they go away.* CAMILLA *sobs hysterically.*)

*Curtain*

## Act II: "Master and Pupil"

HAL*'s rooms.* GUY *and* HAL *just finishing breakfast.*

GUY   You don't give one an appetite, Hal.

HAL   I'm afraid you will have to do without.

(GUY *pours himself another cup of tea and eats some bread and butter.* HAL *looks down.*)

GUY   Hal!

HAL   Shall I order another chop for you?

GUY   What is the matter, Hal, old man? (*Touching him*)

HAL   What should be the matter, do you think? Don't I look as well and happy as I am? Hang it . . . mayn't I be quiet sometimes? I can't be always at high pressure. You have eaten your breakfast . . . can't you smoke now and read the paper and let me think.

GUY   If you thought aloud it might be better for you and more cheerful for me. (*No answer from* HAL)

(GUY *balances his knife etc. Same business as* VIOLET*'s in the first act.*)

HAL   Don't do that. Can't you spare my nerves in the morning? You are as bad as Violet Bond-Hinton: she infuriates my mother with her trick of balancing an inkstand on the edge of a paper knife.

(GUY *sighs several times, partly because he is unhappy, partly to punish* HAL *and partly to obtain some sympathy.*)

HAL   Nice way of beginning the day. Why do you come out to breakfast if you want to sigh and look glum. Have some consideration for me.

GUY   You are a little difficult this morning. And it is hard on me . . . as I want help and advice.

HAL   Don't whimper. There's a good boy. Of course I will help and advise, but there are moments when neither help nor advice are worth much . . . and when sympathy . . . beside being impossible . . . is the worst of all.

GUY   Don't discourage me, Hal. You always had your doleful moods. When the apples were too green your remorse used to be intense; and when it was discovered that you had told Maurice Wyllie . . .

HAL   Spare me those sickening reminiscences if you want me to listen to you.

GUY   You have helped me before, old man . . . *(Bursting out)* The truth is that I am in a worse tangle than ever before; worse than when that girl was expecting me to marry her, you remember.

HAL   Come to the point. I have not over much time this morning.

GUY   Now you look more like yourself. I can tell you everything. I don't know what to do or which way to turn.

HAL   Money of course; your true love I believe runs rather smooth.

GUY   Yes, Violet is splendid; she fights for me, and will stick to me through thick and thin.

HAL   Worried as you are I wonder how you find time to be in love. It puzzles me . . . but yours is a happy disposition, Guy . . . that is why you will get over your troubles more easily than I . . . your worries don't seem to overlap one another as mine do.

GUY   Why are we always bothered about money, you and I? We don't seem to spend much more than other people.

HAL   Whenever any of my people pay my debts it is only on condition that I do impossibilities. Every help I have ever had from them has meant some curtailing of my existence. They have made my life unbearable to me over and over. When my mother paid my debts for the first time she insisted on my leaving Oxford and on my cutting Ned Hounsell . . . because he had lent me two hundred pounds. The second time she raved until I promised to drop Phyllis Preston who had always been most disinterested. Poor little Phyllis. I cannot think of a single instance when I have been helped without being maimed. Even Edward Bond-Hinton made me go to New York.

GUY   I'd go anywhere just now . . . if it were not for Violet.

HAL   That's the worst of being in love; it always makes you wish to stay or go, whichever is not convenient.

GUY   I want five hundred pounds: Travers says that if I don't pay him to-day or to-morrow he will take proceedings against me, that he will make it impossible for me to hold up my head in London. The man is a scoundrel but that only makes my position worse. My uncle will disinherit me, as sure as my name is Guy Joscelyn! And betting, too; which he curses every evening of his life, after dinner: it was the ruin of my youngest uncle.

HAL   There's only one thing for you to do. Go to your uncle to-day; there is a train at three. You will surprise him pleasantly; dine with him, agree with him about betting and then confess that you have lost £500 at *cards* with a scoundrel. He will storm . . . you will show your penitence by promising never to touch a card again. And who wants to touch a card! It is too risky! I am afraid of cards now.

GUY   Do you really think that a good plan?

HAL   If you don't mind the dishonesty of it.

GUY   Debtors mustn't be choosers. If I pull through this time I will be all that is straightforward and honest. But, Hal, you really think my uncle will . . .

HAL   Of course. But first go and tell Travers that you will pay him to-morrow if he holds his tongue.

GUY   Oh, Hal, dear old Hal! I will write to you this evening. Thank you.

HAL   Be off with you! (HAL, *alone, looks after* GUY *kindly and murmurs*) Poor old Guy! He will keep straight some day.

(*He looks at the clock. He frowns. He is nervous, anxious, impatient, he wants* PRICE *to come and yet he does not want to see him. Just as loneliness makes him wish to see* PRICE *he hears* PRICE's *voice outside saying to the man servant):*

PRICE   All right. He expects me.

*(And* HAL *turns away sulkily)*

*(*PRICE *enters, very easy, very pleasant)*

PRICE   Ah! my dear boy; nice to see you looking so well. I hope you were not bored at Lady Wastewater's, but you had to show yourself there.

HAL   Good morning, Claud. How did you like the new Marguerite at Covent Garden? And did you enjoy Gounod's music as much as ever?

PRICE   When we are rich, Hyacinth, one of us must have a box at Covent Garden. *(Putting his hand on* HAL's *shoulder)* What is the matter with this boy? Supper? or was there too pretty a face at the ball? *(Seriously)* Who has been breakfasting here?

HAL   Only Joscelyn: a very old friend. I have known him all my life.

PRICE   I suppose you know that a very old friend is the most pernicious. He sees through you and doesn't take the trouble to conceal his knowledge from the world.

HAL   You don't think Guy Joscelyn would speak to me again if he knew?

PRICE   Don't be foolish. It is time to be in earnest now.

HAL   Yes. I have done it. I imagine that is what you want to know.

PRICE   Done what?

HAL   Claud. I have written that letter and sent it off.

PRICE   *(Impatiently)* What letter? Which letter?

HAL   I wrote what you told me to Mrs. Bond-Hinton. Here's the draft.

PRICE   Let me see: no, read it to me first.

HAL   *(Reads)* Dear Mrs. Bond-Hinton . . . I have to write to you on a matter of some delicacy. You must not be mortified that different circumstances have made me a party to secrets which touch you directly, which naturally do not concern me. The fact is that Mr. Price is in pressing need of ready money. His need is so urgent that he has told me to ask you to repay him £500 you owe him within the shortest space of time from your receiving this letter. He

says that this simple request will be quite sufficient; and that you will make no delay in doing what he asks. Yours very sincerely Halford Dangar.

PRICE   Thanks. I'll take that. *(*PRICE *takes the paper, reads it carefully and puts it in his pocket book, in inside pocket: then he says):* That was neat, was it not, Hyacinth? *(He looks at him steadily and* HAL *smiles at him as steadily as he can.)* Come and sit here, smoke your cigarette and I will explain to you. You see it is all done so *decently.* It is a lovely thing to be a gentleman and decent. Camilla cannot show this letter to anyone, because of the borrowed five hundred pounds. Five hundred pounds! When I think of the time that woman has cost me, the time and the patience. Five hundred pounds is cheap. It is only an instalment of course. *(*HAL *frightened, fascinated, listens)* You are a good boy, Hyacinth, and I don't feel so much alone since we have met. I have been a lonely man. *(He pats* HYACINTH's *head very lightly once or twice.)* And you don't know what that is. You have never been lonely. When I met you you were on the verge of loneliness. No one understood you.

HAL   *(During this becomes more cordial and more at his ease)* You have always been good to me, Claud, more than I deserve.

PRICE   If you are true and intelligent and loyal I can never say that you do not deserve everything. Now, about that other matter, that other letter?

HAL   *(Shortly)* I have not written it.

PRICE   Not? Well then the sooner you write it the better.

HAL   I can't.

PRICE   But Scarsbrook would pay almost anything he had . . . not so very much alas! . . . for the information we can give him about his stepbrother.

HAL   But I had it from the boy when I had given him too much champagne to make him a little amusing. I had no notion he was about to give himself away so completely.

PRICE   Remember, Hyacinth, you told me about him without any fuss. He is a cub; and though his brother is not very high-minded and wants to get him out of his path *he* is worth more. I can't write to him as he doesn't like me much, and he knows I dislike the cub. But you, a friend of both, can in the smoothest and simplest manner arrange everything to our satisfaction. You don't want to be turned adrift, to have to get up at eight and eat in a hurry something so nasty you could not eat it slowly; and then run after a bus and be a respectable citizen.

HAL    No, no, don't suggest such things.

PRICE    That is what I was meant to do by my people. No one has ever cared for me, you know. And that is what you will have to do if you prove for the third time (or is it the fourth?) that you can't live on whatever income you have.

HAL    How can I? I have never had eleven hundred a year! I can't manage with less than a thousand. My mother allows me four hundred if I live with her, three hundred and sixty-five if I live *out*. She says that as I cannot live on three hundred and sixty-five I must work. And I do.

PRICE    And you do. Filling up the gap every year between three hundred and sixty-five and a thousand is as difficult as building up a fortune. Indeed, Hyacinth, if you should ever want five pounds as badly as I have sometimes, you will find five pounds as far from you as five hundred pounds, as unattainable: and in a different class the man who *must* have five shillings or die finds his chase quite as desperate.

HAL    You make me cold. I have a shiver down my back. I have all my life had to struggle for money and against money. I must have clothes. I must eat. I can't live on my friends and drop in when I am not wanted. My mother is half a vegetarian. I must live somewhere within reach of my fellow mortals. I can't walk all day: I should not have time for anything else. I must go to the theatre, to the opera *(you understand that, Claud)*, I can't be stingy towards men who have lent me money. If I owe a friend a hundred pounds I can't help asking him to dinner or to supper. It's only the interest due to him, is it not?

PRICE    Remember, dear Hyacinth, that I have always said you must do all these things, and have these things, and live in a manner consistent with your dignity.

HAL    Yes, yes, Claud; I know it. Only the means and ways are somewhat difficult.

PRICE    One has to be brave to be somebody or something. . . . It is brave of me to trust you, I who have unlearnt to confide in man and in woman.

HAL    *(Flattered and afraid)* And you, so clever, so independent, so bold, have really trusted me, found in me . . .

PRICE    My pupil, my comrade who is to be. Little Hyacinth Dangar, you are getting the man you were meant to be. You are unfolding yourself, freeing yourself from all the trammels of stupidity. I believe in you.

HAL    You make *me* almost believe in myself when you talk like this. There is something infectious in you, Claud, but you must give me time. Have patience with me. I can't tell you how much I suffer when we differ.

PRICE    It is not as if I wanted you to lower yourself, to go down in the world I only want to make the most of you, to remove from you all that darkens your life and blunts your wits.

HAL    I have I know made an awful fool of myself over and over. And I have done things I have been ashamed of before: but I have never felt what I feel now, crushed, elated, intoxicated, lost . . .

PRICE    Saved!

HAL    Perhaps, but ashamed. *(He breaks down.)*

PRICE    *(Kindly)* Child, what a child you are. I don't much mind your childishness now. Don't forget though that it is doomed and bound to fail. Now tell me, Hyacinth, what it is you fear?

HAL    I am not a coward.

PRICE    But you fear detection or at least suspicion. Follow my injunctions and there is nothing to fear and everything to gain. Since you have known me and been led by me you have had more leisure for moral scruples and for your conscience.

HAL    Claud, Claud, don't be cruel. I sometimes feel as if I had been flayed alive.

PRICE    Because you have been able to afford to have a conscience. Don't wince. I was not unlike you once.

HAL    That must have been a long time ago. When we were children you were already fearless and lawless.

PRICE    *(Laughing)* And what is called thoroughly bad you mean! but what may be called bad in a child is all right in a man . . . No, we are here for an end: self-preservation, success. That is the end of creation, and what distinguishes us from brute beasts is that we are not brutishly selfish, that we are not happy unless we have someone to share with. . . .

HAL   Then what the world called villainy has improved until it has reached what the world now calls goodness and loyalty.

PRICE   Honour amongst thieves, my boy.

HAL   *(Recoiling)* Thieves?

PRICE   *(Sternly)* This is a good opportunity. I won't have all this nonsense about words. Theft is a good, an old-fashioned institution, and I won't have you more squeamish than our grandfathers. Write to Scarsbrook now.

*(HAL obeys.)*

HAL   Are you pleased?

PRICE   Yes, of course. *(Laughs)* You know what you are, Hyacinth, don't you?

HAL   What I am? What do you mean?

PRICE   You know the name by which this sort of transaction usually goes . . . even amongst the unprejudiced?

HAL   No. . . . *(Under PRICE's look he falters)* Yes.

PRICE   And it is?

HAL   Spare me! Spare me! Claud!

PRICE   Blackmail. *(HAL is silent.)* What did I say?

HAL   *(Tremblingly)* Blackmail.

PRICE   And you are a blackmailer, my dear Hyacinth. When is this Guy Joscelyn coming back?

HAL   To-morrow.

PRICE   Where is he now?

HAL   Gone to see his people in the country. He is *(Then he gets nervous)* very much in love, and anxious about his love affairs, poor thing! *(HAL is nervous and flounders through his words.)* He comes here and tells me his troubles.

*(PRICE has become indifferent during this speech and he does not listen HAL's words die away.)*

PRICE   Now I am off. You will I daresay receive an important visitor this morning. I expect Camilla to call on you.

HAL   Camilla . . . poor Camilla. She has always been good to me. Can she not be spared, Claud? I don't mind harming some people . . . they deserve it . . . or if they don't they should look out, but hurting Camilla . . .

PRICE   *(Putting his hat on and holding his stick and his gloves)* I am sick of all this sentiment about Camilla. Because she

keeps up appearances and has a nice manner and a nice house she is to be allowed to disgrace herself and her daughter, deceive her husband, desecrate the most respectable ties! I am astonished at your being taken in by this mask, this disguise, this hypocrisy. I detest, I despise the woman who throws away her chances, who might be peaceful, prosperous, quiet, helpful. Oh! women are despicable. I cannot at this moment imagine a more contemptible life than your Camilla's. How that woman has crawled and lied, all for what? To take us all in, her husband, the world and me. Oblige me, my dear Hyacinth, and take a saner view of her.

HAL   I daresay you are right, but I have been used to respect and admire Edward Bond-Hinton's wife. . . . Good-bye, Claud. We meet at dinner, don't we? I shan't be late this time.

PRICE   *(Shakes hands, smiles and goes)* I'll take this. *(The letter to Scarsbrook)*

*(HAL left alone has a scene of tumultuous emotion. "My God! My God!" he cries beating his temple with his fist. This occupies a certain time. SERVANT opens door.)*

SERVANT   A lady, sir.

*(Enter CAMILLA soberly dressed, pale, in a state of suppressed agitation.)*

HAL   Good morning, Mrs. Bond-Hinton.

CAMILLA   Good morning.

HAL   You are out early.

CAMILLA   It is my only opportunity, and I prefer to transact my business with you face to face.

HAL   Business?

CAMILLA   Business, yes; business which is not fit for the daylight. And though this is the most shameful moment of my life, I cannot now afford the luxury of shame.

HAL   I do not understand.

CAMILLA   *(Gives a sniff of derision)* Come, come. Your master would not approve of this affectation. Take off your mask, Mr. Dangar, and show the face of the blackmailer.

*(Emotion of HAL)*

HAL   You said you came on business.

CAMILLA   *(With horrible irony)* That's better.

Business. I do not want to exchange many words over it. This envelope *(From her bag)* contains the money you have asked me for. You named the sum with great cleverness. In order to meet your threatening demand I have been forced to realise from a tiny property I had hoped to preserve for my daughter. I have kept it whole through many years and many needs and temptations. When I married, my trousseau was bought by the charity of my relations.

HAL   Had you laid up other treasures for your daughter . . . a legacy worth having, a mother's purity! . . . she might have had the trousseau in the bargain.

CAMILLA   Hold your poisonous tongue!

HAL   The stains a mother invites upon herself descend to her daughter by strange laws. . . .

CAMILLA   *(Exclamation of disgust)*

HAL   And all the lace and cambric that ever was cannot cover them . . .

CAMILLA   Oh! Oh! . . . I am punished. oh! oh! . . . That . . . that will not suffice *(Pointing to the money)* My God it will not suffice. I shall have to strip the flesh from my bones to feed you two. Oh! Oh! . . . *(*HAL *hurries to give her water)* Thank you, Hal. A small kindness goes a long way with me now. I see the day when I shall be refused a glass of water.

*(A pause)*

HAL   Take the money to him yourself – no, it's no use.

CAMILLA   *(In despair)* No use . . .

HAL   Confess . . .

CAMILLA   Fool!

HAL   I pity you deeply. Couldn't you . . . couldn't you take this money to Claud yourself and say . . . well, you would know what to say.

CAMILLA   It would be waste of breath. No, Hal, take these notes to Mr. Price; and then, for pity sake, help me. Help me, on the ground of your manhood, out of the chivalry I have always given you credit for. He is a clever, a pitiless man. But there is nothing shameful between you and me. There you will have an advantage to compensate his cleverness. Be chivalrous. You have a mother. Think of my poor little girl. Pity her, not me.

HAL   I will help you, Mrs. Bond-Hinton. I will use all the influence I had with Claud.

CAMILLA   You promise me?

HAL   I promise you.

CAMILLA   Tell him what is the fact that I have no more to give him. Persuade him that if he pursues his persecutions too far he will only open my husband's eyes and only gain my husband's suspicions. . . . It is more than likely that Edward knows things about Mr. Price. . . . Hal, Hal, if you make my misery really a personal matter, you can say something to Mr. Price, perhaps, which will make him heed you.

HAL   I will use *very strong* influence, Mrs. Bond-Hinton. Although I know quite well how thankless my trouble will be. *(Very slowly)* Although I know that I shall only get hate for my pains and injury, too, one day, when you can hit me safely.

CAMILLA No, no. *(Falling on her knees)* Hal. I swear to you, I swear to you, the longest day I live . . .

HAL Come, come, Mrs. Bond-Hinton. Don't lose your composure. Go home now and leave me to fulfil my promise, which I will not fail to do.

CAMILLA Yes, I will go home. Thank you, Hal; thank you. I shall always be grateful to you, even for your promises.

*(She goes out; when she is gone* HAL *walks about his room under the play of his emotions.)*

HAL   Wretch that I am. *(He says)*: Blackguard!

*(He punches one hand with the other fist. In the end he shakes his head like a man recovering his senses, and brushes his temples with his hands. Then he goes to the table where the envelope lies, opens it, counts the notes.)*

HAL   The first fruits of intelligence and adroitness. I suppose Claud will be pleased . . . he should be. *(And he puts the envelope in his breast pocket)* I must write him a note.

*(*MR. JOSCELYN *is announced.)*

HAL   *(Angrily)*. What do you want here? I beg your pardon, Guy; but what *do* you want?

GUY   You frightened me, Hal.

HAL   You deserve to be frightened. When I give you advice I give you something real and you must recognise that fact and not treat me flippantly. I consider I am within my right when I ask you why you are not on the way. *(Looking at his watch)* Oh, there's lots of time, you are going, of course.

GUY   I don't know.

HAL   What do you mean, Guy? Make haste and tell me. I have a great deal to do to-day.

GUY   Well, I have heard from my uncle . . .

HAL   Go on.

GUY   . . . that he has made his will in my favour.

HAL   I congratulate you. I thought you had had bad news.

GUY   Wait . . . he says he hopes it won't make me anything but glad if he lives for years, that he hopes I shall never exceed my income by a penny, never ask him for anything above my allowance; and above all never gamble.

HAL   Um! Looks bad, don't it? Still, as far as I see, except for the unpleasantness of broaching your trouble on top of his letter, the situation isn't different from what it was this morning.

GUY   It's very awkward for me. But that's only the first part and by no means the worst.

HAL   Guy, if I had time I'd give you a talking to you wouldn't forget in a hurry. Why don't you out with your wretched difficulties if you want me to help you? Excuse me, don't let us quarrel, there isn't time; but not for goodness sake go straight to the point.

GUY   Yes, be patient with me. I'm going slowly to try to keep collected. I'm nearly beside myself. I have another letter – from Violet. Here they are, both of them. Violet says she can't help it and she's very sorry, but her people won't let it go on any more. They say that from what they've heard *(curse him!)* even if I had my uncle's fortune in my hands they wouldn't let it go on – what shall I do – *(Getting excited)*. Curse him, it's that horrible Travers; it's that cad, he's ruined me, he's ruined me! I shall do something desperate before the day is out.

HAL   Quiet! quiet!

GUY   And half an hour ago he said it was all right.

HAL   Now, look at me. Take confidence. I am quite calm – am I not? and I understand and feel it all. Just work your

wits, it will do you good. What do you *think* you can do? Try.

GUY   If only Travers could be put off till Monday!

HAL   Well, if he could? What then?

GUY   On Saturday I get my quarter – 250. I can get a hundred from Attenborough and I can ask my sister for the other hundred and fifty.

HAL   Good! Now I'll be dead serious with you. That's all stuff of Violet's relations. I don't for a moment believe Travers has spoken. It's an outcome of some family quarrel, with Violet or without her, or perhaps, and more likely, it's simply to hurry things along, to provoke you to get something more out of your uncle – *which you must try to do*. Work that out for yourself. Tell him you want to marry and so on and so on. And I've no doubt he will see the situation with your eyes. Why, the old boy might even have you to live with him, and I'm sure he'd pay you well to live somewhere else.

GUY   *(Smiles with unutterable melancholy)* But Travers, Hal? *(Whispering)* But Travers?

HAL   Travers! a rat! Until next Monday morning the 10th at 11 o'clock I will lend you five hundred pounds.

GUY   *(Stupid with gratitude)* Hal! Hal!

HAL   Go at once and pay Travers. *(Drawing out the notes)* And on the stroke of 11 on Monday I expect you.

GUY   I can't thank you. Where did you get them?

HAL   *(Loftily)* They are not all mine.

GUY   Thanks, thanks – you have saved me.

HAL   *(After GUY has gone out)* The devil's money. I hope it won't burn your fingers!

*Curtain*

## Act III: "A House of Cards"

MRS. BOND-HINTON's *drawing-room.*
CAMILLA *lying back in an armchair seems to be resting. She seems happy. A book and some roses are on her lap.*
EDWARD BOND-HINTON *comes in. He is going out.*

BOND-HINTON   Are you better, Camilla?

CAMILLA   Much better, Edward, quite well. Your roses are so sweet. Thank you so much for them.

BOND-HINTON  Camilla.

CAMILLA  Edward?

BOND-HINTON  You are not too tired for me to talk a little seriously to you, dear?

CAMILLA  (Gently) No, of course not, Edward.

BOND-HINTON  I don't think you have been happy of late, Camilla . . . oh! don't think I blame you. You have been patient and admirable. I have seen you struggling.

CAMILLA  No, Edward.

BOND-HINTON  Yes, I have seen you trying to look pleased and brave, and I don't suppose other people have noticed anything but some languor or some impatience. But I have known. One can't be married to a truthful woman like you without knowing everything that takes place in her.

CAMILLA  Yes, I have been a truthful wife have I not?

BOND-HINTON  Most certainly, and some of our earlier difficulties were due to that very candour of yours. I admired it, I revered it at first . . .

CAMILLA  The beginning of our married life is like a dream, to me. Your goodness, your tenderness. (She cries.)

BOND-HINTON  Forgive me, Camilla, forgive me if I ever was less tender to you. That very honesty of yours, I own, I confess, irritated me. You were too young, I too experienced when we married. The time came when you seemed to me too unbending, too severe.

CAMILLA  Perhaps I was, but I did try to accept the necessities of my new life, to welcome your friends, to please you.

BOND-HINTON  I want to thank you, Camilla . . . sometimes I think I have not thanked you enough. I know why you were unhappy, but will you believe me if I promise that you need never know this trouble again. I am aware that you disapproved of some of my friends. You may have been right, Camilla. Women are so quick, and you were always a judge of character. You never trusted Claud Price.

CAMILLA  (Eagerly). You remember my distrust of him before ever seeing him?

BOND-HINTON  I do; well I think you were not altogether wrong. And I wanted, my dear Camilla, to tell you so and to thank you for your forbearance.

CAMILLA  Edward, Edward, you are too kind to me.

BOND-HINTON  We understand each other, do we not, my dear? What I really wish to tell you . . . don't cry . . . is that your . . . suspicions . . . about . . . Mrs. Finchley, for instance, were quite unfounded.

CAMILLA  I was quite sure of it . . . I too wanted to ask you, Edward. (She looks so tragic that he becomes anxious, and his anxiety terrifies her.) Only be kind to me, Edward, be gentle, and I will forget everything, everything. (She leans back. He looks at her kindly.) You won't forget to send that book to Cissie this afternoon?

BOND-HINTON  No, indeed. On my way to my brother's – he has sent for me – I will order Cissy's book. Adventures and no fairies, the sort of book, she says, that her father and mother could read together.

(CAMILLA smiles. He takes her hand and kisses her cheek.

CAMILLA, left alone, smiles, leans back, smells her flowers, reads her book – a novel – MRS. DANGAR is announced.)

SERVANT  Mrs. Dangar.

(She is in black and does not smile when CAMILLA shakes hands with her.)

CAMILLA  I hope you have no bad news, Mrs. Dangar, you seem worried. I hope your daughter and her children are quite well.

MRS. DANGAR  Quite well, thank you.

CAMILLA  Where will you sit?

MRS. DANGAR  (After some hesitation). You know about Violet of course. I met Edward on his way to her father.

CAMILLA  Violet? Why she dined here yesterday, in high spirits, and I thought her less averse to Mr. Coulson whom her people encourage.

MRS. DANGAR  Indeed? She never went home.

CAMILLA  Mrs. Dangar!

MRS. DANGAR  Don't be so excited. She left your house to elope with Guy Joscelyn.

CAMILLA  Poor children! How foolish, how wrong, but it will be all right, will it not. Guy's uncle likes Violet, and her father and mother will forgive her.

MRS. DANGAR  I imagine that Mr. Joscelyn will disinherit Guy, in spite of Violet. Guy has not only behaved abominably in compromising Violet but he has involved himself in some shady money transactions.

CAMILLA (*Sighs*). Money!

MRS. DANGAR My cousin Dangar Felbert who knows everything and everybody tells me that a Mr. Travers says he has been cheated by Guy.

CAMILLA Guy Joscelyn was never a great friend of mine after I found Violet liked him so much. As she was here constantly and as her people disapproved of him I could not bring them together.

MRS. DANGAR Dangar Felbert says that Guy has only the bankruptcy court to look forward to – Joscelyn Court will be left to those Wearsoms whom Mr. Joscelyn has never been kind to. Conscience and anger will help to ruin Guy and Violet. Violet as you know has no fortune. Nothing that could keep Guy Joscelyn.

CAMILLA If they care for each other and are good to one another they may be happy, Mrs. Dangar, happier than most of us.

MRS. DANGAR How sentimental you are. . . . No, they are done for. Poor Violet: she was like a daughter to me, at least I thought so until now. Now . . .

CAMILLA You alarm me, Mrs. Dangar.

MRS. DANGAR I have not entered this house to-day to speak to you about poor Violet. I have come on a more sacred, on a more dreadful errand.

(CAMILLA *tries to quell her own agitation.* MRS. DANGAR *is very calm.*)

MRS. DANGAR I am here to tell you that you must help me.

CAMILLA Of course, I would always help you, Mrs. Dangar, but don't look so unhappy – I am not very well and you . . . alarm me.

MRS. DANGAR No hysterics. I wanted to help you once and you refused. You shrank from my hand. (CAMILLA *wants to seize* MRS. DANGAR'*s hand who withdraws it.* CAMILLA *quiets down at once.*) Yes, no scenes before me. Keep them for your husband. You will need them. . . . But that is not now nor here. You *must* help me to save my unhappy son.

CAMILLA I don't think your son is in any danger.

MRS. DANGAR (*Fiercely*). That shows your folly if you mean what you say. Do you remember my telling you that you were in danger?

CAMILLA You may be equally mistaken this time.

MRS. DANGAR I am not mistaken. (*Very sternly*) I am not mistaken (*Very sadly*).

CAMILLA My dear friend, you may count on me.

MRS. DANGAR (*Coldly*) You and I must save my son: because he is still so young, because I am his mother, and because you are the only woman in the world who can save him.

CAMILLA I?

MRS. DANGAR (*Imperiously*) You.

CAMILLA I don't understand.

MRS. DANGAR You are the one woman who can tell him what sort of man this Claud Price is.

CAMILLA You should speak to Edward, not to me.

MRS. DANGAR Ah! Edward has found out something. Edward can already give him a character. I thought it would not be very long.

CAMILLA Mrs. Dangar, whatever you may think about . . .

MRS. DANGAR It doesn't require much penetration to form a good general estimate of Mr. Price. I soon formed one, and a day or two sufficed for me to find out enough about him to convince any sane person that Mr. Price is an unconscionable villain. But I repeat to you you must tell my son what he is. Day and night for the last thirty-six hours I have told him nothing else. But what can a poor old mother do with her son, and a son like mine?

CAMILLA Really, Mrs. Dangar! . . .

MRS. DANGAR One person who can tell him, must: Claud Price's mistress. (CAMILLA *looks terror and rage and clenches her hands.*) Yes, be the tragic heroine if it amuses you, that is what you are. (*Pause*) In fact, because you *must* tell him, I have told him to come here this afternoon.

(MRS. DANGAR *rises to leave.*)

CAMILLA I shall tell your son nothing.

MRS. DANGAR (*Turning round*) You will tell him all you know – *because* I know all about you. (*Exit*)

(CAMILLA *makes the beginning of a ranting walk towards the opposite door, where* PRICE'*s head appears.* CAMILLA *a moment aghast.*)

PRICE   Has she gone? *(Entering)*

CAMILLA   How did you come here?

PRICE   *(Seating himself leisurely)* Ah! Camilla.

CAMILLA   How did you get in here? – the servants have orders not to admit you.

PRICE   The servants have orders! I've come to see you. You can't shut me out, little woman. I know the ways of the house – Come, let us have a little chat – No? – How's the baby-girl? – No? – you'll speak presently, I'll wait.

CAMILLA   Leave this house.

PRICE   Camilla!

CAMILLA   Don't call me Camilla. When I hear your treacherous lips speak that word it seems to me that I have no name left. You have destroyed all I valued. You have wrecked my happy life.

PRICE   Yet you complained of our lot when I met you and consoled you. There was a void in your heart, a gap between you and happiness. Your husband did not need you. He had his occupations, his business, his politics, his friends, men friends and women friends. And you allowed him the latter for the sake of this man friend of yours and his.

CAMILLA   I had my child's love.

PRICE   You should have thought of that some months ago.

CAMILLA   What is the use of our talking any more? I may have done wrong.

PRICE   You have, I am as positive on that point as your husband would be if he ever knew, or as your daughter's future husband would be should your sin not destroy Cissy's chance of finding a husband.

CAMILLA   I forbid you to speak of my daughter. . . . How can you be so wicked, so base?

PRICE   You did not always think me so, or if you did you were even worse than I bargained for.

CAMILLA   To my shame, to my eternal shame be it said that you deceived me. I did not think you base or wicked. Would a woman like myself sacrifice herself and everything and everyone for a man she did not . . .

PRICE   Fancy is the word you are seeking, my dear lady.

CAMILLA   Villain! . . . You seemed once to understand the deep pity that filled my breast for you. Oh! the pain, the anguish I felt when I first saw your suffering face brighten because of me. Your sorrow, your loneliness had pierced me. Ever since I have known you I have suffered here. *(She presses her bosom)* Pity at first, compassion: you could not bear the burden of your days alone, you trusted no one, you wanted a friend, a sister. . . . Then the fear of losing you, jealousy, madness . . . I must have been mad to think I had the power, no the right, the duty to save you at the expense of myself. . . . You did not keep me long in ignorance, in criminal peace. I soon learnt to dread you, to loathe you, to despise you. You wanted me to rob my husband for you. . . .

PRICE   You know as well as I know, Camilla, that there is no sense in your displaying temper with me. You and I are grown up; we may grumble at it, but we do not sulk with necessity.

CAMILLA   If you are beginning one of those long, hypnotic speeches of yours I cannot listen to you. The sound of your voice makes simply that old gurgling impression upon me, putting my senses to sleep. I cannot get the meaning of the words.

PRICE   Well, Camilla, as you please: I am in trouble.

CAMILLA   *(Suddenly trembling all over)* What? what? what?

PRICE   I am sorry, dear Camilla, but I want money and at once.

CAMILLA   I have none to give you.

PRICE   Camilla, don't cry to me. You are above that even in misfortune. I used to be proud to tell you and you flattered to hear that you were the only *gentleman* of the female sex I had ever met. Don't lie to me, Camilla.

CAMILLA   I told Hal Dangar it was all I had when I brought him the money you asked for; and it was true.

*(PRICE controls himself when this news comes upon him: he tries to think how the matter really stands.)*

PRICE   Camilla, don't be foolish, don't try to trifle with me. If I am forced to hit you hard you will feel it; don't be mistaken. And I shall not *hesitate* if you attempt to fool me. Now for this transaction with Hal; you got his letter?

CAMILLA   Excuse me, it's *money* you want?

*(PRICE nods his head.)*

CAMILLA   How much?

PRICE   Two thousand pounds.

CAMILLA   I haven't two thousand pence, but I will get two thousand pounds for you, if . . .

PRICE   Ah!

CAMILLA   . . . if you will release young Dangar from all the enterprises he has undertaken with you, and engage not to see him again, and if you see him not to speak with him.

PRICE   (becoming meditative already) Wait a moment.

(The audience will here see the great scoundrel in the act of working out plans in his brain. He counts on his fingers, puts this and that together, finally he has come to his conclusion.)

PRICE   Um? I question very much, Camilla, if you could get two thousand out of the old lady – there, I don't know, perhaps you might. But, my poor child, if you could get two, I could get ten. Dear me, if I weren't so busy! . . . if only I weren't so busy.

CAMILLA   Ah! let me. Let me manage this. You will have what you demand of me. Spare that lad, do spare him. Let him go. Don't take on your soul the weight of the ruin to which he will come one day.

PRICE   Yes, all very fine, but you're wandering away from the subject. No, I don't think there's much in your plan. I'm not in the habit of making promises. When you speak of my letting Hyacinth go, you clearly don't understand what you're talking about. Your two thousand must come from some other source.

CAMILLA   I have no other.

PRICE   I am not hard upon you – you will pay me in four instalments.

CAMILLA   I have lost my reasoning power.

PRICE   You will be able to think it out at leisure. I shall remind you when the instalments are due. On your own statement you answered Hyacinth's letter promptly.

CAMILLA   Yes.

PRICE   You brought him five hundred pounds.

CAMILLA   Yes.

PRICE   I've not had them. I shall have to look into the matter.

CAMILLA   There's no more hope in the world.

PRICE   Don't despair, dearest Camilla.

CAMILLA   You cruel monster.

PRICE   There's hope for you, and perhaps years of honest married life.

CAMILLA   Devil!

PRICE   For Master Hyacinth I can't quite say yet. He has first to answer a little interrogatory of mine. I may have to make him dance . . . but I believe in him, I have great faith in the lad.

CAMILLA   Oh my God, my God!

(HAL is announced.)

SERVANT   Mr. Halford Dangar.

(CAMILLA looks relieved. But when HAL sees PRICE he begins to tremble and shows the greatest nervousness. Physical signs of terror. He looks furtively at PRICE and does not dare to come forward.)

PRICE   Ah! Here is our gentleman.

HAL   (Stands irresolute. At last he says to CAMILLA in a dull voice) My mother says you wanted to see me.

CAMILLA   You have come at the right moment. We both wanted you.

(PRICE goes to HAL and seizes his hand in a fierce grip and drags him a step or two from where he stands.)

PRICE   Are you a traitor, Hyacinth?

HAL   You hurt me. Let go my hand.

PRICE   (Laughs and squeezes his fingers still more and then lets him go and says not unkindly) Have you been a traitor to me, Hyacinth?

HAL   No, I give you my word.

PRICE   Now, Camilla, let the boy explain. He is raw and untrained, but he is not bad. But mind, you two, I am going to sit in judgement and if I discover untruth or deceit in either of you, beware.

(HAL is still frightened. He is not reassured by PRICE's pleasantries, and there is nothing reassuring either in CAMILLA's appearance. CAMILLA seems wearied to death by her anxieties and PRICE makes her sit down.)

CAMILLA   This is the executioner's civility, I suppose.

PRICE   It is also to save time. We must have this over before you faint and before your husband comes back. (He sits down.) I don't ask Hyacinth to sit down. He is young and for the present the guilty party.

*(HAL makes violent efforts to regain his composure and to look at PRICE as if they were equals; when he tries to speak his throat is dry and he feels about to choke.)*

PRICE   We excuse you. Don't trouble to speak yet. This is the most important day of your life. . . . Will you promise to speak the truth. It is your best chance.

HAL   I promise. I have never been a liar or a coward and I am not going to begin now before the pair of you. Why should I value your opinion of me?

CAMILLA   Because you are not utterly lost, my poor Hal.

PRICE   Because you have to regain my esteem, my young Hyacinth.

CAMILLA   Did I come to you with five hundred pounds for your friend?

HAL   *(Looks imploringly at PRICE)* Yes, on Friday morning.

PRICE   I believed her; but now to explain the improbable.

CAMILLA   And what did you promise me when I knelt before you, on my knees?

HAL   To save you from him, and from yourself. I promised to intercede for you, to use all my influence, all my friendship to obtain your release.

*(A pause. CAMILLA and PRICE are both looking at HAL. At last PRICE says):*

PRICE   Foolish boy: but he meant no harm then. *(Then he turns fiercely and furiously on HAL.)* And then, sir, and then what did you do with the money, with my money, with my four hundred. One hundred you know was yours, and you were aware of how I wanted my money. Should I have wasted so much time on this poor specimen of unconventionality *(Pointing to MRS. BOND-HINTON who has been gazing at them with eyes of scorn.)* if I had not wanted my four hundred pounds badly; and should I not have claimed more if I could have done with less?

HAL   It is no use bullying me. I have made a mistake, but I did it for the best. I did not intend to cheat either of you, either you, Claud or you, Mrs. Bond-Hinton. When you gave me those five hundred pounds I

meant to carry out my promise loyally. I meant to save you and to get out of the toils of . . . him. I was sick of the whole thing. Then Guy Joscelyn.

PRICE   *(Through his teeth)*. I always hated Guy Joscelyn even although all I knew of him was his empty chair after breakfast that morning.

CAMILLA   Guy Joscelyn, I begin to understand.

HAL   Guy came to me in despair. He was worse off than I or you, or you. He wanted five hundred pounds until Monday in order to pay Travers, so keep his uncle's favour, and not to lose Violet. He might have committed suicide if I had not helped him.

PRICE   I should have let him.

*(HAL turns towards him with disgust.)*

CAMILLA   Until Monday you said.

HAL   Yes, but when Monday came Guy had run away with Violet without paying Travers.

PRICE   *(Excited)* Travers, Travers, all this on account of Travers. Travers! whom I carry in my waistcoat pocket. Oh, Hyacinth, you young idiot, you damned amateur. Mightn't your poor wits *(addled as they are)* have told you that I would know a way to treat with Travers. Travers! I could chew him up. Five hundred pounds of *my* money wandering about looking for Travers!

HAL   Speak a little more civilly, will you? *I* am going to take on myself, Mrs. Bond-Hinton's responsibility to you. I have promised it, and I will not fail. I promised her; I told her she would hate and harm me for my generosity, and I will keep my word. *(PRICE is surprised and interested. CAMILLA only looks up sadly.)* Here, then, Claud, *(Drawing a packet from his pocket)* are your four hundred pounds.

PRICE   No? Where did you . . . how did you come by this? . . . Speak . . . speak, where did you get them? . . . it doesn't matter before *this. (Mrs. Bond-Hinton)*

*(HAL does not answer.)*

PRICE   *(in a whisper)* Scarsbrook? . . . *(HAL does not answer.)* I beg your pardon, Hyacinth.

HAL   Mrs. Bond-Hinton, your first instalment is paid.

CAMILLA   I will be no party to your scoundrelly treaties. I have a duty to perform, a punishment to undergo. I have flinched often enough, now I will flinch no more. I am going to make my husband a full confession. . . .

HAL   And involve us?

PRICE   You will not confess to your husband.

CAMILLA   I shall tell him everything.

HAL   I prophesied your treachery. Had I not been kind to you . . .

PRICE   You will think of your little girl and you will *not* confess.

CAMILLA   I love my child. I have a duty to my child. But I love my husband with a greater love; I have a higher duty to the man I have treated so basely. I shall tell him everything.

HAL   Take care you are not too late. It is my duty to tell Mr. Bond-Hinton if he is to be told.

PRICE   Excuse me, Hyacinth, this is my deal. Pardon me, Mrs. Bond-Hinton, while I indicate to you your proper course. If you *yearn* to tell your husband what kind of woman his wife is be guided by me into doing it in proper form and with the address of a grown up person.

CAMILLA   I want none of your advice.

PRICE   If you yearn, as I said . . . *(CAMILLA has a gesture of silencing him with her hand)* . . . and I do not deny altogether that your course is a wise one. *(CAMILLA cannot help being interested)* you can do it madly, completely give everybody away, be divorced, never see husband or child again, be cut by everybody, retire God knows where, on nothing a year and be an old woman before you reach your hiding place –

HAL   Take Claud's advice, I implore you.

PRICE   – Or take council with poor, diabolical, infamous Claud and you shall eat your dinner to-night an honest, shriven woman, humid with tears of repentance, rosy with a husband's forgiveness. *(CAMILLA stares at him.)* Will you take my advice? *(CAMILLA looks away.)* Ah! you want it – how coy you are. Your plan, my dear, is to sell your husband to me.

CAMILLA   Never.

PRICE   Leave me the telling of your story. I will do my work with "good taste." Sell your Edward to me, the merchant of morals. *(CAMILLA looks at him again.)* Commission me, dear lady, and rest assured your work will be well done. Your defence against your virtuous lord is in the way of recrimination. But you shall not need even to name the lady.

CAMILLA   Ah! You're very clever. I know all about her and Edward knows I know.

PRICE   And the *other*?

CAMILLA   *And* the other, *all* the others.

PRICE   A woman in your *own* set? a woman you see very often and know quite well?

CAMILLA   What do you mean?

PRICE   *(Triumphantly)* Ah! we shall yet come to terms. *(Changing his voice and position.)*

*(Enter BOND-HINTON)*

PRICE   *(gravely)* How do you do?

*(BOND-HINTON bows)*

HAL   How do you do, Mr. Bond-Hinton?

BOND-HINTON   Quite well, thanks. *(To CAMILLA.)* How tired you look. You should not have seen anyone to-day. Won't you go to your room and rest a little? This evening will be tiring for you.

CAMILLA   Thank you, Edward, I will.

*(CAMILLA looks anxiously at PRICE, at HAL and at her husband, and seems about to carry out her intention to confess, but she does not and leaves. A moment after PRICE leaves, too.)*

BOND-HINTON   *(Following PRICE with his eyes)* I would give five hundred pounds to know if what these women tell me about him is true.

HAL   *(Who has listened with undisguised interest to BOND-HINTON's exclamation smiles as if he knew something. As BOND-HINTON does not look at him, HAL is reduced to say):* I don't think I caught what you said.

BOND-HINTON   *(Laughing).* You incorrigible boy: as curious as ever. You know quite well I was thinking aloud. But there is no need for any secrecy between us.

*(BOND-HINTON and HAL sit down comfortably.)*

HAL   Oh! how I wish I could have had a young father like you. You have always been kind and good to me, but only since I was a big boy. If I had had you as a young father when I was a child things would have been so different.

BOND-HINTON   If I had married when I was your age I might almost have been your father, and things as you say might have been very different with me also. I was a little old *(in heart)* when I married Camilla. Yes I should have liked a tall son – with more sense though in his good-looking head than you have in yours.

HAL   *(Pleased)* If you don't get too tired of me you might put more sense into my head. I would do anything for you. You have always helped me. Now can't I help you just for once.

BOND-HINTON   Very kind I am sure, but how is it to be done?

HAL   About . . . *(He hesitates)* Price.

BOND-HINTON   Ah! You know something.

HAL   *(Quickly)* You said that some women had told you about him.

BOND-HINTON   *(Smiling)* I said that I would give five hundred pounds to know if what Mrs. Finchley had told me about him was true. . . . I never thought him very highminded, or very first rate, but he was thoroughly useful to me, and pleasant, yes pleasant as a companion, and he knew his place well. . . .

HAL   *(Disappointed at* BOND-HINTON's *apparent indifference)* You joked when you said you would give five hundred pounds to know. . . .

BOND-HINTON   Not at all. I would give a thousand.

HAL   *(To himself)* A thousand!

*(A manservant brings some letters. Whilst* BOND-HINTON *reads his letters,* HAL *says to himself):*

HAL   A thousand, a year's income, a year's independence, safety! Ah!

BOND-HINTON   Well, Hal, why this abstracted air? *(*HAL *looks down.)* Mrs. Finchley tells me that Price tried to blackmail her. He had her letters – not that she ever cared for him, but he was a sort of go-between during that adventure of hers with Lord John Tedworth, you remember – And she showed me a note of his asking for the money he had lent her. *(*HAL *starts)* Did you know about that?

HAL   No.

BOND-HINTON   The note was not really compromising, she is so extravagant and

such a borrower, but she swore to me that he had never lent her a farthing. She said it was his trick in order to shield himself should she show the letter. But she had no proofs. And . . .

*(A pause.* HAL *looks at him inquiringly.)*

BOND-HINTON   *(With studied calm)* And another woman in a very different position has also become involved with Price. And this is a case which touches me much nearer than Mrs. Finchley.

HAL   *(Huskily)* Who is she?

BOND-HINTON   A friend of mine and of my wife. *(*HAL *gives a breath of relief.)* No use to mention names, is it?

HAL   Oh! no, not yet.

BOND-HINTON   Price pretended to be her friend and mine – and in order to save us from annoyance, from danger even, he undertook to destroy any evidence against her. She is innocent of course, but she is married and appearances, Hal, appearances.

HAL   Curse appearances!

BOND-HINTON   She now tells me that she is more afraid of Price than of her former traducer, that he is quite as likely to blackmail us, that he is only waiting for some opportunity. She is so afraid that she refuses to see me alone. She grows hysterical at the thought of Price. She made me drop him saying he was even more dangerous as a friend than as a foe. He has not taken any steps yet. What is he waiting for? Is he waiting for anything?

HAL   I think I know.

BOND-HINTON   If you tell me what you know you may be saving our married happiness. I care for Camilla more than for any other woman in the world. I intend her to be happy in future. It takes time, Hal, for a sensible man to work off all the foolishness of which he is capable. But, thank Heaven, that moment has been reached, and henceforth . . . *(He smiles)* I know that Camilla would not heed any calumny, but I want our life to start fair and fresh. I will not have a man like Price possibly preparing vile insinuations. And that is the reason of my wish to be primed with the truth about this man.

HAL   If I tell you, if you buy my knowledge, will not that be a horrid transaction? Shall I not seem to you something of a blackmailer too?

BOND-HINTON  *(Laughing)* A blackmailer! No, my boy!

HAL  It is so unmanly to sell one's information.

BOND-HINTON  You may count on my understanding you. This will be an excellent moment for you too to start fair, pay all your debts, clear your path.

HAL  How kind you are to me. . . . Yes . . .

BOND-HINTON  Well?

HAL  You know why he is waiting to blackmail you and . . . that friend of Mrs. Bond-Hinton's.

BOND-HINTON  *(Eagerly)* Why?

HAL  First of all he is afraid of a well armed man like you, who would not stand either humbug or threats. You could expose him, checkmate him if you were bold and unafraid. He is too wary – until he is very hard up. Then he becomes reckless.

BOND-HINTON  Why does he want so much money?

HAL  *(Sighing)* Because he hasn't any at all to start with. Why do I spend so much money? Because I want £365 to become £1,000.

BOND-HINTON  Poor boy. Don't be unhappy. I will help you. Go on.

HAL  He always wants money. Sometimes I wonder whether he saves, whether he has a passion for money.

*(BOND-HINTON looks very much interested but says nothing.)*

HAL  *(Reflectively)* Of course many successful operations are needed to obtain a capital. *(He starts up.)* The truth is, Mr. Bond-Hinton, that Price is engaged on something very ticklish just now, and he may be waiting until he succeeds before attacking you.

BOND-HINTON  Yes?

HAL  A married woman – a respectable woman – quite in our world.

BOND-HINTON  Yes.

HAL  She is in his power completely. She has a child, *(He corrects himself)* children, a very good husband, and Price has threatened her with exposure unless she gives him two thousand pounds, in four instalments. She has paid him the first.

BOND-HINTON  The scoundrel.

HAL  Yes, of course. How have people the heart to do such things? I could never hold up my head again.

BOND-HINTON  Yes?

HAL  I want to make an offer, a suggestion. If I could procure you proofs, documents, that would make London, England impossible for Price. . . . I could do it. . . . would you in that case promise me . . .

BOND-HINTON  What?

HAL  To respect this woman's incognito.

BOND-HINTON  How does she concern me?

HAL  Precisely. She does not, and that is why I want you not to lift her mask, not to find out her name, to shut your ears to any innuendo.

BOND-HINTON  But I am a man of discretion. If I knew what would happen?

HAL  *(Excitedly)* Ah! poor woman, if any one knew her secret – and she is not a bad woman I assure you. You would call her a good woman. He preyed on her very virtues. If I should discover her secret!

BOND-HINTON  You know it – why should I be less trustworthy than you?

HAL  Her secret, yes – but I don't know her name.

BOND-HINTON  My dear boy!

HAL  If I must be truthful, I do, but nothing, nothing would induce me to betray her.

*(BOND-HINTON observes his emotion inquiringly.)*

HAL  *(With some confusion)* Mr. Bond-Hinton, let us unite, let me help you to send Price away from England and save . . . his victims. Oh! will you not join me?

BOND-HINTON  This woman's name?

HAL  *(Getting up)* I can't tell you.

*(He walks away from BOND-HINTON. BOND-HINTON stares at the door through which CAMILLA left the room, and as he stares the situation dawns on him. All this while HAL is walking up and down, striking the floor with his heels as he walks. BOND-HINTON rings the bell. HAL turns round as the man servant comes in and BOND-HINTON with apparent composure takes up his letters and says to the servant):*

BOND-HINTON  If the man who brought this begging letter asks for me always say I am not at home. *(HAL turns his head and BOND-HINTON says to the servant in a low voice):*

Ask Mrs. Bond-Hinton to come here for five minutes? And don't shut the door after you. *(As the man leaves the room* BOND-HINTON *says):* Come here, Hal, and sit down.

*(*HAL *obeys and sits down facing* BOND-HINTON *and turning his back to the door through which* MRS. BOND-HINTON *is expected.* BOND-HINTON *is silent.* HAL *lies back, thinking. He is tired by all he has gone through and does not quite know what to say.)*

BOND-HINTON   You would like to get rid of Price?

HAL   Oh! . . . He does not touch me, it is for others that I speak.

*(*CAMILLA *comes in very ill and anxious. The door being open she comes in noiselessly.* BOND-HINTON *sees her.* HAL *does not.* BOND-HINTON *watches* HAL *as he says):*

BOND-HINTON   And so, my dear Hal, you were saying that this unhappy woman has betrayed her trusting husband and forgotten her duty for her daughter for the sake of that mean scoundrel Price? *(*HAL *looks terrified.)* I don't know what you their accomplice deserves, but I know what she deserves.

*(His voice is so threatening that* HAL *pushes back his arm-chair. At that moment* CAMILLA *who has been listening in the most appalling agitation falls headlong on the ground.* BOND-HINTON's *first impulse is towards her. Then he restrains himself and says to* HAL *who has also been exhibiting the greatest emotion.)*

BOND-HINTON   You, *I* can't.

*(*HAL *kneels and tries to raise* CAMILLA.)*

*Curtain*

## Act IV: "A Perfect Scoundrel"

MRS. DANGAR's *drawing-room in Chester Square. A jardiniere with some plants before the window.*

MRS. TAUNTON   *(Mrs. Dangar's daughter, and* HAL's *elder sister) in some dark travelling dress. She is good-looking, but very severe and* unamiable, – *and* SUSAN, *Mrs. Dangar's parlourmaid.*

MRS. TAUNTON   Was Mrs. Bond-Hinton any better?

SUSAN   Oh, no, m'm, the butler told me she was that worse they don't expect her to keep her head if she do get better. She eats nothing, and does not sleep, and cries if anyone looks at her. Mr. Bond-Hinton is in Germany with Miss Cissy. She is to finish her education abroad and only come home to be presented at Court, so the butler says 'm – and all the servants are so sorry. They had nothing ever to complain of before I'm sure, 'm.

MRS. TAUNTON   But of course the doctor thinks she will recover. She is certain to get well.

SUSAN   *(Mysteriously).* If you won't be offended, 'm, I could tell you something.

MRS. TAUNTON   Tell me, Susan, if you think I ought to know. I have not my mother's nerves as you are aware.

SUSAN   *(Hesitating)* Well 'm, James, the butler, told me *(She lowers her voice impressively)* that he had heard Mary, Mrs. Bond-Hinton's maid who had been sent away, and whom he met by accident, say that it would be a good thing for all concerned if Mrs. Bond-Hinton never got any better.

MRS. TAUNTON   *(Who has listened with grim interest – says coldly):* Don't bring any tea, Susan, unless I ring. And see that my mother's room is ready if she wants to go to bed before dinner. Don't tell the cook, because Lady Felbert or Miss Alcyra may stay and dine. . . . Was that a ring at the front door?

*(*SUSAN *goes.* MRS. TAUNTON *takes out a note book and writes her expenses down.)*

SUSAN   *(Announces)* Lady Felbert and Miss Felbert.

*(*LADY FELBERT *is 70 but very coquettish, many bangles on her arms, and dressed in the fashion of many years ago. There are flowers on her bonnet or hat, and she has a passion for bows and dangling ribbons. She is exceedingly affected and sprightly. The* HONOURABLE MISS ALCYRA FELBERT *is 35, but looks much older – older than her mother in her gestures and in her words, but she has the same tricks of speech. They don't*

*pronounce their Rs and their final Gs, etc.*
MISS FELBERT *is plainly dressed, rather short-skirted, has a man's boots, driving gloves, a man's Tyrolean hat with a cock's feather. Her eccentric plainness of attire contrasts with* MRS. TAUNTON's *quiet simplicity.*)

LADY FELBERT  *(Gives her hand to* MRS. TAUNTON) How are you, dear, how is May?
MRS. TAUNTON  My poor mother is not bearing up very well, but she will be with you very soon.

(MISS FELBERT *and* MRS. TAUNTON *kiss.*)

LADY FELBERT  *(Sitting down)* I was not astonished.

(MRS. TAUNTON *sighs.*)

MISS FELBERT  Does Cousin May cry very much?
MRS. TAUNTON  Not yet. Tears will be a relief to her, but she won't cry until it is all over.
LADY FELBERT  We have to leave by the eight o'clock train. We put off our departure to be with you on this sad occasion, although of what earthly use we can be to my poor niece and to you . . .
MRS. TAUNTON  We are so grateful to you for coming. We look on you as the head of our family, don't we, Alcyra?
MISS FELBERT  I own I am nervous. I hope your mother don't cry. I hate crying, it don't do any good.
MRS. TAUNTON  *(Rings the bell)* My poor mother, poor, poor mother. *(The* SERVANT *comes in.)* *(To the* SERVANT.*)* No dinner to-night, Susan – or . . . I will tell you later.
SUSAN  Yes'm. Please'm, cook says she will be so glad to have definite orders.
MRS. TAUNTON  It was high time I paid a visit to this house.
MISS FELBERT.  Yes, she's a very good woman.
MRS. TAUNTON  Not at all.
LADY FELBERT  *Aren't* you, Harriet?
SUSAN  Sir Felbert Dangar!

(THE ADMIRAL *is very much of the Lord Nelson type. Very blind and doddering.* MRS. TAUNTON *motions* SUSAN *to remain – she rushes up to him.*)

MRS. TAUNTON  My dear uncle!

(*She puts up her face to be kissed on both cheeks, but* THE ADMIRAL *doesn't see.*)

SIR FELBERT  Is Lady Felbert here?
MRS. TAUNTON  Of course you'll dine with us, dear Uncle.
SIR FELBERT  Yes, my dear, certainly I will.
MRS. TAUNTON  *(To* SUSAN*).* Dinner for two.
SIR FELBERT  Is Lady Felbert here?
MRS. TAUNTON  Yes, dear Uncle.
SIR FELBERT  In which direction? *(*LADY FELBERT *has come near him.)* Ah, cousin, delightful, delightful. Thank you so much for the butter.
LADY FELBERT  Thank you for sending back the basket.
SIR FELBERT  How young you are, Lady Felbert. Going to do all the theatres, I suppose?
LADY FELBERT  Going back tonight, alas. Alcyra is getting so infirm.
MISS FELBERT  We don't approve of running about, Sir Felbert. How are you, Sir Felbert? I see you are going to preside at the commemoration of the battle of Majorca.
SIR FELBERT  Yes, we had no torpedoes, or any of that nonsense, just round shot and plenty of 'em. We did very well.

(MRS. DANGAR *has entered very tragic, dressed in black. She goes up to* SIR FELBERT DANGAR.)

MRS. DANGAR  Sir Felbert, I cannot thank you sufficiently for standing by me this awful day.
SIR FELBERT  Very pleased, May, I'm sure. I've got the paper with me. I've had it copied out in plain writing . . . but I think I know it all.
MRS. DANGAR  How are you, Aunt Betty? Did the journey tired you? How are you, Alcyra? . . .
MISS FELBERT  No, mother likes it. She likes trains, I don't like the jolting. But when it's for a shocking thing like this . . .
MRS. TAUNTON  *(To her mother)* Are you better, dear?
MRS. DANGAR  No, my dear. I shall never be better again.
MRS. TAUNTON  Now, don't upset yourself wilfully, dear. Sit down quietly, and don't talk. *(Lower)* You shouldn't have come in so soon.
MRS. DANGAR  It's time, isn't it?

SUSAN   Mr. Dangar Felbert.

*(An old dandy of 48 with a beard.)*

MR. DANGAR FELBERT   I hope I'm not the last.

MRS. DANGAR   No, the *last* has yet to come. He is indeed the last of all men. How are you?

MR. DANGAR FELBERT   How are you, Mrs. Dangar? Bear up, we may save the poor boy yet.

SIR FELBERT   *(From a distance).* I see you, Felbert.

MR. DANGAR FELBERT.   Glad to see you, Sir Felbert. How are you? *(He turns to talk again to* MRS. DANGAR.*)*

SIR FELBERT   Will you dine with me this evening at Boodles'?

*(*MRS. TAUNTON *hears this, looks up and puts her hand on the bell.)*

MR. DANGAR FELBERT   I beg your pardon, Sir Felbert?

SIR FELBERT   I said: will you come and have a bit of dinner at Boodles' this evening, just a bite at Boodles', you know, a bit of dinner.

MR. DANGAR FELBERT   Yes, I should like to. *(*MRS. TAUNTON *listens with interest to this.)* You must have courage, Mrs. Dangar. Many a good man has begun queerly.

MRS. DANGAR   I thank you for your wish to console me, Mr. Felbert, but, ah, I fear he has missed the last hope of his turning. I have been a good mother to him.

MR. DANGAR FELBERT   The offer we have agreed upon is a hope. It gives him a chance; if he takes it . . .

MRS. DANGAR   I shall thank God with all my heart.

MR. DANGAR FELBERT   Even if you never see him again?

MRS. DANGAR   I forego that willingly if it will save him.

*(Enter* HAL, *very defiant and apparently self-satisfied, a flower in his buttonhole.)*

HAL   My dear mother! . . . Ah! Harriet. *(To his sister)* How is your husband? Not here? . . . Cousin Alcyra, have you converted many sinners since I saw you, or do you let them convert themselves now? . . . Aunt, I can let you have a small alligator for your menagerie. It is quite alive, and bites: a delightful companion. . . .

LADY FELBERT   If it were a dear little monkey now, my nephew. . . .

*(*MRS. TAUNTON *and* MISS FELBERT *look at her reproachfully.)*

MRS. DANGAR   You have not spoken to Sir Felbert nor to your cousin.

HAL   *(Turning round)* A family party, quite a family party. How do you do, Sir Felbert? I have not seen you since that Covent Garden ball last year. And you, old man, how are you? Still anæmic?

*(*SIR FELBERT DANGAR *scarcely shakes hands with him, but* MR. DANGAR FELBERT *laughs and stops abruptly short.)*

MRS. DANGAR   We have all been waiting for you.

MRS. TAUNTON   You are late.

HAL   Am I? I must apologize. I was lunching with some friends at the Savoy and could not get away. As it is, they thought me particularly rude.

MR. DANGAR FELBERT   However, here you are. *(Cheerily)*

HAL   This is all very pleasant, seeing all one's nearest and dearest collected together is of course bewildering and charming. *(He finishes his sentence turned towards* LADY FELBERT *who struggles against an inclination to grin back at him.)*

SIR FELBERT   Shall we be seated. *(All sit down)* Halford Dangar, we, representatives of your outraged family, have summoned you here to express to you our displeasure at your late manner of life, our abhorrence of most of your recent acts.

HAL   I will change my place, Sir Felbert, if you will excuse me. *(He moves nearer.)*

SIR FELBERT   I will trouble you, sir, not to speak again until you are bidden.

HAL   I am one accused among many accusers. I can make no promises.

SIR FELBERT   You are asked for obedience, not promises . . . to express our abhorrence of most of your recent acts.

HAL   You said that before, Sir Felbert.

SIR FELBERT   The words I employ are mild to express that abhorrence. They are temperate for the very reason that we are met, not to reprove you; our purpose, which is far graver, you will learn later. *(Movement of approval)* I will not dwell upon the distress, the humiliation, the infamy you have brought upon an honourable family. You know that as a general fact sufficiently well already.

HAL   I deny it.

SIR FELBERT   Neither will I refer to your conduct at Oxford.

HAL   I have great respect for you personally, Sir Felbert.

SIR FELBERT   Nor to your refusal to remain in the profession which has twice been selected for you.

HAL   Go on.

SIR FELBERT   My accusation, which is also made on behalf of those here present, shall date only from the beginning of the present year. The first item, *(Referring to his paper)* is a blackmailing transaction, which you conducted under the tutorship of a Mr. Price, against whom I believe a warrant is being issued to-day. This machination was against an unfortunate woman who will soon be beyond your threats. I refer to Mrs. Bond-Hinton.

HAL   I deny it.

SIR FELBERT   You deny complicity?

HAL   I deny complicity. I deny everything.

SIR FELBERT   Would you like to be shown *(Rummaging among the papers)* a letter you wrote her, in the matter of a loan, as it was called.

HAL   I acted straightforwardly.

SIR FELBERT   You acted in a manner to bring you to the Old Bailey.

HAL   I employed all I knew to save Mrs. Bond-Hinton.

SIR FELBERT   With money extorted from that wretched woman. You put means into the hands of a very much younger man than yourself. . . .

HAL   Two years younger.

SIR FELBERT   Of carrying out a wicked plan, no doubt inculcated by yourself. . . .

HAL   Bosh!

SIR FELBERT   . . . which jeopardised every prospect he had in the world.

HAL   Guy Joscelyn, a thief, who robbed me when I tried to help him.

SIR FELBERT   You then attempted a bargain with Mr. Bond-Hinton: to sell him infamous secrets for a sum of money. When he delayed, in his grief, to pay you, you employed a discharged butler, a

notorious blackmailer, too, to threaten Mr. Bond-Hinton that you would publish his story.

HAL   I deny it.

SIR FELBERT   Your friend, the butler, was ejected by Mr. Bond-Hinton himself, who next day sent you a cheque: Pay to the scoundrel Halford Dangar £1,000. That cheque I may inform those present, you had the impudence to present for payment.

HAL   Mother!

*(MRS. DANGAR drops back.)*

MRS. DANGAR   Produce the cheque, Sir Felbert, confront him with it.

SIR FELBERT   Would you rather withdraw, May?

MRS. DANGAR   No, thank you, Sir Felbert, I will remain.

SIR FELBERT   I have the cheque here, indorsed by you.

HAL   It is a forgery, a joke.

SIR FELBERT   In the meantime, you had disgraceful transactions with a Mr. S. which are believed to have been the origin of his brother's social ruin. Your victim of this very occasion you afterwards lured into the clutches of a card-sharper, a known one, named Travers, who finished the poor young man.

HAL   My only encounter with Travers was one day when I thrashed him.

SIR FELBERT   Mere brag, I think. Your remaining blackmailing adventure I shall mention was the one which brought about your discovery to us. You tried an older quarry, and happily failed. When this old gentleman's daughter's engagement was announced you came to him . . .

HAL   Name him.

SIR FELBERT   That is pure malice. If you insist upon it I will name the gentleman to Mr. Felbert, and show him the proofs I have here. The ladies, I am sure, would be sorry to be acquainted with any of the details – I can assure them. To continue the narrative; when the daughter was engaged, you came to her father with a minute account of a very old and, I am pained to say, discreditable business, demanding hush-money with the greatest insolence. The old gentleman knew his man. He feigned great alarm, *thanked* you even, as I understand, gave you £200 on account, and before you were hardly down the street, had his detectives after you. Within twenty-four hours *my* detectives too were on your heels. *(HAL gets fidgety.)* I have the two reports here of your doings during eight weeks, and a pretty record it is. I may add as what is, unfortunately, a *small* detail, that you are about to be warned off every racecourse in England.

HAL   Anything else?

SIR FELBERT   There are some minor matters I will not mention: that is the whole of my accusation. What do you say?

HAL   The whole story is a fabrication. I claim to examine the whole bundle of lies, if you are my relations.

SIR FELBERT   Hal, Hal, poor Hal! Your position is perilous, awful. Be a man, face the thing, give us a little truth.

HAL   *(Bowing gravely)* I thank you all for your patience which I will not vex much longer. Yes! the time has come now for a little truth, a little right, a little of all the things you talk of so glibly. You are glib and virtuous and respectable and moral, are you not, all of you? I am to live up to the traditions of the family and not disgrace your name or mine. I am to be worthy of you, my worthy sister. Well, I am quite worthy of you. What are you? Who are you? A petty tyrant, a penny-grubbing, money-loving woman. Ask my mother, your husband, your children, your servants. Is there anything in this world you like better than authority? Yes, yes, money. Do you imagine I don't know why you invited Lady Felbert and the Admiral *(This is said with much scorn)* to witness my discomfiture? No, I deserve to be your brother, Harriet, I can read your avaricious, revengeful thoughts.

MRS. TAUNTON   You are mad! Let us leave him, Lady Felbert, Mamma . . .

HAL   *(Laughing)* Lady Felbert is too fond of enjoying herself – and she has enjoyed herself! – to leave now. She came expecting to be bored, at the best hoping to be able to amuse her country neighbours with the latest London cackle on her return; and now she finds she is in for something better even than a first night at the theatre. *(LADY FELBERT laughs involuntarily.)* Ah! you can't help grinning. Don't think I am forgetting you, Harriet, or your motive. You know that with the exception of Cousin Alcyra, who is wedded

to celibacy – *(ALCYRA starts as though shocked)* we are Lady Felbert's nearest relations – the Admiral's also. You know that Lady Felbert has a sense of humour, an impatience of being bored – and you bore her, Harriet, you bore her. Oh! how frightfully. *(LADY FELBERT is in fits of wicked old delight at this: let her grin and twinkle – rub her hands if she likes, pull up her mittens – for very joy.)* I have – I had – rather – some chance with her because I made her laugh; because I went into smarter society than you, because I was less afraid of being contaminated. You counted on her age, her fear and my disgraceful conduct. As to the Admiral, he has been a humbug too long not to be violently shocked at what I say.

SIR FELBERT   When you have done insulting your sister, sir!

HAL   My sister – my enemy, who hates me.

MISS FELBERT   When he was a little boy, Harriet used to carry him in her arms and say: look at my baby.

HAL   Because I amused her like a doll. But since we grew up when did she ever prove my friend? I was never in any grown-up trouble or sorrow without finding in her the most stubborn of adversaries. Deceitful too – and with a vengeance! *(MRS. TAUNTON puts her handkerchief to her eyes. MISS FELBERT whimpers. HAL turns fiercely on MISS FELBERT.)* Cousin Alcyra, stop that. You are thinking of your brother Reggie, whom you and your mother and my mother and the Admiral drove mad. Don't whimper about him now. Because he disgraced you – *disgraced you* – you cast him forth. You were proud of him once, you petted him, you spoiled him, pampered him, pandered to him – until the day he *needed* you. Then his mother refused to see him. He had disgraced her. His sister shuddered when she thought of him. He had disgraced *her*. What if he had disgraced himself? And a disgraced man needs all you can give. *(A pause)* Not that I want anything you can give me. *(Looking at MR. DANGAR FELBERT)* Fancy asking *him* for anything, except a pin for one's buttonhole, a pencil to write an address, a plover's egg, or a glass of champagne at supper! What have you ever done for anyone, except be an example? When I was young you were held up to me as a warning: keep off the grass and don't break your toys. Don't tell lies at home. Don't be like Dangar Felbert. Oh! we are a nice crew, we Felberts and Dangars and Halfords. See yourselves now! A nice family for an honest man to spring from.

MRS. TAUNTON   You don't know what it is to be an honest man.

HAL   Don't I? Don't I? I am honest now, honest, do you hear. If I scream, it is because you are so deaf, body and soul, that you can't understand. Don't think I am excited or hysterical. My brain is calm. I know quite well what I am saying. What chance have I ever had? What intelligent love have I ever had?

SIR FELBERT   Your parents, unnatural boy.

HAL   The only intelligent affection ever wasted on me was the affection of a scoundrel like myself, not a scoundrel, mark me, like one of you.

SIR FELBERT   We did not come here to be insulted, I think.

MISS FELBERT   Mamma, let us go. You will have a headache if you stay.

LADY FELBERT   Not yet. I must see him chastised for talking of Reggie in that shameless fashion.

MR. DANGAR FELBERT   Have some consideration for your mother or you will live to regret it.

MRS. DANGAR   Don't stop him. He is a fiend. He is not my son. I have *no* son. *(She stretches her arms out to* MRS. TAUNTON.*)* Let him blaspheme! Let him say that his mother is to blame.

*(*MISS FELBERT *weeps.* LADY FELBERT *looks interested, the* ADMIRAL *angry,* MR. DANGAR FELBERT *nervous.)*

HAL   Yes, I am your son. Am I not what you have made me? You did not love my father, you married him because in our family the women used always to marry. *(With a vicious look at* MISS FELBERT*)* You did not love him. I don't accuse you that you did not care for him, but I do accuse you for not hiding your antipathy from your children. When we were little, Harriet and I, you never disguised from us your dislike of our father. You drew our attention to his bullying, vulgar voice, his heavy tread, his untidy moustache, his physical delinquencies, his moral deficiencies. You sapped his power, and our love

at the same time, and when we were older, and you needed his authority as a weapon against us, you called us unnatural because we despised him! How can you disobey your father? You taught me first to know how contemptible a man he was. Then you went over to his side, and encouraged his tyranny over me. Who will blame me?

[Who can ask me to humour his memory? Come, I summon you, come and stand by your own, come and take *your* share of my disaster. You cannot lie easily in your grave, your sin is scarlet, come up and answer it. You are not dead, you cannot die. I see you now, the brutal pompous poltroon you were. I smell the tobacco you smoked incessantly. I feel the physical dread I had shaking hands with you. You do not like it! I see your look of sullen fear when my mother accused you before me, in innuendoes I penetrated easily. I never trusted you! I never confided in you. Indeed I never had anything to say to you. But I have now. Why did you marry my mother? Why in God's name, having married her, did you not understand her? What did you ever do for me? You never showed me how to speak straight or look straight. You gave me nothing but your worthlessness. Curse you, curse you, wake and walk for ever with my curse! You shall rot with me when I come to penal servitude; you shall hang with me when I come to that. Curse you!][3]

MRS. DANGAR   He is mad!

HAL   *(Impetuously)* You never understood me, mother. *You* fostered all my vices, all my vanities – *you* treated me as if the world belonged to me. "My boy is not like other boys," you used to say. You did not like my giving up anything to anyone. You hated my modesty, you destroyed my unselfishness. You were ambitious for your son, for yourself. You did not want me happy and young, but prosperous and approved of. "Succeed, succeed," you said, and you scorned me when I failed. "Do what pleases you, enjoy yourself, but above all, beware of an imprudent marriage. Go to church, don't be found out, and be a credit to yourself and your family." That is the moral staff you gave me. As to the heart and brain you had given me, you know their quality. I could not do everything you told me to do, but

I have done most, and I have done my best. I was not born very good nor very brave nor very straight, I suppose, and I was ordered to be all that and successful – when I did something which I thought good or brave or straight, I was usually bullied or disbelieved or sneered at. Prosperity, on the contrary, or any sign of it met with a cordial reception. And so I drifted more and more towards trying to be successful. And here I am in trouble. That is the long and the short of it.

MRS. DANGAR  *My* son so base, so heartless, so unlike us all.

HAL  *(Roughly)* Mother, that's a little too much. I am what you all of you have made me, and I am not ashamed to look at any of you. I am every bit as good as anyone.

SIR FELBERT  *(Solemnly and a little shakily)* After this criminal outburst against your excellent mother, there is no doubt left in me, and I trust in none of us here present that you are, I regret to say . . .

HAL  *(Insolently)* Put on the black cap, I don't mind.

SIR FELBERT  . . . Incorrigible, incorrigible.

*(The relations all sigh approval.)*

HAL  Then why try to correct me?

LADY FELBERT  I never heard of anyone so cynical.

MISS FELBERT  Harriet, you hear what mamma says.

*(MRS. TAUNTON has a tragic gesture of assent. MR. DANGAR FELBERT presses MISS FELBERT's hand.)*

SIR FELBERT  We have heard your defence – no defence but a string of stupid, irrelevant calumnies. You have not enough intelligence to counterbalance your bad heart.

HAL  As you please. I am tired of talking to you.

LADY FELBERT  We are tired of hearing you break with all the traditions of our family.

*(MISS FELBERT looks enthusiastically at her mother.)*

HAL  As you please, only let me go. I want to lie down before dressing for dinner.

SIR FELBERT  Wretched boy. We have decided – and nothing can alter our decision; is it not so, Mrs. Dangar?

MRS. DANGAR  Nothing.

*(MRS. TAUNTON clasps her hand in her two [hands].)*

SIR FELBERT  There are two alternatives before you. *(HAL listens eagerly)* You have proved yourself unfit to remain in any civilised community as one of us, as one of an honoured and honourable family.

HAL  Spare me these commonplaces.

SIR FELBERT  If you remain in England you remain at your cost and peril: an outcast, almost an outlaw. Your unhappy mother herself will have the courage never to hold any communication with you, your sister will teach her children to forget their uncle's existence, we will not only reject you, but *we* will expose you, pursue you with our scorn.

*(HAL shrugs his shoulders.)*

SIR FELBERT  *(Pursues with even greater sternness)* There is not one decent man or woman who would hold converse with you, scarcely a rascal who would think it worth his while to plot with you – if you remain in England.

*(Silent approval of the relations. MRS. DANGAR wails, HAL turns to her despairingly. She wails again without noticing his appeal.)*

SIR FELBERT  *(More quickly)* However, if you go to New Zealand – *(Small pause)* where we have some connections – if you go to New Zealand . . .

HAL  I cannot stand the sea voyage.

SIR FELBERT  I believe there is no other way to New Zealand.

HAL  Going to New York almost killed me. I am not going to New Zealand.

*(The women seem violently shocked.)*

MISS FELBERT  Coward.

LADY FELBERT  Poltroon.

MRS. TAUNTON  Impostor.

MRS. DANGAR  Ah! my dear poor husband did right to die. I never thought so before.

SIR FELBERT   And you will not go there like a young man who travels idly for pleasure or for instruction.

(SUSAN *comes in timidly, with a note.*)

MRS. TAUNTON   Don't disturb us.

SUSAN   This note was brought in by a messenger for Mr. H. Dangar. Immediate, he said.

(HAL *takes the note carelessly, says: "Thank you, Susan," looks at the envelope, starts, flushes, and tries to seem calm and indifferent. He straightens his back and smooths his hair with his hand.*)

SIR FELBERT   No, you will go as some one who has to rough it, to renounce all the luxuries of life, all the pleasures of refinement, – I do not say that you will like your new life, but it will be a new life, it will give you the chance to repent, to change, to work. Work, miserable Hal, work, that most blessed of cures for a guilty heart. And perhaps out there, (*With a vague gesture*) far from the corrupting influences of a great city like London, out there alone with your conscience and with God, you will turn with a purified heart to your deceived and injured relations in England. And it may not be impossible – no – nay, we will all hope that after long years of separation, your mother may be able to cross the seas and at last, bending over the cradle of an innocent child, see in that sleeping babe your innocent childhood, and as you kneel there at her feet – two good women, your mother and your wife, will meet and be kin, linked by the love of a good man.

(SIR FELBERT *wipes his forehead,* MRS. DANGAR *seems transfixed with hope.*)

HAL   (*Coolly*) You will allow me to have a glass of wine? I am tired. Port for choice. (MRS. TAUNTON *rings the bell.*) And if I consent to New Zealand? . . .

SIR FELBERT   You leave London to-night for Liverpool.

(HAL *starts violently, then he opens the envelope slowly and says quietly*):

HAL   Excuse me; it is about a supper party this evening.

(*Whilst he reads* SUSAN *has put a plate with a glass of port wine near him. He takes out of his pocket a little flask and pours something in the glass.*)

MRS. DANGAR   (*Cries*) Hal!

HAL   Only my new mixture for my heart.

MRS. DANGAR   Don't you take your capsules any more?

HAL   This is more efficacious, I fancy. (*He puts the glass to his lips but does not drink.* MR. DANGAR FELBERT *is looking at him.*) You make me nervous, staring at me. (HAL *touches the glass as if to drink, then he reads his letter through. He leans back, then he says in a tired voice*): Can I be given a little time to make up my mind? You don't expect me to choose in a hurry.

MRS. DANGAR   There is no choice, there is no choice.

SIR FELBERT   No choice.

MRS. TAUNTON   It may be as well to spare my mother the next few minutes of indecision. There is no choice of course, but he will like to torment us until the end.

(*They all walk out of the room,* SIR FELBERT *last.*)

SIR FELBERT   Five minutes.

HAL   (*Left alone*) No choice – my mother said no choice. (*He puts the glass to his lips. He shudders – he says*): Not yet . . . (*He reads the letter.*) Claud has been true. He always swore I should know his staunchness in my hour of sorest need. (*He reads aloud.*) My dear Hyacinth, I send this by someone who will know where to find you. You have the keys of my rooms, and of the left-hand top drawer of my desk. Go there at once, and you will find enough money to bring you comfortably to where you can meet me. Stop the night in Paris, at the house you have heard of. You are expected there, and you will be told where to find me. We are on the eve of success, of real success, but I don't want to triumph without you, my pupil, soon to be my equal. Come. We understand one another now and the World. (HAL *gets up.*) Is it a trap? Does he want to destroy me? If I go to his rooms shall I be arrested? . . . Claud, Claud, if you were here to advise me . . . (*In the greatest*

*agitation)* I can't go to New Zealand. I can't.
I should die on the boat. I'd rather die than
live such a life. Yes, die . . . *(He looks at the
glass.)* Die, die, and I am still so young and
I could be so happy. At any rate I could
enjoy myself. *(He gives a great sob.)* I can't
die, I can't die. I can't bury myself alive in
New Zealand and work, work. *(He gives
another sob.)* I won't die. I will join Claud.
*(He smiles.)* Claud will help me. He has
never deceived me. He has been patient
with me. He would not trap me now,
betray me. *(He gets up.)* What if he does? I
can take of myself . . . . *(He begins to hum.)*

*(He walks backward and forward once or twice,
then gathering up his hat and stick and gloves,*

*he creeps on tiptoe out of the room.
Enter the file of the ancestors, they look round,
with growing terror.* MRS. DANGAR *drops on
the sofa in uncontrolled grief. The other women
surround her.)*

SIR FELBERT   The scoundrel!

*(*MR. DANGAR FELBERT *goes over mysteriously
to the glass of port, carries it carefully to the
jardiniere and pours it away.)*

MR. DANGAR FELBERT   Do you think it
would have been better if he had taken it?

*Curtain*

# Documents

*Review by Addison Bright in* The Theatre,
*1 July 1894, pp. 37–8*

*The Blackmailers*

A play in four acts, by JOHN GRAY and
ANDRE RAFFALOVICH. First produced at
the Prince of Wales's Theatre, on Thursday
Afternoon, June 7th, 1894

Admiral Sir Felbert Dangar
   Mr. JULIAN CROSS
Mr. Dangar Felbert
   Mr. C. COLNAGHI
Edward Bond-Hinton
   Mr. A. BROMLEY DAVENPORT
Guy Joscelyn
   Mr. HARRY EVERSFIELD
Claud Price
   Mr. W. L. ABINGDON
Servant to Hal Dangar
   Mr. FRANK WEATHERSBY
Servant to the Bond-Hintons
   Mr. E. BELLENDEN
Hyacinth Halford Dangar
   Mr. CHARLES THURSBY
Lady Felbert
   Miss EMILY MILLER
The Hon. Miss Alcyra Felbert
   Miss MARY CALLAN
Mrs. Dangar
   Mrs. THEODORE WRIGHT
Violet Bond-Hinton
   Miss M. T. BRUNTON
Susan
   Miss HENRIETTA CROSS
Camilla Bond-Hinton
   Miss OLGA BRANDON

What the authors of this play intended us to
see, and what we actually did see, are, it
seems, two different things. What we saw was
a party of males and females, labelled
"modern life," but never, as *Mrs. Gamp*[4]

remarked, "be'avin' as sich." Prominent
amongst these was a loathly object, played
with due artistic loathsomeness by Mr. W. L.
Abingdon, who levied blackmail upon a
married woman whose lover he had been.
Then we traced the brief career of an
acquaintance of both, an amiable and
apparently innocuous product of the public
schools and universities. This, by name
*Dangar*, overheard a startling conversation
between his hostess and the blackmailer.
What did he do? Offer *Mrs. Bond Hinton* the
protection of his presence? Kick *Mr. Claud
Price* out of the room? Oh, dear, no; just
shared *Mr. Price's* confidence and took to
blackmail himself as a duck takes to water!

From this picture of "modern life" we
proceeded to another, in which *Dangar's*
friend, for whom he had, we charitably
concluded, bled the wretched *Mrs. Bond
Hinton*, bolts with the spoil! and thence to a
third, wherein Blackmailer No.2, for a
consideration, betrays Blackmailer No.1 to
*Mr. Bond Hinton*, and, after the lapse of an
entr'acte, is solemnly arraigned before his
sisters and his cousins and his aunts, whom
he finally deserts for the flashier joys of Paris
and his blackmailing guide, philosopher, and
friend – his mother, as he vanishes, uttering
the pious lament, "Oh, why didn't he kill
himself!" upon which the curtain falls.

This was the drama as played. What it was,
as written, the Licenser and the authors, Mr.
John Gray and Mr. André Raffalovich, alone
can tell. As a mere matter of gossip, it may be
noted that these two gentlemen utterly
repudiate the piece as it appeared on the
boards. It was, they assert, only "a mangled
and mutilated version of the first four acts,"
and they further protest that "It was only a
consideration of honour which prevented us
from withdrawing the play when we found to
what a state it was being reduced from
rehearsal to rehearsal. We saw scene after

scene ruined by cuts, omissions, impoverishments and slip-shod. It is no wonder that we refused to own the play by answering the kindly call of a disconcerted audience. We wish to add to our apology from writing this letter that we hope shortly to submit to the public the original version of "The Blackmailers," and show how we trace the makings and downward career of a scoundrel."

The obvious comment upon these statements is that rehearsals no less than actors are part and parcel of a play; and that if authors choose to delegate their authority to unreliable people, or to resign their power of control, they have only themselves to thank for any mangling done on the theatre premises. Imagine the case of a book bearing the name of Tennyson or Meredith. Imagine page after page and volume after volume of incoherent formless rubbish, a weary waste of unmeaning words. Then picture your feelings upon reading a disclaimer from the author in these or some similar words: "It is entirely the fault of the printers. They submitted proofs in a chaotic state. Indeed I was almost tempted to withdraw the book. But please reserve judgment upon my work, for I intend shortly to publish it in its original form." Pray, why publish at all, unless it be in the form that gives you satisfaction, that represents you truly, my dear Authors?

*Review in* The Times, *8 June 1894*

The description 'new and original' was hardly needed in connexion with *The Blackmailers*, a play by Messrs John Gray and André Raffalovich, which was tried at the Prince of Wales' Theatre yesterday afternoon. It would be hard to name any source to which the authors could have been indebted, or, indeed, any society which their sketch could be said to resemble. Like Jean-Jacques' "Confessions" their work is without precedent and may very well hope to remain without imitators. The story is a sordid and repulsive picture of blackmailing practices carried on in society. The principal adventurer is one Claude [*sic*] Price, but he has obtained a sinister influence over, and makes a tool of, a foolish youth, Hal Danger [*sic*], a member of an influential family, who has vainly tried to solve by honest means

the distressing problem of how to live on an allowance of four hundred a year. By these two scoundrels, whose game appears to be perfectly well understood by the society in which they move, and which, nevertheless, tolerates them, blackmail is levied right and left; there is nothing but that in the play. In the last act the young culprit is soundly rated for his offences by a sort of family council who propose that he should emigrate. He thinks of taking poison, but in the end, being left to himself to consider the situation, he merely walks out of the house, leaving the family council, which is headed by a garrulous old admiral, to its own devices. The greater culprit apparently escapes molestation of any kind. The curtain thus descends upon the "note of interrogation" beloved of Ibsenites. Of the acting in the piece it is unncessary to speak, though it was in the hands of such an excellent company as Miss Olga Brandon, Mrs. Theodore Wright, Mr. W. L. Abingdon, Mr. Colnaghi, and Mr. Julian Cross.

*Review by Clement Scott*[5] *in* the Illustrated London News, *16 June 1894, pp. 766–68.*

I may be rather stupid, but I do not quite understand the assumed position of the young authors of "The Blackmailers," two able and enthusiastic young men, fond of the stage, students of dramatic literature in all countries, but who, having written a play on a disagreeable subject, turn round and say, "It is no child of mine." Mr. John Gray and Mr. André Raffalovich clearly believed in the subject of "The Blackmailers," or they would not have written it. They certainly had faith in its success, or they would not have taken a theatre in which to produce it. They evidently had confidence in their judgment, or they would not have asked their friends to come and see it. I cannot conceive they would have been so unwise as to leave the poor play alone at rehearsals unattended; nor do I understand the position of an author who having taken and paid for a theatre in order to show his own work, in which he believed, allows any stage manager or director in existence to alter the motive or the fabric of the play. Suggestions at rehearsal from practical people are of the greatest possible value. They often help a play on to success. But no stage manager or director is ever permitted to change the tone, style, or dramatic method of a play. That would be intolerable. It must stand or fall by the author's intention, and it frequently fails because the author's ideas are not in the least carried out by the actors and actresses. On the other hand, more often than not, clever actors and actresses help the lame dog of an author over the stile. What I should like to know is in what respect the play as it was written and intended to be acted by the authors differs from the play that we all saw produced at the Prince of Wales's Theatre? Apart from the subject, which I consider essentially disagreeable, and unnaturally forced for the purposes of the stage, it was the character of the hero that fogged me completely. What was he, this young Blackmailer? A good man, a weak man, or a detestable scoundrel? I could not make him out. He started full of virtuous sentiment; he tried hard to struggle against and resist temptation; he argued with and lectured a young friend as if we were his own tutor at the University or the head master of a public school; he became the catspaw of a scoundrel, but he ever refused to pick the chestnuts out of the fire. Then all on a sudden this much-tempted youth and hater of blackmailing in any forms turns out the most outrageous rascal who ever appeared in dramatic print. Out at elbows as he is, with cash and credit gone, threatened with a criminal prosecution on the instant, his family comes very nobly to his assistance. Men in this predicament are generally allowed to sink without a helping hand. But when the family offer to get this reprobate out of his hobble and send him off to the Colonies, what does he do? He turns round like a cur and snaps at the assisting fingers. He bullies and blackguards a venerable old gentleman whose grey hairs should at least be respected, he insults his uncles, his cousins, and his aunts, and, worst of all, he turns round and grossly insults his own mother, whose one sin has been her leniency towards this cub. Having grossly insulted his family, and by inexcus-able cruelty brought tears into his mother's eyes, he thinks he will commit suicide. But he is too much of a coward for that, and sneaks off to Paris to cheat and blackmail more people, rather glorying in his power of imitating the criminal classes. The play ends with the mother's regret that such a blackguard should disgrace humanity. Well, it is not a cheerful subject, however we consider it. There may be University and public-school men who would blackmail innocent women and blackguard their own mothers. But they are in hopeless minority, and it is scarcely worth while to write plays in order to advertise such abnormal cases of depravity. At any rate, this is not holding the mirror up to nature. It is showing an unnatural monster in a very dirty and dusty looking-glass. It will be a grievous thing if our clever young men who would and could write well for the stage are led away into the fool's paradise full of faddists and eccentrics. The public has not called for this kind of work, and does not want it. They want pictures of men and women, not monsters. The public taste is not diseased, it is healthy; and in my humble opinion, the men and women who waste their talent over "Mrs. Lessinghams"[6] and "Blackmailers," and these kind of people, waste their time also, and the time of the public, which is worse.

*Marc-André Raffalovich, from* In Fancy Dress *(1886)*

Because our world has music, and we
    dance;
Because our world has colour, and They
    gaze;
Because our speech is tuned, and schooled
    our glance,
And we have roseleaf nights, and roseleaf
    days,
And we have leisure, works to do, and rest;
Because They see us laughing when we
    meet,
And hear our words and voices, see us
    dressed
With skill, and pass us and our flowers
    smell sweet; –
They think that we know friendship,
    passion, love!
Our peacock Pride! And Art our
    nightingale!
And Pleasure's hand upon our dogskin
    glove!
And if They see our faces burn or pale,
    It is the sunlight, think They, or the
      gas,
    – Our lives are wired like our
      gardenias.[7]

*Marc-André Raffalovich,* It is Thyself *(1889),*
*no.cxx*

> Put on that languor which the world frowns
>> on,
> That blamed misleading strangeness of
>> attire,
> And let them see that see us we have done
> With their false worldliness and look up
>> higher.
> Because the world has treated us so ill
> And brought suspicion near our happiness,
> Let men that like to slander as they will;
> It shall not be my fault if we love less.
> Because we two who never did them harm,
> And never dreamt of harm ourselves, find
>> men
> So eager to perplex us and alarm
> And scare from us our dove-like thoughts,
>> well then
>> Since 'twixt the world and truth
>>> must be our choice,
>> Let us seem vile, not be so, and
>>> rejoice.

*From John Gray, "Poem XVII," from*
Silverpoints *(1893). The volume was dedicated*
*to Wilde, who had subsidized the edition:*

> Did we not, darling, you and I
> Walk on earth like other men?
> Did we not walk and wonder why they spat
>> upon us so?

## Notes

1 This incorrect information appears on the title page of the typescript. Presumably, the theater that Raffalovich had intended to lease was unavailable and the performance had to be postponed and transferred to the Prince of Wales's.

2 The authors no doubt expected to instruct the actors in the precise stage business in the course of rehearsals.

3 The passage in brackets was written into the typescript as an after-thought.

4 The drunken nurse-midwife in Dickens' *Martin Chuzzlewit.*

5 Clement William Scott (1841–1904) was one of London's most conservative, anti-Ibsenite dramatic critics; his indulgence to the authors is remarkable.

6 *Mrs. Lessingham* by "George Fleming" (pseudonym of the American novelist Constance Fletcher) opened at the Garrick Theatre on 7 April 1894. It concerns an adulterous woman whose second marriage to her former lover ends in her suicide.

7 Raffalovich, whose first language was French, must have known that *feuille de rose* [rose-leaf] was brothel slang for anilingus.

# *At Saint Judas's*

*by*
*Henry Blake Fuller*

(1896)

*At Saint Judas's* is reprinted from Henry B. Fuller, *The Puppet-booth. Twelve Plays*, New York, The Century Company, 1896

# Introduction _____

In *Dayneford's Library*, James Gifford's
elegant study of American homosexual
writing from 1900 to 1913, you will look in
vain for the name of Henry Blake Fuller
(1857–1929).[1] He belongs there, however, for
he shares with Henry James and E. M.
Forster an evasive homophilia fascinated
by innocents in thrall to European
decadence.

Fuller's first experience of Europe came
during a year's excursion in his youth: he was
otherwise a Chicagoan born and bred, the
child of a well-to-do bank cashier. Chicago,
following the Great Fire, had rebuilt itself
into a cosmopolis and despite the rawness of
its meat packing, immigrant quarters, and
rough-and-tumble politics, it prided itself on
its progressive cultural aspirations.
Millionaires such as the Potter Palmers were
among the first to collect Impressionists, and
by the turn of the century Chicago was home
to some of the most advanced schools of
poetry and fiction in the country. Fuller,
despite his attraction to the traditions of
Europe and his professed hatred of his
birthplace, resided in Chicago all his life; he
managed his family's business affairs, taking
an active part in real estate holdings, and
participated in the city's lively journalistic
scene, serving on the advisory board of
*Poetry: A Magazine of Verse*, editing the book
review section of the *Chicago Evening Post*,
and penning editorials for the *Chicago Record-
Herald*.[2]

Fuller's toing-and-froing between the poles
of his native Chicago and the grand-tourist's
Europe (which he revisited for six-month
periods in 1883, 1886, 1894, 1896 and again
briefly in 1924) is evident in his fiction. His
first novel and its sequel centered on a
cultivated Italian gentleman and a French
noblewoman. It was the next two, however,
*The Cliff-Dwellers* (1893) and *With the
Procession* (1895) which established his fame

and assigned him to the naturalistic camp.
Those novels were well-observed and mildly
sardonic portraits of the newly rich of
Chicago, and the tension between capitalism
flexing its muscles and high culture trying to
make itself heard. They can easily be ranked
with similar studies of Boston and New York
society by William Dean Howells and Edith
Wharton.

Just when the literary world had firmly
classified Fuller as a "genteel realist," he
issued *The Puppet-Booth: Twelve Plays* in 1896.
Brief, allegorical, Maeterlinckian in
technique and mood, they were characterized
by Fuller as "Phantasy" sketches, idle dreams,
mere ephemera; critics have adopted his
dismissive tone and seen them primarily as a
"pivot" to his later fiction. Certainly they
were not intended for the stage, and when
two of them were given a full presentation by
a class from the Chicago Conservatory in May
1897, the audience, at first awed and
confused, eventually burst into laughter.
"Pre-Raphaelite" was enlisted as a term of
abuse. "They carry no real conviction, and
their treatment is uniformly derivative" is the
damning verdict of one modern critic who
attributes Fuller's dabbling in Maeterlinck to
boredom and frustration with contemporary
life.[3] Edmund Wilson is more tolerant: he
judges that they "depart from the realistic
without managing to achieve the poetic."[4]

One play, however, was singled out for
praise by James Huneker, the American
propagandist for decadence and symbolism
in art. This was *At Saint Judas's*, which, he
told Fuller, was wonderfully subtle. The fact
is, that when an established author suddenly
veers in a new direction but attempts to
downplay the importance of his
experimentation, our critical senses should
be sharpened, not lulled. For *At Saint Judas's*,
rather than being an attempt "to express the
egocentric essence of evil," as Bowron puts it,

struck the blow? In any case, the recourse to the sword with its bloody outcome provides a proto-Freudian touch: the phallic weapon effecting a fluid discharge which resolves the tension.

Interestingly, one of the Best Man's strategies to prevent his friend's marriage is anonymous blackmail, slandering his reputation to a higher purpose. It is a curious reinvention of the bane of the clandestine homosexual as a means for advancing same-sex love. The Best Man's behaviour parallels that of Erich in Otto Ernst's *The Youth of Today* (see 'General Introduction') who writes anonymous newspaper articles belittling his friend's scientific discoveries so that his friend will give up research and stick to him. The intrication of love and jealousy is well observed.

The ambiguity of the ending extends to Fuller's attitudes. Does he share the Bridegroom's revulsion at this revelation of an impure passion, or is it only the revelation and not the passion that appals him? The play, with its *double entendre* dialogue, may be saturated with irony, so that it is the changed attitude of the Bridegroom, once wholly devoted to his friend, which is the butt. In any case, when one contrasts the heightened histrionics of *At Saint Judas's* with what we know of Fuller's personality, one must say, as the Victorian lady did after a performance of *Antony and Cleopatra*, "How different, how very different, from the home life of our own dear Queen."

Fuller's sentimental life is something of a mystery. A lifelong bachelor, he was highly sociable, a regular at literary and artistic gatherings, and an enthusiastic mentor of young talents. For all his comfortable income, he spent much of his time in a succession of boarding houses and restaurants, and, for all his charm and gentility, gave off an air of finicky fastidiousness. He was reluctant to write love scenes, a bar to popularity with the greater public, and his treatment of passion is always tinged with irony. He probably identified with his character, the Freiherr von Kaltenau in *The Refuge*, who travels with an adored youth: "The book of life had been opened wide before him, but he had declined to make the usual advance that leads straight on from chapter to chapter; rather had he fluttered the leaves carelessly, glanced at the end before reaching the middle, and

*Plate 3* Postures of male affection in American *carte-de-visite* and tintype photographs of the latter half of the nineteenth century. The proliferation of such poses, even when meant facetiously, suggests that physical intimacy between males was a common occurrence that did not necessarily imply sexual relations to the world at large. (Laurence Senelick Collection.)

is an effort to find a literary outlet for its author's homophilic longing.

*At Saint Judas's* is a duologue between a Bridegroom and a Best Man in the sacristy as a High Anglican wedding ceremony is celebrated offstage. The two men are military officers, the dearest of friends, whose closeness, stopping short only at physical intimacy, would have been wholly acceptable to Victorian sensibilities. In the course of an intense scrutiny of the recent past, it is revealed that the Best Man is desperately in love with the Bridegroom and has been the hidden enemy who has tried every possible ploy to smear his name and have the engagement broken off. Appalled, the Bridegroom draws his sabre, the Best Man offers his breast to the blade, but the final tableau of the stricken lover weltering in gore is left ambiguous. Which of the two has

*Plate 4* Portrait of Captain Frederick Gustavus Burnaby by James Tissot (1870). Tissot's painting elegantly presents the image of the officer and gentleman preserved in the minds of Fuller's protagonists. (Burnaby, a swart, coarse-featured man, disliked having his portrait made; Tissot obviously flattered him.) (National Portrait Gallery, London.)

thoroughly thwarted the aims and intentions of the great Author."

Again, it was Edmund Wilson who was the first to declare baldly, "He was evidently homosexual" and points out that in his writings, Fuller dwells more circumstantially on the physiques of his heroes than of his heroines. But "homosexual" is inaccurate; given Fuller's "reluctance about committing myself – a touch of dread about letting myself go" (words of another character, a novelist), he probably had sexual relations with no one in his lifetime. Like a great many bachelors of the period, he could conceal his passional nature as a refined commitment to art, repressing his libido to conform with social norms though at some expense to his psychic health. "The natural 'paradigm' was the homosocial dream of the Bachelor and Brotherhood," Gifford writes of American literary treatments of the theme in the early twentieth century.[5] Clubland and other fraternal venues were forged into modern equivalents of chivalric brotherhood, and

foreign travel offered both an opportunity and a metaphor for untrammeled experimentation. At the same time, a more overt band of initiates was spreading the gospel of Edward Carpenter in parts of America. Their reformist notion of "homogenic love", a male–male intimacy close to nature and socialist in its sympathies, echoed much already to be found in Walt Whitman.

Consequently, *At Saint Judas's* may be overwrought but it is not necessarily "absurd," as Wilson would have it. The intensity of the two men's relationship is quite in line with the tradition of "passionate friendship" handed down from David and Jonathan and embodied by the late nineteenth century in a spiritualized male bonding.

On the other hand, *At Saint Judas's* was written at a time when such relations were characterized in most print-matter as deranged and criminal behaviour. Between March and May of 1895 the newspapers were filled with reports of the trials of Oscar Wilde, while André Raffalovich's essay on "Uranism" was being much discussed in medical journals. A spate of case studies and sensational accounts of aberrant sexual conduct gorged the popular press, and at least three novels appeared based on a widely-publicized murder of a lesbian by her lover.[6] The public discourse treated same-sex love – now designated clinically as "homosexuality," – either as a ghastly crime or a serious disease.

The most lurid of these cases was that of Guy T. Olmstead. On 28 March 1894, on a street in Chicago at noon, 31-year-old Olmstead fired several shots at his fellow letter-carrier William L. Clifford, as part of what he had conceived to be a lovers' suicide pact. Attacked by an angry mob, he was prevented from turning his weapon on himself. Olmstead's history included a deranged family and an abusive childhood; he had walked out on his wife and his job as a schoolmaster after falling in love with her male cousin. Following a stint in a Kansas insane asylum, he became a postman in Chicago and carried on a brief affair with his fellow-worker Clifford. When Clifford ended the relationship, Olmstead bombarded him with *billets-doux*, which the exasperated Clifford laid before the local postmaster. Olmstead was asked to resign.

Hoping to stifle his passion, Olmstead had his testicles surgically removed, but to no avail. As he wrote to a Dr Talbot from Mercy Hospital,

Heaven only knows how hard I have tried to make a decent creature out of myself, but my vileness is uncontrollable, and I might as well give up and die. I wonder if the doctors knew that after emasculation it was possible for a man to have erections, commit masturbation, and have the same passion as before. I am ashamed of myself; I hate myself; but I can't help it. I have friends among nice people, play the piano, love music, books, and everything is beautiful and elevating; yet they can't elevate me, because this load of inborn vileness drags me down and prevents my perfect enjoyment of anything. Doctors are the only ones who understand and know my helplessness before this monster.[7]

A few days later, he made his attack on Clifford and was committed to an asylum for the criminally insane. Since his victim did not die and Olmstead appeared rational, he was discharged, whereupon he returned to Chicago and demanded his testicles from the City Postmaster. His paranoia remanded him to the Cook County Insane Hospital. "Going postal" is not just a twentieth-century phenomenon.

An intense six weeks in November and December of 1895 saw Fuller writing the dozen plays that comprise *The Puppet-Booth*. This is probably not coincidental. He could hardly have avoided hearing debates about Wilde's guilt in his own artistic circles, and, given his involvement in journalism, would have read the on-going accounts of the Olmstead affair and similar *faits divers*. *At Saint Judas's* vividly displays his own inner conflicts over whether a man's love for another man is a noble and disinterested passion, a morbid form of insanity or a criminal action. Olmstead's self-disgust at his "inborn vileness" is echoed again and again in the case histories of well-educated, cultured men recorded in the medical literature of the period. It is not unlikely that Fuller shared, in some small degree, this kind of inner recrimination.

However, to remove his characters from the sordid world of examination rooms and police courts, Fuller is careful to set the melodrama of their actions within a framework of religious imagery. Each episode between Bridegroom and Best Man is played out against an allegorical background, keyed to a pictorial change in the postures of the stained-glass angels and an auditory change in the intoning of psalms. This lifts the situation from a mere dossier, a sensational crime of passion, to a symbolic statement of the impossiblity of fully-consummated love between men in an ethos that condemns it. The title "Bridegroom" evokes the "Beautiful Bridegroom" lovingly delineated in the homoerotic art of Simeon Solomon. The epigraph from Dante and the allusion to the fall of Lucifer award the Best Man status as a Fallen Angel, though in his case his sin is not pride but – what? Not lust, but love, which counts as a virtue. The enigma of Fuller's message remains.

Fuller's self-admitted reticence and inhibitions were such that it comes as a surprise that at the age of 62 he published a novel dominated by its homosexual characters. *Bertram Cope's Year* (1919) was an intentional rejoinder to magazine fiction fixated on love stories; he regarded his narrative of obsession as innocent in comparison with James Branch Cabell's doggedly Rabelaisian *Jurgen*. The central characters are Bertram Cope, a young English instructor at a thinly disguised Northwestern University, who exercises a potent attraction on several persons, not least Basil Randolph, a stock-broker and dilettante art collector. Randolph's hopes of having Cope move in with him are thwarted by the arrival of Cope's friend Arthur Lemoyne, a plump and dark-eyed rival. Lemoyne wins success as a female impersonator in a college drag show, but makes advances to the male lead backstage and is expelled. Cope himself leaves for a better job at an eastern university, abandoning all his admirers of both sexes, and presumably moving in with Lemoyne. Throughout the novel, Cope is portrayed as a rather egoistic but ordinary young man, and the infatuation of his friends, who worship him as an Adonis, something outlandish and irrational.

Once again, it was Huneker who best appreciated the novel for its "portraiture and psychological strokes," but most of Fuller's intimates were horrified.[8] Reviewers avoided it and the public didn't buy it. Fuller, having daintily tested the waters of audacity, quickly drew back into his shell, burned his mansucript and the unsold two-thirds of the first edition, and waited ten years before writing another novel. *Bertram Cope's Year* has never been republished, and is all but impossible to find in libraries or at second-hand dealers. No wonder Fuller fails to make an appearance in *Dayneford's Library*. Yet his furtive sorties to explore homophilic attractions and anxieties introduce an oblique approach to the subject that will recur in much American fiction and drama.

## Notes

1 J. Gifford, *Dayneford's Library. American Homosexual Writing, 1900–1913*, Amherst, University of Massachusetts Press, 1995.
2 Reminiscences of Fuller can be found in A. Morgan (ed.), *Tributes to Henry B.Fuller from Friends in Whose Minds and Hearts He Will Always Live*, n.p., Ralph Fletcher Seymour, 1920. The standard biographies are C. M. Griffin, *Henry Blake Fuller: A Critical Biography*, Philadelphia, University of Pennsylvania Press, 1939, and B. R. Bowron, Jr., *Henry B. Fuller of Chicago. The Ordeal of a Genteel Realist in Ungenteel America*, Westport, Conn., Greenwood Press, 1974. Neither is very perceptive, but Griffin is the more comprehending about Fuller's personal anxieties.
3 Bowron, Jr., op. cit., pp. 174–5.
4 E. Wilson, "Two neglected American novelists," in *The Devils and Canon Barham*, New York, Farrar, Straus and Giroux, 1973, p. 29. Wilson's remains the best short study of Fuller's life and work.
5 Gifford, op. cit., p. 12.
6 For a good selection of excerpts, see J. N. Katz, *Gay/Lesbian Almanac. A New Documentary*, New York, Harper and Row, 1983, pp. 258–88.
7 19 March 1894, in Havelock Ellis, *Studies in the Psychology of Sex*, New York, Random House, 1936, vol. 2, part 2, p. 171.
8 Bowron is typically obtuse is calling this fascinating, semi-comic study of sexual magnetism, "not a very interesting novel" (p. 227).

# At Saint Judas's

*Henry Blake Fuller*

(1896)

> . . . al fondo che divora
> Lucifero con Giuda . . .
>
> *(Inferno, XXXI)*

> . . . in the abyss which swallows up
> Judas with Lucifer . . .
>
> *(Longfellow's translation)*

## Characters

THE BRIDEGROOM

THE BEST MAN

THE SACRISTAN

A PROCESSION OF PRIESTS AND ACOLYTES

EIGHT PAINTED WINDOWS

*The sacristy of the church of St. Judas. Time: ten minutes before noon. A pealing of bells is heard. The sacristy is a great octagonal room of sculptured stone; its groined vaulting is upheld by one central column which is wreathed from base to capital with a band of pale carven flowers, and its eight windows – broad and high, trefoiled and quatrefoiled – flood both floor and roof with an endless dapple and ripple of variegated light. Under one of these windows an open door leads into the church. Through this doorway one sees the chancel banked with flowers; and above the decorous murmur of a thousand tongues one hears the tones of the organ and the voices of the choirboys.*
*Present in the sacristy: the* BRIDEGROOM *and his* BEST MAN. *Both in full uniform; each wears white gloves and carries a sword.*

THE BRIDEGROOM   *(Gaily)* In ten minutes – ten minutes more!

THE BEST MAN   *(With constraint)* In ten minutes – as you say.

THE BRIDEGROOM   *(Fastening his glove)* Is that a long time, or a short time? A long time, I think.

THE BEST MAN   A short time. But much may happen within a short time; much may happen in ten minutes.

THE BRIDEGROOM   How soberly said! Are you as jovial as one's closest friend should be?

THE BEST MAN   Perhaps not. This day – it means so much for me.

THE BRIDEGROOM   *(Unfastening his glove)* As much as it means for me?

THE BEST MAN   As much, yes. Quite as much. Perhaps more.

THE BRIDEGROOM   Not more. For it means everything in the world for me.

THE BEST MAN   It means everything in the world for *me.*

THE BRIDEGROOM   *Now* that voice vibrates with such a degree of interest as I have felt this day demanded! *Now* I begin to recognize you! – the first time for a month.

THE BEST MAN   I am the same. I am unaltered.

THE BRIDEGROOM   *(Refastening his glove)* No, no; you have never been quite the same since I told you – since you heard of the great change in store for me.

THE BEST MAN   How did you tell me? In your sleep – your own pillow close to mine. I felt myself an eavesdropper; I felt that I had betrayed your confidence.

THE BRIDEGROOM   Not betrayed; only anticipated. You would have known within a day. You have known everything else. You have shared my thoughts, my ideas, my secrets, my ambitions. We have eaten together; we have slept together; we have fought side by side. We are of the same age, the same height – my eyes have always been able to look level into yours. We are of the same bulk as well; – who shall say that even at the present moment I am not wearing your coat and you mine?

THE BEST MAN   That has happened more than once.

THE BRIDEGROOM  You have saved my life; I have saved yours. Have we not pledged an unbreaking friendship?

THE BEST MAN  We have.

*(The* FIRST *of the* EIGHT WINDOWS *comes to life; there is a flux of color and of outline among its mullioned lights. Gradually two figures among its ranks of churchly warriors become strangely secularized; they raise their crossed swords on high, while their left hands meet in a clasp of friendship. The colors upon the pavement shift in correspondence, and from the church, or from spaces far above and beyond it, there come the tones of the* Ecce, quam bonum.*)*[1]

THE BRIDEGROOM  But for *you* my bones, hacked by African sabers, might now be bleaching upon the desert sands.

THE BEST MAN  But for *you* my own, gnawed by nameless fishes, might now be lying at the bottom of the sea.

THE BRIDEGROOM  Your arm, sweeping through that burning air, saved me for to-day.

THE BEST MAN  Yours, cleaving through those angry waters, saved me for – for – *(To himself)* for – what?

THE BRIDEGROOM  Yes, you have saved me for to-day. A moment more, and I shall stand where I have long hoped to stand, and shall take the vow that so long has been ready on my lips. At last all obstacles are brushed aside – at last the way stands clear. Those obstacles – you know my combat with them as well as I myself. At every step, on every hand, this mysterious opposition, this determined and unceasing enmity. From what source could it come? From what motive? What enemy have I? The worst should stay his hand at such a time as this.

THE BEST MAN  *(Vaguely)* True – true.

THE BRIDEGROOM  I pass over the attempt to embarrass my fortune; and I will say nothing of the efforts made to transfer me to another regiment and to have me sent back to the wars. Nor will I dwell upon the conspiracy disclosed by the repeated advice from so many friends to forgo this marriage. For few of these advisers were close enough to me to have the right to speak; fewer still had any definite reason to tender; and all were but too plainly moved – some of them unconsciously, perhaps –

by one hidden yet dexterous hand. Let all that pass. How did the real attack begin? What was the first thing to be insinuated?

THE BEST MAN  *(As before)* Yes, I remember.

*(The* SECOND *of the* EIGHT WINDOWS *is endowed with a moving consciousness. Ten honorable Knights rise in a semicircle and look down, with an open apprehension in their pure young eyes, upon the pair beneath. An indignant diapason rolls in from the organ, and distant voices are heard to chant the* In quo corriget?*)*[2]

THE BRIDEGROOM  A shameful whisper, creeping hither and thither, named me a cheat, a trickster, a gamester. I have played – yes; it is the privilege of my order, of my profession. But I have never played otherwise than honorably.

THE BEST MAN  None otherwise than honorably.

THE BRIDEGROOM  A hundred tongues came to my defense. Only one was silent – yours. I can never thank you enough for that. Your perfect confidence would not deign . . . Your certainty of my innocence made it seem . . .

THE BEST MAN  Unnecessary to defend.

*(The Knights look into one another's eyes and shake their heads and turn away their faces.)*

THE BRIDEGROOM  I strangled this slanderous report – though *she* indeed had never doubted me; and I struck down the only man who dared repeat it openly. But what came next? After defending my honor as an officer, I was compelled to defend my honor as a suitor.

*(The* THIRD WINDOW *sets itself in motion. A band of chaste young Damsels brush forward through ranks of tall and rigid lilies and curve their lustrous palms before their ears to hear the coming words of ill-report. Voices (not theirs) intone the words of the* Noli æmulari.*)*[3]

THE BRIDEGROOM  A score of lying words placed in an honest hand – a villainous bit of paper brought to the gaze of a pair of trusting eyes. Who could have done it, I ask – and why?

THE BEST MAN  We never learned.

THE BRIDEGROOM  I have indeed lived

freely, but who shall say that I have seriously overstepped the bounds?

*(The Damsels blush, and stoop to hide their faces among the lilies. But their blushes are repeated upon the pavement.)*

THE BEST MAN   No one.

THE BRIDEGROOM   I went to her brother. What I told him satisfied him. But who could have written that letter? and why?

THE BEST MAN   You never learned.

THE BRIDEGROOM   But as bad followed – or worse. What was next attacked? My courage as a soldier. Mine – mine!

*(The* FOURTH WINDOW. *An army with banners. The leaders of the host rest on their swordhilts and gaze downward with satirical and contemptuous smiles. Above the ranks rise flags of scarlet and purple that flaunt in airy derision and dapple the sculptured pillar.)*

THE BRIDEGROOM   I demanded a hearing. I combated the unworthy charges sent back across those wastes of sea and sand. I summoned my witnesses. *You* spoke for me; briefly, quietly, one might almost have said reluctantly.

THE BEST MAN   You were above such accusations.

THE BRIDEGROOM   Your words, added to those of others, sufficed. And that evening Angela kissed me for the untarnished soldier that I was.

THE BEST MAN   Then I said enough. *(To himself)* Too much, perhaps.

*(The leader of the Army lifts a foreshortened sword, and makes a movement as if of warning. But neither of the pair interprets his movement, for neither sees it.)*

THE BRIDEGROOM   I came at last, then, to stand forth whole, sound, unscathed. I. But the others? – my bride? her parents? . . .

*(The* FIFTH WINDOW: *A rising of the sheeted Dead. The sun, half hidden by a passing cloud, but partly penetrates the dull and spectral panes.)*

THE BRIDEGROOM   A rumor ran that my orphaned bride had been born out of wedlock – that no priest had ever blessed the union of . . . O, it was foul! I beat at the doors of townhalls; I rained blows upon the portals of parish churches: my Angela should not be thus doubly and disgracefully orphaned. I searched the records, dim and dusty as they were. And I brought the truth triumphantly to light.

*(The sun reappears. The Dead shove back their cowls. Their eyes sparkle, their cheeks are flushed with life. They raise their full-fleshed hands in benediction.)*

THE BRIDEGROOM   But who could have started that rumor? And why?

THE BEST MAN   Who, indeed? You have never learned.

THE BRIDEGROOM   But even that was not enough. Worse followed – you know what. Word passed that Angela herself . . . No, no; I cannot say it. I – I heard that she was false . . .

*(The* SIXTH WINDOW: *A trio of female figures – Love, Truth and Purity – entwined in one another's arms. Their eyes are startled; their garments quiver and scintillate in reds and ambers and pale greens. Their mouths open, but whether in condemnation or in defense it is too soon to say. From that quarter or from another, there comes the chant:* Iniquos odio habui.)[4]

THE BRIDEGROOM   – that she was untrue . . . impure . . . Yes, but the last great lie was faced and routed. Here I await her; one moment more and she will have come. *(Happy tears course iridescently down the cheeks of the three Virgins.)* Hark, hark! I hear even now their carriage-wheels without.

*(The* SACRISTAN *enters.)*

THE SACRISTAN   Noon, and past noon. And the bride does not come.

THE BEST MAN   The chimes have long since ceased pealing.

THE SACRISTAN   The whole church questions, and whispers; – do you not hear?

THE BRIDEGROOM   Nothing can prevent that. Let the bells be heard too.

*(The* SACRISTAN *closes the door leading into the church, and retires by means of a second one opposite. Through walls, or doors, or windows*

*are heard the words:* Quare fremuerent gentes?)[5]

THE BEST MAN    The bells may ring, but they will bring you nothing.

THE BRIDEGROOM    What do you mean, my friend?

THE BEST MAN    She will not come.

*(The* SEVENTH WINDOW: *The Seven Cardinal Virtues; they change, with a slow but relentless movement of color, of outline, of feature, into the Seven Deadly Sins. This transformation, like all the others, passes unheeded.)*

THE BEST MAN    She will not come. Have you not heard?

THE BRIDEGROOM    Heard what?

THE BEST MAN    What every one else has heard; what fills the church with smiles and whispers even now.

THE BRIDEGROOM    What have you to tell me?

THE BEST MAN    It is always thus. The most concerned is ever the last to learn.

THE BRIDEGROOM    What have I to learn?

THE BEST MAN    This: that she has sinned.

THE BRIDEGROOM    That should have been said before. Or, better and more truly, not at all.

THE BEST MAN    They say that she has sinned, and sinned – with me.

THE BRIDEGROOM    O, my enemy! unseen, but unrelenting! And what is your response?

THE BEST MAN    Were the other reports true?

THE BRIDEGROOM    Not one of them.

THE BEST MAN    Ah . . . Perhaps the chimes will begin again. Perhaps the bride will yet appear. Perhaps those whisperings will cease. Do you hear them?

THE BRIDEGROOM    Yes – even through that door.

THE BEST MAN    Do you hear the bells?

THE BRIDEGROOM    No.

THE BEST MAN    Do you hear the bride arriving?

THE BRIDEGROOM    Not yet.

THE BEST MAN    Ah . . .    *(A pause)*

THE BRIDEGROOM    Is it true – what you say? Is it true? Is it true?

THE BEST MAN    Why need that matter? It is nothing; let is pass.

THE BRIDEGROOM    Nothing? . . . Let it pass? . . .

THE BEST MAN    Yes. *I* am here. And *she* will

never be. You may wait, but you shall wait in vain. *(He places his hand on the other's shoulders.)* If she were to come, I should not let her have you. She shall not have you. Nobody shall have you.

THE BRIDEGROOM    What is your meaning, Oliver?

*(The Deadliest of the Seven Sins hides her face; it is too hideous for contemplation.)*

THE BEST MAN    I shall not let you go. Our friendship has been too long, too close, too intimate. It shall not be destroyed; it shall not be broken. No one shall come between us.

THE BRIDEGROOM    Peace, Oliver, in heaven's name!

THE BEST MAN    Why have we lived so long together – why shared each other's every thought? To be completely sundered now? – Why did I save your life? To have it taken from me thus? – Why did you save mine? That you might cast this blight upon it in the end? – She shall not have you! I will do everything to prevent it! I *have* done everything to pre . . .

THE BRIDEGROOM    Ha! It is *you* who have attacked my honor?

THE BEST MAN    Your honor is secure.

THE BRIDEGROOM    It is *you* who have questioned my courage?

THE BEST MAN    You are brave; I believe that.

THE BRIDEGROOM    It is *you* who have insulted my love?

THE BEST MAN    No one loves you more than I.

*(The sculptured wreath entwined round the great central column writhes in descending spirals, like a vast serpent.)*

THE BRIDEGROOM    You are a liar, a traitor, a perjurer, and you shall die.

THE BEST MAN    One of us shall die.

THE BRIDEGROOM    One of us two shall die. It shall be you.

THE BEST MAN    One of us shall die – one of us three. *She* shall die; it is she who has come between us.

THE BRIDEGROOM    *(Drawing his sword)* You shall die. I shall kill you with my own hands.

*(The chimes begin to ring. A sound of rumbling*

*wheels and trampling hoofs is heard outside. A procession of priests and acolytes crosses the sacristy on the way into the church. They pause at the signs of combat.)*

THE BRIDEGROOM    Ah! She comes! She believes in me! And so shall all the others! They do, already; I will not believe the throng makes sport of our fair fame. *(To the priests)* Move on; move on! I will follow you within a moment.

*(The procession traverses the sacristy and moves on toward the high altar.* THE BRIDEGROOM *shuts the door behind it. The* BEST MAN, *springing forward, thrusts him from it, and then stands staunchly with his own back against its panels.)*

THE BEST MAN    You shall not pass. You shall never pass – to her.

THE BRIDEGROOM    Stand aside. Let me through.

THE BEST MAN    I do not mean to fail at the last moment. I shall not allow so many good endeavors to go for naught.

THE BRIDEGROOM    Stand aside. I hate you; I detest you; I despise you; I loathe you.

THE BEST MAN    You hate me? That cannot be!

THE BRIDEGROOM    I hate you with my whole heart. I loathe you with my whole soul.

THE BEST MAN    You loathe me? I, who have done so much . . .

THE BRIDEGROOM    You are not fit to live. You are not fit to die. But die you shall. I shall not kill you. You shall kill yourself. You shall do it now, and I shall see you do it. You have no other road to redemption.

THE BEST MAN    We have been friends always . . . I have loved you all my life . . . The thought of *her* made me mad . . . made me desperate . . .

THE BRIDEGROOM    Times presses. Use your blade.

*(The* EIGHTH WINDOW. *The Angelic Host trumpeting from the clouds, while Lucifer plunges headlong toward the Pit: the wonder is that he can fall so long, so fast, so far.*

*When* THE BRIDEGROOM *opens the door into the church,* THE BRIDE *is seen coming up the aisle, while the choirboys and the organ unite in a resounding Gloria. Upon the floor of the sacristy lies the body of a man in a pool of blood. As* THE BRIDE *and* THE BRIDEGROOM *meet before the altar rail, the* EIGHT WINDOWS, *dappling the floor of the sacristy with a thousand varied splotches of color – (but there is one, broader and brighter than them all) – shudder back convulsively to their pristine selves.)*

*Curtain*

# Documents

*Letter of the failed murderer Guy T. Olmstead from Cook County Jail to Dr Talbot of Chicago, 23 April 1894 (from Havelock Ellis,* Sexual Inversion, *1897, History XXVI)*

I feel as though I had neglected you in not writing you in all this time, though you may not care to hear from me, as I have never done anything but trespass on your kindness. But please do me the justice of thinking that I never expected all this trouble, as I thought Will and I would be in our graves and at peace long before this. But my plans failed miserably. Poor Will was not dead, and I was grabbed before I could shoot myself. I think Will really shot himself, and I feel certain others will think so, too, when the whole story comes out in court. I can't understand the surprise and indignation my act seemed to engender, as it was perfectly right and natural that Will and I should die together, and nobody else's business. Do you know I believe that poor boy will yet kill himself, for last November when I in my grief and anger told his relations about our marriage he was so frightened, hurt, and angry that he wanted us both to kill ourselves. I acquiesced gladly in this proposal to commit suicide, but he backed out in a day or two. I am glad now that Will is alive, and am glad that I am alive, even with the prospect of years of imprisonment before me, but which I will cheerfully endure for his sake. And yet for the last ten months his influence has so completely controlled me, both body and soul, that if I have done right he should be blamed for the mischief, as I have not been myself at all, but a part of him, and happy to merge my individuality into his.

*Letter from an anonymous case history in Havelock Ellis,* Sexual Inversion, *third edition 1915*

It is with the greatest reluctance that I reveal the closely guarded secret of my life. I have no other abnormality, and have not hitherto betrayed my abnormal instinct. I have never made any person the victim of passion: moral and religious feelings were too powerful. I have found my reverence for other souls a perfect safeguard against any approach to impurity. [. . .] My friendships with men, younger men, have been coloured by passion, against which I have fought continually. The shame of this has made life a hell, and the horror of this abnormality since I came to know it as such, has been an enemy to my religious faith [. . .] The power which gave me life seemed to insist on my doing that for which the same power would sting me with remorse. If there is no remedy I must either cry out against the injustice of this life of torment between nature and conscience, or submit to the blind trust of baffled ignorance. [. . .] I am nearly 42 and I have always diverted myself from personal interests that threatened to become dangerous to me. More than a year ago, however, a new fate seemed to open to my unhappy and lonely life. I became intimate with a young man of 20, of the rarest beauty of form and character. I am confident that he is and always has been pure. He lives an exalted moral and religious life dominated by the idea that he and all men are partners of the divine nature, and able in the strength of that nature to be free from evil. I believe him to be normal [. . .] He is poor, and it was possible for me to guarantee him a good education. I began to help him from the longings of a lonely life. I wanted a son and a friend in my inward desolation. I craved the companionship of this pure and happy nature. I felt such a reverence for him that I hoped to find the sensuous element in me purged away by his purity. I am, indeed, utterly incapable of doing him harm; I am not morally weak; nevertheless the sensuous element is there, and it poisons my happiness. He is ardently affectionate and demonstrative. He spends the summers with me in Europe, and the tenderness he feels for me has prompted him at times to embrace and kiss me as he has always done to his father. Of late I have begun to fear that without will or desire I may injure the springs of feeling in him, especially if it is true that the homosexual tendency is latent in most men. The love he shows me is my joy, but a poisoned joy. It is the bread and wine of life to me; but I dare not think what his ardent affection might ripen into. I can go on fighting the battle of good and evil in my attachment to him, but I cannot define my duty to him. To shun him would be cruelty and would belie his trust in human fidelity. Without my friendship he will not take my money – the condition of a large career. I might, indeed, explain to him what I explain to you, but the ordeal and shame are too great, and I cannot see what good it would do. If he has the capacity of homosexual feeling he might be violently stimulated; if he is incapable of it, he would feel repulsion. [ . . . ]

What I long for is the right to love, not for the mere physical gratification, for the right to take another into the arms of my heart and profess all the tenderness I feel, to find my joy in planning his career with him, as one who is rightfully and naturally entitled to do so.

When I read what I have written I see how pointless it is. It is possible, indeed, that brooding over my personal calamity magnifies in my mind the sense of danger to this friend through me, and that I only need to find the right relation of friendliness coupled with aloofness which will secure him against any too ardent attachment. Certainly I have no fear that I shall forget myself. Yet [ . . . ] I rebel inwardly against the necessity of isolating myself as if I were a pestilence, and I rebel against the taint of sensuous feeling. The normal man can feel that his instinct is no shame when the spirit is in control. I know that to the consciousness of others my instinct itself would be a shame and a baseness, and I have no tendency to

construct a moral system for myself. I have, to be sure, moments when I declare to myself that I will have my sensuous gratification as well as other men, but, the moment I think of the wickedness of it, the rebellion is soon over. The disesteem of self, the sense of taint, the necessity of withdrawing from happiness lest I communicate my taint, that is a spiritual malady whch makes the ground-tone of my existence one of pain and melancholy. . . .

*From a letter of the socialist Robert Allan Nicol in California to Edward Carpenter in England, March 1896 (in J. N. Katz,* Gay/Lesbian Almanac, *New York, Harper and Row, 1983, pp. 250–4)*

I long for glorious comradeship – a band of brothers, men and women – each for their art, who would co-operate and picture and utter for the race – sing the glad day which dawns and lead the people to the reconstruction of society – and humanity. Of myself I can do so little – as you once said to me – and with my comrades I could do so much.

[. . .] Slowly but surely, the nucleus of the new society [. . .] is gathering in Young America. . . . we young fellows are coming together, tho' we have not met one another yet [. . .] we are frank and open with each other – as Walt [Whitman] says, no "venereal taint, rum-drinker" or untrue man or woman can come – and tho' we present "no stainless perfections," yet we must be *honest* even in our seeming animalism, weaknesses [. . .] impurity simply consists in knowingly abandoning reality for illusion. [. . .]

*From* The Social Evil in Chicago. A Study of Existing Conditions with Recommendations by the Vice Commission of Chicago, *Chicago, Gunthrop-Warren Printing Co., 1911, pp. 296–8*

At the very outset of the Commission's investigation, its attention was called by several persons to a condition of affairs with regard to sexual perversion which was said to be enormously prevalent and growing in Chicago. In reporting their impression of their work on the Municipal bench at the Harrison street court, Judges [. . .] said that the most striking thing they observed in the last year was the great increase of sex perversion in Chicago. Police officers said the same thing [. . .]

It must be understood that under the law, the perpetrators of these various forms of sexual perversion can be regarded as those who may be punished by application of Section 47, Chapter 38, of the Revised Statues of Illinois (1909), the wording of which remains unchanged since the statutes were revised in 1845.

> The infamous crime against nature, either with man or beast, shall subject the offender to be punished by imprisonment, in the penitentiary for a term not more than ten years.

The Commission's investigator was, of course, unable to gain entrance in those circles of the very well-to-do, which are engaged in these practices, nor did he concern himself with the lowest stratum of society, which is the class more observable in our courts. Nor did he gain any information about the much more occasional cases among women, of which the Commission heard something from other sources. He most readily, however, became acquainted with whole groups and colonies of these men who are sex perverts but who do not fall into the hands of the police on account of their practices, and who are not known in their true character to any extent by physicians because of the fact that their habits do not, as a rule, produce bodily disease [. . .]

[. . .] it appears that the law framed in 1845 should more definitely recognize the dangers of this latter day growth of degenerate traits.

It should be so altered and made specific, under the guidance of scientific men who understand these practices, as to make it clearly understood that society regards these abhorrent deeds as crimes. Better definition would probably make it more possible to readily obtain conviction when desirable.

It would appear very doubtful, however, whether any spread of the actual knowledge of these practices is in any way desirable. Probably the purity or wholesomeness of the normal sexual relationship is all that is necessary to dwell on.

## Notes

1 *Ecce, quam bonum*, from Psalm 133, verse 1: "Behold, how good and how pleasant it is for brethren to dwell together in unity!"
2 *In quo corriget?* from Psalm 119, verse 9: "Wherewithal shall a young man cleanse his way? [i.e., keep himself pure] by taking heed thereto according to thy word."
3 *Noli æmulari*, from Psalm 37, verse 1. "Fret not thyself because of evildoers, neither be thou envious against the workers of inquity."
4 *Iniquos odio habui*, from Psalm 119, verse 113. "I hate vain thoughts [alternatively, two-faced men]: but thy law do I love."
5 *Quare fremuerunt gentes?* from Psalm 2, verse 1. "Why do the heathen rage, and the people imagine a vain thing?" [Alternatively, "Why do the nations so furiously rage together?"] This psalm is often intoned at Christmas and Good Friday matins.

# *"Mistakes"*

*Dramatic study in three acts*
*by*
*Herbert Hirschberg*

(1906)

translated from the German by Laurence Senelick

*"Mistakes"* is translated from Herbert Hirschberg, *"Fehler", dramatische Studie in 3 Aufzügen*, Strassburg and Leipzig: Josef Singer, 1906.

# Introduction

Germany in the 1890s was more open than England in its discussion of homosexuality and freer with the word itself, at least in legal and medical circles. From the publication of Richard von Krafft-Ebing's *Psychopathia Sexualis* in 1886, awareness of a wide spectrum of sexual activity coexisted with fear that these newly conspicuous variations bespoke a corresponding moral decline of society. In 1897, perhaps partially in response to Wilde's conviction and in the face of attempts by moral purity organizations to tighten the legal strictures on homosexuality, Dr Magnus Hirschfeld founded the *Wissenschaftlich-humanitäres Komitee* (Scientific-Humanitarian Committee) to militate for the reform of §175.[1]

Given the heated pamphlet wars over these questions, problem plays seemed a natural means of taking the debate to a wider audience. The first of these was Ludwig Dilsner's *Jasminblüthe* (*Jasmine Blossoms*, 1899), a thesis drama which falls back on melodramatic reversals and climaxes to dramatize the problem.[2] (Imagine one of Shaw's "unpleasant plays" minus a sense of humour and you get some idea of Dilsner's approach.) *Jasmine Blossoms* is prefaced with a long apologetic essay that in many respects echoes the Scientific-Humanitarian Committee's 1897 petition to moderate §175. Hirschfeld argued that homosexuality was an innate condition; Dilsner explained that it cannot therefore be considered a sin. Half of mankind is homosexual, he declares, but trapped between law and religion, with little outlet for its feelings. The great manage to escape §175 but the respectable middle class fall prey to blackmail and failed marriages.

Since the law did not specifically penalize mutual masturbation, Hirschfeld, somewhat disingenuously, had contended that oral and anal sex and pedophilia were uncommon among homosexuals, no more widely

*Plate 5* A homosexual blackmailer well known to the Berlin police. This photograph appeared in Magnus Hirschfeld's study of "the third sex" in Germany, 1904. (Laurence Senelick Collection.)

practiced than among heterosexuals. Dilsner adopted this argument, while offering some eccentric *obiter dicta* based more on fine feeling than on scientific observation. According to him, only perverted heterosexuals prefer pubescent boys. Mutual masturbation or coitus *inter femora* is more aesthetically pleasing than coitus with women; but anal intercourse and fellatio are

*Plate 6* "The Blackmailers," a cartoon which appeared in *Lustige Blätter*, 1 February 1905. The caption reads: "Now I asks yez! They wanna drop Paragiraffe 175 from da penal code" Den how's da middle classes s'posed to make a livin'?" (Laurence Senelick Collection.)

disgusting. Opinions such as these, despite their well-meant effort to elevate homosexuality to a position superior to the norm, cast the shadow of the crackpot over the play itself.

*Jasmine Blossoms* is essentially a set of dialogues voicing prevailing views of "uranism": a headmaster's relatively enlightened approach, a pastor's ignorance, a father's benighted authoritarianism, a mother's tardy tolerance. The jasmine blossoms of the title, their stunted stamens half turned to petals, are the headmaster's metaphor for homosexuality as a transitional stage. They are incarnated in Rudolf Welcke, a shy, dreamy sixth-former who is precociously aware of his own predilections. Unable to get anything from his pastor but unreasoning condemnation, he decides to live life according "to his nature" and falls in love with Schröder, a workman. Schröder proves to be a scoundrel who demands money from the lad's father on the pretext that Rudolf seduced him to commit an indecent act (all they had done in fact was embrace). Rudolf, threatened by the scandal and ordered by his father to go to America (the solution imposed on Hal in *The Blackmailers*), prepares for suicide but is talked out of it by the headmaster. A doctor

prescribes hard work, mental distraction, and early marriage to efface any trace of "the transitory madness of youth."

In Act IV, some years having gone by, Rudolf is financially independent and established in his profession, when family and friends urge him to marry an old acquaintance, Marie. Unable to resist the requests, entreaties and exhortations, he becomes engaged but realizes that he will be unable to consummate the marriage. Even after he explains the situation to his fiancée, she refuses to release him from his pledge, confident that her love will win his in time. Unwilling to marry with a lie in his heart, Rudolf shoots himself. His mother pronounces the peroration, stressing the dead youth's right to live "according to his nature"; could it have saved his life, she personally would have brought him the object of his affections.

"The play has for the first time directly and literally dealt with homosexuality in a dramatic format," wrote Numa Prætorius in the *Yearbook for Sexual Transitional States*.[3] It also set the pattern for subsequent plays on this subject. In *Jasmine Blossoms*, tendentious debates rise to dramatic action only by means of melodramatic techniques; the treatment is entirely superficial, and the psychic conflicts within the protagonist – his inner life – are never shown in action. Because Rudolf is depicted as a youth wise beyond his years, fully conscious of his desires and temperament, the betrothal seems an implausible plot device to trigger the suicide, which is itself incredible, given Rudolf's economic and mental independence. The blackmail device, although meant as a counterblast to §175, is rather a damp squib, with no serious consequences except to disclose Rudolf's homophilia to his father.

What comes across loud and clear, however, is the notion that there is such a thing as an inherent "homosexual nature" and that to thwart and deny it will produce dire consequences. In this respect, Dilsner and the playwrights who followed him clearly espoused the position of Hirschfeld and his supporters, that "homosexuality was deeply rooted in a biological imperative [with] no escape from sexual desires for individuals of the same sex."[4] Unfortunately, Hirschfeld himself predicated a view of the urning as an unhappy individual, tormented from without by intolerant persecution and from within by intolerable passion. This view, popularized by the Scientific-Humanitarian Commitee's widely disseminated publications, recurred in drama well into the 1960s.

The debate over rescinding §175 became more heated in the first years of the twentieth century, and the authorities more entrenched in their resistance to reform. Since the Committee's petition against the law had been rejected every year since 1899, it sought to educate the populace at large to support its work. In 1902 it published a pamphlet entitled "What Should the Ordinary Person [das Volk] Know about the Third Sex?" and distributed over 30,000 copies over the next two years. In 1903 it conducted inquiries about male homosexuality among Berlin high-school students and ironworkers. The backlash was immediate. After perusing the manuscript of a lecture on "Those Disinherited of Life's Blessings or The Third Sex," the Chief of Police of Hanover forbade its public presentation lest it put the listener in "moral peril." Five students accused Hirschfeld of molesting them via his questionnaires, and he was sentenced to a fine of 200 marks or twenty days in prison.

Finally, on 31 March 1905, the Committee managed to get its petition scheduled for debate by the Petitions Commission of the Reichstag. Its spokesman Adolf Thiele explained that this was a matter not simply of concern to homosexuals, but to society at large, for "what if homosexuals were in the majority and said: heterosexual activity in sexual life is abnormal?" However, a great many called this homosexual propaganda, and the petition was tabled. Despite the negative outcome, Hirschfeld declared a kind of success, in view of the fact that a parliament had discussed the welfare of homosexuals in an open forum for the very first time. Other members of the Committee refused to submit any more petitions and proposed instead to organize "a mass self-denunciation." "A large number of homosexuals – around a thousand – should be publicly charged in a common cause. Then the untenability of the legal paragraph would be demonstrated."[5]

It was against this backdrop that several new plays about the homosexual's plight were published, though not performed. Blackmail and bad marriages continued to be their melodramatic pivots, but always with an eye to legal reform. Herbert Hirschberg's 1906 three-act drama, *"Mistakes"* (*"Fehler"*), is typical.[6] It concerns a young lawyer, Edmund Manhard, who marries money to save his father from bankruptcy. Fully cognizant of his homosexual "nature," he nevertheless weds Elsa, the sweetheart of his old friend Kurt, whose lowly origins had caused him to be rejected by the girl's father. Edmund's servant has long blackmailed his master over their sexual relations; when he is dismissed by Edmund's father, he sends an incriminating letter to Elsa, now Frau Manhard, and demands a thousand marks – or else he will denounce his master to the authorities. Kurt, who is a doctor, informs Elsa of Edmund's true proclivities; at first, full of aversion for her husband, she wants to let things take their course. Finally she decides to pay the extortionist and sue for divorce, but this line of action is forestalled when Edmund shoots himself, leaving Elsa and Kurt free to marry.[7]

A variation on this theme was played out in Siegfried Moldau's 1907 four-act play *Wahrheit* (*Truth*).[8] Count Hector von Hemstedt has married in ignorance of his "true nature" but gradually awakens to his feelings. A dismissed servant who has made off with two love letters from von Hemstedt to his friend Theodor, denounces the count to the state's attorney. Von Hemstedt is tried, sent to prison, and divorced by his wife who takes custody of their son Kurt. After serving his sentence, the count, whose property has all gone for court costs, alimony and child support, takes refuge with Theodor, where he dies broken in body and spirit. At his mother's insistence, young Kurt marries the highborn Countess of Frankenfeld, whom he finds unappealing, solely to rehabilitate the family and suppress any hereditary unnatural longings he may harbor.

The play may have been inspired by Count Gunther von Schulenberg's letter to another nobleman, suggesting they found a league of aristocratic uranians. He opined that "well-born uranians suffer more than others [from blackmail] because of their sense of honour" and noted that the world would suddenly revise its opinion of homosexuality if 10 percent of the nobility "outed" itself.[9]

Like Dilsner, Hirschberg and Moldau subscribed to the Hirschfeldian thesis that there was a homosexual nature independent of environmental or morbid factors, which was both compulsory and compulsive. In *Jasmine Blossoms*, precocious Rudolf decides to live "according to his nature"; in *"Mistakes"*, Edmund is aware of "his true nature" but tries to suppress it; in *Truth*, the count is unaware of his true nature and acts in opposition to it. Despite this insistence on the inner emotional drives of the characters, the catastrophe that invariably ensues, however, is precipitated not by internal contradictions but from without by a blackmailer or a forced marriage. Because the protagonist is isolated, never shown with an equal who shares his predilections, the "naturalness" of his feelings remains undemonstrated. Complex psychological states and questions of interpersonal relationships are reduced to crude, stagey clichés. Hirschberg even undermines his own argument by the recurrent reference to a "mistake," as if it were an Aristotelian character defect that Edmund could overcome by force of will.

Still, the playwrights did not endorse Magnus Hirschfeld's ideas in every respect. None of them embraced the doctrine of homosexuals as a "third sex" with identifiable physical characterics. The count, Edmund, and, despite his hypersensitivity, even Rudolf all pass in ordinary society, and it requires an external agency to reveal their difference. Moldau also contradicted Hirschfeld by

suggesting that homosexuality may be passed down from father to son, a concept of hereditary taint that the Scientific-Humanitarian Committee actively combatted. Here Moldau as a dramatist seemed to be employing an Ibsenite metaphor for the sins or, in this case, the sorrows of the father being passed on to the younger generation.[10]

Such contradictions, along with the clumsy workmanship of these plays, led the reviewer for the *Yearbook* to suggest, "Perhaps the homosexual question is still too much an issue of contention, still too much an object of passionate struggle as a result of the idiotic clause in the legal code, for a dramatic treatment to set aside the message and subordinate it to purely artistic considerations."[11] Tendentiousness was, of course, inherent in any didactic *pièce à thèse* (in *"Mistakes"* the characters quote newspaper articles at length and dip into the *Psychopathia Sexualis* for answers). It was the eruption of the sensational into these debates, in lieu of a more organic or dynamic dramatic principle, that undermined the plays' purpose of reform. Playwrights eager to put this fresh material on stage fell back on tried-and-true devices of the well-made play and limned their character with the commonplaces of histrionic tradition. The first-act curtain of *"Mistakes"*, for instance, is another crude echo of Ibsen's *Ghosts*. Edmund has agreed to marry, despite his sexual bent, and now *"in great excitement he lays both hands on his head and stares after his father with the fixed gaze of a lunatic; brokenly*): – Too late! – a mistake – a mistake!" At the same time, the playwrights were handicapped by the inchoate nature of the temperament or psychology that they were trying to render stageworthy. Since the leading thinkers on the subject had not reached a consensus about homosexuality, Dilsner and the other authors, who seemed to be informed less by observation than by reading, were hard put to provide the "homosexual" with a sharp outline.

The critic Hanns Fuch, writing in 1902, complained that, whereas modern drama was dominated by the complications and conflicts of heterosexual love, no playwright had yet dared to feature a homosexual love story.[12] Reciprocated affection and genital activity are absent from these plays. Rudolf's sole physical audacity is to embrace a workman;

the count merely writes sentimental letters (which would not, *de jure*, incur the punishment that the play inflicts on him). Only Edmund in *"Mistakes"* has actually committed an illicit sexual act, and that was with his manservant Gerhard, an indolent and insolent lackey who characterizes their dealings as "*Schweinerei.*" Class and gender are rigidly maintained in these plays, aimed as they are at a bourgeois reader or spectator. Obedient to the common notion of homosexual blackmail, the authors always draw their protagonist from either the professional or the upper classes; the blackmailer is always a plebeian. (Gerhard speaks the Berlin equivalent of cockney, which has overtones both of comedy and criminality – a perverted Enery Stryker, perhaps?)

Hirschberg does seem to have vague socialist tendencies, for he credits his hero's downfall as much to the economic pressures represented by his rapacious father, as to the law's inflexibility. The older generation in *"Mistakes"* is characterized as social-climbing and money-grubbing, willfully blind to the desires of its children. Much of the contempt for its values is put in the mouth of the doctor/*raisonneur*, a self-made man and staunch heterosexual, who in his own way has suffered badly from these inequities.

Within these schematic boundaries, there is little room for sophisticated treatment. Not until Ferdinand Bruckner's *Die Verbrecher* (*Criminals*) of 1929 would homosexual victims be portrayed as charming, normal young men, whose unreliability and mood swings were due entirely to their oppression under the law. By that time, there was no longer an Imperial censorship to prevent such depictions from reaching the stage. There was also a vigorous and vociferous homosexual subculture in Berlin.

## Notes

1 See J. C. Fout, "Sexual politics in Wilhelmine Germany: the male gender crisis, moral purity, and homophobia," *Journal of the History of Sexuality*, 1992, vol. 2, p. 389; H.-G. Stümke, *Homosexuelle in Deutschland: eine politische Geschichte*, Munich, C. H. Beck, 1989, pp. 21–52; Freunde eines Schwulen Museums in Berlin e.v. (eds), *Die Geschichte des §175: Strafrecht gegen Homosexuelle*, Berlin, Rosa Winkel, 1990; and J. D. Steakley, *The Homosexual Emancipation Movement in Germany*, Salem, NH, Ayer Co., 1975, pp. 21–61.

2 L. Dilsner, *Jasminblüthe: Drama in fünf Akten*, Berlin, *c.* 1899.

3 Numa Prætorius (pseud. of Eugen Wilhelm), "Reine Bellestristik," *Jahrbuch für sexuelle Zwischenstufen*, 1901, vol. 3, pp. 431–8.

4 Fout, op. cit., p. 398.

5 M. Baumgart, "Die Homosexuellen-Bewegung bis zum Ende des Ersten Weltkrieges," in Berlin Museum (ed.), *Eldorado. Homosexuelle Frauen und Männer in Berlin 1850–1950. Geschichte Alltag und Kultur*, Berlin, Frölich and Kaufmann, 1984, pp. 19–23; E. Kraushaar (ed.), *Hundert Jahre Schwul: eine Revue*, Berlin, Rowohlt, 1997, pp. 14–17.

6 Herbert Hirschberg (b. 1881) was a prolific minor dramatist who wrote a history of the court theatre of Coburg and Gotha. His clinical interests suggest he may be identical with the Dr Herbert G. Hirschberg who wrote a propaganda attack on British recruiting during the First World War (1915).

7 H. Hirschberg, *"Fehler" (Dramatische Studie in drei Aufzügen)*, Strassburg and Leipzig, Josef Singer, 1906. See also Numa Prætorius, "Belletristik," *Jahrbuch für sexuelle Zwischenstufen*, 1907, vol. 9, pp. 604–7.

8 S. Moldau, *Wahrheit*, Leipzig, M. Spohr, 1907. See also Numa Prætorius, "Belletristik," *Jahrbuch für sexuelle Zwischenstufen*, 1910, vol. 11, pp. 95–6.

9 See A. Raffalovich, "Chronique de l'unisexualité," *Archives de l'anthropologie criminelle*, 1909, vol. 24, pp. 378–9.

10 Raffalovich quotes from Féré's work on castration as a remedy for sexual inversion, in which Féré noted, "The progeny of inverts is certainly tainted by degenerescence in reasonably observed cases; but one may be sure that some inverts have engendered normal children exclusively: a diseased heredity is not predestined." Raffalovich, "A propos du syndicat des uranistes," p. 286.

11 Numa Prætorius, "Belletristik," *Jahrbuch für sexuelle Zwischenstufen*, 1907, p. 604.

12 Hanns Fuchs, "Die Homosexualität im Drama der Gegenwart und der Zukunft," *Die Kritik*, 1 Aug. 1902, p. 513.

# "Mistakes"

Dramatic study in three acts

## Herbert Hirschberg

(1906)

"Μάχεσθαι χρὴ τὸν δῆμον
ὑπὲρ νόμου ὅπως ὑπὲρ τειχους."

Heraclitus[1]

dedicated to Dr Magnus Hirschfeld, M.D.

## Characters

KONRAD MANHARDT, banker
DR EDMUND MANHARDT, a junior civil
   servant, his son
ELSA WALDENBERG
DR KURT KLEEFELD, physician
GERHARD, a servant in the Manhardt
   household
PATSCHKE, a policeman

*Time: The Present [1906]*
*Between the first and second acts three months
elapse.*

*Place of action: Berlin*

### Notes on the staging

KONRAD MANHARDT, average height and
   weight, mid-40s, military moustache,
   balding, white strands of hair, carefully and
   greasily combed over his head.
EDMUND MANHARDT, slight, late 20s, clean-
   shaven, long black hair, piercing eyes and
   long prominent nose.
ELSA WALDENBERG, pale, frigid blonde, 23.
DR. KURT KLEEFELD, handsome, well-built,
   late 20s, smart moustache.
GERHARD, slender blond youth, early 20s,
   clean-shaven, elegant livery.
PATSCHKE wears the uniform of the Berlin
   constabulary.

## Act I

*Scenery:* EDMUND MANHARDT'*s study,
furnished in an up-to-date style in fumed oak. In*
front of the very wide window in the corner left,
a diplomat's desk, at which Edmund is seated,
reading the newspaper with his back to the
audience. Right a door, and next to it the
bookcase, on top of it a messy heap of
documents. Against the wall, centre, set around
the desk a comfortable leather sofa and two deep
club chairs. On the walls opulent oil paintings.
It is 10 o'clock in the morning.*

*Curtain up!*

EDMUND   (*Reads his paper, occasionally
   reacting with a gesture – after a while he
   rings,* GERHARD *appears*) Why haven't you
   dusted, why haven't the files been put in
   order?
GERHARD   Sorry, boss, I didn't figger you'd
   be up this early.
EDMUND   I like everything to be in place by
   9 o'clock. For the last time – this loafing
   has got to stop. I'm sick to death of your
   excuses. Tidy up the files and put the first
   five documents on the desk here – I've got
   to get to work – by the way, if I find any
   more signs of imbroglio in my room,
   you'll be out on your ear! – I've had to put
   up with your slovenly ways for far too
   long.
GERHARD   The way I figger, boss, a man like
   me can get this kinda job anywheres – call
   this a job! And as for this army discipline
   you're suddenly tryin' to innerduce, I'm
   fed up to here. What d'ye mean anyway,
   bimbolio? I don't see nuthin' wrong. (*He
   puts five documents on the desk.*)
EDMUND   Shut up, and get out!
GERHARD   You take that kinda tone with me
   once more, boss, and I go to the cops. Then
   the gloves'll be off. I may be a red, but it
   don't stop me from goin' to the boys in blue
   and lettin' all the nasty li'l skellintons outa
   the closet!
EDMUND   (*Gets up very excited, pulls out his*

*handkerchief and wipes the sweat of fear from his brow)* Listen, Gerhard!

GERHARD   See, boss, it don't pay to be throwin' me out. And talkin' o' blue, your big-mouth highbrow words is gonna cost you another hunnert in blue banknotes – now! *(Sticks out his hand)*

EDMUND   *(Pulls out his wallet, removes a hundred-mark note and gives it to Gerhard)* Here – now shut up and go! I see in the paper that Dr Kleefeld, – you remember he used to visit, – is back from his trip abroad. He's planning to settle here. Get dressed, you're going to take him a letter from me and some flowers, you can buy them on the way. The doctor's address is 46 Joachim Street. Take a cab.

GERHARD   Yessir, I'll git dressed right away! *(Goes out)*

EDMUND   *(Walks nervously back and forth and then sits at the desk and starts to write; a bell rings. Gerhard appears with a calling card on a silver salver)* What is it now?

GERHARD   That Doc Kleefeld – I think he's outside.

EDMUND   *(Joyously grabs the card and reads)* You're right, he is. Show him in.

*(Exit Gerhard, Kurt enters shortly.)*

EDMUND   *(Hurries up to kiss him)*

KURT   *(Parries him with a hand)* Let's have a friendly handshake, my dear Edmund. My first free day is devoted to my dear old chum. Well, how've you been these last two years?

EDMUND   Is it two years already? . . . *(Musing)* Completed your odyssey in two years? Then it's your turn to tell the stories. You know, whenever anyone's been on a sea voyage . . .

*(They sit down.)*

KURT   And what a voyage! My boy, do you have any idea what the women were like? In America! Especially when you're a ship's doctor in a white uniform. . . . It works like a charm. Total power. One woman even left a wedding-ring in my cabin, a symbolic gesture! . . . First stop, Atlantic City. Compared with what's available there, the Tiergarten is a wilderness.

EDMUND   Kurt, you know those conquests of yours don't interest me. What with my tendencies, another man's happiness can only make me feel miserable.

KURT   Please forgive me, I completely forgot *(He looks at him sympathetically.)* Incidentally – when I was in America I ran into plenty of cases like yours. There was an abundance of material there. So I thought about you a lot, and I think I've figured it out. I'd like to give you my diagnosis soon, for even if there's no complete cure, I can offer you encouragement. *(Pause)* But that's enough about that. I'm glad to see you aren't too proud to go on being friends with the son of the porter at your bank.

EDMUND   Why, Kurt, I was just about to send some flowers to your apartment as a housewarming gift.

KURT   Thanks, but it doesn't change the circumstances! My father was a working-man and his biggest mistake was to try and turn me into a man of learning. Blinkered as he was, he didn't realize the humilation in store for me when he sent me here to the Wilhelm Academy, the "High Hat Kid Glove School," where I was treated like an untouchable by the sons of purse-proud snobs. You were the only boy who stood up for me like a man and offered to be my friend.

EDMUND   I always shared your feelings. Anyway, when it comes to pedigrees, you know that my own grandfather was nothing but a drum major in the infantry reserves. And, if you like, I can prove to you in no time that I'm the untouchable now and you're the fair-haired boy, the man of the hour.

KURT   Well, my only consolation is that I'm a totally self-made man. Given my parents' slender resources I had to earn my own living. Whenever my classmates went out for a good time, I'd be giving private lessons . . . working myself to death *(He sweeps a hand over his brow)*, thank God, I got through it, and when I was ready, I went into the world to make myself useful and earn my bread. Imagine, as a ship's doctor I could see the world free, gratis and for nothing, and even put by a tidy sum, which I can now use to set up in business.

EDMUND   Does a ship's doctor make that much money?

KURT   Not likely! But there are perks! Believe you me, dollar millionaires on their travels are just as close-fisted with doctor's fees as they are with dollar heiresses. Not to mention that Berlin is diabolically expensive. In the two weeks I've been ashore, it's as if I've sworn off patients, ha ha ha, and my office hours could better be christened leisure hours. I planned to pay you a visit as soon as I'd found and furnished an apartment – so here I am.

EDMUND   Don't let it get you down, Kurt. Patients here in Berlin don't come in droves, that's true. But if you can keep at it and make your way, things'll fall into place. Come to think of it, Papa might be able to do something for you, some job like house doctor at the bank.

KURT   (Interrupts) I would really be grateful for that.

EDMUND   Then I 'll put the wheels in motion right away. But I can't offer you much in the way of prospects. It pays – if I remember the pay-scale correctly – 25 pfennigs per appointment, with reimbursement for bandages and the like thrown in. You won't get rich. But for a start it'll keep you off the streets.

KURT   I know. It's always tough getting started, don't I know it! America was my biggest lesson in taking life seriously. There profit is written in capital letters and only the go-getters make it. (Pause) Sooner or later all the fun I had globetrotting will prove to be an advance I'll have to pay back with interest. What I want is real serious, regular activity, lots and lots of work! – But here I am nattering on about myself without asking about your ups and downs. What are you doing now? Are you a civil servant? I see files. (He points to the desk)

EDMUND   Not even close! I'm on the board of the Conrad Manhardt-Berlin Banking Firm. My father may believe that Civil Servant is the finest title the Prussian state can bestow, but he can pay me better than the state can. (Indicating the documents) Those are mortgage deeds waiting for my inspection.

KURT   Then I'm disturbing you (About to get up).

EDMUND   Not at all, there's no hurry, do stay. (He rings. [Gerhard] appears) Cherry brandy and cigars. ([Gerhard] exits)

KURT   Please, don't make a fuss!

EDMUND   It's no trouble, dear boy, we have to sample our good old Havanas.

(GERHARD puts the liqueur, two liqueur glasses and cigars on the table, fills the glasses and exits.)

EDMUND   (Raising his glass) Cheers, to a firm friendship!

KURT   (Takes a glass and touches EDMUND's with his little finger) Bless all who sail in her!

(They drink and put the glasses down.)

EDMUND   (Hands him the cigar box; they both take a cigar and start to smoke) Who's her?

KURT   Our friendship, what else?

EDMUND   I thought you were referring to Elsa Waldenberg, your childhood sweetheart. Or have you put her out of your thoughts?

KURT   What choice have I had! You think Alderman Waldenberg would bestow his daughter on an over-educated prole? (He sighs deeply) You see, we're back to that original mistake that keeps dogging my steps. If I had been a manual labourer, I would never have gone into society, never have met her and never been so unspeakably unhappy. (Groaning) Ah, it really hurt to have to give her up!

EDMUND   You must have one in every port! – You used to be famous for your conquests.

KURT   Ah yes! – To obliterate the painful memory I tried to drown myself in a whirlpool of pleasures and sink deep into the swamp of pleasure. But a week ago, when I saw her on Tiergartenstrasse and she passed close by me, everything that seemed to be dormant in here (He indicates his heart) awoke again. I thought I'd forgotten her, but her eyes taught me otherwise.

EDMUND   Didn't you propose to her before you set sail? So far as I know, she reciprocated your affection. Whenever we'd meet, at her place or ours, and I'd drop your name, she'd blush bright red and break off the conversation. If I'd been in your shoes, I would have talked to her old man.

KURT   Which is what I did with a heavy heart and do you know the old snob's response? First he laughed which made the blood rush to my head, and then he said, "My dear doctor, you're a very pleasant companion, a very amusing guest, but I see absolutely no reason to let that and your alleged love for my daughter influence my choice of son-in-law. My son-in-law must be cut from other cloth – my respects – dinner's on the table!" and left me standing there.

EDMUND   That must have been a bitter pill!

KURT   And until now I believed it had done the trick. Get away, get far away was my only thought, which I soon put into practice.

EDMUND   Old Waldenberg has tripled his fortune in the last year by shrewd investments. He made an incredible amount of money out of the Russo-Japanese war.

KURT   I dreamed about his losing it all and becoming poor as a churchmouse. That was the only hope I had left. But this news makes everything more hopeless than it was before.

EDMUND   I'm afraid so! He's full of crazy ambitions, obsessed with ranks and titles. He's set on buying himself some ghastly lieutenant in the guards.

KURT   Then the fellow can trade in his sabre for a scissors, and cut stock coupons for Waldenberg.

EDMUND   My poor boy, try to forget her. Drown your sorrows in someone else's unhappiness, which far outweighs yours. The high-water mark of your misery can't come near mine! Believe me, Kurt, your visit is a great comfort. I'm grasping at straws like a drowning man. You have to advise me, Kurt, help me!

KURT   Stop talking in riddles, are you speaking to me as a doctor or as a friend?

EDMUND   Both!

KURT   Then please – don't hold back!

EDMUND   These last two years I've felt like a stag at bay, always on the point of ending my life. My abnormal tendencies have made me the victim of a wretch who's squeezing me like a lemon. I've tried every possible way to get out of his clutches, but it's no use. No matter how I try to deal with the fellow, kind words or energetic actions, the result is always blackmail.

KURT   And who is this nemesis of yours?

EDMUND   Gerhard, my servant!

KURT   Edmund, how could you sink so low? – *(Pause)* I realize that passions aren't easy things to control – But as a lawyer you should know . . .

EDMUND   You'd better hear the worst. Of course I ought to know better, but listen to the case of a wiser lawyer than I, listen to the *Berlin Daily* report on the case of a district judge from Breslau *(He goes to the desk, takes the paper and reads)*: "Last night at 6 o'clock a gunshot rang out near St Hedwig's Church. The police hastened to the spot and arrested two men, one an individual from Hamburg of no fixed abode, who was loafing about. The other was district judge Dr G., a visitor from Breslau and chronic victim of blackmail, who, in his desperation, made use of a revolver. The wounded man, a 'casual laborer' named Blaffke, was taken to the charity ward, while Dr. G. was imprisoned pending investigation. – This sensational occurrence will shortly come before our criminal court." *(He lets the paper fall from his hand.)* That's what happened to a lawyer who was actually a criminal court judge.

KURT   There we have another mistake!

EDMUND   As a doctor how you can call such tendencies mistakes?

KURT   Don't get me wrong! What I'm calling a mistake is the law which punishes such unhappy men! It is a legislative mistake, a disastrous mistake, a gap in the education of the legislators. Believe me, the case of this district judge, which tells an appalling tale, this dreadful, awful case will change the government's mind. The papers will raise a hue and cry, a bill will be introduced, the bill will become law, it has to become law. . . .

EDMUND   Never. As a lawyer I've had plenty of opportunity to see what goes on backstage. – For years now there's been a "Society for Human Rights," headed by a physician, to agitate for just such a bill.

KURT   Where does this "Society" hold its meetings, and what is the name of this noble humanitarian?

EDMUND   *(Takes out his wallet and after a long search hands out a calling card to* [Kurt]*)* This'll give you the details!

KURT   *(Takes the card from* EDMUND, *reads it and puts it away)* Thanks; I shall immediately become an ally of this good Samaritan. This is a wonderful field where I might do some good. Don't you see, don't you share my view that every judge has to study psychology above all, that psychology must become an obligatory subject for the bar exam?

EDMUND   These reforms speak so persuasively for themselves that I'm persuaded you must have spent time in prison as a modern-day martyr.

KURT   All right then, Edmund! I want to take up the fight. I want to correct the mistakes. For now God bless you! *(Extends his hand, which* EDMUND *shakes)*

EDMUND   Good-bye, Kurt, I hope to see you soon. *(*KURT *exits)*

EDMUND   *(Rings –* GERHARD *appears)*

EDMUND   Clear the table, Gerhard. I am in to no one. If it's business, tell them to see me at the counting-house during my office hours; if it's private, I cannot receive visitors. *(He sits at the desk and riffles through the documents.* GERHARD *clears the glasses from the table. The bell rings loudly.)*

GERHARD   *(On his way out)* So the gent's not in to nobody.

EDMUND   No!

GERHARD   *(Goes out, comes right back and announces)* "The Privy Councilor" would like to see the "Junior Civil Servant".

EDMUND   *(Astonished, looks at the clock)* Papa, at this hour? . . . Please come in!

*(*GERHARD *exits, soon afterwards the* FATHER *enters very excited and drops into an armchair.)*

FATHER   Good morning, Edmund, matters of great urgency bring me to my legal counsel.

EDMUND   *(Who has risen to greet his* FATHER, *sits down at the desk)* Please, Papa, you know that my abilities are always at the service of the Conrad Manhardt Bank *(Indicating the documents)*. I was working for the firm at this very moment.

FATHER   God grant you haven't worked in vain, God grant that I haven't built all this up in vain. *(He rises excited and struggles with a resolve. After a long pause.)* I have to inform you as my firm's lawyer of my imminent bankruptcy. *(*EDMUND *with a gesture of surprise tries to interrupt him.)* Don't interrupt me, please. I hesitated until now to let anyone know of this, I hesitated until I was sure, until I was absolutely sure. The latest balance sheet which I drew up last night confirmed my death sentence. And that's why I hastened to you so early. Only you can save me, save me I say, for in addition to my fortune, Russia has cost me my honour. My life is at stake. And now, my beloved son, I come to you as a father and look to you to make the

sacrifice, the only one that can save me, save us – *(He breaks into tears.)*

EDMUND   What shall I do, father? I am ready to do anything necessary to intercede for you. Poverty is no disgrace, shall I go to work? I can earn enough for both of us as an attorney.

FATHER   I crave more than what you propose. My honour is to be cleared only by Mammon. Is the fraudulent bankrupt . . . I can't hold off the stock market for more than a fortnight . . . is the fraudulent bankrupt who heads the Conrad Manhardt Firm to make a field-day for the scandal sheets of Berlin? I know that I am asking something monstrous of you, but Edmund, remember that everything I've done was done for you, for you, my son! . . . Twenty-eight years ago, when your dying mother raised her dimming eyes to me, laid you in my arms and departed this life, when the young bank clerk was alone, alone with his child, it became clear to me that all my ideals were buried with her in the cold grave, that the world had become stale, flat and unprofitable. So I became a cold, hard-hearted apostle of selfishness, and my life was devoted only to business and to your upbringing, in that order. After I had earned enough and reached the top, after I had built up everything here for you, fate the cheat comes to snatch it all away again. So I am defending my, our hoard, for there is a way to stop this from happening.

EDMUND   And what, father, do you want of me?

FATHER   *(Slowly and seriously)* Marriage.

EDMUND   *(Cries out)* Father, you know that . . .

FATHER   *(Sighing deeply)* I know, my son, what I ask of you is a sheer impossibility. *(He kneels before him.)* Edmund, are you willing to stake your life to save your father's life? Is your father's honour, which is yours as well, not worth a sacrifice?

EDMUND   You know, father, that I am one of fate's disinherited, you also know that any girl I take to wife, that unfortunate victim whose name I don't even know, will be accursed.

FATHER   The girl doesn't matter! My honour and this firm, which is my life's work, my fortune are what's important! Even someone disinherited has a legal right to a portion of the estate, and so do you, and

89

you are willing to give it up? Must I ask you again?

EDMUND   *(Stands motionless, pensive. His whole being presents a picture of misery. After a long silence.)* So be it, father! You have my word. . . . To ransom your life I will enchain another to my miserable existence.

FATHER   *(Kisses* EDMUND, *joyously excited)* Thank you, Edmund. All will be well. I'm saved. Today the Conrad Manhardt Bank has been shaken to its foundations. You, my son, have made it secure more once. The assault has been repelled.

EDMUND   And the name of the unlucky woman?

FATHER   Banker Waldenberg has had his eye on you for the last two years. He wants his daughter's alliance to you to effect a merger of the Manhardt and Waldenberg firms.

EDMUND   *(Who shrieked aloud on hearing the name)* Never, father, Elsa Waldenberg must never be my wife.

FATHER   *(Abruptly)* I have your word! *(Coolly exits, his head held high)*

EDMUND   *(In the greatest distress puts his hands on his head and stares after his* FATHER *with the fixed gaze of a madman; staccato):* . . . Too late! . . . what a mistake . . . what a mistake!

*Quick curtain*

## Act II

*Same setting as Act I. It is 5 o'clock in the afternoon. At the rise of the curtain* EDMUND's *room in seen in twilight.* KURT *and* GERHARD *enter from outside.* GERHARD *turns on the electric light.*

GERHARD   Please, if the Doc don't mind waitin' a while, the master' ll be in shortly.

KURT   So, the couple returned from their honeymoon yesterday?

GERHARD   Yeah, last night. The ol' man was sure surprised. More work fur me, clean up the apartment, up to my neck in work. Ackshly they're s'posed to stay away four weeks, but they came back yestiddy. Just before I went to bed, the boss gimme a letter to mail to you. . . . I'll jes' take a peek 'n' see if he's up yet! *(About to go out when* EDMUND *meets him,* GERHARD *withdraws):* Mornin', boss, *(indicating* KURT*);* Doc Kleefeld's here.

EDMUND   *(Goes up to* KURT, *without taking notice of* GERHARD*)* Good morning, my dear, dear KURT. *(He nods to* GERHARD *to get out, and* GERHARD *does so.)*

KURT   Good morning. . . . You asked me to come here, Edmund, and I came, but I didn't come on your account. After what has happened there's nothing more to be said. If I came, I did so out of alarm and concern for someone who was a goddess for me and whom you stole from me *(Groaning)*, worse than that, whom you cheated me of.

EDMUND   There's nothing you can say that's bad enough. No, go ahead, hit me and trample on me like a worm. Humiliate me, do with me what you will; for I know I've destroyed, crushed the happiness of your life. But I didn't do it for my own sake. A double game, call it duty versus nature, call it heaven versus hell, angels versus demons, call it whatever you like, this double game that goes on in every human soul has been won by filial love. And if you do trample on me now, if you do hit me, if you do spit on me, then at least, dear Kurt, offer me the hope of forgiveness.

KURT   Don't play-act on my behalf! I won't and can't believe you. So it was your father and his insatiable greed that destroyed all my prospects. . . . I thought as much the minute I read the notice of your engagement in the papers. Of course you didn't say a word of it to me. And I, poor fool, believed in your sympathy, while you were probably gloating in secret over my heartache. But revenge is still mine . . . and I shall have it.

EDMUND   *(Convulsively recoils in some dismay)* Kurt! . . . I thought you were a bigger person.

KURT   Think of me what you like. I don't care whether you think me a clod or a perfect gentleman.

EDMUND   Hear me out, Kurt. One last time I want to speak you as friend to friend. . . . What drove me to that unholy step, spare me from saying. Enough, believe me, that owing to urgent complications I had to marry Elsa against my will. It was a plain matter of business between our fathers, which I was driven to accept for the only reason that meant anything, filial love. But you know that . . . I can be nothing to my wife, that I can only . . . offer her friendship. And if I behaved badly to you, commonly and shabbily, if I am detestable in your eyes, then for the sake of the woman you love, I implore you for the sake of Elsa, who must never hear of it, for the sake of this noble woman's soul, which it would be a crime to destroy, I beseech you to say nothing.

KURT   Man, have you any idea the sort of disgusting crime you've just committed? Can't you imagine how it looks in my mind? But what difference does that make to you and your business deals? What do you care if a thousand poor people lose all their happiness, all their hardwon savings, this marriage which you yourself describe as a business matter is nothing but business as usual. But in spite of all this I intend to behave more honourably than you did to me. I shall say nothing. If, however, your wife were to ask me, I would not hesitate to enlighten her without equivocation.

EDMUND   *(In great alarm which he masters with difficulty)* But Kurt, aside from any moral obligation, you have no legal right to do so. Paragraph 300 of the penal code . . .

KURT   Allows a doctor to reveal medical secrets to married couples.

EDMUND   *(Livid with anger)* Liar! The paragraph allows the revelation of medical secrets only with the permission of the couples concerned, and I don't permit it! Watch out!

KURT   *(Looks at him contemptuously, very calmly)* Then I shall take whatever steps are necessary.

*(A knock,* GERHARD *enters and announces)*

GERHARD   The Councilor.

*(*GERHARD *exits, the* FATHER *enters.)*

EDMUND   *(As he enters)* Kurt, you wanted . . .

FATHER   Good evening, gentlemen.

EDMUND and KURT *(Bowing)* Good evening.

*(All three sit on the sofa and in armchairs.)*

EDMUND   Papa, I'm glad that you came in just now.

FATHER   That goes without saying. Slept soundly in your new home? And where's little Elsa?

EDMUND   Elsa will be here soon. She hasn't finished dressing yet.

FATHER   Ah, yes, women! *(To* KURT*)* So, Doctor Kleefeld, how are you? Lots to do already.

KURT   Thank you, sir, it's a living! . . . I take this occasion to thank you for the position I acquired owing to your kind offices.

FATHER   Don't mention it, dear doctor! How's the private practice going?

KURT   All right, thanks.

FATHER   In no time it'll be a bed of roses. The main thing is to lay down a firm foundation. And where there's honey, the bees fly to it! You know, Doctor, once you start earning money, there are always investments to be made.

EDMUND   Papa looks at everything from a business standpoint.

KURT   Well, that's his business!

*(All three laugh heartily.* ELSA *appears and the gentlemen rise.)*

ELSA   Good evening, gentlemen.

THE FATHER and EDMUND   Evening!

*(*KURT *bows)*

EDMUND   *(Indicating* KURT*)* Dr Kurt Kleefeld knew you in the old days, Elsa?

ELSA   Oh yes, very well! *(She extends her hand to* KURT, *who kisses it.)*

KURT   Allow me, dear lady, to offer you my congratulations on your recent marriage. Unfortunately I've had no earlier opportunity . . .

EDMUND   What difference does that make, Kurt? You know that our wedding was attended only by the immediate family.

KURT   To which a friend of your youth naturally does not belong.

ELSA   I accept your well-meant congratulations now as gladly as I would have on my wedding day.

FATHER   But, my dear doctor, why so formal? As Edmund's friend you can drop the "dear lady" and say "Frau Elsa" without more ado, right, daughter?

ELSA   Of course, Papa dear!

EDMUND   I think I have something to say about that as well.

KURT   Quite right, dear Edmund, we'll leave it at "dear lady" and now allow me, dear people, to take my leave.

ELSA   But at least wait for tea . . .

EDMUND   Kurt has patients to attend to!

(KURT *looks boldly at* EDMUND, *then bows to* ELSA, *kisses her hand and, bowing coolly to the gentlemen, exits.*)

FATHER   That was a bit too obvious, Edmund. I gather that, now you're married, his visits are no longer agreeable. Such social climbers don't suit your house. It was all right when you were a bachelor.

EDMUND   You're wrong, Papa, I invited him here. But he overstepped the bounds and that's why I wish to have nothing more to do with him.

FATHER   Y'see, that's what I was saying. The mistakes made in early childhood are always unpleasantly obvious in that sort of person. But all the same that hint you dropped was pretty heavy. "If you can't say something nice about a person . . . "

ELSA   Edmund must be mistaken, for I know that he and Kurt Kleefeld have been friends for years; people can't suddenly break it off like that. I've known the doctor a long time too, and never have I noticed anything tactless in his behaviour.

FATHER   That's true, my boy, Elsa's quite right. You must give him up gradually.

ELSA   That's not what I meant.

EDMUND   I'll settle it with him in private. To begin with, no more of his solo visits. Elsa, that smug visitor's smile he always loves to turn on you can get on my nerves. But now, happily, he's gone. So, end of discussion.

FATHER   Sweep it under the carpet! And now, children, we are alone, so tell me frankly, why did you come back home so suddenly – so higgledy-piggledy? Did you have a falling-out, your first matrimonial tiff? What?

(ELSA and EDMUND *embarrassed, look at one another, after a long silence.*)

FATHER   Well, out with it, whose fault was it?

ELSA   Daddy, you're guessing up the wrong tree. No, no! The reason we returned from Italy was that Edmund missed you so much.

FATHER   I don't believe it, it's simply not true!

EDMUND   Yes it is, Papa! I . . . neither of us could rest, Elsa and I, we missed you!

FATHER   You never felt that way before!

EDMUND   But now all the more so, Papa! We got homesick.

ELSA   And those uncomfortable hotels that I can't stand! I agreed at once when Edmund suggested we go home and move into our cozy house, which he'd been raving about.

FATHER   *(Laughing)* So my person was not the only attraction after all.

EDMUND   *(to ELSA)* Now was I exaggerating? Isn't our nest to your taste?

ELSA   On the whole I'm very pleased with it. Naturally there are all sorts of alterations to be made.

FATHER   Well, it's your own fault with your hasty homecoming. You took all the joy out of it for me. I had a heap of surprises in store for you, but you were in such a hurry I couldn't get to them. And father Waldenberg was really angry: he also had lots of plans brewing for the welcome home.

EDMUND   Papa, it's all right as it is! We'll take it as done. A woman's hand works wonders . . . Elsa will make our house truly comfortable all by herself. Am I right, Elsa?

ELSA   Whatever lies within my feeble powers I shall do, and bye and bye you'll learn to love it. . . . By the way . . . before I forget . . . the first reform is to dismiss that rude lout.

EDMUND   Gerhard?

ELSA   Yes, is that his name, the servant? He's a very impudent, cheeky fellow! The insolent way he answers back!

FATHER   Of course he'll be dismissed. He got in the habit of being outspoken during Edmund's bachelor days. I didn't think he'd last long under the new regime. He's out directly! *(A knock and* GERHARD *appears)*

GERHARD   Councillor Waldenberg would like to see the mistress for half a hour. The carriage is waitin' downstairs.

ELSA   But we're just having tea!

FATHER   We'll forego it on behalf of your dear father. Get ready now, Elsa. Edmund insists on having you back for supper.

EDMUND   I'd really like to accompany Elsa, I don't like to let her travel on her own.

ELSA   Please do come.

FATHER   No, nothing doing! First you miss me and then you want to leave me all alone! Leave Edmund here. I want to talk over some business matters.

ELSA   All right then, see you this evening! *(Makes her farewells and exits)*

FATHER and EDMUND   Good-bye!

FATHER  (To GERHARD, who is on his way out) You stay here.

(GERHARD takes a stand provocatively facing the Father.)

FATHER  You have behaved insolently to the mistress of the house. How dare you do a thing like that?

GERHARD  Councillor, never, me? . . . I'd never dare nothin' like that, so there's nothin' to esplain.

FATHER  Fellow, don't be so impertinent and stand up straight when you're talking to me.

EDMUND  Papa, there's no need to get so overwrought!

FATHER  Leave me alone, this is unheard of! (He walks angrily to and fro)

GERHARD  Sir, this ain't the first time you've talked about kickin' me out. You don't need to look for a reason. I gotta go do my military service in July. An' since I can't stand the womenfolk, I'll be leavin' here soon enough.

EDMUND  There's no great hurry.

FATHER  You think not? I'm of another opinion. The man goes and this very day.

GERHARD  Go ahead, the sooner the better! Sir, on accounta my three years' service in your house, I gotta get severance pay.

EDMUND  I'll make sure you get everything coming to you, Gerhard!

FATHER  Severance pay! Fellow, have you gone crazy? Haven't you always got your wages on the dot? He'll pay you as usual up to August 1.

GERHARD  Is that so? I really figgered (With a penetrating glance at EDMUND) I earned myself a bonus what with all my extra services.

FATHER  This is going too far. You are a completely shameless fellow. Your wages will be paid to you at the office up to August 1. And (He points to the door) now get out and make it snappy!

EDMUND  (Greatly alarmed) Papa, the fellow . . .

FATHER  . . . must get out. You've got to put your foot down around here. This is ridiculous! (To GERHARD) Pack your bags and leave at once!

(EDMUND looks at him with an imploring glance)

GERHARD  I'm goin' right now – but I got ways of gettin' that bonus o' mine.

*Curtain*

## Act III

*Same scenery as in Act I. The bookcase is open. ELSA is sitting in an armchair, reading, holding a handkerchief to her face. After a while she takes a thick book that lies on the table, and reads it. Suddenly she drops it from her hand, rises and takes a letter lying on the table, and walks back and forth, as if struggling to come to a decision. The bell rings, she pulls herself together and goes to meet KURT, who enters through the door. KURT walks into the room and bows.*

ELSA  I sent for you, Doctor.

KURT  And I came, albeit unwillingly!

ELSA  (Pointing to an armchair) Take a seat, please! (They both sit) I won't keep you long. If I were to presume on your love for me and ask a favour, would you refuse?

KURT  Dear lady, you found someone worthier of your love than I. He was my best friend. (After a pause) However, be that as it may, I am at your disposal.

ELSA  (Upset) You must promise to grant my wish.

KURT  (An uncanny glint in his eyes) I promise. (Gives ELSA his hand)

ELSA  Then listen. I insisted that the servant in our employ be dismissed because of his insolent behavior. As is typical of such nasty creatures, he has taken revenge by accusing my husband of all sorts of incredible things in this letter (Hands him the letter) and at the end threatens to denounce him to the police if I . . . are you paying attention? . . . if I don't pay him 10,000 marks hush money by tomorrow morning. At first I hesitated . . . I wasn't sure how to act. . . . But certain peculiarities of my husband's hadn't escaped my notice, and he had been so insistent that the servant be retained . . . I had a sudden suspicion that the man's charges might not be slanders. Just before you arrived, I was reading Krafft-Ebing's *Psychopathia Sexualis* and it bolstered my suppositions and fortified my doubts of Edmund's normality . . . and now I ask you, Doctor, who as his friend and physician must have a stake in solving the riddle . . . show me a way out of this quandary.

(KURT *sits in silent amazement, avoiding* ELSA's *gaze*)

ELSA  You'll find I am completely calm and collected, Doctor. Speak to me frankly! . . . I am prepared for the worst, if I . . . *(She breathes deeply.)* . . . if I have been the victim of a conspiracy. We will not be disturbed. My husband will be home late. There is a general audit at the bank.

KURT  Even before I came here, I knew what you would ask of me. I've known for a long time that the day would come when you would summon me and put this question to me. In fact I have gone over in my mind whether or not I should answer it. My mind is made up. I will not answer your question. I cannot, I dare not do it.

ELSA  But you just promised . . .

KURT  I promised, for the sake of love, to do you a favour, but not to break a sacred trust, which it is any physician's first, most proper obligation to uphold.

ELSA  Coward!

KURT  Not so, Elsa!

ELSA  But you once swore to me that your love was the greatest love, a love beyond description!.

KURT  *(Struggling with himself, looks at* ELSA *beseechingly)* Believe me, Elsa . . .

ELSA  *(Abruptly)* More than once that love gave you the courage to cut through old red tape, to bend the strict letter of the law. *(She tries to be more gentle.)* Kurt, remember the night you brought me home from the tennis courts . . . the walk through the Tiergarten? It was just before you went away! Three years ago, Kurt. At that time you swore to me . . . if I should ever wish it . . . , you would make the greatest sacrifice for me, you would lay down your life for me *(She draws near him and clutches his hand).*

KURT  *(Barely able to master his distress)* Elsa, believe me, the greatest favour I could do for love of you is to keep silent.

ELSA  *(Feverishly overwrought)* Doctor, I suspect . . . *(She seizes his arm.)* I implore you, allay my doubts!

KURT  All right then: Edmund, your husband, is one of those unhappy men denied the ability to love women – denied it by nature. Nevertheless, as a man of noble character, which he is in every fibre of his being, he can be your friend and companion.

ELSA  *(Having turned away during* KURT's *revelation, passionately goes back to him)* I will never go on living with this madman!

KURT  Edmund is not a madman, Frau Elsa. I have . . . unwillingly . . . answered your question, and been guilty of a serious breach of confidence, of malpractice. But I have answered your question as conscientiously as if I were standing before a judge, the same judge who would punish me for providing that answer. I do not wish to appear more noble in your eyes than I am. My love for you, which still smoulders, Frau Elsa, is mingled with feelings of revenge. . . .

ELSA  Never, Doctor!

KURT  I am very sorry for you! When your fathers prearranged your marriage, no one paid the slightest heed to your personal natures! But then you share much of the blame, Frau Elsa. You did not dispose freely of your heart, which . . . I know only too well . . . belonged to me at the time and still belongs to me today.

ELSA  It was the fondest wish of my old father, who had no idea he was shoving me into the arms of a criminal . . . *(She sobs deeply)* a madman for a husband.

KURT  But Edmund was also carrying out "his father's fondest wish".

ELSA  He should have given some thought to his disease.

KURT  This has nothing to do with disease. Edmund is completely normal except for his emotional proclivities. . . . His only fault was to get married, and for that he will either be punished or have his union annulled.

ELSA  And what about this letter!

KURT  Ye-es . . . there's the rub. Edmund's instincts went haywire and he'll be sorely punished for it, if it comes to the attention of the authorities.

ELSA  Now at last I understand it all. . . . But wouldn't it be better if such . . . people were harmlessly interned in madhouses, instead of being punished so harshly for their quirky natures? There were a lot of demonstrations lately . . . I read about it in the papers . . . to introduce a bill in parliament. . . . But aren't you on the wrong track? . . . Don't you see the mischief it makes, no, you don't share my feelings. (*She sobs deeply again and puts her head in her hands.*)

(KURT *tries in vain to calm her.*)

ELSA  (*Suddenly regains control and straightens up with a stony expression*) I have made up my mind, Doctor! I shall leave this house at once and file for divorce.

KURT  What about the letter? . . .

ELSA  (*Stands up proudly*) I no longer consider my fate to be bound up with that of a madman. . . . I shall let matters take their course.

KURT  But then he goes to jail!

ELSA  (*Coldly*) To the penitentiary, if it were up to me. So far as I'm concerned, he no longer exists!

(*The door to the hall is clearly heard to open.*)

ELSA  There's Edmund! (KURT *moves to withdraw*) Please stay!

EDMUND  (*Hurries in and heads for the desk*) Just forgot my briefcase, Elsa dear! (*As he notices* KURT) You . . . here!

ELSA  (*Coolly steps between them*) Read this letter.

EDMUND  (*Takes the letter from her with trembling hand and, greatly alarmed, reads it. After he has read it*): So you know, Elsa? (*The letter falls from his hand.*)

ELSA  (*Without any sign of feeling*) I know it all, and today I am going back to my father's house.

(EDMUND *looks frantically at* KURT)

KURT  (*Looking down at the floor*) I couldn't help it!

EDMUND  (*Stands vacillating for a moment, looks around with the mien of a lunatic, walks to the desk as in a dream and takes the briefcase from it. Idiotically.*) There's a man waiting for me at the office with the balance sheet! (*He slowly exits. We can hear the latch on the door to the corridor snap to.*)

KURT  For heaven's sake, Elsa, at least try and save him from punishment. Give me the letter. I'll send the wretch the money out of my own pocket. Only don't . . .

ELSA  No, my dear. You once said that no judge has the right to dissolve our marriage

because it is legally valid. Even so, don't *I* have the sacred right, for that which I ask, to demand love in return for my total submission?

KURT  You do, you do above all other women.

ELSA  And am I never to enjoy the career of wife, companion and mother? Is there no power, no means of freeing me from that madman?

KURT  If you leave his house forever, the court can declare a separation.

ELSA  Then wait here. (*She hurries out, is soon back holding a checkbook, goes to the desk and writes a check.*) Here, Doctor, cash this check at the bank and tomorrow morning take the money to the man at the designated spot. (*She hands him the check and the letter*) You know what he looks like.

KURT  Thank you, Elsa, for forgiving Edmund. After all it is not his fault.

ELSA  And when I'm back home, you come there . . . as you used to do . . . and help me care for my father and beautify the evening of his life. Believe me, Doctor, only now am I mature enough for this life.

KURT  Elsa, you could even make me forget my grudge against your father.

ELSA  So you will come? Without you, who has so manfully shared this deep pain with me . . .

KURT  (*Abruptly seizes her hand and kisses it*) Then I dare hope . . .

ELSA  Leave me now, Kurt.

KURT  (*Joyously excited*) Elsa! (*He embraces and kisses her as* ELSA *sinks in his arms. The bell rings,* ELSA *and* KURT *draw apart. Shortly the* FATHER *enters, hurries into the room and . . . when he sees* KURT *. . . steps back in amazement.*)

FATHER  What's keeping Edmund so long?

ELSA  He was here a while ago, but had to go back to the office. (*She is interrupted by a loud and prolonged noise.*)

FATHER  He is at the office. Maybe he's on his way now. (*He goes to the door, for there is a loud knock. The* FATHER *opens the door and* PATSCHKE *enters in his service uniform and helmet.*)

PATSCHKE  (*Puts his hand to his helmet*) Constable Patschke of the 13th Precinct Krone Street. A man just shot himself in a cab in the Tiergarten and the corpse was

95

identified as being that of Councillor Edmund Manhardt. Should the body be brought here or to the morgue?

FATHER  *(Screams like a madman; to* KURT*)* Murderer, you drove him to desperation. You have him on your conscience!

*(*KURT *is silent and stares at the floor.)*

ELSA  No, father, he paid off all his old debts!

*Curtain*

# Documents

*M. Kaufmann, review of "Mistakes",* Jahrbuch für sexuelle Zwischenstufen, *1908, vol. 9, pp. 606–7*

A praiseworthy attempt at a dramatic treatment of a homosexual conflict.

If this attempt, like some previous ones by various other writers, is not entirely successful on the artistic plane, the fault lies in its all too obvious penchant for tendentiousness. Perhaps the homosexual question is still too much an issue of contention, still too much an object of passionate struggle as a result of the idiotic clause in the legal code, for a dramatic treatment to set aside the message and subordinate it to purely artistic considerations.

[*There follows a plot summary*]

The various conflicts and dramatic events follow one another all too swiftly and are not given firm enough motivation. One senses all too clearly the intention to curtail development and get to the preconceived basic ideas. The characters have too little life as personalities. Their decisions and actions are not seen to grow out of themselves, they progress suddenly and without preparation.

The whole drama therefore seems too sketchy, too schematic. It may perhaps achieve an estimable realization on stage – but this can only be rightly judged in production. In any case it is to be wished that the manager of a theatre dare make the experiment of a public presentation of a timely treatment of the homosexual question, which is dealt with so with much interest and understanding.

To this end it may be pointed out that the author has depicted a delicate subject with great aplomb, in so decent and earnest a way as to avoid all graphic sexual or passionate moments that even the most prudish spectator could not take offense and the drama need not be kept from the general public.

*Contemporary cases*

*From* Jahrbuch für sexuelle Zwischenstufen, *1900, vol. 2, p. 1255*

A prominent member of a local theatre was surprised to no small degree the day before yesterday when during the performance the stage-doorman handed him a letter which had been turned in at the stagedoor and which contained mysterious hints about an embarrassing affair. The contents said that the sender had to reproach the actor, who weeks before had enticed him to commit an act which was punishable by law, and now he – the writer – was ill. He demanded that the actor send 400 crowns to him at his home. The letter was signed "Konrad Ludwig Böhmke." Now the actor knew nothing about the behaviour he was charged with nor was he in any way acquainted with Herr Böhmke. He therefore took the letter to the police. They established that the undersigned Konrad Ludwig Böhmke actually lived at the address given. A police agent conveyed him to the authorities and at the arraignment the prisoner confessed without more ado that he had written the letter. He declared, however, that the facts contained in the letter were true. But since the artist stuck by his statement, Böhmke was brought before the man he had implicated, and for the first time he attested that he didn't know the wrongfully accused indivdiual. The man who had led him to the punishable action had later falsely given him the name of this actor. Böhmke, a 22-year-old waiter, is now under arrest and consigned to the county court. The search for the man whom Böhmke indicated as his seducer is under way.

*From* Jahrbuch für sexuelle Zwischenstufen, *1904, vol. 5, part 2, p. 1249*

*Inveterate Blackmailer* A landed nobleman who has lived in this province for some time engaged in impure relations with the journeyman blacksmith Sebastian Lieb of this locality. Lieb had used this circumstance for some years to exact lucrative blackmail on the Baron. In 1900 he solicited a loan of 150 marks, first politely, then under the covert threat of informing the Baron's lady wife as well as the police about the past relations. Through the mediation of a local lawyer, Lieb obtained the sought-for 150 marks. For a long while the Baron was left in peace, then Lieb started his extortion once more and in his letters went to work in a superficially refined manner. He usually obtained large amounts of money and finally requested 5 to 600 marks for a trip to America. He was also promised a not inconsiderable amount which he could, however, collect only in Hamburg. Lieb came straight to Hamburg, but not to America; he was watershy, turned around and began his blackmail again, to relieve the Baron of a thousand. Since Lieb did not stop, he was finally denounced and today was sentenced for blackmail, theft and forgery to 3 years and 6 months in prison and 5 years loss of civil rights.

*From* Der Tag, *29 April 1907*

For infractions of Paragraph 175 of the State Penal Code the photographer Henry Gretschmer along with the mechanic's apprentice, 16-year-old Paul Gerhardt, brought before the County Criminal Court. The 34-year-old photographer Gretschmer had run a photographic studio for about two years in the building at 81–82 Oranienstrasse. The residents of the building noticed that this studio was frequented exclusively by male persons. As was later demonstrated, G. had for a considerable time played a certain role as specialist photographer in homosexual circles. In order to procure the necessary models, G. used the following means. He had accomplices distribute gift certificates for his studio in pubs frequented by young people.

By means of these gift certificates G. obtained the necessary models and put the young people at the disposal of certain libertines. In November of last year G. made the acquaintance of the co-defendant Gerhardt. The 16-year-old let himself be led astray and followed the invitation of the dangerous seducer to the studio, and soon the young man was fully drawn into the morass. An even sorrier fate befell another young person, who fell into Gretschmer's clutches. This was the 15-year-old apothecary's apprentice Fritz Siering of Wilmersdorf. Through an American living in Wilmersdorf, who also played a role in perverse society, Siering obtained a gift certificate for Gretschmer's studio. Then Siering too was drawn into sinister practices. These scandalous goings-on finally came to the attention of the criminal police. – The result of the police investigations has now led to charges of offences against §175 against Gretschmer, Gerhardt and Siering. The last, out of fear of punishment, poisoned himself.

*Contemporary blackmail letters, from Magnus Hirschfeld's collection. Published in Hans Ostwald,* Männliche Prostitution, *Leipzig, Ernst Müller, 1905, pp. 49–50*

Worthy sir!
Because I'm presently in difficulties, I turn to you. Be so good as to send me by tomorrow, Sunday, June 23, 8 o'clock 300 marks – care of Code H. B. 17 at the Dorotheestrasse Post Office (No. 7), namely post-paid in a plain sealed envelope. If you're not willing to help me out, then on Monday the District Attorney's office will have in hand information concerning offences against §175 of the Penal Code in 17 separate and specific instances. In return I promise to keep silent and also take it upon myself to make no use of any knowledge I may have of you or a third party. With the hope that you will comply with my request, I should like to point out that a refusal on your part means long incarceration for you and ruin of your whole way of life, whereas if I should be punished for blackmail, it won't be any loss to me since I'll be ruined anyway if I don't get the 300 marks by Sunday.

H.B.17

Most respected sir!

Forgive me for taking the liberty of troubling you with these lines. Since I've had no answer from your respected son to my letter, the enclosed document, I am making my request to you, to be helpful [*sic*] to me in order to get it back. Since I'd like to acquaint you that previously your respected son was intimate with my person, the following circumstances will explain.

[*There follows a detailed description in garbled German of how they become acquainted and the things that allegedly happened.*]

He dismissed me while he put a little sum in my pocket. Then he told me that in three weeks he would take rooms at the Hotel . . . There I learned that he was out, I wrote to him there and got an answer from ---- . That's how I learned that your respected son lives with his brother in ---- St. Since I find myself momentarily in very great need, I wrote to your respected son to lend me some money, so that I could buy a suit and boots. And promised to pay it back as quickly as possible in installments, since the high holy days are coming up soon, I'm Mosaic, and unemployed and don't like running around in so reduced a state, I have to fight hard for the necessities of life. Who and what I am, your respected son knows, for I showed him all my papers. But I put in the letter a few more documents precious to me as a guarantee. But as I already said he didn't give me an answer, although I asked him real hard.

Now I'd like to ask you poltly [*sic*] to tell me his address in . . . . . . which I asked for, since I get no anwer from him at . . . . , where he made off that night. And I now still don't

have no in phormation. I promise you above all *to keep strictly silent to any other person*, and also ask you pltly for discretion. I ask you pltly to send me an answer soon as possible, to leave it, I'll wait till tomorrow, Wednesday, at Post Office. . . . Please forgive me for the extremely important revelation for you. That my words are grounded in truth, I can prove by a letter of your son's.

Your most obedient servant
[Name]

Most respected sir!

A gentleman known to you possesses photographs which portray your person in the most intimate conjunction with a handsome youth. These pictures were taken at a time when you did not think you were observed.

The gentleman in question has already sold a large number of these pictures to his acquaintances. Merely in your interest I have persuaded him to turn over the plates together with all the unsold pictures, for I am firmly convinced that you will do your utmost to prevent the sale of these pictures which compromise you to the uttermost.

If you will deposit 100 marks to me poste restante, you will immediately get the pictures. Unfortunately I cannot tell you my name, for I belong to the nobility.

Your sincere sympathizer

v.G.

## Notes

1 This can be loosely translated as "The people must fight for the law as much as they fight for the city walls."

# The Dangerous Precaution

*Comedy in one act with songs*
*by*
*Mikhail Kuzmin*

(1907)

Translated from the Russian by Laurence Senelick

*The Dangerous Precaution* is translated from the text published in Volume 2 of M. Kuzmin, *Teatr v chetyrakh tomakh*, ed. A. Timofeev. Berkeley: Berkeley Slavic Specialties, 1994.

# Introduction

In an angry polemic against what he called the pornographic element in Russian literature, the critic N. S. Novopolin set aside a special chapter to attack the "idealization" of "the sin of Sodom." His prime targets were the lesbian writer Zinovieva-Annibal and the elegant aesthete Mikhail Afanasievich Kuzmin (1872–1936). Novopolin sneered at the hero of Kuzmin's homoerotic novella *Wings* as its "heroine" and was appalled that the protagonists should be attracted to a gymnast. The truly deplorable thing about this novel, the critic complained, is not its depiction of such "unnatural relations" which "I am told are widely practiced in the Caucasus and in aristocratic circles in both our capitals." It is the open propaganda for and glorification of homoeroticism through philosophical disquisitions among cultured and educated men and the apotheosis of its hero: when he finally consummates his romance, his lover beholds him endowed with wings. Novopolin was particularly disturbed by Kuzmin's appeal that "a man develop all the faculties of his body and soul to the uttermost possibility and seek out ways to apply his capacities, if he does not wish to remain a *Caliban*." Are such practices part and parcel of human self-fulfilment?[1]

Although laws against *muzhelozhstvo* (literally, lying with men) had been on the books since the reign of Peter the Great, they were sufficiently vague and imprecise in their definition of the crime to be less severe and less frequently imposed than their Western European counterparts. By 1903, reformers, led by Vladimir Nabokov (father of the novelist), were calling for repeal of such laws, and characterizing intrusion into the sanctity of the private sphere as a form of serfdom.[2] Homosexual behavior, as Novopolin noted, had long been tolerated in the upper echelons of society, though it was one of those things not talked about in polite

conversation. Moreover, as far back as the sixteenth century, *muzhelozhstvo* had also been singled out as a standard feature of peasant life. Adam Olearius in his seventeenth-century description of an itinerant puppet show deplored that "their Puppets, representing their brutalities and sodomies, make sport to the Children, who are thereby induc'd to quit all sentiments of shame and honesty."[3]

During the so-called Silver Age of art and literature, a period roughly stretching from the late 1890s to the outbreak of the First World War, there was a cult of Oscar Wilde in

*Plate 7* Portrait of Mikhail Kuzmin by his friend Konstantin Somov, 1909. Gouache and water-color, original in the Tretyakov Gallery, Moscow.

*Plate 8* The cover for Kuzmin's novel *Wings*, designed by N. P. Feofilaktov, and published by Scorpion Press, Moscow, 1907. From Feofilaktov, *66 risunkov* (1909).

Russia. Mikhail Lykiardopoulo, the secretary of the staid Moscow Art Theatre, published translations in elegant limited editions, and the younger actors of the company clubbed together to buy these expensive works and share them round. Several directors planned stagings of *Salomé*, but ran afoul of the Holy Synod, which prohibited such productions. One of Wilde's most enthusiastic admirers and epigones was Kuzmin.[4] A central figure in *Wings* (first published as a serial in 1906, then in a separate volume in 1907, and reprinted in 1908), is Larion Dmitrievich Strup, a wealthy, cosmopolitan half-Englishman, somewhat on the order of Lord Henry Wootton in *The Picture of Dorian Gray*, who becomes the hero's travelling companion and mentor.

Kuzmin had taken advantage of a relatively censor-free period in Russian literature, when questions of sexuality could be treated with a degree of openness. A *Bildungsroman* depicting a young man's coming to awareness and acceptance of his true nature,

*Wings* is also a paean to paganism, the cult of "Zeus–Dionysos–Helios." However, for all its literary references and refinements, the novel does not shy away from reality; the carnal practices of the cult occur as a financial transaction with a bathhouse attendant or as a hasty interchange between master and servant. Contemporary critics could not decide whether they were more disgusted by the "idealization" of homosexuality or by this quantum of reality.[5]

1906 was a busy year for Kuzmin: in addition to *Wings*, he published a collection of poems and finished the words and music for his play *The Chimes of Love* (*Kuranty lyubvi*). Like so many Russian writers, including Gogol and Chekhov, Kuzmin had been a stage-struck child, attending operettas in Saratov and running his own puppet-theatre. When the family moved to St Petersburg in 1885, his theatre-going increased, as did his composing. Among the other pieces he wrote in 1906 were two for the theatre, a "mime ballet" *The Choice of a Bride* (*Vybor nevesty*) and *The Dangerous Precaution* (*Opasnaya predostorozhnost*). The latter was dedicated to his close friend and fellow homosexual Walter Nouvel who composed music for it. When the two pieces were published in 1907, with a third play, "a pastoral for masquerade" *Two Swains and a Nymph in a Cottage* (*Dva pastukha i nimfa v khizhine*), the collection was promptly confiscated by the government, probably because of the insouciant pederastic sentiments of *The Dangerous Precaution*.

1906 was also the year in which Kuzmin began to attend Saturday gatherings at the Latyshky Club in the studio of Vera Kommissarzhevskaya's theatre. Kommissarzhevskaya, a actress of luminous talent and neurotic personality, had become fascinated by the Symbolist movement and had invited the young director Vsevolod Meyerhold to run her new theatre in Officer Street. The first season under Meyerhold (1906–7) was one of gaiety, masquerades, and galas, in which Kuzmin became friendly with many of the most prominent poets of the time, including Blok and Sologub. He also carried on a number of brief affairs, yielding to momentary infatuation and living, as his friend Somov said, as if tomorrow we were to die. This was the acme of Kuzmin's dandy period, his epigonism of Wilde, in which he appeared in society in colourful waistcoats (never the same one twice), a cherry-red velvet, tight-fitting jacket, a jet-black goatee and a touch of artfully applied rouge, heightened by musky perfumes and exquisite manicures. A diary entry for 1905 records:

> Sunny today, and I strolled along the Morskaya after the hairdresser's. When I saw my face in a shop mirror, I tried out an oblique glance and what I saw was a gentleman with black eyes behind gold-framed pince-nez, a clean-shaven powdered chin, a fresh, not puckered but dryish mouth, a certain covert wariness, a face which hides something and conceals idealistic asceticism or vice, new learning or charlatanry.[6]

This foppery advertised his sexual preferences, for, although he enjoyed the company of women, his love life involved men exclusively. (He claimed that in love he preferred the known to the unfamiliar.)

The exuberant optimism of the first Meyerhold season at Kommissarzhevskaya's Theatre was dispelled by the second season, when it became clear that Meyerhold's increasingly stylized staging ran counter to the actress's interest in social betterment and the tastes of her fans. The director was an admirer of Kuzmin's drama, crediting him as one of those who created the New Theatre in Russia; but when he asked to stage one of Kuzmin's pseudo-miracle plays, *The Comedy of Alexis, a Man of God*, Kommissarzhevskaya replied in the negative: "I have read Kuzmin's play, and this is my impresison: a dull, totally pointless picture in a fancy frame. Lost in admiration of the frame, your attention unconsciously says to you, 'I could paint that picture myself,' but it actually isn't worth it, and it's dangerous to waste oneself that way."[7] Although Kuzmin's own plays received no production, he was in demand as a composer, providing incidental music for such important works as Blok's *Little Showbooth*.

As Meyerhold's situation deteriorated, Kuzmin had less to do with this theatre, and he transferred his attention to the World of Art movement and his services to the Imperial theatres, translating libretti (*Elektra, Faust, Benvenuto Cellini, The Gipsy Baron* and *Abduction from the Seraglio*). He also began a long career as a drama critic. When Meyerhold staged studio productions in nonce spaces, Kuzmin took part as actor and composer, and eventually a number of his short pieces were put on: pastorals, comic operettas, ballets. His fairy-tale operetta *Maids at Play (Zabava dev)*, set in a harem, even managed to be staged at Suvorin's Maly Theatre, a privately owned but important playhouse, in 1911, and one of its songs became a hit. Kuzmin was later a leading light of the artistic cabarets, the Stray Dog, writing its anthem, and the Comedians' Rest. After the Revolution, he carried on his stage activities at children's and puppet theatres, and served as dramaturge of the Bolshoy Dramatic Theatre in Leningrad.[8]

In short, of all the poets who warmed themselves at the bubbling crucible of art in the days before the Revolution, Kuzmin was the one most devoted to the theatre and especially to its lighter forms, what the Germans call *Kleinkunst*. Meyerhold had called for a return to *cabotinage*, a stage of multi-talented performers capable of a high degree of theatricality; like so many artists of the time, Kuzmin shared this desire to escape realism and naturalism and recover the frank playfulness of the *commedia dell'arte* and the Baroque and Rococo stages.

Homoeroticism contributes to his early plays a touch of naughtiness, a provocation, an amorality which helps to evoke a time before Ibsenite tendentiousness and Victorian moralizing took over the theatre. Michael Green suggests that *Three Plays* was suppressed whereas *Wings* was not, simply because the treatment of same-sex love in the former is light-hearted and off-handed.[9] I would add that plays, meant to be shown to a variegated public, were always of more concern to the Russian censor than was coterie literature printed in limited editions.

Green also points out that Kuzmin's first published play *The Story of Cavalier d'Alessio* (1905) is a misogynistic pageant, culminating in a tableau of idealized homoeroticism reminiscent of Stefan George. The hero visits and escapes a number of *femmes fatales* before arriving at a Masonic Temple where a chorus confirms his admission to the elect by singing, "A boy spirit touched him with his lips and his soul became ardent and winged, and the kisses of women became cloying to him." The astral youth as spiritual guide is a constant throughout Kuzmin's writing.

In *Two Swains and a Nymph in a Cottage*, the shepherds Mirabel and Dorabel find their close attachment threatened by an encroaching female and drive her away. A similar intrusion occurs in Kuzmin's later play *The Venetian Madcaps* (*Venetsianskie bezumtsy*, 1915), in which the romance between Count Stello and his lover Narcisetto, who are discovered in an embrace at rise of curtain, is intentionally broken up by the actress Finetta. After seducing Narcisetto, Finetta tells him she doesn't love him. The youth, heartbroken at having betrayed his true lover, appears with the Count in a masquerade as Arlecchino and Columbine. Narcissetto stabs the Count, kisses him and tosses his body into the canal, declaring to Finetta, "I love no one but the Count, I never loved anyone but him." Kuzmin intended this play to be a pederastic and Goldoniesque variation on Lermontov's tragedy of jealousy *Masquerade*.

If *Two Swains* imitates the pastoral *opéra-comique* of pre-Revolutionary France and *The Venetian Madcaps* draws on the *commedia* of Goldoni and Gozzi, *The Dangerous Precaution* hearkens even farther back to the transvestitic comedies of Shakespeare and the Spanish Golden Age. (Kuzmin was much later to write a poetic interlude "Willie Hughes as Rosalind," adopting Wilde's hypothesis that the fair youth of the sonnets was a boy player of that name, and depicting the boy in love with the actor playing Orlando.) Although the title seems to echo the subtitle of Beaumarchais' *Barber of Seville* – *The Useless Precaution* – the characters' names, Posthumous and Floridal (evoking Florizel), are reminiscent of Shakespeare's late romances *Cymbeline* and *A Winter's Tale*, and the action takes place in a fairy-tale kingdom. The boy player disguised as a girl disguised as a boy receives a particular complication here: Floridal, an actual boy (played by a boy) goes about in boy's clothes, but is supposed by the courtiers to be Dorita, a girl in boy's clothing. Kuzmin's paradox is that the sophisticated court, alert to such disguises, is actually deceived, for as his spokesman, the poet laureate Gaetano, notes, there is scant difference between a youth and a woman. Prince René, troubled by his love for Dorita, suddenly comes to terms with the fact that he is infatuated with a youth, and calls for masculine music, a jig, rather than the more heterosexual gavotte. This carnival overthrow of convention, without any overtones of tragedy, makes *The Dangerous Precaution* the most guiltless of all modernist plays of same-sex love.

## Notes

1 G. S. Novopolin, *Pornograficheskij élement v russkoj literature*, St Petersburg, M. M. Stasyulevich, 1909, pp. 155–62.

2 See L. Engelstein, *The Keys to Happiness. Sex and the Search of Modernity in Fin-de-Siècle Russia*, Ithaca, NY, Cornell University Press, 1992, pp. 56–71. For an overview of Russian homosexuality at this period, see S. Karlinsky, "Russia's gay literature and culture: the impact of the October Revolution," in M. B. Duberman, M. Vicinus and G. Chauncey Jr. (eds), *Hidden from History. Reclaiming the Gay and Lesbian Past*, New York, New American Library, 1989, pp. 348–56. A variant appeared in *Gay Sunshine*, Summer–Fall 1976.

3 A. Olearius (1637), quoted in C. Kelly, *Petrushka. The Russian Carnival Puppet Theatre*, Cambridge, Cambridge University Press, 1990, p. 50.

4 The standard biography of Kuzmin is that by J. E. Malmstad, which appeared in the third volume of Kuzmin's collected poetry: J. E. Malmstad and V. Markov (eds), *M. A. Kuzmin. Sobranie stikhov*, Munich, Wilhelm Fink, 1977.

5 An English translation of *Wings*, as well of the play *The Venetian Madcaps* and other works can be found in M. Green (ed. and trans.), *Mikhail Kuzmin, Selected Prose & Poetry*, Ann Arbor, Ardis, 1980.

6 Quoted in Malmstad and Markov, op. cit., vol. 3, p. 109.

7 *Vera Fedorovna Kommisarzhevskaya. Pis'ma aktrisy. Vospominaniya o ney. Materialy*, Leningrad-Moscow, Iskusstvo, 1964, p. 165.

8 In addition to the Malmstad biography, see M. Green, "Mikhail Kuzmin and the theatre," *Russian Literature Triquarterly*, Winter 1974, vol. 7, and A. G. Timofeev, "Teatr 'nezdeshnikh vecherov'," in V. Markov and G. Sheron (eds), *M. Kuzmin. Teatr*, Berkeley: Berkeley Slavic Specialties, 1994, vol. 3, pp. 383–422.

9 M. Green, "Kuzmin and the theater," op. cit., p. 252.

# The Dangerous Precaution

Comedy in one Act with songs

*Mikhail Kuzmin*

(1907)

## Characters

POSTHUMOUS

FLORIDAL, his son (presumed to be his
daughter Dorita)

RENÉ, a young prince

CLORINDA, his inamorata

GAETANO, courtier to Posthumous

FIRST COURTIER

SECOND COURTIER

COURTIERS, LADIES, SERVANTS

*Period: XVIIth century*
*Scene: a garden on René's estate*

## Scene 1

(Enter POSTHUMOUS, FLORIDAL, GAETANO
*and a few of* POSTHUMOUS's courtiers)

FLORIDAL   Once and for all I'm sick of this!
POSTHUMOUS   Calm yourself, my son, be
patient but a while longer . . .
FLORIDAL   I'm fed up with this game, this
deception! Everyone assumes I'm a
woman, and, in obedience to you, I'm not
allowed to prove them wrong.
GAETANO   O, you might prove it very easily
and graphically!
FLORIDAL   It's ridiculous! That poor wretch
René is losing his mind . . .
POSTHUMOUS   The precaution is only a
precaution, my son: once our affairs are
wound up and Clorinda is out of the
picture, I shall be the first to reveal your
disguise, with a laugh.
GAETANO   Just three more days of flirtation,
Prince.
FLORIDAL   Just three more days of sighs,
reproaches, tender rambles. After all, I feel
sorry for him, for René.

GAETANO
O Floridal!
  Compare a woman and a man of tender
  years,
  You'll find the difference not so very
  great,
  No more so than 'twixt hill and dale
  appears,
  Than hands from ears in likeness
  deviate.
    Nothing but trivia,
    Nothing but trivia,
  Narrow hips, lissom waist, and a trim
  rump
  Are god's gift to a youth, to a fair youth,
  Women are prized when they're buxom
  and plump – ,
  And there the difference lies – I tell the
  truth.
  For us the gaze of both may prove a
  danger,
  The kiss of both with poison may us fill,
  A handsome, well-built youth, close
  friend or stranger,
  May truly cause of the heart of us to
  thrill.
    Nothing but trivia,
    Nothing but trivia;
  Narrow hips, lissom waist, and a trim
  rump
  Are god's gift to a youth, to a fair youth,
  Women are prized when they're buxom
  and plump – ,
  And there the difference lies – I tell the
  truth.
Or to put it otherwise:
    Heads or tails, in this game
    Top or bottom's all the same.

POSTHUMOUS   I find your song indecent,
Gaetano.
GAETANO   I'm a free versifier; decency is a
matter of convention . . . *ergo*: my verses
scan decently . . . that's one. What's more,

they're accurate . . . that's two. What's more, they possess measure, grace and mirth.

POSTHUMOUS In short, they possess everything except modesty. But hush . . . I hear the singing of our fowler. Patience, my son, this is naught but a precaution, in three days all will be revealed. Good-bye!

GAETANO Best wishes for your success!

*(Exeunt)*

## Scene 2

*(*FLORIDAL *is alone; offstage* RENÉ *is singing.)*

RENÉ

To woods, to woods
We flee from boring rooms and cumbrous
  goods!
The sun shines bright,
No one but you and I, friend, basks in its
  light.
The grass grows green, mottled with
  flowers the mead,
The wind blows, fluttering bird's wings
  help it speed.
The freshet shimmers, the valley romps
  amain
And suddenly subsides, and melts into the
  plain.
To woods, to woods
Let's look on love, when skies are blue we
  should!
The birds are singing there as they soar
  by,
At night the lightning flashes streak the
  sky.
We watch the sun go down, come up so
  high above,
While prowling near us, keeping look-out's
  Love.
To woods, to woods!
Sharp eyes will find out miracles for
  good.
Wound round with ivy dense there stands a
  cell
Where I and my Dorita close shall
  dwell.
Dorita's flown – as in a dream, I falter and
  decline.
Dorita's here – flame-like, I come to life,
  for she is mine.
To woods, to woods,
Come ye, like me, and freshen your life's
  blood.

## Scene 3

*(Enter* RENÉ, CLORINDA *and a few ladies and courtiers)*

CLORINDA *(to* FLORIDAL) Greetings, prince.

FLORIDAL Haven't we met before?

CLORINDA How observant you are! As if you were in love and had lost sight of your beloved for more than a hour.

FLORIDAL I was listening to the singing of our host and fell into a reverie.

CLORINDA O yes! that Dorita intrigues me, I should like to see her.

RENÉ You might do that at once.

CLORINDA O Prince, you are too complimentary.

RENÉ I was not referring to a mirror. *(To* FLORIDAL) Are you bored, Prince? Perhaps you would like to tread a measure?

FLORIDAL 'Tis all the same to me.

RENÉ There are musicians on the terrace.

*(Exeunt)*

## Scene 4

FIRST COURTIER He'd be keen to dance a saraband with her, if she weren't wearing breeches.

SECOND COURTIER Breeches get in the way not only in a saraband, but in a sailor's hornpipe.

FIRST COURTIER They get in the way of the imagination.

SECOND COURTIER Yes, when it's as stunted as yours . . .

*(Exeunt; the music has faded away.* CLORINDA *returns in a while and sits on the bench.)*

## Scene 5

CLORINDA Although she calls herself Floridal, although her face recalls the faces of schoolboys, although she lacks women's attire with its frills and furbelows, his heart has turned to her. O René! yet once, once upon a time!

O'ershadowed by leaves of a spruce tree,
My love and I sat carefree,
Singing, full of glee.
When the sky would redden suddenly,
To the pan-pipes' strains would we
Swoon with ecstasy . . .

What has caused those happy days to flee?
The years, hours and weeks, how can it be
Each one's a refugee?
Did my beloved lose his sanity?
For, after all, he gave up loving me.
Didn't he? Didn't he?
Hidden shoals lurk deep buried in the sea,
From treach'rous reefs our ship we could
   not free
Down went we, down went we . . .
The sky's turned dark, alas, I cannot see,
I can sustain my life in no degree,
Or barely, barely . . .
Ah!

*(Enter* FLORINDA)

## Scene 6

CLORINDA  Two words, Floridal.
FLORIDAL  You wish to speak with me?
CLORINDA  Yes, Prince.
FLORIDAL  I'm at your service.
CLORINDA  It is no secret to you that René was once in love with me. it is no secret to you that he no longer loves me, attracted to you, who is not Floridal but Dorita, and as a woman you can understand my torment and support me, and so I implore you.

O pray return his love to me,
That once again I'll gladly see,
Forgetting his past slips,
The smile upon his lips.
O pray return the warmth of his embrace,
So I may have the strength and grace
The flame of passion to contain
That courses through my veins.
O pray return to me that ardent kiss,
That said, "I love you, jealousy's amiss."
(In kissing I am fain
To mingle love with bane!)
For like a monarch's crimson seal,
My lips must close and naught reveal.
O heed my heart-felt plea,
And give him back to me!

FLORIDAL  I am no less distraught than you, Clorinda, but you overestimate my influence, if you think that I can give you back René.
CLORINDA  You can, sister, you can, only you must want to; do you promise?
FLORIDAL  Very well, I promise.
CLORINDA  May Heaven bless you for this.

*(Exits)*

## Scene 7

FLORIDAL  That woman's words move me well and truly. This game is beginning to go too far, and besides, I feel a certain agitation, which cannot be explained merely as pity for René. What is it?

I am not Dorita, for a start,
Why should René forever haunt my
   dreams!
Is this a waking state, where it but seems
My flesh is harbouring a woman's heart?
What Fate's designs are, who can say?
Can love's caprice be truly reckoned?
Is honour wronged, when glances beckon
And rouse me, glances from René?
Alas! not mine, Dorita's are his sighs!
Dorita's traits he looks for in my face.
Dorita is a myth – love fades in space,
And, loving, I return to my disguise.

Cost what it may, today I shall reveal myself to him without equivocation. Both that maiden's words and my own feelings demand it.

*(*RENÉ *enters rapidly)*

RENÉ  Dorita, don't go away, don't contradict me! I know that you are a woman, that you are Dorita the daughter of Posthumous, whom he, for precaution's sake, for fear of censure that you influence his decisions, has dressed in man's clothes. Not a word, don't contradict! For every secret comes to light, and old men's subtle stratagems prove to be futile, therefore I know that you are Dorita, and I speak, I shout it to you along with the fact that I love you, do you hear, I love you!
FLORIDAL  Of course, I hear you.
RENÉ  Not a word! I love you and will crack the skull of anyone who says that you are not Dorita, that I do not love you and that sort of thing. Why are you silent? I have spoken.
FLORIDAL  I'm afraid that you will crack *my* skull, because all I can say is that I am not Dorita . . .
RENÉ  You do not love me, you despise me!
FLORIDAL  I didn't say I didn't love you or I despise you, I only said that I am not a woman, and I speak in deadly earnest, I swear by your love as well as by mine.
RENÉ  Not Dorita, not Dorita!

FLORIDAL  O youth, though your plight
   makes me cry,
      I am not Dorita, Floridal am I.
      Do women have such ruddy lips
      As I do?
      Do women have such slender hips
      As I do?
      Do women cuddle up so snug
      As I do?
      Do women with such passion hug
      As I do?
   I weep with you, René, but what are we to
   do?
      Though your plight makes me cry,
      I am not Dorita, Floridal am I.
   Do you still disbelieve me, tell me true?

RENÉ  No, I don't believe it . . . but what of
   that? I gaze on you and does my heart beat,
   does my head spin as when I thought you
   were Dorita?

FLORIDAL  Do they?

RENÉ  They do. Forgive me, it will pass . . .

FLORIDAL Of course, it will pass. And since
   I'm not Dorita, let me kiss you. *(Slowly
   kisses him.)*

RENÉ There are no Doritas.

FLORIDAL Perhaps there never was anyone
   but Floridal.

RENÉ Music! Music! *(Musicians strike up a
   gavotte.)* To hell with the gavotte! A jig, an
   English jig! Not the shuffling of slippers but
   the trampling of boots is what I want to
   hear. My grief has fermented, and its cork
   has popped. I want to be absurdly merry,
   because today I am insanely happy! A jig,
   a jig!

*(The musicians strike up a jig.)*

*Finis*

# Documents

*"Homosexuality in pre-Revolutionary Russia,"* from Prof. Benjamin Tarnowsky, Anthropological, Legal and Medical Studies on Pederasty in Europe, *New York, Anthropological Press, n.d., pp. 135–8*

In Russia, notably in Saint Petersburg, there are many bathing establishments containing numerous private rooms. These have a regular staff of attendants, among whom there are many mercenary pederasts forming private associations, so to speak [. . .] A catamite in Saint Petersburg receives about the same fee as a prostitute. Blackmail on the part of bath-house boys is practically unknown, because they operate by associations and share the profits. Aside from bath-house attendants the ranks of catamites are recruited from amongst young coachmen, janitors, apprentices in the various trades who have not been working for a long time, etc. According to what all pederasts have told me, uneducated common people in Saint Petersburg appear to be extremely indulgent in indecent solicitations. These are "gentlemen's pleasures," they say. These simple creatures do not consider such propositions as at all insulting, and whether they accept or decline them, they would never denounce them on their own initiative, or complain about them to the authorities. [. . .]

Four years ago a former soldier, Aleksey M . . . , aged 55, [. . .] was accused of having excited three of his young apprentices to perform anal and oral coition. One of the victims, V. Ch . . . , in whom the judicial investigation disclosed undenial signs of passive pederasty and who frankly admitted the whole affair, testified as follows: "A short time ago I came from a village to Saint Petersburg. I did not know what the general practice of this place might be, so I didn't complain. In fact I supposed that all masters acted the same way here."

*From Kuzmin's manuscript memoirs, quoted in J. E. Malmstad and V. Markov (eds), M. A. Kuzmin,* Sobranie stikhov III, *Munich, Wilhelm Fink, 1977, p. 22*

And my first puppet theatre! Wonderful! Even now I blush all over with delight. The magical spotlight, and the Chinese shadows, and the opera, and the drama. The operas I always made up, and sang them myself in my thin, shrill voice, I always made up my own plots. The dramas I took from Shakespeare, I was an absurd and pretentious little Fauntleroy, but I was so bashful, so happy and hot-headed! And the silhouettes, my perennial allurements! Among others I had a girl-friend, a little bluestocking named Zina. She wrote and persuaded me to copy out my fantasies. She wrote a long, moralistic story for children, I wrote novellas (three), over-the-top imitations of Hoffmann. . . .

*From a letter to V. V. Ruslov, Nov. and Dec. 1907*

. . . I don't care for Beethoven, Wagner and especially Schumann. I don't like Schiller, Heine, Ibsen and most of the Germans except for Hofmannsthal, Stefan George and their schools. I don't like Byron. I don't like the 1860s and the Itinerants.

In art I like things that are either indelibly alive, even if coarse and vulgar, or else aristocratically unique.

I do not like moralizing bad taste. . . . I incline to the French and the Italians. I love both sobriety and an unabashed accumulation of luxuriousness.

And so, on one hand I love the Italian novella-writers, French comedies of the seventeenth and eighteenth centuries, the theatre of Shakespeare's contemporaries, Pushkin and Leskov, on the other hand certain German Romantic prose writers (Hoffmann, J. P. Richter, Platen), Musset, Merimée, Gautier, Stendahl, D'Annunzio, Wilde and Swinburne. I love Rabelais, Don Quixote, 1001 Nights and Perrault's fairy tales, but I do not like old Russian legends and epics. I love Flaubert, A. France and Henri de Regnier.

I like Bryusov, parts of Blok and some prose of Sologub. I love old French and Italian music: Mozart, Bizet, Delibes and the latest French – Debussy . . . above all I love Berlioz. I prefer vocal and ballet music, I prefer chamber music, but not quartets.

. . . I love the sounds of a military orchestra in the open air.

I love ballets (traditional), comedies and comic operas (in a broad sense, operettas – only the old ones). I love Swift, the comedies of Congreve and the like. I worship Apuleius, Petronius and Lucian. I love Voltaire.

In painting I love old miniatures, Botticelli, Beardsley, eighteenth-century painting, I used to love Klinger and Thomas (but not Boecklin and Schtuka), I love Somov and some of Benois. I love old Russian wood-cut broadsides and portraits. I seldom like landscapes.

I love pussy-cats and [indecipherable].

I love pearls, garnets, opals and also semi-precious stones such as "bull's eyes," "moonstones," "cat's eyes." I love roses, mimosas, narcissi and gilly-flowers, I do not like lilies-of-the-valley, violets and forget-me-nots. Plants without flowers I do not like. I love to sleep on fur without sheets.

*Kuzmin's diary entries for 1906 and the correspondence between him and his close friend Walter Nouvel[1] not only express his frame of mind around the time he wrote* The Dangerous Precaution; *it also sheds light on the private life of a prominent propagandist for homosexuality in the first years of this century. The excerpts are drawn from N. A. Bogomolov,* Mikhail Kuzmin: stat'i i materialy, *Moscow, Novoe Literaturnoe Obozrenie, 1995, pp. 61, 101–2, 230–37.*

*From Kuzmin's diary, 27–28 February 1906*

This afternoon some fellow turned up in a beret, a green velvet peasant-blouse worn under a jacket without a waistcoat, and bright red curls, obviously dyed. It appears he is the artist's model Valentin, who has read *Wings* somewhere, found out my address and made an appearance, for no clear reason, before "the Russian Wilde." Greater vulgarity and affectation in speech and manner I have never seen. He offered me his journal as raw material. It may be interesting. But he so lisped, swooned, used up about 40 minutes, promising to call again, that I was overcome with the most eerie horror . . .

Valentin's diary is something incredible, highly mannered, akin to dreams about life in a boulevard novel, the style is unusually comical, but there are unexpected patches of exposé and tattle. . . .

*On 3 July 1906, Kuzmin, Nouvel, and two other young men visited a restaurant out-of-town*

We travelled in two cabs. On the steamboat in the rain we arranged to write an apochryphal page in the diary to intrigue the Ivanovs.[2] Nouvel wanted to sit on the upper balcony where he once got lucky with Kolya Zinoviev, but it was windy there; the interior was laid out the way out-of-town restaurants probably had been in the 1860s, booths, one large room, kitchens, cupboards. No other customers. Somov[3] apparently liked it. We ate, drank Chablis and mulled wine and coffee without chicory. All four of us went back in one cab under a hood and everybody kissed, as if in Hafiz's tent. Somov even kissed Pavlik,[4] said that he had to become better friends with him and he would give him some advice about cosmetics. I found that his strong point was that nose, very Pierrot and *bien taillé* [finely sculpted], that the cheeks respond to the touch and that the lips, so severely criticized by Nouvel, are remarkably adept at kissing. I found that as a kisser I am *pas fameux* [not so great], but I kissed him all the better for that. "*Mais c'est déjà beaucoup mieux et vous n'êtes qu'un orgueilleux qui cache ses baisers.*" [Well, that's a good deal in itself and you're simply a proud fellow who conceals his kisses.] They came back with us and we went to Nouvel's. Pavlik stayed till morning. In the morning I could barely manage to wake him up.

*On 13 July 1906, Kuzmin left St Petersburg for Vasil'sursk where the cost of living was less expensive.*

*Kuzmin to Nouvel, 18 July 1906*

Dear Walter Fedorovich,
Now the wish you once expressed to see me in Vasil'sursk has come to pass. But if you were to see me, feel how I feel, you would be surprised by the cruelty of your wish. What can I do here, what can I write? If you love me, write to me more frequently, although best of all would be if the need to do so ended as soon as possible. Write me tender things about your meetings, about the *pays du tendre*,[5] about friends, about Pavlik. Do you see him? is he sad? is he happy? or like an April day? is he now pale or of the same peach-bloom? does he remember me? where has he been? with whom? what kind of new cravats is he wearing? not to see most of all his dear eyes, round shoulders! what writing is in that!? What can I tell you? What is there in the world, that would not be far from me?

My regards to friends: Ivanov, Bakst[6] and dear Somov. Write me. I kiss you. Address: Vasil'sursk, Nizhegorod St., Yushkevich Building.

Mikh. Kuzmin

*Nouvel to Kuzmin, 22 July 1906*

Dear Antinous!
How glad I was to get your letter, but alas! such a sad one and with a hint of reproach, as if I am at fault for it all. How am I to console you? With news of Pavlik? Here it is. After I took leave of you, I headed for my *rendez-vous* (which did not especially satisfy me), and from there to the *Pays du Tendre*, where Pavlik was to be. (In this case things went in reverse: *voyage des pays chauds au pays du Tendre* [journey from the torrid zone to the land of tender feeling]). Pavlik was depressed. To my question, which of us did he like best, he answered: Mikhail Alekseevich! Then I saw Pavlik the next Saturday at the Tauride with Kostya Somov. That day I made another backwards journey, i.e., I arrived at the *pays du Tendre* after a visit to Vyacheslav.[7] Finally, the last time I saw him was on Thursday, two days ago, in the same place. He was surprised that he had had no letter from you and said that, though he had no news, he would write you first.

He looked as if his face were somewhat thinner, but just as fresh as before. We spoke a lot about you. He said, among other things, that you are able to love, but I am not, which, I'm afraid, is true, at least for now. [. . .]

Don't grieve, my dear friend. You are too much the fatalist. Therefore you take what is to be inevitable. It may be that the value of this experience will give you new joy. I think Pavlik is seriously attracted to you, and when you come back again, the joy will be all the more intense after a long separation. [. . .]

Write more often.

Cordially yours,
V. Nouvel

*Kuzmin to Nouvel, 25 July 1906*

Dear Walter Fedorovich,
In my exile your letter with news of Pavlik was a real holiday, although I earlier had some tidings of you . . .

*Nouvel to Kuzmin, 1 August 1906*

My dear friend,
Forgive me for taking so long to answer your letter. Almost the whole week I've been staying in Peterhof and therefore could not see Pavlik. To write to you without recalling the dear name would be cruel – and I waited till I met with him.

Finally, two days ago, I saw him in the Tauride. Unfortunately, I could not talk with him for long, i.e. I wasn't alone, but I can tell that he is the same as before. The Pierrot nose and the shrewd eyes and the succulent mouth – all in place (I had no chance to observe the rest). Of course, we thought about you and sympathized with your longing. But why, my dear, such gloomy thoughts? I understand your present mood, that you are in a desert with no way to slake your thirst. But ahead of you lies a return and a new meeting with him, which will be all the sweeter the longer and more oppressive the separation. Of course I won't comfort you with Kuropatkin's patience, but you will soon be back (I hope!) and then everything will be transfigured. [. . .]

Your letter moved me deeply. But your tragic outlook alarmed me. Why, what for?

What's the reason? Explain it, for god's sake! Where is that buoyancy of life, which you constantly stood for? How can it lead to such fatal conclusions? Then everything will collapse, and you will have betrayed "the colours of merry earth." And Pierrot's nose and Marivaux and "The Marriage of Figaro" – you are only temporarily estranged from all this, and you must fall out of love with them definitively if you are to lose hope of seeing them again and soon.

I feel that my feeble consolation will not chase away your depression, but thanks to those favourite details, I pray you, do not lose hope, especially since the end of the ordeal is nigh.

What am I to say about myself? My Vyacheslav is on manoeuvres, I have no other escapades. It was boring in Peterhof. And there's not much fun here at the moment. Besides I don't feel very well physically. [. . .]

Cordially yours,
V. Nouvel

*A letter to Kuzmin from a schoolboy admirer, early 1908*

Great one, accept these roses as flowers of my heart . . .

I never expected to have such happiness befall me. The singer of the immortal (I say it boldly) *Wings* has written to me. First of all great thanks from my soul for those rare moments in life which I experienced while reading *Wings*. With what choking excitement I drank in that rose-coloured book, for in that year I was still a naturalist. Some of my school-mates, whom I propagandized with these new, lofty ideas, were even dizzy with excitement. Everyone was attracted by this beauty of a new life, the thrilling talent of the prophet of the awaited winds of the coming "Third Kingdom." And somewhere there in the distance, within the twilight of evening reality, enters the beckoning figure of the poet . . . You have given me these wings. Thank you, thank you . . . Now I know the paths which one must travel to seek a soul. I shall not stray from the true path that leads to the "Beauty of Life" . . .

But meanwhile everything around me is still so dark, the breaking of the new dawn is still so far away, somewhere lost in the distance the cock crows. But the day is far off.

Very much so. I cannot go it alone. Cannot spread my Wings.

> For the sake of the new beauty
> We transgress all laws and lines.

But I am lonely. Where is that evening star, which Wagner's Wolfram[8] sang of? . . .

Balmont[9] says that the most important moments in one's life he considers 'the sudden epiphanies.' I once had something like that happen. When for the first time I heard

> "The soul strives
> To distant heights."

As if through a dream at daybreak I understood everything at once. From that time on I've been wandering in search of the guiding star. I've had enough of merely moving. I repeat, you gave me wings, but where is that fascinating remoteness whither I must fly? . . .

How passionately I should like to touch that hand capable of wresting sounds from those songs of the earth that are not boring. But this is so crudely realistic. I consider you so remote that it is impossible to reach you. And one can see you only bathed in moonlight in a receding perspective . . .

Your Distant One . . .

If you would like to let me experience those unforgettable moments once more, this is my conventional address:

Nikolaev Station, to the bearer of ticket No.27 of Boginsky Technical High School.

[*There is no information that Kuzmin ever took up this invitation.*]

## Notes

1 Walter Fedorovich Nouvel (1871–1949), a musician and wit, was considered the arbiter of elegance and the life of the party in St Petersburg artistic circles.

2 The poet and philologist Vyacheslav Ivanov and his wife Lidiya Zinovieva-Annibal held a Wednesday afternoon salon in their apartment "The Tower" near the Tauride Palace. It was a gathering place for symbolist, acmeists and aesthetes of many stripes.

3 Konstantin Andreevich Somov (1869–1939), Russian painter and designer prominent in the World of Art movement.

4 Pavel Konstantinovich Maslov, Kuzmin's lover at the time, to whom he dedicated the poem cycle "This summer's love." In his diary, Kuzmin described him as "A positively unpleasant, even repulsive, Jew boy, but on second thought, despite the obvious homeliness and sallowness of his face today, he's got something that forces you to intuit something better . . . My expectations are fully justified, he seemed very merry and affectionate, and even the homely face, when he flushes and laughs into the pillow, and the blatantly naked body pleased me at once. But he wriggled and romped, as before, freezing in the most impossible and recherché poses. By and large I was very pleased: one can speak with him, he does not lie there like an impassive block of wood, he is in control of his own art and is not unresponsive (not to me, of course, but to caresses), and then I plain and simply like even his ugly face . . . " Kuzmin worried about Pavlik's taking up with Nouvel and Somov when he was away.

5 The land of tender feeling, from the *Carte du Tendre*, a map of loveland devised by the French *précieuses* of the seventeenth century; Kuzmin and friends used the term to designate the cruising grounds of the Tauride Gardens in St. Petersburg.

6 Leon Bakst (Lev Rozenberg, 1866–1924), Russian painter and designer, co-founder of the World of Art movement, famous for his work with Dyagilev's Ballets Russes.

7 Nouvel's lover of the time, a regimental medical orderly he picked up in the Tauride Gardens.

8 Wolfram von Eschenbach in Wagner's *Tannhäuser* sings a baritone aria to a guiding star; the opera was especially popular with Decadents because of its contest between erotic and divine love.

9 Konstantin Dmitrievich Balmont (1867–1942), a symbolist poet of spectacular ego.

# The Gentleman of the Chrysanthemums

*Play in three acts*
*by Armory (Carle Dauriac)*

(1908)

Translated from the French by Laurence Senelick

*The Gentleman of the Chrysanthemums* is translated from Armory, *Le Monsieur aux chrysanthèmes, pièce en trois actes*, Paris, Librairie Molière, 1908.

# Introduction _____

In England, prior to the Wilde trials, the aesthete, male and female, had been a figure of fun, from the *Punch* cartoons of George Du Maurier to such stage comedies as Francis Burnand's *The Colonel* and Gilbert and Sullivan's *Patience; or Bunthorne's Bride* (both 1881). At first, the targets of the mockery were largely sartorial: long hair, velvet knee-breeches on men, pre-Raphaelite fringes and shapeless brocade gowns on women, and the ubiquitous sunflower motif. A mock pantomime in the 7 January 1882 issue of *Punch*, entitled "Harlequin King Cultchaw," pilloried Wilde for his pretensions to classical learning and his long hair, but the only whiff of sexual deviance was his entrance *"in the midst of pale lavender fire."*[1] This is the earliest association of the color lavender with effeminate posing that I have found in English.

Although Du Maurier's laughing stocks were depicted in willowy poses, with the limp wrist, deboned posture and asymmetrical bearing later associated with effeminate homosexuals, the passional nature of these misfits was fixated exclusively on blue china and lilies. In *Patience*, Bunthorne's "attachment à la Plato" is to a "bashful young potato or a not too French, French bean,"[2] though here the "vegetable passion" is a fraud, masking a perfectly acceptable attraction to a wholesome milkmaid. In the 1887 burlesque *Frankenstein; or, The Vampire's Victim*, a catchall of topical satirical butts, the popular comedian Fred Leslie as the Creature guyed Oscar Wilde in his "special police number." At first sight, there seems something suggestive in this reference to the new Metropolitan Police and the endowment of the creature with a vampire mate named "Mary Ann," standard slang for a male hustler; but in fact these shafts were aimed at a venture, with no special heed to Wilde's temperament. Photographs of Leslie show him in a garish sportman's outfit, more an attack on social climbing philistines than on aesthetes.[3]

A mere two years before the trials, the stage depiction of Wilde as a minor poet Cyril Vane in John Todhunter's *The Black Cat* (1893) is still relatively benign, satire targeted primarily at eccentricities of dress, utterance and literary precocity. The English comic treatment of the aesthete suggested that he was a harmless poseur, whose noxious fads would evaporate in a confrontation with plain common sense.

*Plate 9* "And my talent . . . as a bonussss! . . ." Caricature of a homosexual aesthete by Paul Iribe, from *L'Assiette au beurre*, 21 April 1903. The sibilance is already in place as a token of the effeminate fop. (Laurence Senelick Collection.)

*Plate 10* "The Temptation." Jean Lorrain, on whom Armory's hero was partly based, remarks to the nude lady, "Why tempt me? Are you trying to turn me into a man like any other?" Collage of cartoons by Moriss and A.R. in *L'Indiscret*. (Laurence Senelick Collection.)

Of course, spectators who chose not to ignore the obvious could read deviant sexuality into these characters and poses. As Linda Dowling has pointed out, in all the artistic scandals of the late Victorian age, there was a "pervasive and habitual coincidence of sexual and aesthetic categories" and "at times it is difficult to determine whether the problems of art are being discussed in the vocabulary of sexuality, or whether issues of sexuality are being vented in the vocabulary of art."[4] The American librettist Harry B. Smith recalled a performance of *Patience* in Texas in the early 1880s, where "derisive comments greeted the lady-like poets, Bunthorne and Grosvenor; but the climax of disorder was reached when the three military officers entered as aesthetes gazing enrapt at sunflowers. At moments, prospects looked promising for a lynching. Public sentiment in Texas is against that kind of folks."[5] The cowboys read the brand as unmanliness, which itself implied sexual unorthodoxy.

In France, aestheticism, disseminated in the poetry of Baudelaire and Verlaine, was regarded as a more sinister symptom of decadence – perhaps because art was taken more seriously there than across the Channel. "Homosexuality is the noble disease of the artist," Théophile Gautier is supposed to have said.[6] His status as pariah, as anti-social outlaw, a legacy from the Romantics, was confirmed by his sexual abnormality. Exhibitionists such as Wilde and the Comte Robert de Montesquiou, effeminate, languid, ultra-refined, were taken as its icons.

Cartoons in illustrated papers depicted aesthetes as "Les Sans-Sexe," not so much sexless as sexually ambivalent, the women mannish with their cropped hair and tailored suits, the men effeminized by their unbarbered locks and flaccid postures. What later became caricatures of bulldykes and fairies began as mockery of fringe poetasters, as in the chorus of Jean Meudrot's song "Les Esthètes":

Ce sont les esthètes vannés,
Tous leur sentiments son fanés
Il ne font jamais de conquêtes (bis)
Le beau sexe avec ces appas
Pour ces Messieurs n'existe pas
Ce n'est qu'entre eux, ce n'est qu'entre eux
Que se fréquentent les esthètes.[7]

("These are the enervated aesthetes/All their feelings are washed out/They never make conquests/The fair sex and its attractions/Do not exist for these gentlemen/They only hang out with one another,/Do the aesthetes.") As one French critic has remarked, "Not every homosexual is a dandy but most dandies of the *fin de siècle* are notorious homosexuals."[8]

Harmless enough in their own circles, these aesthetes were seen as dangerous and corrupting when their tastes and manners infiltrate the bon ton. Such fears saturated the porous fabric of nineteenth-century society, wary lest its ill-defined ranks be penetrated by bounders and bawds. French drama was full of impostors and fallen women imposing on the middle class, as in Augier's *Le Mariage d'Olympe* (1855), which demonstrated the destruction wrought upon a respectable family when a liminal figure, a courtesan, marries into it. By the end of the century, this fear of infiltration was complicated by the notion that what had been clandestine and marginal (and therefore relatively easy to control) would, through modern media of publicity, become familiar to the general public and prompt widespread imitation.

There is much in common between Augier's problem drama and Armory's three-act society comedy *Le Monsieur aux chrysanthèmes* (*The Gentleman of the Chrysanthemums*, 1908), the first modern play with a homosexual at centre stage to be produced. The title alludes to both Dumas *fils' Lady of the Camellias*, who renounced her contamination of good society, and to a more exotic courtesan, Pierre Loti's geisha *Madame Chrysanthème* (1887). Armory's comedy sets out to illustrate how both human relationships and cultural values are perverted when society's arbiter is homosexual. It rehashes the aesthete character and employs a number of melodramatic devices, but is still remarkable for its wit and even-handedness.

The play's heroine, an eccentric young widow named Marthe Bourdon, rejects any number of suitors, because she has fallen in love with Gill Norvège, a feared and pampered critic, columnist and novelist who wears a yellow chrysanthemum (a Gallic green carnation) in his buttonhole as a badge of his refinement. Gill's amorous predilections tend elsewhere, but he strings Marthe along and even has sex with her to get 30,000 francs to pay off a troublesome blackmailer.

Marthe has borrowed the money from a well-heeled provincial poet named Jacques Romagne, who is genuinely in love with her; when she fails to reciprocate, he decides to go to South America. Marthe is therefore obliged to repay the loan at once, but cannot get Gill to admit his indebtedness. He is smitten with the young poet's beauty and has already made his partiality known, although to no avail. When he learns that it was Jacques who lent the sum, Gill suggests to Marthe that the poet himself request the repayment. In an instant she realizes just what a dupe she has been and that all the rumours about Gill are true. Aware that Gill has merely bartered her, she vilifies him as a monster and a puppet and orders him out.

Although Armory denied the connection in his memoirs (see Documents), contemporaries claimed that the character of Gill Norvège was based on Jean Lorrain, a heavily made-up, bejewelled celebrity-author who emblazoned his tastes with astute showmanship. Rich, adulated, he brazenly flaunted the rough trade he would pick up in the slums; his "Raîtifs" were columns of gossip and innuendo which would flay his best friends, preludes to profuse apology afterwards. What Gill and Lorrain also have in common is an admiring circle of women, much like the Rossettian damozels who besiege Bunthorne. But Lorrain was flamboyant in proclaiming his pederasty; he would hardly have been the victim of blackmail.[9] Gill, on the other hand, is careful to go into society chaperoned by a matronly duenna and to advertise his liasion with Marthe.

Wilde seems to be a likelier model for Gill's cynicism, although Armory also denied claims that the English writer or even the epicene Romanian-born actor De Max were exact parallels. De Max was another flamboyant type with an ardent following, which included Jean Cocteau. Anecdotes about him were rife. He drove in the Bois de Boulogne with blue ribbons for reins, and entertained the American actress Jane Cowl in his drawing-room naked except for a small leopard skin around his hips. Gide reports that the three costume roles he coveted were Julian the Apostate, Heliogabalus and Henri III. When De Max played Prometheus almost in the nude at the amphitheatre in Orange, the hairdresser who had depilated him placed the cuttings for sale in a shopwindow, advertised as "Tuffts [*sic: poiles*] from the great tragedian de Max."[10]

Gill, Armory insisted, "is a character made up to satirize not so much the vice itself as its ridiculous exhibitionism and the complaisance with which it is met in Parisian society."[11] Within society, the cult of exquisite taste was shown to have replaced earlier touchstones of birth, breeding, wealth, talent, or moral probity. Gill effaced previous dramatic impostors such as Robert Macaire, the felonious pretender to nobility and honest sentiments, and, more appositely, Tartuffe, the felonious pretender to sanctity. As it happens, Burnand's anti-aesthetic comedy *The Colonel* had been based on an earlier play, Bayle Bernard's *The Serious Family*, in which the inrusive imposter was not an artistic fraud but a religious charlatan.[12] This play in turn had been adapted from a French original by Bayard and Rouvier, *Le Mari à la campagne*, itself based on Tartuffe. When a community treasures fashion over piety, the confidence man's *modus operandi* requires different camouflage. *The Gentleman of the Chrysanthemums* builds somewhat like *Tartuffe*: the title character is kept offstage for a good while, to build expectation and to suggest by absence a larger-than-life presence. The removal of an eligible woman from the marriage market by her alliance with an unsuitable outsider is a central feature of both plots. As in *Tartuffe*, the scene in which the deceived victim comes to an awareness of the villain's real nature and denounces him as a monster, ordering him out of the house, shifts the mood from social comedy to domestic tragedy and even melodrama. In Molière, the Argus-eyed Sun King is evoked to bring his impostor to justice; in his republican age, Armory was more realistic in depicting the resilience of his social climber.

Gill is described as *"looking very young, glabrous, his lips painted and outlined . . . A peculiar elegance."*[13] In public, he is subject to vapours and other signs of frailty; in private he wears purple-lined suits of fantastic cut, silk shirts and lace jabots. His name (Norway) alludes to the fad for Scandinavian drama among the French avant-garde and perhaps to the homosexual Danish novelist Herman Bang, who was literary adviser to Lugné-Poe's Théâtre de l'Oeuvre. Gill's domestic interior is *"très artiste et très 'cocotte',"* advertising the mixture of finicky fastidiousness and tacky flash that characterizes the effeminate aesthete.

Armory's depiction of Gill was not unsympathetic, since his moral blemish lies less in his "vice" than in society's eager endorsement of it. One character admits, "He is necessary to our age of decadence," and Gill himself explains that "what our age needed was a man who speaks his desires, writes his desires, sets the fashion . . . I live in a glass cage so that everyone can see me. Better still, I live for others . . . ." This is where Gill is most like Jean Lorrain, of whom a modern biographer remarked, "The paradox is that Lorrain resorted to journalism in order to support himself as an aesthete, but as an aesthete he became a slave to journalism."[14] Gill's personal tastes can be sustained only by exploiting them as public diversions. Halfway to the "fairy" as society's jester, Gill Norvège is a remarkable forecast of the homosexual media celebrity, the sexual outlaw as arbiter of taste, a portent of Jean Cocteau, Truman Capote and Andy Warhol.

Gill's posing does some violence to his own artistic tenets; he pledges sincere if florid allegiance to an aesthetic cocktail of Ruskin, Pater and Wilde (an interest in Ruskin is also Proust's). His models are such Renaissance painters as Leonardo da Vinci and Il Sodoma. He envisages a new Greece, "a paradise beneath an open sky, beneath free laws respectful of art . . . And to think that never shall we know that paradise, we who are blasphemed against, hunted down, condemned . . . unable to slake our thirst or spread our wings without their being torn." The imagery was part of the Zeitgeist; one thinks of *Wings*, the homoerotic propaganda novel published by Mikhail Kuzmin two years before Armory's play, and the numerous seraphs that flit through homophilic periodicals (and, later, Wing Biddlebaum exiled from Sherwood Anderson's *Winesburg, Ohio*). Armory made it clear, however, that this kind of aestheticism, however genuine, is nourished by lust and nourishes it in turn. Connoisseurship commingles with Gill's desire for Jacques.

Except for the financial burden it imposes on him, Gill is not much troubled by extortion. Unlike the German characters, crushed by the weight of their guilty secrets, he survives, for he is closer to Vautrin than Werther. Still, the intrusion of blackmail is a reminder that for all of Armory's well-observed detail and the multifaceted psychology of his protagonist, he too must fall back on the familiar convention to propel his plot. The blackmailer, who never appears, is given the ugly name Durch and described as "an infamous man . . . dirty . . . repulsive." *"Infâme"* had been synonymous with "sodomite" in the French language since the Reformation.[15] While Armory seems to be drawing a distinction between polished, well-bred deviants (such as Gill, his devoted secretary Edgard, and his colleague Lantigny) who are presentable in good society and the likes of Durch and Georges the blackmailing shoeshine boy who emerge from an unsavoury subculture, he is also hinting that the *haut*mosexual is not fundamentally different from the hustler, and that same-sex love, stripped of its pretensions to refinement, is bestial.

Of the early modernist dramatic treatments of the male homosexual, only Armory's shrewd blend of comedy of manners and society melodrama was staged successfully – so successfully that it helped to crystallize a particular image of the homosexual dandy as feline, neurasthenic, underhanded and manipulative in his dealings with others, producing an unreasoning adoration in women and a somewhat more reasoning abhorrence in men. Although more genuine than Bunthorne's, his tastes in art were clues to his depraved nature, and his milieu, filled with flowers and *objets d'art*, was a hothouse where selfish passions were bred. The combination of an uplifting credo with an sybaritic egoism makes Gill, like Hal and Claud in *The Blackmailers*, an early exponent of a "homosexual sensibility."[16] Unlike their doomed German brethren, the French and English characters share a defiant and amoral attention to the trivial and the amusing that announces the advent of camp.

These became signs easily read by theatre and cinema audiences: a fussy boutonnière, an interest in bric-à-brac, a prissy elegance announced the sinister deviant who casts a blight on the growth of normal loves. His epicene nature encodes self-centered sterility and misanthropic cynicism. He later appeared as the malevolent man-milliner Jacquelin in Edward Knoblock's *My Lady's Dress* (1915) and as the effete Mr. Dulcimer in Mordaunt Shairp's *The Green Bay Tree* (1931). In *film noir*, Clifton Webb's Waldo Lydecker in *Laura* (1944) was an exceptionally envenomed example: Waldo, like Gill, is a society columnist. Their fields of activity were relatively circumscribed. Soon, however, the evil aesthete was transferred to more influential spheres, intent on world domination. It may not be fetching things too far to see the louche gracility of Gill Norvège as a shadow behind Ernst Stavro Blofeld in the James Bond saga, dealing death and destruction as he languidly strokes the pussy in his lap.

## Notes

1  J. Savory and P. Marks, *The Smiling Muse: Victoriana in the Comic Press*, Philadelphia, Art Union Press, 1985, p. 154. A good account of this phase of Du Maurier's work can be found in L. Ormond, *George Du Maurier*, London, Routledge and Kegan Paul, 1969, pp. 243–307. She makes the point that Du Maurier is unconcerned with "the unhealthy preoccupations with self . . . nor of the strain of perversity and unnaturalness . . . which was latent in aestheticism . . . The real implications of the Wilde story would always have escaped him" (p. 258).

2  W. S. Gilbert, *Original Plays, Third Series*, London, Chatto and Windus, 1913, p. 10. Reviewing the "aesthetic quadrille" in an 1882 pantomime, G. A. Sala noted that the satire was off target: "There are a good many gentlemen who wear velvet coats, knickerbockers and coloured hose when they play lawn-tennis or go bicycling; but did you ever see persons dressed like Bunthorne in society? I never did. Even that good-natured eccentric Mr. Oscar Wilde did not venture to wear knee-breeches in public until he crossed the Atlantic." G. A. Sala, *Living London*, London, Cassell, 1883, pp. 63–4.

3  S. E. Forry, *Hideous Progenies: Dramatizations of Frankenstein from Mary Shelley to the Present*, Philadelphia, University of Pennsylvania Press, 1990, pp. 54–6, 63–72.

4  L. Dowling, "Ruskin's pied beauty and the constitution of a 'homosexual' code," *Victorian Newsletter*, 1989, vol. 75, p. 7.

5  H. B. Smith, *First Nights and First Editions*, Boston, Little, Brown, 1931, pp. 88–90.

6  Quoted in G. L. Mosse, *Nationalism and Sexuality: Respectability and Abnormal Sexuality in Modern Europe*, New York, Howard Fertig, 1985, p. 34. It is unlikely that Gautier used the word "homosexuality," however.

7  J. Meudrot, "Les Esthètes," *Gil Blas*, 6 Aug. 1897, p. 8. The defeminized woman of Parisian bohemia is discussed in M. Wilson, " 'Sans les femmes, qu'est qui nous resterait': gender and transgression in bohemian Montmartre," in J. Epstein and K. Straub (eds), *Body Guards: The Cultural Politics of Gender Ambiguity*, New York, Routledge, 1991, pp. 195–222.

8  M. Delbourg-Delphis, *Masculin singulier*, Paris, Hachette, 1985, p. 23.

9  See the anecdotes in Willy, *Le troisième sexe*, Paris, Paris-Edition, 1927, pp. 124–7.

10  A. Stevens, *Actorviews*, Chicago, Covici-McGee, 1923, pp. 306–7; A. Gide, 4 February 1902, in *Journal (1889–1912)*, Rio de Janeiro, Americ-Edit, 1943, p. 148; Willy, op. cit., p. 135. One of the *succès de scandale* of the 1926 Parisian theatre

season was Bouissac de Saint-Marc André's comedy *Sardanapale*, whose central character was unmistakably based on de Max.

11 Armory, *Cinquante ans de vie parisienne (souvenirs et figures)*, Paris, Jean-Renard, 1943, p. 96.

12 *The Colonel* may even have lent something to *The Blackmailers*, since its humbug aesthete Lambert Stryke is teamed with an equally objectionable nephew, Basil Giorgioni.

13 Armory, *Le Monsieur aux Chrysanthèmes*.

*Pièce en trois actes*, Paris, Librairie Molière, 1908, p. 40.

14 P. Kyria, *Jean Lorrain*, Paris, Seghers, 1973, p23.

15 M. Lever, *Les Bûchers de Sodome. Histoire des "infâmes,"* Paris, Fayard, 1985. A 1906 novel of homosexual life in Berlin by the pseudonymous Fritz Geron Pernhaum was entitled *Die Infamen*.

16 See J. Dollimore, *Sexual Dissidence: Augustine to Wilde, Freud to Foucault*, Oxford, Oxford University Press, 1991, chapter 20.

# The Gentleman of the Chrysanthemums

Play in Three Acts

## Armory (Carle Dauriac)

First played at the Palais Royal, Paris, under the auspices of the "Nouveau Théâtre d'Art," 17 June 1908

---

To Jean Ayme and Jeanine Zorelli, as a token of sincere gratitude.

## Characters

GILL NORVÈGE

PIERRE BOURDON, known as SAINT-LOUP

JACQUES ROMAGNE

SUMÈNE

TOURNY

EDGARD

GERMAIN BERGE

LANTIGNY

MARTHE BOURDON

REINE DE VIGNEUX

MADAME ARMIDE

LINON DE LONDINE

GEORGETTE PERRAULT

HENRIETTE DE VILLERVILLE

*Paris, the present time [i.e., 1908]*

## Act I

The home of PIERRE and MARTHE BOURDON

*A not very opulent reception room, hung with modern works of art.*
*A side-door at right, another door farther along, opening into a drawing-room. A double-door upstage, opening onto a corridor. In the left corner, a window. A piano near the window. Up right, a tea table set for an informal luncheon. A mantelpiece down right.*
*Centre, all sorts of furnishings , tables, straight chairs, armchairs, rocking chairs, etc. Down left a sofa. Vases of flowers all over the place.*

## Scene 1

PIERRE BOURDON, *alias* SAINT-LOUP, *30, rather hearty and quite attractive; then* MARTHE, *25 to 30, pretty, somewhat eccentric.*

*As the curtain rises,* SAINT-LOUP *is standing near the mantelpiece nailing up a piece of cloth embroidered with a Maltese cross.*
MARTHE BOURDON *enters, carrying flowers. She stops at the threshold, aghast. A few seconds slip by.*

MARTHE   What on earth is that?
SAINT-LOUP   It's a cross, isn't it obvious?
MARTHE   *(Dumbfounded)* A cross! . . . Over the mantelpiece! Have you gone crazy?
SAINT-LOUP   Not in the least.
MARTHE   But we've got friends coming!
SAINT-LOUP   That's right, it's our open house day . . . Well, let 'em come.
MARTHE   Is your head on straight?
SAINT-LOUP   Straight as a die, my dear. *(He adjusts the cross.)* How about yours? *(Coming center)* Well, that doesn't look bad at all.
MARTHE   Do you have to be an incorrigible eccentric? *(Saint-Loup laughs.)* That cross!
SAINT-LOUP   I promised it to you . . .
MARTHE   You did?
SAINT-LOUP   We agreed that when you fell in love. . . .
MARTHE   *(Nonplussed)* When I . . . So I'm in love?
SAINT-LOUP   So it seems; just like everybody else. . . . Although I have to admit there is a difference.
MARTHE   *(Sarcastic)* Is that so?
SAINT-LOUP   You're worse at it than everybody else.
MARTHE   *(Annoyed)* What do you mean by that?
SAINT-LOUP   *(Clasping his hands, and gazing at the cross)* Sweet Jesus, look who you picked to fall in love with!

MARTHE   Don't be ridiculous. Just what do you mean? How do you know I'm in love with anyone?

SAINT-LOUP   You don't even bother to hide it.

MARTHE   *(Making up her mind)* All right, let's suppose . . . I say, suppose . . . that your assumptions have some slight foundation based on appearances, that's no reason for you to feel sorry for yourself.

SAINT-LOUP   I don't feel sorry for myself; I feel sorry for you.

MARTHE   And why, may I ask?

SAINT-LOUP   Because . . . because . . . hum! just one of those things, my love . . .

MARTHE   *(Arranging flowers in vases)* Yes, I know . . . those absurd rumours about him that are going round.

SAINT-LOUP   There aren't any rumours about me.

MARTHE   Because he's more refined than the rest of you and makes a pose of being special. Besides, you don't like him. Which doesn't keep you from being overjoyed whenever he pays us a visit.

SAINT-LOUP   Overjoyed, hah . . . I'd call it . . .

MARTHE   Be honest; it sets you up in the right circles.

SAINT-LOUP   It sets me up . . . and gets me down . . . Whenever I'm Saint-Loup, man of letters, he can be useful to me . . . whenever I'm plain Pierre Bourdon, he rubs me the wrong way.

MARTHE   Oh, come now, you're not a cat.

SAINT-LOUP   Yes, yes, there are even times when he gets my back up *(Gesture)* like that, meow . . . Besides, what does he get out of coming here?

MARTHE   Charming. What about me?

SAINT-LOUP   *(Staring at her)* You? No, the more I think about it, the less I understand it. He comes here because of you?

MARTHE   I'm able to lure him here, for your sake, as I've done with plenty of other men.

SAINT-LOUP   Thanks a lot. . . . The plenty of other men doesn't surprise me; he does . . . *(A pause)* And it's been going on a long time . . .

MARTHE   But I'm not his mistress yet.

SAINT-LOUP   Oh! I know, I know.

MARTHE   *(Angered)* What! You know?

SAINT-LOUP   I assume . . .

MARTHE   Because you believe that absurd slander. Well, matters have gone much

farther with us than you think. Besides, I can hardly believe that Gill would shun a woman who was frank, sincere and . . .

SAINT-LOUP   *(Astonished)* No! Really?

MARTHE   And I won't allow anyone to meddle in my affairs, is that clear?

SAINT-LOUP   Clear enough. . . . May I ask you, though, how long you've been in love with him?

MARTHE   You insist on my being in love with him.

SAINT-LOUP   I don't insist all that hard. I'd much rather you weren't. But facts are facts . . . and though I'm not a professional psychologist . . .

MARTHE   *(Making a face)* Is it all that obvious?

SAINT-LOUP   Obvious . . . obscure . . . You really have me going. Just yesterday I was at George Petit's and saw his portrait by Sandarini, the one who specializes in painting women! Not that he'd made an exception in this case. Oh, that portrait, a regular poem! If you were out to catch a man, you've caught a winner. Congratulations.

MARTHE   It's my business.

SAINT-LOUP   I won't argue with you. You're in love and that's what matters. *(He looks at the cross.)*

MARTHE   Your joke is in bad taste. You'll have to take that down.

SAINT-LOUP   Oh no; it looks very good. It's a symbol, a work of art. I could have put up a crucifix . . . but this cross has more class.

MARTHE   Take it down!

SAINT-LOUP   Never.

MARTHE   I don't want it there.

SAINT-LOUP   I'm sorry but there it stays.

MARTHE   Against my wishes?

SAINT-LOUP   Against your wishes.

MARTHE   *(Looking at the cross)* Oh, you are hateful. I'll find a way to get rid of it.

SAINT-LOUP   I'll replace it.

MARTHE   It's ridiculous.

SAINT-LOUP   Not as ridiculous as all that . . . For two years you were married to my brother, a delightful fellow, you didn't mind loving him . . .

MARTHE   *(Sarcastic)* Go on: after your brother died, when we decided to share this apartment, you had hopes. . . .

SAINT-LOUP   *(Irritated)* Skip it.

MARTHE   All right, we'll skip it. . . . You won't forgive me. I bet you're still jealous . . . and because of that cheap jealousy . . .

SAINT-LOUP   You couldn't be more mistaken! Besides, other admirers of yours . . .

MARTHE   Charming ones.

SAINT-LOUP   Quite right, came on the scene. Nothing doing. Next!, you'd say. . . . Then one day, you remember, you were sitting over there in that armchair, and I was over here smoking. After I had seen the latest list of my friends' failures both as candidates for lover and candidates for husband, I remarked . . . *(He stretches his arms towards the mantlepiece.)* The day you fall in love, I shall erect a cross over the mantlepiece. *(He points to the cross.)* And there it is. . . . But I never expected the lucky man to be . . . No, that's too rich!

MARTHE   What's wrong with you?

SAINT-LOUP   I'm in stitches.

MARTHE   You'll be in traction.

SAINT-LOUP   Gill Norvège! Ha, ha! The Gentleman of the Chrysanthemums, the gentleman who . . . Oh, oh! Aren't you afraid he might break?

MARTHE   You're really going too far. That's enough. . . . Yes, you're jealous, jealous of him, and his talent, his art, his notoriety . . . his success. Because you never got close to me. Because I wouldn't love you any more than I loved your brother. . . . There, I said it!

SAINT-LOUP   Shut up!

MARTHE   I married him against my will.

SAINT-LOUP   Please.

MARTHE   I must tell you everything today so that you'll leave me in peace from now on.

SAINT-LOUP   I'd rather leave you in peace in advance. Ah! now you're scaring me. You really are the most selfish, dangerous woman, capable of doing as much harm as you can. God, the only one you could love would be a Gill Norvège! You're right.

MARTHE   Oh! So now you consent?

SAINT-LOUP   Do I? . . . *(A pause. He looks at her, considers and seems to be mulling over a diabolical scheme.)* Yes, you are right. Maybe you'll get somewhere with him. *(Casting a sidelong, sly glance at her)* I might even lend you a hand.

MARTHE   *(Surprised)* Really . . .

SAINT-LOUP   *(Unconvinced)* After all, he might be in love with you too.

MARTHE   Why not?

SAINT-LOUP   When you consider his pride. You could match his pride in spades. *(Sincerely)* It wouldn't be hard for you.

MARTHE   And you intend to be my adviser!

SAINT-LOUP   Why not? *(Amiably)* Unless you don't want me to be.

MARTHE   Not at all. . . . You seem to have calmed down. I've hopes of domesticating you yet.

SAINT-LOUP   Domesticate the other fellow. I'd enjoy seeing that.

MARTHE   I don't understand! Someone would think you were encouraging me now.

SAINT-LOUP   Yes. I misjudged the situation. Quite sincerely, I wouldn't mind a bit.

MARTHE   What a creature you are! Next thing you know, you'll be offering to be my confidant.

SAINT-LOUP   At your service.

MARTHE   You no longer think I'm crazy?

SAINT-LOUP   Certainly not . . .

MARTHE   Then admit that he can't resist a love that's true and openly declared.

SAINT-LOUP   *(Hands in his pockets)* Try it and see.

MARTHE   But, if what people say of him is true . . .

SAINT-LOUP   What do they say?

MARTHE   Oh, you know . . . If only I could . . . steer him in a different direction . . .

SAINT-LOUP   Hmm! What's the point?

MARTHE   *(Convinced)* It would be a good deed.

SAINT-LOUP   A genuine achievement, in fact; that's all you'd need. . . . Since you're already smitten with him, you might as well do a good deed. . . . *(Sarcastic)* Ah! it's a rotten shame!

MARTHE   Huh?

SAINT-LOUP   *(Violent)* Go ahead and love him, love him, do. Throw yourself at him, for pity's sake!

MARTHE   *(Laughing)* At least wait till he gets here.

SAINT-LOUP   Fair enough.

MARTHE   He'll be here any minute, I'm counting on him.

SAINT-LOUP   Damn! so am I.

MARTHE   There, you see, you are too.

SAINT-LOUP   I want to introduce him to Jacques Romagne.

MARTHE   Jacques Romagne . . . He'll be bored by him.

SAINT-LOUP   Norvège will bore Jacques?

MARTHE   No, Jacques will bore Norvège.

SAINT-LOUP   Why? Anyway, I'll let you do the honours. . . . That'll give you an opportunity to test your influence. . . .

There now, admit that you've got a model brother-in-law.

MARTHE   One who wants me to introduce Jacques Romagne to Gill Norvège? What's come over you today?

SAINT-LOUP   *(Pretending delight)* I'm all a-flutter . . . because you're in love!

*(Door bell)*

MARTHE   *(Indicating the cross)* What are you going to tell people about that? It's stupid!

SAINT-LOUP   I'll tell them the truth.

MARTHE   Meaning?

SAINT-LOUP   That it's an altar cross from Burgos and I managed to acquire it thanks to an antique dealer in Rue de Sèvres. . . . We'll stick some bric-à-brac at the corners, and there you are. . . .

## Scene 2

THE SAME, REINE DE VIGNEUX

REINE DE VIGNEUX   *(Elegant, refined, very down-to-earth)* Oh, I'm the first!

MARTHE   *(Pressing her hand, somewhat ironically)* You usually arrange to be the first.

REINE   *(Candidly)* Goodness, yes, when I don't have a rehearsal. *(Going to* SAINT-LOUP*)* Good afternoon. *(Noticing the cross)* Oh! something new!

MARTHE   *(Quickly)* Yes, an altar cross from Burgos Pierre managed to acquire from an antique dealer in Rue de Sèvres.

REINE   *(A connoisseur, applying her lorgnette)* Very classy! *(Turning around and inspecting the room)* But, if I were you, I would have put it on the piano. It would go better there.

SAINT-LOUP   True enough, but . . .

MARTHE   Pooh! no, I don't think so.

REINE   *(Insisting)* Oh! yes, definitely.

MARTHE   *(Annoyed)* Anyway, it's where it is. Now is not the time to change things around! *(Leaving)* I'll leave you alone. *(She exits)*

## Scene 3

SAINT-LOUP, REINE DE VIGNEUX

*(*REINE *makes sure that the door is tightly shut, then throws herself into* SAINT-LOUP's *arms.)*

REINE   Bonjour, you! . . .

SAINT-LOUP   *(Hugging her)* Bon . . . jour, Reine my dear.

REINE   *(Still in his embrace)* Say, what's the matter with her?

SAINT-LOUP   *(Seriously)* She's in love.

REINE   *(Pulling out of the embrace, surprised)* She's in . . . !

*(*SAINT-LOUP *nods "yes," then points to the cross.)*

SAINT-LOUP   Get it?

REINE   *(Still surprised)* Not really! And who's the guy?

SAINT-LOUP   Somebody famous! . . . but it's a secret.

REINE   Oh! I won't ask the name. . . . But I really would like to know. . . .

SAINT-LOUP   This secret is on the verge of making a public appearance. Yes, it's about to become an open secret. But far be it from me to arrange its debut.

REINE   Ha, ha! . . . Just what are you hinting at?

SAINT-LOUP   No comment.

REINE   You're jealous!

SAINT-LOUP   Oh no! . . . not this time.

REINE   But you *were* in love with your sister-in-law? Don't say you weren't!

SAINT-LOUP   Yes, I did love her. *(With effort)* But it's all over now. . . .

REINE   Is it?

SAINT-LOUP   Don't be stupid. You're the only one I love!

REINE   *(Delighted, throwing her arms around his neck)* Me too!

SAINT-LOUP   You're the only one you love?

REINE   No, you, you big silly! *(They kiss)* All the same, it isn't normal.

SAINT-LOUP   What isn't?

REINE   The two of you living together like this.

SAINT-LOUP   Yes, it is kind of funny. At first, when she came from the provinces and suggested we live together to save money, I did think . . .

REINE   She was asking you to shack up with her.

SAINT-LOUP   Or marry her, at least. . . . Well, I was totally wrong. . . . My beloved sister-in-law simply turned out to be a woman of brains. . . .

REINE   A woman of brains, yes, but not of heart: she'll never come to grief on that score.

SAINT-LOUP   She made the overtures.

REINE   Did she make your poor brother suffer horribly?

SAINT-LOUP   Quite a bit. . . . He killed himself on account of a ballerina.

REINE   Marthe was cheating on him the whole time?

SAINT-LOUP   I have no idea. . . . (Bitterly) with the servants maybe or with . . .

REINE   You're being malicious, you must still love her. (Putting her hand over his mouth) Now keep still, you're about to say something obscene. (After a moment's thought) Never mind, Marthe in love is the novelty. Ah! yes, it is a novelty. As Berge would say, "Life has its turning-points" . . .

SAINT-LOUP   Dangerous crossing. Cyclists beware. (Thinking out loud) Actually, it's not a bicycle built for two.

REINE   Aha! . . . He doesn't love her?

SAINT-LOUP   He couldn't possibly. . . . No, the more I think about it, the less I understand it.

REINE   Listen, I think I'm beginning to get it. . . . Only it seems awfully weird.

SAINT-LOUP   You got it.

REINE   Really? Could it be . . .

SAINT-LOUP   (Signalling that someone's coming) Yes, be quiet.

## Scene 4

THE SAME, MARTHE , crossing in the corridor to the left where JACQUES ROMAGNE enters. He is 25, very good-looking, but shy and polite rather than elegant, a true type of the country gentleman. They pass each other and speak upstage.

JACQUES ROMAGNE   (Somewhat startled by this abrupt encounter) Ah! Good afternoon, Madame. . . . How are you today?

MARTHE   The same as yesterday and the day before.

ROMAGNE   (Confused) But yesterday and the day before I didn't have the pleasure of . . .

MARTHE   (Not listening, heading downstage) Are you through? May we come in?

REINE   (A bit offended) Oh!

SAINT-LOUP   We are not through. But you may come in, to prove it. . . . Well, Romagne . . . (Rising and going to shake his hand effusively) How are things?

ROMAGNE   So-so.

(MARTHE comes and goes, exits and re-enters, preparing the tea-table.)

SAINT-LOUP   (Indicating REINE) Do you know one another?

ROMAGNE   No, I haven't had the honour. . . .

SAINT-LOUP   (Introducing) Reine de Vigneux, the hardest worker at the Folies Françaises, who will, with little urging, I think, have the pleasure of reciting you.

ROMAGNE   (Protesting) Oh! I . . .

SAINT-LOUP   I have spoken. (Introducing ROMAGNE) Jacques Romagne, a newcomer to Paris, a poet in the true sense of the word, a robust, manly talent . . .

MARTHE   (At a distance) Oh, come on now!

REINE   (Joking, extending a hand to ROMAGNE) Delighted to make your acquaintance, monsieur.

SAINT-LOUP   (Arranging the armchairs) There . . . woo her.

ROMAGNE   (Embarrassed, looking towards MARTHE) But . . .

SAINT-LOUP   (to REINE) Don't damage him for me, he's a sincere sort, a delicate blossom. Let's not abuse our betters. . . . Now, try some flirtation. The word is idiotically symbolic: it doesn't mean a thing. (REINE and ROMAGNE laugh. SAINT-LOUP joins MARTHE.) Don't you want to flirt today? That gentleman with the posies poses so well . . . what with all his different posies; he smells good anyway.

MARTHE   Norvège? At the moment he wears nothing but chrysanthemums.

SAINT-LOUP   Of different colours . . . like the camellias of Marguerite Gautier . . . to warn his admirers when he's having his period.

(REINE is eavesdropping, while talking to ROMAGNE.)

MARTHE   What are you getting at?

SAINT-LOUP   When he isn't having his question mark.

MARTHE   Which means?

SAINT-LOUP   Which means: zero, zip, zilch. . . .

MARTHE   Don't be stupid, I don't like riddles.

SAINT-LOUP   Oh really! . . . you could have fooled me!

(He makes a pirouette and winds up face to face with SUMÈNE.)

## Scene 5

THE SAME, SUMÈNE , *a type of the all-purpose journalist, a gossipy social climber, a fluttering yes-man.*

SAINT-LOUP   Sumène! *(He shakes his hand)* What tidings do you bring, Marlborough?

SUMÈNE   Tidings of great import. . . . Only don't call me Marlborough when they get here. . . .

SAINT-LOUP   When the news gets here?

SUMÈNE   No, when Georgette Perrault gets here . . . she's on her way.

MARTHE   Georgette!

SAINT-LOUP   *(To* ROMAGNE*)* She runs the Folies Françaises.

REINE   Honestly, if I had known . . .

SAINT-LOUP   Was it Berge who talked her into coming?

SUMÈNE   Not at all, it was me.

SAINT-LOUP   You! Get out!

SUMÈNE   I did. I told her that she'd meet Gill Norvège here.

MARTHE   *(Whisper to* SAINT-LOUP*)* There, you hear that, you ingrate! He'll lure all of them to you.

SAINT-LOUP   Yes, I grant you that.

SUMÈNE   She wants to touch him for an article about herself. . . . Ssh! *(To* SAINT-LOUP*)* By the way, it seems that Gill's stock is on the way down. . . . Did you know?

SAINT-LOUP   No, who told you that?

SUMÈNE   An anonymous tip.

MARTHE   *(Drawing near)* What has Gill done?

SUMÈNE   *(Drawing away from her)* I can't tell it with ladies present.

*(*MARTHE *shrugs and goes up to the piano.)*

SAINT-LOUP   *(Joining* SUMÈNE*)* Well?

SUMÈNE   Well, all sorts of stories are going the rounds, a huge scandal is about to explode any day now, it appears. . . . People are even daring to attack him!

SAINT-LOUP   Blackmail?

SUMÈNE   Something of the kind. At any rate, it ought to dissuade disciples from trying to follow him in his groove of glory.

SAINT-LOUP   His debts are mounting?

SUMÈNE   To the stratosphere. His reputation may prove to be a nuisance when it comes to creditors.

SAINT-LOUP   Creditors? Hah! Besides, he'll put them on a false scent. *(Rubbing his hands)* This should be interesting.

SURMÈNE   What's it to you?

SAINT-LOUP   Me? . . . Nothing.

## Scene 6

THE SAME, GEORGETTE PERRAULT, *34, a very pretty woman,* HENRIETTE DE VILLERVILLE, *20 to 25, a pseudo-ingenue: both very elegant.*

MARTHE   *(Rushing to* GEORGETTE PERRAULT*)* How good of you to come!

GEORGETTE   Don't mention it. . . . *(Shaking* SAINT-LOUP*'s hand)* Good afternoon, Saint-Loup. *(Introducing* HENRIETTE DE VILLERVILLE*)* I took the liberty of bringing one of my young friends, Mademoiselle Henriette de Villerville.

*(*MARTHE *and* HENRIETTE *shake hands.)*

SAINT-LOUP   Pleased to meet you, Mademoiselle.

HENRIETTE   It's good of you to have me. *(Whisper to* SAINT-LOUP*)* Is he here yet?

SAINT-LOUP   Who?

HENRIETTE   Gill Norvège.

SAINT-LOUP   Not yet.

SUMÈNE   You are well, mademoiselle?

HENRIETTE   Of course.

GEORGETTE   *(Going towards* REINE*)* Well, well, de Vigneux . . .

SAINT-LOUIS   *(Following her)* Is she rehearsing with you tonight?

GEORGETTE   *(Very amiable)* Why, of course, and in your play, with your co-author Germain Berge. We expect you to be there too.

MARTHE   *(Who has just brought a cup of tea to* ROMAGNE*)* A cup of tea?

GEORGETTE   Please. *(She goes up towards* MARTHE*)*

REINE   *(Whisper to* SAINT-LOUP*)* Isn't she friendly to you!

SAINT-LOUP   *(Whisper)* It's Gill Norvège . . .

REINE   Gill?

SAINT-LOUP   It's all due to him.

REINE   We can be together tonight.

SAINT-LOUP   Yes, ordinarily when I'm around she's in a foul temper and nothing goes right, so I let clever Germain take over.

REINE   And here he is, right on cue.

## Scene 7

THE SAME , GERMAIN BERGE, *the elegant man of letters, a skeptic, quite in the swim, and* TOURNY, *the famous "collaborator," very bald, very fat, a hard drinker who speaks pidgin French.*

BERGE   Here we are!

*(They greet* MARTHE.*)*

TOURNY   *(Bursting out laughing)* Ha! ha! ha! Georgette Perrault! What the hell are you doin' here?

GEORGETTE   You're surprised that I should pay a call on my author?

TOURNY   *(Bluntly)* Yes.

BERGE   It's a surprise for the co-author.

GEORGETTE   I knew I'd meet you here, Berge.

SAINT-LOUP   *(Tapping* BERGE *on the shoulder)* Touché, old man!

GEORGETTE   I came to see both of you.

SAINT-LOUP   *(Whisper to* REINE*)* And Gill Norvège.

SUMÈNE   *(to* MARTHE*)* What sweetener did you feed the lady?

*(Everyone laughs.)*

GEORGETTE   Ah! watch out, Sumène, I'll stop telling you my secrets.

SUMÈNE   She was selling me shares in them.

TOURNY   *(To* REINE, *indicating* ROMAGNE*)* Say, whozat sad kid over there, dipping his cookie in his cup while his mind's miles away? I'll bet there's no tea left in the cup, but he don't pay it no mind . . . he's poured it full o' melancholy and it's overflowin'!

REINE   Keep still, that's . . .

TOURNY   A poet, right, one more of 'em. . . . Damn, he'd better spill it out or else he'll drown in the depths of his dream, and come to a bad end!

SAINT-LOUP   He's a pedigreed artist, no jokes, Tourny, he writes very fine verse.

TOURNY   Oh, swell!

*(He goes to* BERGE, *slips his arm through* BERGE*'s arm and drags him off, whispering the while.* SUMÈNE *exits upstage,* SAINT-LOUP *and* REINE *join* GEORGETTE *and* HENRIETTE, *right.* MARTHE *and* ROMAGNE *come down to the forestage.)*

MARTHE   Don't push too hard with Georgette. You aren't trendy enough for her.

ROMAGNE   *(Sincerely)* I never will be. . . . But I haven't said two words to you yet.

MARTHE   You're all right.

ROMAGNE   It's good of you to take an interest in me. *(Energetically)* You do take an interest in me?

MARTHE   Pierre's friends are my friends.

ROMAGNE   Oh, Pierre's . . . does he have a lot of them?

MARTHE   You know he doesn't . . . not with his temper. . . . So, shall I introduce you to Gill Norvège?

ROMAGNE   *(Timidly)* Oh! there's no hurry.

MARTHE   Yes, yes, I shall introduce you. *(Impatient)* . . . But what can be keeping him?

*(*ROMAGNE *stares at her a long time. Bursts of laughter from the group.)*

MARTHE   What are they on about now? *(Leaving him to join the group)* They must be pulling to pieces someone new.

ROMAGNE   It's butchery!

TOURNY   *(Who has heard him, crossing near him)* Refinery, young man, refinery *(Imitating sprinkling a sugar-caster)* 'cause of all the sugar; they start by pouring in the sugar.

ROMAGNE   Perhaps they put in more sugar than Attic salt.

TOURNY   Both, sometimes; it works like a tenderizer, and the meat's all the easier to carve up afterwards, because they also do their own slaughtering.

BERGE   *(Laughing)* Talking about food, are you!

TOURNY   Take Berge, for example! They tried to serve him up that way at Gill's.

BERGE   *(Laughing)* So I've heard.

TOURNY   You can laugh, but they almost gobbled you up, big boy, your life and your works. . . . One afternoon they felt like makin' a dog's dinner of our colleague here. . . . The lot fell to the youngest of those absent, and after telling a few home truths about you as appetizer, they were just about to pluck you bare when I showed up. I put a stop to the operation.

ROMAGNE   *(Hearing* MARTHE *laugh louder than the others)* Perhaps I ought to stop that lot the same way . . .

131

TOURNY  *(Going upstage)* Yes, let's see who they're operating on.

ROMAGNE  *(To* BERGE, *who is about to follow* TOURNY*)* Monsieur, is it like this here every day?

BERGE  Oh no! . . . They don't hold open house every day.

SUMÈNE  *(Re-entering)* Linon de Londine is in the lift!

MARTHE  She's not wanted here!

SUMÈNE  That's what I told her. But what I say doesn't count. Norvège asked her to come, she said.

SAINT-LOUP  *(Watching* MARTHE*)* His mood today probably requires a numerous and . . . varied company. Besides, we'll see it right away from his signal.

MARTHE  What signal?

SAINT-LOUP  Why, his pansy!

TOURNY  *(Pretending to be shocked)* What did you say?

SAINT-LOUP  *(Whisper to* MARTHE*)* Whatever the colour, go for it.

MARTHE  Ah!

SAINT-LOUP  Yes. *(He moves away and approaches* HENRIETTE.*)* I'm sorry, Mademoiselle, that in my home you have to meet Linon de Londine, whose reputation is as bad as those of her girl friends.

HENRIETTE  On the contrary, dear sir, I'm eager to meet her.

SAINT-LOUP  *(Astonished, staring at her, then changing his mind)* In that case . . . *(He bows and moves away.)*

SUMÈNE  *(Stopping him)* What were you telling her?

SAINT-LOUP  I thought she was a young lady of good society. . . .

SUMÈNE  The best, her father is the leader of the right-wing faction. . . . And she's a close friend of Georgette Perrault.

SAINT-LOUP  She's a goer?

SUMÈNE  Not exactly: she's a galloper.

SAINT-LOUP  With you?

SUMÈNE  I jog . . . the streets . . . from eight on the dot. . . .

SAINT-LOUP  *(Moving away)* The preliminary atrocities.

## Scene 8

THE SAME , LINON DE LONDINE, *then* GILL NORVÈGE *and* MADAME ARMIDE

*(*TOURNY *who has gone to the upstage door,*

returns, hilarious, his hand in front of his mouth.)*

TOURNY  Pfff! Here they come, and him too! In evening dress!

ALL  Him?

SAINT-LOUP  And the signal?

TOURNY  White.

SAINT-LOUP  White, steady on! Perfect.

*(*LINON DE LONDINE, *a famous beauty, makes a noisy entrance. Very elegant, a big snob. Greetings, introductions, handshakes, except for* ROMAGNE, *who stays on the periphery.)*

LINON  Five minutes, I can only stay five minutes. My dogs are downstairs in the vestibule, they wouldn't go in the lift.

SAINT-LOUP  Seeing that it had a cage.

LINON  That's right. . . .

*(She sits down preciously, but almost immediately turns her head towards* GILL NORVÈGE *who enters, folowed by* MME ARMIDE. GILL, *40, looking very young and glabrous, his lips painted and outlined. He is in evening dress. A special elegance. A white chrysanthemum flowers in his buttonhole.* MME ARMIDE *is a mature individual, with tiny gestures, self-effacing.)*

GILL  *(To* MARTHE*)* A short visit, dear madam, before I dine at Prince Ibrahim's. . . . *(He shakes her hand and moves farther downstage, escorted by everyone, whom he squints at as if they were far away.)*

GEORGETTE  Good afternoon, Norvège.

GILL  Aha! Georgette Perrault!

GEORGETTE  You know I still have something to ask you in private.

GILL  Later, if you don't mind. . . . *(He moves farther downstage.)* What about you, Linon?

LINON  Dear master. . . . Did you get my last novel?

GILL  You know I did, Linon.

LINON  You see I have to tell you . . .

GILL  *(Weary)* Don't tell me, not today. . . . By the way, I dropped your name.

LINON  *(Charmed)* When was that?

GILL  Tomorrow, read it and thank me. *(He shakes* SAINT-LOUP*'s hand.)*

LINON  How can I thank you?

GILL  By being kind to me: send me some flowers you picked out yourself, come and tell me about your loves. . . .

LINON  Oh!

GILL  Your lovely loves. *(Seeing* MARTHE *nearby, he suddenly stops and stares at her at length.)*

SAINT-LOUP  What would you like to drink, whisky, straight from Danzig?

GILL  Might I have an eggnog? On behalf of my throat.

SAINT-LOUP  Marthe will whip one up for you; she's only too happy to!

GILL  *(Delicately putting his hand in his pocket)* My friends, I cannot shake all your hands. . . . There are too many of them! *(He pulls out a dainty handkerchief and dabs himself with it.)*

MADAME ARMIDE  You would wear yourself out by going to see that boxing match.

GILL  True enough. *(He installs himself in an armchair next to* LINON. *Everyone surrounds him. He remains silent, takes the pose of a 'man of sorrows', with affected elegance.)*

MARTHE  *(Bringing the drink, stirring it up in the glass with a straw)* Here you are. Is this what you wanted?

SAINT-LOUP  *(Sardonic, whisper to* MARTHE) Marthe, I'm pleased with you. . . .

MARTHE  Ha! ha!

*(She hands the glass to* GILL *who takes it without thanking her and starts to drink daintily, watching those around him with mild scorn.)*

TOURNY  I'd like a drink too, but easy on the milk for me. . . .

REINE  I'll find some spirits to raise your spirits: come on.

*(They head for the drinks table. The others remain to worship* GILL, *except for* ROMAGNE *who, on the periphery, cannot manage to disguise the disgust it all inspires in him.* GILL *slides a glance of curiosity in his direction.* SAINT-LOUP, *for his part, watches his friend stealthily.)*

GILL  *(Handing the empty glass to* SUMÈNE) Please.

SUMÈNE  *(Taking the glass and handing it to* BERGE) Do you mind, Berge?

BERGE  Of course not! *(Taking the glass and handing it to* SAINT-LOUP) Only too honoured!

SAINT-LOUP  *(Taking the glass and passing it to* MARTHE) The imprint of his lips!

*(MARTHE *puts the glass on the table.* BERGE *and* SAINT-LOUP *come down right.)*

BERGE  *(To* SAINT-LOUP) He drinks the way he thinks! Look at la Georgette whirling around him. . . . She's bright-eyed and bushy-tailed for Gill Norvège. Craving his blessing.

SAINT-LOUP  Surely she doesn't need that sort of thing any more.

BERGE  Yes, but they're all the same, until he's conferred fifty lines of soft-soap on them or let their hair down in a headline column, they don't think they've 'arrived'.

SAINT-LOUP  Incredible!

BERGE  Stop whining, you're already in Georgette Perrault's petticoats. Latch on to her garters, she's got long legs.

SAINT-LOUP  Pooh! her underwear's too frilly.

BERGE  Don't look down on cheap frills. Bah! let's be part of our times. It's not for us to judge.

SAINT-LOUP  You're turning into a social climber.

BERGE  Let me climb, I promise I'll stop once I've reached the top. Come on, I could do with some tea. . . .

*(They go back upstage.* ROMAGNE *comes forward to be near* MARTHE.)*

TOURNY  *(Who has drawn near* LINON DE LONDINE) You, you're copying the manners of Gill Norvège.

GILL  Copying me. Ah! God, you are witty.

TOURNY  The original is a unique.

GILL  You're going to make me angry, Tourny.

TOURNY  No offence meant . . .

MADAME ARMIDE  *(Running to* GILL) Oh! don't get excited, you're not supposed to.

GILL  *(Prettily)* Tourny, you are a nasty piece of work.

TOURNY  *(Laughing)* One of your productions then. *(He turns to* LINON.) And you, lovely Linon, yesterday you wouldn't open your door to me. . . .

LINON  I was having migraine.

TOURNY  Is that your girl-friend's name?

LINON  You really are rude, my dear! I'm telling you the truth.

GILL  Which is a luxury.

LINON  *(To* TOURNY) And since with you one has to be emphatic . . .

GILL  Do so, you're too flimsy, Linon.

TOURNY   True enough.

LINON   You're spoiling for a fight! But all right, I shall be emphatic. . . . Very well, my little white cat had just been brought to me – disembowelled . . . !

GILL   (*Almost turning ill, which makes* MADAME ARMIDE *hurry to him*) How ghastly. . . . How ghastly! And didn't you faint?

MADAME ARMIDE   Oh! good heavens!

LINON   (*Ingenuously*) No . . . I forgot to. . . . And besides, I was alone.

TOURNY   Well done. If you had let me in . . . you could have fainted.

GILL   Poor dear Lesbia! Some ruffian, I suppose?

LINON   Don't talk about it; she fell on to a kitchen knife . . .

GILL   (*Who appears to have the vapours*) God!

TOURNY   Impaled. . . . The pale imp or the death of the anguished angora of Linon De Londine. Sumène, you should compose a column on that; that'd earn you a fiver.

SUMÈNE   If you'd be willing to sign it, it would earn me fifty.

TOURNY   I'm on my way, boy. We'll drink up the profits.

GILL   (*Rising from the armchair using his wrists*) Don't bother, there's no need, I shall write of it myself. . . .

SAINT-LOUP   (*Returning to the group*) You?

GILL   Why not? It will amuse me. It might have died of love. (*He looks towards* ROMAGNE.) Love, all is love! (*He bangs his fists on the armchair.*) To love! . . . You know nothing about love, you moderns! . . .

LINON   (*Delighted, clapping her hands*) Are you really going to mention it?

GEORGETTE   (*Annoyed, to* SAINT-LOUP) Now I'm going to be passed over for a pussy-cat!

SAINT-LOUP   The dead always have a head-start on us. (*Aloud*) Marthe, my dear, would you send for a kitchen knife? (*General amazement*)

MARTHE   (*Nonplussed*) What did you say?

SAINT-LOUP   For Madame Georgette Perrault . . . desirous of following Lesbia in her glory.

(*A pause.* GILL *turns around and stares at* SAINT-LOUP, *then* GEORGETTE.)

GILL   (*Laughing*) Oh! you do amuse me! So be it! Madame Armide, remind me that tomorrow we must go to Georgette's dressing-room.

GEORGETTE   Ah!. . . Yes, there'll be flowers there, Norvège; there'll also be Adrien, that gymnast you find so charming, and those chocolates you're so fond of.

GILL   Then I shall come.

GEORGETTE   (*Squeezing* SAINT-LOUP'*s hand*) You've got brains, you do! Now I've got to run.

SAINT-LOUP   Why 'now'? You've got what you came for?

GEORGETTE   (*Squeezing his hand again*) Yes. (*She takes leave of* HENRIETTE.)

GILL   (*To* GEORGETTE) Are you going?

GEORGETTE   Yes. . . . (*She shakes his hand and goes upstage.*) Coming, Sumène?

SUMÈNE   (*His mouth full . . . holding a glass*) But . . . I haven't finished . . .

GEORGETTE   Then stay! I leave Henriette in your care.

SAINT-LOUP   One last cookie?

GEORGETTE   No, wait, a sugared almond. Thanks. Good-bye. (*She exits.*)

MARTHE   (*Escorting her*) Are you in such a hurry? . . . (*Her voice fades out in the corridor.*)

## Scene 9

THE SAME , *minus* GEORGETTE PERRAULT

MARTHE   (*Returning, to* SAINT-LOUP) You're turning this into a farce!

SAINT-LOUP   Leave me alone, I am out of favour today, the chrysanthemum is white. . . . What about you, where do you stand with him?

MARTHE   I don't know.

SAINT-LOUP   Come on. . . . (*He crosses down left and espies* HENRIETTE. *To* GILL) Do you know Mademoiselle de Villerville?

GILL   (*Aloof*) Guy de Villerville's daughter, I believe? . . . The Senate must be a torment for a man of his breeding.

(SAINT-LOUP *shrugs*)

HENRIETTE   Papa, no, he takes it rather well.

MARTHE   May I present another one of your admirers?

GILL   (*Ogling* ROMAGNE) You certainly may!

MARTHE   (*Trying to get* ROMAGNE *to move forward, but he resists being introduced*) A poet. . . .

(*But* ROMAGNE *hangs back*)

GILL *(Charmed)* A trifle shy. *(To* MARTHE*)* Very nice indeed! *(Aloud)* It's a fine thing to be a poet. . . .

ROMAGNE *(At a distance)* When you are a poet, it makes you feel more acutely the ugliness you encounter and you suffer all the more.

GILL *(Preciously)* Suffer all the more! You're telling me! I who am composed of tender feelings, who dreams only of beauty and who too often is forced to behold all sorts of ugliness! . . . Ah! ugliness, we are beset by ugliness. I do suffer from it . . . oh, how I suffer from it. . . . Madame Armide, have you got my vial of ether?

MADAME ARMIDE Here it is, but don't overdo it, you've already had plenty today.

*(At a gesture from* GILL*, the others withdraw, either upstage or to the buffet.* LINON*,* HENRIETTE *and* REINE *move into the next room.)*

MARTHE *(to* GILL*)* Oh! don't use too much. . . . *(She moves away a bit.)*

MADAME ARMIDE *(to* GILL*)* There's another one eager to take care of you!

GILL Isn't she though?

MADAME ARMIDE *(Urgently)* Naive, discreet . . . and . . . primed for action. It won't be your gentlemen friends, your noble lords, your male admirers or whatever who'll get us out of our fix. You have to showcase a woman to put them off the track.

GILL *(Pretending to inhale the ether to keep the others at bay)* But that's the only reason I'm here.

MADAME ARMIDE Really? . . . Who knows, that girl is peculiar.

GILL Why? Because her opinion of me runs counter to the one in circulation? . . .

MADAME ARMIDE The one you put in circulation. . . . Never mind, your exchequer is scraping bottom.

GILL I'm not impoverished.

MADAME ARMIDE No. But in another week you'll be rich in more than fifty thousand francs worth of scandal. . . .

GILL Tomorrow I shall show myself off at Georgette Perrault's.

MADAME ARMIDE Tomorrow, yes. . . . But today let that girl have her way.

GILL *(Bored)* Ah! you think so?

MARTHE *(Drawing near)* Oh! you're overdoing the ether.

GILL *(Returning the flask to* MADAME ARMIDE*)* Never enough . . . alas!

MARTHE If I dared, I would beg you to be more careful. . . . It will do you harm, I'm sure of it.

*(*MADAME ARMIDE *withdraws, but keeps an eye on them.)*

GILL And what do you care if it does me harm!

MARTHE True enough, you are an egoist. . . . It will do others harm.

GILL Oh! you're wrong about that.

MARTHE Listen to me, I'm not the same sort of woman they are, or perhaps you've already noticed that?

GILL Perhaps.

MARTHE I know that you are powerful, more feared than loved; too many people adore you for anyone ever to dream of loving you.

GILL Perhaps. *(He takes her hand.)* What about you?

MARTHE *(Proudly)* Why not me?

GILL Oh! indeed, indeed! You are a proud creature, a pretty creature, a pitiless creature, so they say . . . would you come to poor Norvège if he were defamed, detested? . . .

MARTHE Who defames you, who detests you?

GILL Everyone.

MARTHE Ah! . . . And what if someone said she was the exception.

GILL You?

MARTHE Yes. . . . Don't turn me away.

*(*SAINT-LOUP *is watching this scene from a distance, as is* ROMAGNE*.)*

GILL *(Taking* MARTHE*'s arm and leaning on her as they walk)* The lady friend of Gill Norvège, doesn't that frighten you?

MARTHE I have come of my own free will.

*(He draws her aside.)*

ROMAGNE *(Hurt and indignant)* Oh! oh!

GILL *(To* MARTHE*)* And we shall be friends?

MARTHE *(Resolutely)* Whatever you'd like. . . .

*(*GILL *makes a gesture which* MADAME ARMIDE *misunderstands; she runs to him.)*

MADAME ARMIDE   Did you want your ether?

GILL   Later. . . . *(Moving with* MARTHE *back to the armchairs at right)* Just who is that young man?

HENRIETTE   *(Coming out of the drawing-room)* Oh! she's monopolizing him!

BERGE   That is odd! *(He follows the couple with his eyes.)*

SUMÈNE   *(To* HENRIETTE*)* What do you think of him?

HENRIETTE   Very handsome.

SUMÈNE   Ah! . . . Still I'd prefer to look at you.

HENRIETTE   Don't be stupid, I'm speaking as a man. . . .

SUMÈNE   Ha, ha! as a man. . . . By the way, if you'd like to monopolize me the same way, I'm at your service, and you know, I'm said to have my attractions, as a man.

HENRIETTE   *(Moving away)* Keep quiet! *(She returns to the drawing-room.)*

TOURNY   Madame Armide is making the most of the food . . .

SUMÈNE   And the poet over there, look at him eating away . . . oblivious to what he's doing.

TOURNY   He don't seem to be able to swallow Gill though. Say, Saint-Loup.

SAINT-LOUP   What is it?

TOURNY   Your sister-in-law is monopolizing Norvège and I gotta talk to him.

SAINT-LOUP   Of course she is . . .

TOURNY   You're not surprised?

SAINT-LOUP   I am. I can barely recognize . . .

TOURNY   Our gentleman of the pans . . . of the chrysanthemums, eh?

*(*LINON DE LONDINE, REINE DE VIGNEUX, HENRIETTE *return from the drawing-room at this point.)*

LINON   We've just had our cards read.

SAINT-LOUP   And what did they foretell?

LINON   A marriage of two queens . . . to one another. There must have been a misdeal.

HENRIETTE   I'm sure there wasn't.

TOURNY   That's very funny!

LINON   And loss of money.

BERGE   Whose?

REINE   The king of diamonds.

BERGE   Your cards are pretty vague.

HENRIETTE   No, no more than usual.

SAINT-LOUP   True enough.

LINON   *(To* SAINT-LOUP*)* Do you enjoy seeing Gill ditch us for the sake of your sister-in-law?

SAINT-LOUP   Tremendously. . . . Would you like some more tea and cakes?

LINON   *(Disdainfully)* Oh! Madame Armide has polished them off, with the assistance of your poet.

REINE   I'm going. *(To* SAINT-LOUP*)* Shall I disturb them?

SAINT-LOUP   No, be careful! . . .

*(She moves away, he calls her back.)*

REINE   *(Charming)* What now?

SAINT-LOUP   *(Whisper)* I love you.

REINE   Oh! that's nice. *(False exit, she returns, and points out* GILL *and* MARTHE *to him)* This wouldn't happen to be jealousy, would it?

SAINT-LOUP   No.

REINE   In that case . . . I love you too. *(With a gesture, to* MARTHE*)* Good-bye.

MARTHE   *(Absent-mindedly)* Good-bye.

*(*REINE *exits.)*

## Scene 10

THE SAME, *minus* REINE DE VIGNEUX

SAINT-LOUP   Excuse me, Norvège, but our friends are beginning to complain that there's no more tea and not enough of you.

MARTHE   I shall return him to them. . . . *(She separates from* GILL*.)*

SAINT-LOUP   *(Whisper, to* MARTHE*)* And I was giving *you* advice!

MARTHE   *(Whisper)* Don't give me any more, please.

GILL   *(A weary and hieratic gesture)* It is late, Madame Armide.

MME ARMIDE   *(Closing a magazine she was reading)* I believe it is.

*(She exits upstage. Everyone surrounds* GILL *again.)*

SAINT-LOUP   Would you like a drink or something?

GILL   *(Capriciously)* No.

TOURNY   *(Drawing him aside)* Want to talk to me tonight about that thing you were asking about?

GILL   *(Fatigued)* Tonight? No.

LINON   Gill, would you like me to pick you up in my car and drive you to the wrestling matches?

GILL   No. . . . *(Resolved)* I'm leaving.

SAINT-LOUP  What?

GILL  (Looking at ROMAGNE) Don't cross-examine me . . . my nerves are shot, (Shaking his hand in farewell) really shot.

EVERYONE  (Crying out) So soon!

GILL  (Casting one last glance at ROMAGNE and, after a sigh) Come, Madame Armide . . .

MME ARMIDE  (Who brings GILL his elegant cape) Wait. Put your cape on before you go out.

GILL  Yes. (He indolently shoulders the cape, aided by MME ARMIDE and a few others.)

MME ARMIDE  Your scarf . . .

GILL  (Putting on the scarf) Thursday I shall be at home. (He heads upstage solemnly, following MME ARMIDE and accompanied by the others who simultaneously and very quickly take leave of SAINT-LOUP and MARTHE.)

TOURNY  I'm taking off too . . . dinner party.

LINON  I have to stop by the skating-rink.

SUMÈNE  I'm escorting Mademoiselle de Villerville. Are you coming, Berge?

BERGE  No, I'll stay a while, I haven't talked to Saint-Loup yet.

SUMÈNE  Neither have I, sorry but . . .

BERGE  (Shaking his hand and HENRIETTE's) Let's go then, let's go . . .

(They make their exits, surrounding GILL NORVÈGE. MARTHE accompanies them, as does BERGE. . . . SAINT-LOUP takes a few steps in their wake. ROMAGNE, without seeing him and thinking he is alone, shakes his fist indignantly at the upstage door.)

## Scene 11

SAINT-LOUP, ROMAGNE

SAINT-LOUP  (Returning) Well, well, well . . .

ROMAGNE  (Choking) Oh! . . . you . . .

SAINT-LOUP  (Smiling) Yes, I . . . (Offering him an armchair) Have a seat. A cigarette? (He settles into another armchair.) You aren't too put out?

ROMAGNE  (Abashed) How do you mean?

SAINT-LOUP  Everything you saw pained you, I can understand that. . . . (To himself) Still, once you're inured to it, you stop noticing. You're too far inside it to observe it. They are rather a disgraceful lot, aren't they?

ROMAGNE  (Astonished) But . . .

SAINT-LOUP  Gill Norvège disgusts me too, for all his talent.

ROMAGNE  (Enthusiastically) You too?

SAINT-LOUP  But I need him; we all need him. He is all-powerful. Would you believe it?

ROMAGNE  It's outrageous.

SAINT-LOUP  It's how things are. . . . None of us is strong enough to resist. To do that you'd have to be totally independent. . . . Alas! (A pause) Why are you looking at me that way?

ROMAGNE  Excuse me, it's as if I had never seen you before.

SAINT-LOUP  Ah! so, could it be you take me for a Sumène or a Tourny?

ROMAGNE  Of course not.

SAINT-LOUP  You should have stayed in your mountains.

ROMAGNE  I think you're right.

SAINT-LOUP  You're better off there! Anyone is, far away from here. . . . You see, I'm too sensitive, there are some things I still can't accept, things that revolt me. And sometimes I suffer here, you have no idea.

ROMAGNE  (Convinced) Oh! I do.

SAINT-LOUP  (Drawing closer to him) Anyway, things happen, old man, let's not talk about them any more. Tell me about your plans. . . . Oh! there are too many lights here; hard to feel at home. (He gets up and puts out a few lights.) There, let's create a little intimacy. . . . (MARTHE is heard singing offstage. ROMAGNE quivers. SAINT-LOUP observes him for a moment and recovers.) Ah! so . . . (Abruptly, staring him in the face.) You've taken a shine to Marthe.

ROMAGNE  You guessed it then?

SAINT-LOUP  Damn!

ROMAGNE  Pardon?

SAINT-LOUP  I said damn!

ROMAGNE  (Distressed) What of it?

SAINT-LOUP  What of it, what of it, I couldn't see it coming! But then, whom have you chosen to love, my poor old chap? . . . An eccentric creature . . . basically very naive, but she stubbornly refuses to recognize that fact.

ROMAGNE  Listen, don't spoil her for me.

SAINT-LOUP  (Gesture) So you love her 'passionately'?

ROMAGNE  (Sad but positive) Yes.

SAINT-LOUP  Hell! . . . For crying out loud, with your looks, your personality, you had a winning hand.

ROMAGNE  Ah!

SAINT-LOUP   Would you like to win her?

ROMAGNE   Of course! . . . She isn't in love with anyone else?

(SAINT-LOUP *makes a vague but angry gesture and a muffled exclamation.*)

ROMAGNE   Is that a no?

SAINT-LOUP   It's a yes, sort of . . .

ROMAGNE   Gill Norvège? (*Sorrowfully*) Oh! that man!

SAINT-LOUP   He can't be a rival!

ROMAGNE   (*Candidly*) But if she loves him.

SAINT-LOUP   It takes more than that. . . . (*A pause*) No, why couldn't you have told me this right away, instead of letting me encourage her in that ridiculous love. . . .

ROMAGNE   What? You encouraged her?

SAINT-LOUP   Yes, out of revenge, spite . . . I loved her myself . . . madly!

ROMAGNE   Oh! my poor friend, I didn't know.

SAINT-LOUP   It doesn't matter. Never mind. . . . But, as for you, I'm afraid it's too late.

ROMAGNE   (*Crushed*) Ah!

SAINT-LOUP   No, what a long face! . . . Listen: wait!

ROMAGNE   I'd rather leave Paris.

SAINT-LOUP   Stay with us instead. . . . Why . . . if I were you . . .

ROMAGNE   Well?

SAINT-LOUP   Well, instead of running away, I'd go ahead, I would get the upper hand even over myself . . . I . . .

ROMAGNE   Ah!

SAINT-LOUP   Far from hiding, I would be conspicuous everywhere . . . I would . . . go for it . . .

ROMAGNE   (*Astonished*) What's come over you?

SAINT-LOUP   (*Sadly*) Ah! true enough . . . I was putting myself in your place, I would win Marthe's love.

(MARTHE's *singing is heard again.*)

ROMAGNE   (*After a pause, with effort, to himself*) Yes, I will stay.

## Scene 12

ROMAGNE, SAINT-LOUP, BERGE

BERGE   (*Entering*) Did Marthe come into some money? . . . She's in such a cheerful mood!

SAINT-LOUP   A fortune! And to think I sold her the lottery ticket! . . . Haul yourself over here, Germain, I'll introduce you to Romagne. I didn't introduce you earlier because I wanted to let him pass the test on his own. This was the first time he'd come in contact with those people. I insisted on letting him shift for himself. (*To* ROMAGNE.) You were pitiful.

ROMAGNE   I'm flattered.

BERGE   Bravo!

SAINT-LOUP   Shut up, you! . . . Instead, give him some good advice. . . . (*Pointing to the right*) Wait. . . . Go over there and talk, babble about poetry. As for me, I'm going to write my humour column. (*He moves away a bit.*) What about Marthe? (*Looking at* ROMAGNE) I ought to talk to him . . . all the same. (*He snaps his fingers in annoyance, and, while the young men move away, goes to the upstage door and calls.*) Marthe! . . . Marthe?

*Curtain*

## Act II

GILL NORVÈGE's *home*

An interior both very arty and very "tarty." *Art nouveau* furniture. Paintings by masters. Bookcases on both sides of the fireplace. Small round tables centre. A great quantity of flowers, especially assorted chrysanthemums in all sorts of vases. On a large table left, lots of newspapers, books and letters, a small vase of orchids. Door downstage right and left, door upstage. Window in the corner right, opening onto a garden. A stylish sofa downstage.

## Scene 1

GILL , EDGARD

As the curtain rises, GILL and EDGARD, his secretary, are opening the mail. GILL is dressed in an at-home suit of violet, of a very fantastical cut, open over a silk shirt and a lace jabot. EDGARD is a slender, supple young man, his face clean-shaven beneath dark ringlets.

GILL   (*Looking at the clock*) Almost four. Is there much more?

EDGARD   All of this, look.

GILL   Toss it, toss it. . . . Uh, no, let me see it first.

EDGARD   (*Scornfully*) Women's handwriting!

GILL   (*Picking up a letter and reading it*) Toss it, toss it. . . .

EDGARD   (*Suddenly, rising a bit*) Master . . . Master?

GILL   What?

EDGARD   It's good of you, Master, to let me live here with you.

GILL   (*Reading, worried*) Yes, yes, it is good of me . . .

EDGARD   (*Taking courage, more scornful*) Are those letters all that interesting?

GILL   Oh, for heaven's sake, boy, don't be absurd!

EDGARD   (*Emphatic*) No, no, I'm not being absurd, but . . .

GILL   (*Preoccupied, interrupting him*) Let's move on to the newspapers.

EDGARD   (*Handing him a stack picked up from a round table*) There, I've underlined every mention of you.

GILL   The whole stack!

EDGARD   (*Admiring*) The whole stack, yes.

GILL   (*Laughing*) Ah! they're concerned about me.

## Scene 2

THE SAME, MADAME ARMIDE, *entering left*

MME ARMIDE   Others are also concerned about you.

GILL   Ah! there you are! What's your news?

MME ARMIDE   Bad news. What are you going to do? (GILL *gets up with a gesture of anger.*) Gracious, what a mess! It's a common enough mistake to underestimate the temper of your creditors. You chose yours very badly. But if you were anyone else . . .

GILL   Which means?

MME ARMIDE   Which means that someone else, another man, whatever, would have known how to get out of this.

GILL   Don't you realize that if I make my financial embarrassments known, we lose our credit.

MME ARMIDE   Credit that's already exhausted! Besides, you know there's a way out. All you have to do is find a woman in your crowd who . . .

EDGARD   (*Irritated*) Ah! excuse me while I laugh . . .

MADAME ARMIDE   (*Looking at* EDGARD) A woman . . . you know this already . . . yes, a woman. All great artists have always been surrounded by them.

GILL   I have all the women.

MADAME ARMIDE   All and none. . . . Not an individual one.

GILL   Oh, go to blazes! After all, you're a woman, get me out of this mess.

MADAME ARMIDE   Instead I'm going to lock the front door.

GILL   Don't. Someone may show up today. Did you order the cakes?

MADAME ARMIDE   The cakes are here. The pastry-cook wrapped them up in his bill. A baker who wants his dough.

GILL   So witty, Madame Armide.

MADAME ARMIDE   To keep up with you.

GILL   What about the bonbons?

MADAME ARMIDE   Here they are. It's a pity we don't like the same kind. (*She takes a caramel and shoves it in her mouth.*) Until the day we can no longer indulge.

GILL   We shall go on indulging, Madame Armide. Let some time pass. We shall emerge from this deadlock.

MADAME ARMIDE   From this dead end. How? Oh, Lord, where will this end?

GILL   So selfish, you're afraid to be deprived of comforts and attention.

MADAME ARMIDE   You bully me. Oh! Lord. . . . And I do so much. . . . What would become of you if not for me? . . . I left Arlette de Sangoli for you; and she treated me like her mother!

GILL   She was paying you to play that role. The reason you're here is to . . . to go out with me and see to my health.

MADAME ARMIDE   And I wish I could have seen to the health of your budget. . . . Oh dear, are we sick! At least Arlette de Sangoli had a lover. You don't even have a woman, one woman!

GILL   Leave us to ponder, and go prepare our collation.

EDGARD   Oof!

MADAME ARMIDE   (*To* EDGARD) Easy for you to breathe. *You'll* never want for anything in this house!

EDGARD   (*Laughing*) Ha, ha!

MADAME ARMIDE   And you won't even try and help us out. . . . Do you have any ideas?

EDGARD   No.

MADAME ARMIDE   (*Testily*) I'd better go. . . . Ah! if only Arlette were here. . . . But the danger isn't so great that we have to let her in on our affairs. . . . (*She leaves repeating*) A woman . . .

## Scene 3

THE SAME, *minus* MADAME ARMIDE

GILL  *(to* EDGARD) Quick, let's proceed. . . .
*(*EDGARD *brings him the papers; he leafs through one.)* Ah! Here it is. *(He hands* EDGARD *the paper.)* Read it?

EDGARD  No. *(He takes the paper, reads and is outraged)* Why, this is infamous! Who is the wretch? . . .

GILL  *(Laughing)* Tourny. Don't get upset. It's useful.

EDGARD  *(Sincere)* You think so?

GILL  People only attack the strong. *(He passes his hand across his brow languidly.)* I must be a muscle-man.

EDGARD  *(Bleating)* Master . . .

GILL  Yes, I *am* a master, a master of perspicacity. I might have been nothing but a talent, oh, dear, dear, dear . . . but I had instinct. That's what's needed nowadays, a man who says what he wants, writes what he wants, sets the tone. . . . The man Paris finds indispensable. The *de luxe* model of a man, eh! So I handed my private life over to them. Better. I live in a glass cage so that everyone can see me. Better yet, I live entirely for them, my tastes are entirely for them, my vices are entirely for them, they may not care for them but in the end they find them as thrilling as those of a spoiled child. I talk to them about nothing but me. Everything about me interests them, the colour of my clothes, the people I see, my favourite restaurant, the little shoeshine boy who blacked my boots at the corner of the Rue Royale. . . . If I stayed home with you, I'd talk instead about your eyes, your beautiful hair. . . .

EDGARD  Master . . .

GILL  Or the sensual orchids that embellish my table. . . . And I've been successful. . . . All the women read me. . . . By the way, do you know Marthe Bourdon?

EDGARD  *(Particular emphasis)* A slut!

GILL  *(Shrugging his shoulders, making a weary face)* No, no, not at all. . . . She's a paragon!!

EDGARD  *(Anguished)* What do you mean?

GILL  She has a passionate crush on me!

EDGARD  *(Grimacing)* Ah!

GILL  Ah! listen, there's no need to be more fastidious than I am! *(Mocking)* She's very nice, this Marthe Bourdon. . . . Given her heart to no one up to now, so they say. . . . It's very flattering, after all.

EDGARD  You think so?

GILL  Do I think so! *(Dreamily)* . . . Besides . . . *(Changing his tone)* Tell me, did that fellow Durch come back?

EDGARD  He did. . . . He's a villain. He dared to make threats. . . . I threw him out, he was filthy.

GILL  *(Scratching his brow)* And he wants thirty thousand.

EDGARD  Forty.

GILL  Oh, yes, that's right, forty . . . Well! I don't have forty on hand at the moment! No, people of his sort are amazing, they think one has the wherewithal to pay them, just like that!

EDGARD  They're disgusting!

GILL  I'd like to see them keep up the pace I keep. . . . And nobody, nobody will help me out. . . . They don't even pay my expenses. . . . Is he coming back tomorrow?

EDGARD  Yes. And he threatens to mount an opposition to your columns. . . .

GILL  So that I'll have to blackmail him in turn. . . . Oh, no, no!

EDGARD  What then?

GILL  *(Unguardedly)* What then, what then, I'll have to find someone. . . . *(Letting his thought run its course)* Yes, I do make mistakes about people. And you want me to get rid of the women. No, no, Armide is right, one woman will do. . . .

EDGARD  Oh!

GILL  Shut up. I don my mask again. It has to be pink today. . . . The latest whim of Gill Norvège. . . . Come on, let's hurry and get through this mail. . . . *(He leafs through the letters, news clippings.)*

## Scene 4

THE SAME, MADAME ARMIDE

MADAME ARMIDE  *(Returning)* Someone's come in by the garden gate. *(Whisper to* GILL) She's here. . . .

GILL  *(Looking at the clock)* Five o'clock, yes. *(To* EDGARD) Get rid of all these papers. *(He takes a part in this and moves to the window, raising its curtain.)* Madame Armide, our role is secondary, the lady is escorted by a young man. *(Aside)* I expected as much!

MADAME ARMIDE  *(Looking)* That poet. If you knew a way to pry her away from him . . .

*(A pause)*

GILL   I'll find a way. *(The bell rings.)* There they are. *(*MADAME ARMIDE *goes to the entrance. He runs off carrying the papers. Just as he exits right, he turns to* EDGARD *and points to the vases of chrysanthemums.)* Display the mauve ones. . . . *(He exits.)*

## Scene 5

EDGARD, MARTHE, ROMAGNE

*(*EDGARD *changes the placement of the flowers.* MARTHE BOURDON *and* ROMAGNE *enter.* ROMAGNE *is fretful, miserable, he casts a hostile glance at the walls. He is carrying a book.)*

EDGARD   *(imperious and aggressive, putting a vase of mauve chrysanthemums on the table)* Gill Norvège will not be here for another fifteen minutes.
ROMAGNE   *(with effort)* Are we intruding?
EDGARD   No . . . no. . . . He isn't in the mood to receive until then, that's all. . . .
MARTHE   *(Aside, questioning)* Mauve chrysanthemums? *(Aloud)* Your master is indisposed?
EDGARD   *(Indignant)* My master? *(Correcting)* The master is not indisposed, I would have told you. . . . *(Scornfully)* You have only to wait like everyone else. *(He exits.)*

## Scene 6

THE SAME, *minus* EDGARD

MARTHE   How tiresome!
ROMAGNE   Since we're alone, let me repeat: all I desire, all I ask of you is to believe that the feelings I have for you are sincere. . . . Yes, I do love you. Why should that offend you?
MARTHE   I'm not offended. *(Waving a glove)* There's nothing offensive about it. And, for my part, I believe I deserve to be loved.
ROMAGNE   Well then?
MARTHE   *(Continuing)* You don't need to apologize for loving me.
ROMAGNE   Apologize? I never did that!
MARTHE   I do deserve your love, believe me. . . .
ROMAGNE   *(Relieved)* Oh! I'm so . . .
MARTHE   *(With a decided chilliness)* However I want no part of it.
ROMAGNE   *(Downcast)* Huh?!

MARTHE   I want no part of it. Not that it isn't very pleasant. . . . *(Sitting)* Your love has a lot in common with you in that respect.
ROMAGNE   *(With a wry smile)* Oh! thanks ever so.
MARTHE   Yes, yes. . . . And I do feel something for you I have never felt for the others. . . . Why do you look at me like that?
ROMAGNE   I'm waiting.
MARTHE   Where was I? Oh, yes, the something I feel is . . . flattered gratitude. . . . True, I am grateful to you for loving me; coming from the others, it got on my nerves, but coming from you, it gives me pleasure.
ROMAGNE   Oh! keep talking: it's the first time you haven't lumped me with the others. . . . So I do have some hope.
MARTHE   Oh no, no, don't have hope . . . take a friend's advice, don't have hope. All I'll say is, if you've got nothing better to do, well, go on loving me, you have my permission, it doesn't bother me. . . . *(Bursts out laughing)* Ha, ha! you are funny. Now you're happy.
ROMAGNE   I love you, by special authorization.
MARTHE   *(Flirting)* Go ahead.
ROMAGNE   *(Coming close to her)* The fact that I can say it to you is terrific.
MARTHE   *(Watching the doors)* But that's not the reason you escorted me here. Bear that in mind. I want to be useful to you. Complain of me after that!
ROMAGNE   Thanks, but . . .
MARTHE   I'm being frank. You have to earn me, by becoming a somebody. What have you done?
ROMAGNE   Nothing.
MARTHE   Yes, you have. You've written a book: it's not much, but yours is a good book. You have to get Gill Norvège to put a price on it.
ROMAGNE   What for?
MARTHE   Gill Norvège dispenses fame! To win him over is almost the same as capturing Paris, and then you're in . . .
ROMAGNE   *(Impatient, grabbing her arms)* Listen . . .

*(The doorbell rings.)*

MARTHE   *(Quickly)* Ssh, behave. You've got to be serious and try to achieve success.
ROMAGNE   I've got to, I've got to! Ha, success! If it were success with you! Well, I

escorted you here for your pleasure. Otherwise I never would have come.

MARTHE They all say that, and they all make a mad dash to get here!

ROMAGNE For pity's sake, don't make fun of me, I love you.

*(More ringing)*

MARTHE *(Gesture)* Hush! hush!

## Scene 7

MARTHE, ROMAGNE, SUMÈNE *and* LANTIGNY, *an old fop, a mincing caricature with feline gestures*

SUMÈNE *(First to enter)* Good afternoon. *(He shakes hands with* ROMAGNE, *then* MARTHE.) And where has the great man got to?

LANTIGNY *(Greeting* ROMAGNE *and going to present his respects to* MARTHE) He's been sighted on the horizon.

SUMÈNE *(Indicating the side doors)* Ah, yes! . . . Perhaps he's busy digesting Tourny's article. . . . Did you read the "Three Star" this morning?

LANTIGNY *(Vaguely)* Yes, yes . . .

SUMÈNE Tough, but fair, right? *(Movement from* MARTHE) First of all, my dear Monsieur Lantigny, you are too much one of his circle, and too musical at that to appreciate it. . . . Never mind, I have a feeling that Tourny had a collaborator. . . .

ROMAGNE Who would that be?

SUMÈNE Gill Norvège.

ROMAGNE *(Shocked)* No! you think so?

SUMÈNE In any hatchet-job that systematic, o neophytes, learn to read between the lines.

MARTHE Would you happen to have that article on you?

LANTIGNY, SUMÈNE, ROMAGNE *(Simultaneously pulling the paper out of their pockets)* Here!

MARTHE One will do! *(She takes one and, shrugging, sits somewhere to the side.)*

SUMÈNE Anyhow, Tourny's going to be here presently.

*(GILL, a hand in the pocket of his jacket, a cigarette in his mouth, gently opens the door right, without being seen, and steps forward.)*

## Scene 8

THE SAME, GILL

GILL And why shouldn't Tourny come here? *(The others start.)* What has he done? . . . I'll wager he's uttered some more obscenities about me. Tell me what they are.

MARTHE They are all such cowards!

GILL *(Very amiably)* Oh! it's you! How are you? *(He goes to her, takes her hand and gently kisses it.* ROMAGNE *mimes a gesture of anger.* GILL *notices it and turns towards him, smiling.)* And this young man? *(He stares at him, squinting.)*

MARTHE Jacques Romagne has come to present you with his latest volume.

*(Seeing that* ROMAGNE *is about to steal away, she turns to him abruptly. He makes no gesture. Then she takes the volume from his hands. He is loath to give it up, she snatches it from him.* GILL, *who has watched this scene closely, takes the volume from* MARTHE's *hands.)*

GILL Look, it's slightly dented. . . . Well, I shall try to read it. Come back and talk about it with me.

ROMAGNE Oh! don't read it! For heaven's sake. In fact *(He holds out his hand)*, give it back to me!

GILL *(Withholding the book, impish)* Not for the world! *(*ROMAGNE *takes another step towards him.)* Come back. Come, if you like, tomorrow, I'll be waiting for you. . . . *(Displaying the volume)* You can write a dedication. . . .

ROMAGNE Oh, it's not worth the trouble.

GILL It is, it is.

ROMAGNE *(Who can't contain himself any longer)* No . . . no . . .

MARTHE *(Offended by him)* Don't be silly!

*(*ROMAGNE *is about to lose control.* SUMÈNE *runs to him and restrains him.)*

SUMÈNE Are you crazy?

ROMAGNE No, I am not crazy. . . .

*(GILL *joins* MARTHE *who makes excuses)*

SUMÈNE *(to* ROMAGNE) Take it easy . . . take it easy!

ROMAGNE *(Turning around, savagely)* Excuse me. . . .

SUMÈNE My poor boy, you'll do yourself an injury.

ROMAGNE   I can't help it! . . . I don't know any more . . .

LANTIGNY   (*Drawing near them, to* SUMÈNE) The atmosphere's too stormy here, I'm off. I'll just slip out.

SUMÈNE   Just a minute! (*To* ROMAGNE) Run away when he does.

ROMAGNE   That's all I ask. (*To* LANTIGNY) I'll leave with you, Monsieur. (*They take leave of* SUMÈNE *who accompanies them upstage.* GILL *follows* ROMAGNE *with his eyes.*)

## Scene 9

GILL, MARTHE, TOURNY, *then* MME ARMIDE, SUMÈNE *and* EDGARD

GILL   (*to* MARTHE) The boy's a wee bit fierce. (*On seeing* TOURNY *come in, who is somewhat astonished to have bumped into* ROMAGNE) Good, here comes the other one, now!

(SUMÈNE *follows* TOURNY. EDGARD *enters next, behind* MME ARMIDE. GILL *leaves* MARTHE *and goes to* TOURNY; *he takes him by the arm and leads him downstage, speaking in an undertone.*)

GILL   . . . Even so you said more than was proper. It'll turn the younger generation against me.

TOURNY   (*Patently drunk*) And how! . . . Ah! listen, butch, once I get started, I write whatever comes into my head.

GILL   Too much came into your head. And I don't like it, particularly today.

TOURNY   Oh, tough!

GILL   You're drunk! You've come from a bar-room again.

TOURNY   Think so? Maybe. (*Aloud*) Anyway, if you ain't happy with it . . . (*He drops his arm and takes a stand in front of him*) you can always challenge me to a duel. . . .

GILL   Pardon me?

MADAME ARMIDE   (*Running over*) My God, what's going on?

TOURNY   You leave the menfolk's talk, Duchess.

MADAME ARMIDE   Good grief!

SUMÈNE   (*Bustling around them*) What's going on?

TOURNY   Sumène, come have a drink.

SUMÈNE   What's wrong with you?

GILL   I was wondering that myself.

TOURNY   (*Letting it all out*) He is accusin' me of being the "Three Stars" this morning. (*He pulls a paper from his pocket and waves it in the air.*)

EDGARD   Master, they're insulting you again!

GILL   Me? I haven't even read it!

EDGARD   Yes, yes, this is the gentleman who dared . . .

TOURNY   This gentleman! You can get stuffed. (*He tries to kick him in the behind.*)

SUMÈNE   (*Catching hold of* TOURNY) Calm down!

EDGARD   He's still drunk!

GILL   (*Trembling a bit, very feminine*) My dear chap, do me the favour of sleeping off your wine somewhere else. I shall read your article later. (*He suddenly recovers, and, very high and mighty, marches on* TOURNY *who retreats.*) Much, much later!

TOURNY   I get it, I'll beat it. Who's gonna go with me? . . . Nobody! Good night! . . . (*He exits.*)

GILL   (*Coming back and dropping into an armchair, pulling out his handkerchief and fanning himself with it*) Oof!

## Scene 10

THE SAME, *minus* TOURNY

MADAME ARMIDE   The skunk, the skunk, the skunk!

MARTHE   It's insane. You should have had your servant slap his face.

GILL   Drop it, drop it . . .

EDGARD   I will slap him myself.

SUMÈNE   (*Ironically*) You owe him one!

GILL   I'm exhausted, my children, you must all leave me.

MADAME ARMIDE   Are you in pain?

GILL   A bit. (*Whisper to* MARTHE) Come back right away, if you will, you can look after me.

(MARTHE, *triumphant and happy, acquiesces with a gesture and presses his hand.*)

SUMÈNE   We're off.

GILL   That's right, leave me alone. (*In a faltering voice*) Sumène, be prepared to second me in this affair. Ah! how tiresome! I'd shoot him if it weren't too disgusting to bore a hole in such a beer-barrel!

SUMÈNE   I'm at your service. What about Lantigny?

GILL    Impossible, his principles formally prevent him from being my second.

SUMÈNE    *(Whisper to* MARTHE*)* Let me tell you what they call his principles!

*(*GILL *gestures toward the upstage door; they leave, accompanied by* MADAME ARMIDE*.)*

## Scene 11

GILL, EDGARD

EDGARD    *(Rushing to* GILL*)* You're going to fight a duel!

GILL    I am? Who told you that? As if I had the time to stoop to his level! . . . Oh, by the way, Marthe is going to come back.

EDGARD    Marthe? That woman?

GILL    Yes, and I insist that you give her a warm welcome. . . . She is refined, shrewd and 'smitten'. . . . She'll know how to shut them up. And then . . .

EDGARD    And then?

GILL    And then there is another thing . . . *(He stops suddenly, looking at* EDGARD*.)*

EDGARD    She has a lover?

GILL    No . . . quite the contrary . . . but who knows? *(A pause)* Let's talk about something else. You told me Durch is supposed to show up again tomorrow.

EDGARD    Yes, but I didn't promise him anything.

GILL    *(Annoyed)* That doesn't alter the situation. *(Listening)* Someone's coming upstairs. *(Making a quick exit)* Give her a warm welcome . . . I insist. *(He exits through the door left.)*

## Scene 12

EDGARD, MARTHE

MARTHE    *(Confused to find* EDGARD*)* Oh! excuse me . . . Monsieur Norvège isn't alone?

EDGARD    He is, madame. . . .

MARTHE    Ah! . . . May I see him, I'd like to talk to him . . .

EDGARD    *(Hands in his pockets, impertinent)* He'll be back. . . . *(Sarcastic)* Do have a seat!

MARTHE    Ah!

EDGARD    *(Between his teeth)* So he relies on you that much!

MARTHE    *(Shocked)* Pardon?

EDGARD    *(About to speak, but doesn't)* Nothing! *(He sits at some distance from her*

*and watches her. She watches him. Embarrassed silence which should be comic. A pause.)*

## Scene 13

THE SAME, GILL

GILL    *(Aloud, feigning surprise)* What! are you here!

MARTHE    *(Approaching him, smiling, her hand held out)* So you see.

GILL    *(To* EDGARD*)* Leave us alone, my boy. . . .

EDGARD    *(Drily)* Very good. *(He leaves in a rage.)*

## Scene 14

GILL, MARTHE

MARTHE    Here I am.

GILL    It's good of you to come back.

MARTHE    You didn't expect me to?

GILL    Yes and no. . . . How can one tell with women?

MARTHE    *(Looking at him, smiling)* Oh, don't say that, you can always tell. . . . Despite what people say about you.

GILL    What do they say about me?

MARTHE    Of course, you have a deplorable reputation.

GILL    *(Smiling)* Ah, yes! . . . *(Bored and with a vague gesture)* Still, you came all the same.

MARTHE    *(Candidly)* Yes, . . . I'm not afraid of tattle. . . . But, may I forget your standing as an author and a celebrity?

GILL    Ye gods! let's forget it, let's forget it with all our might and main.

MARTHE    Well then, you impress me as being a big baby.

GILL    I am one.

MARTHE    I'm glad you admit it.

GILL    I admit everything. It's a habit of mine. So I will admit that I'm peeved with you on account of young Romagne. You should teach him better manners.

MARTHE    I brought him here at your request; I never expected him to make such a scene. I am still confused and puzzled by it. For heaven's sake, how do I get you to forgive me? . . . Deep down I'm just an ordinary woman.

GILL    *(Coarsely)* That's true.

MARTHE    Would you like me to go?

GILL    Of course not. . . . *(He sighs, then,*

*resolved, he pulls forward an armchair for her.)* Sit down. Why do you look at me with those eyes?

MARTHE   They're the only ones I have. . . . Yes, you are a big baby. And I feel attracted towards you. There's something mysterious about you . . . a mystery that charms me.

GILL   Indeed!

*(MARTHE sits in the armchair, very moved, taking GILL's hand to draw him to her. He remains standing, unresponsive, and drops her hand.)*

MARTHE   Ah! what is pricking me? . . . The hat! *(Taking it off)* Sorry, I'll take it off.

*(She gives it to GILL.)*

GILL   *(Crossing to put the hat on a table, somewhat anxious)* Was it misbehaving?

MARTHE   *(Who goes and sits on the sofa, flirtatiously)* What if it was? *(Summoning him with a gesture)* Come here. You're allowed.

GILL   I should hope so.

MARTHE   Come here, next to me, if I'm not unworthy of it.

GILL   *(Approaching slowly, shaking his head)* What a woman you are!

MARTHE   Of course I am. . . . Don't you like it?

GILL   *(Rather enigmatically)* I'm mad about it. *(He moves felinely, and sits negligently beside her.)*

MARTHE   How good it feels here! It's as if you perfume the air. . . .

*(He smiles. She lets her hands droop towards him; he takes them.)*

GILL   You'll lend them to me?

MARTHE   *(abandoning herself)* Since we have to give in to your whims.

*(He takes her fingers one by one, observes them minutely and caresses them.)*

GILL   They are dainty.

MARTHE   You think so. *(Sighing)* Ah! *(A pause)* Perhaps they became even daintier today for your sake.

GILL   No one, absolutely no one can sense, no one knows how to sense the poetry of hands better than I. (MARTHE, *her eyes half-closed, lies back a bit, waiting for a kiss which*

*never comes.)* Your fingers are slender. *(He kisses them.)* Oh! such rosy nails. . . . Look, a white patch, a truly telling mark. You must have a taste for vice.

MARTHE   Perhaps.

GILL   *(Continuing the examination)* They are like a complex of individual entities, each with its own charm, its special contour.

MARTHE   *(Leaning back and sighing)* Ah!

GILL   The joints are barely visible. . . .

MARTHE   *(Withdrawing her hand)* Excuse me, are you making love or giving an anatomy lesson?

GILL   But . . .

MARTHE   *(Delicately provocative)* My hands . . . only my hands have the power to attract you?

GILL   *(Murmuring)* Not so fast. . . . Oh!

MARTHE   What's wrong?

GILL   Nothing, it'll pass.

MARTHE   *(Looking at him)* What a woman you are!

GILL   *(Stiffening a bit)* Beg pardon?

MARTHE   I said perhaps we ought to switch roles.

GILL   Perhaps . . . you're going a bit far.

MARTHE   It annoys you?

GILL   On the contrary. *(A short pause)* I thought, given what people say about you . . .

MARTHE   Yes, I am frigid, I know. Do you want me to dot all my i's?

GILL   Dot them . . . gently.

MARTHE   All right, I do need love, of course I do. But I want a love capable of satisfying my pride, and since today . . . I have the chance . . .

GILL   I should be very flattered, should I?

MARTHE   Very.

GILL   Hell!

MARTHE   Don't make fun. Being the great artist that you are, you mustn't make fun. *(Flirting)* Not to mention that the gift is worth the taking. *(She rests her elbows on him.)*

GILL   Of course, of course . . . *(A pause)*

MARTHE   *(Rising abruptly)* You must be made of marble!

GILL   *(Not moving, with aplomb)* Thank heaven I am, you won't make me blush.

MARTHE   I make you blush, do I! *(Laughing, somewhat nervously)* Ho, ho! . . . No, there's nothing commonplace about you.

GILL   That's right, tear me to pieces like all the journalists. Actually, I ought to be more worried about them.

MARTHE   Will you fight a duel?

GILL   So it seems. *(Weary, very 'feminine')* You can't imagine. *(Pretending sorrow)* A person thinks he's understood and then . . . *(He flicks his middle finger.)*

MARTHE   Oh! excuse me. You're right. I'm sorry, I wasn't thinking. . . . But if you'd like . . .

GILL   If I'd like?

MARTHE   To have Marthe Bourdon for a friend. . . .

GILL   A rather rude friend.

MARTHE   I had a moment of madness, passion, abandon. I thought that was what you'd need . . . I surrender to you. Understand me in return!

GILL   *(Bored)* Of course.

MARTHE   What do you want of me then? *(GILL doesn't answer.)* What's wrong now? Why are you looking at me like that? . . . You have some funny ways of looking at people, I must say!

GILL   Flirt! *(Abruptly)* I want nothing of you.

MARTHE   Oh! . . . Still I can guess that the Gentleman of the Chrysanthemums is unhappy, he must be miserable, he's worried about something.

GILL   *(Brutally)* Something outstanding! Well, yes! *(He rises, puts his hands in his pockets and strides back and forth, speaking to the ceiling.)* Yes, Gill Norvège, the plaything of Paris, the object of envy, the man all his colleagues drool over, has his problems like everybody else, problems which won't wait. *(Bitterly)* He dons his smile, he gives of himself and keeps on giving. He is hated. . . . You've just had a demonstration of that.

MARTHE   Yes, that's true.

GILL   You see, I unbosom myself to you, you should be pleased!

MARTHE   *(Seriously)* No.

GILL   *(Ironic)* No?

MARTHE   How malicious you are! I come to you as a friend. . . .

GILL   Well, I've spoken to you as a friend.

MARTHE   No, no. Come here and ask my pardon for your malice. *(A pause)*

GILL   *(Coming back to her)* Fair enough, I have been malicious, poor child, forgive me. You know . . . I just don't know . . . tedium, annoyances . . . give me your hands. There, thank you. That's good. . . .

MARTHE   Poor friend! . . .

GILL   There's so much affection in you! You have a fragrant soul.

MARTHE   The things you say!

GILL   My dear, let us forget men and their brutality. Ah! I feel at peace, serene. And yet if you knew . . . if you only knew all that was in me of sorrow, pain, vulnerability to life's hard knocks. *(Grimace of disgust)* Ah, sweet misery of life! . . .

MARTHE   Oh! if I could help you to endure it!

GILL   Yes, but you can't.

MARTHE   Seriously?

GILL   Seriously.

MARTHE   But then, then you'll go on suffering?

GILL   A little more, a little less . . . what else can I do?

MARTHE   You could . . . I don't know. I want you to be less unhappy, I want you to purchase your fame at a cheaper rate.

GILL   It's more impossible than ever.

MARTHE   Then let me do something for you.

GILL   What?

MARTHE   I don't know: what should I do?

GILL   *(Playing surprise)* Why, who do you think I am?

MARTHE   Oh dear! *(Most urgently.)* You must really despise me if you won't accept a favour from me?

GILL   On the contrary . . .

MARTHE   Then let me . . . let me be with you and transcend any prejudices. . . . Grant me the joy of being able to say that I, Marthe Bourdon, helped Gill Norvège to . . . be comforted. *(She smiles at him.)*

GILL   *(Refusing very 'coquettishly')* No, no . . . Gill Norvège will suffer alone. . . . *(A pause)* You would really like to do something for me?

MARTHE   If you wish it.

GILL   And you would take on the task of ridding me of the importunate . . . *(Gesture)* it would be too absurd! I compromise people, remember. . . .

MARTHE   I expect that.

GILL   My follies may surprise you.

MARTHE   No, no. *(She takes him by the hands, he lets her do so.)*

GILL   But . . .

MARTHE   *(Speaking directly to his face)* Yes . . . yes . . . I want to.

GILL   Oh! *(He drops onto her shoulder and embraces her.)*

MARTHE   Ah!

GILL   *(Briskly)* All right then, you want to? *(He pulls her towards the door right.)* You want to . . . *(He opens the door.)*

MARTHE  Ah! your boudoir . . . let's do it . . .
GILL  *(Showing her in – aside, eyes upturned)*
What an experience!!

*Curtain*

## Act III

*Same setting as Act I, minus the cross over the mantlepiece. More intimate arrangement, the doors are closed; a few chrysanthemums on the tables.*

## Scene 1

BERGE, SAINT-LOUP, *then* MARTHE

SAINT-LOUP  I can't get over it.
BERGE  First you cut out the dressmaker's bills?
SAINT-LOUP  Yes. She made me cut out lots of other things too.
BERGE  You still love her?
SAINT-LOUP  I assure you I do not, but . . .
BERGE  Tell the truth.
SAINT-LOUP  No, quite honestly, it's really over now!
BERGE  Does she know who lent you the money you gave her?
SAINT-LOUP  A man doesn't have three dozen friends who'll lend that kind of money. . . .
BERGE  You know, it would be a great token of affection. *(Feeling in his watch-pocket)* Unfortunately . . .
SAINT-LOUP  You have to be a friend from the country to cough up like that!
BERGE  *(Briskly)* True enough.
SAINT-LOUP  Ah, damn that Norvège!
BERGE  Actually, he flabbergasts me; I admire him.
SAINT-LOUP  Shut up! Paris will eventually get tired of putting up with creatures like that. One of these days these swollen bladders will burst and there'll be nothing but air.
BERGE  The air of the period. *(Lighting a cigarette)* Personally, my friend, I think we ought to be proud of having our Gill, just as the ancients had theirs. In our heart of hearts – I'm talking hearts, not arts now – we all resent Gill, we're horrified by him; in public we acclaim him, we gobble him up. He is needed by our decadent age . . . and by us! Don't protest, it's the truth. I'm resigned to it.

SAINT-LOUP  I might be resigned to it too if it weren't for this business. . . . Poor Romagne!
BERGE  He made the wisest decision.
SAINT-LOUP  I don't dare look him in the face. I feel as if I'd played him a disgraceful trick. Oh, if Romagne knew that this fellow indulges in chrysanthemums on money that comes from him . . .
BERGE  What's done is done . . .

*(MARTHE enters at that moment and remains unnoticed upstage.)*

SAINT-LOUP  I have to find a way, I don't know how, but even if I have to go into debt I want to return the money to him before he leaves.
BERGE  Did you tell him it was for Marthe?

*(MARTHE makes a movement.)*

SAINT-LOUP  If I hadn't, he would have refused, I'm sure. . . . *(He turns around and notices* MARTHE, *who immediately pretends to have just entered.)* Ah! . . . there you are! . . .
MARTHE  What did you want, my dear?
SAINT-LOUP  Nothing. We were talking about Romagne. You know he's leaving us.
MARTHE  Ah! he's going back to the provinces?
SAINT-LOUP  No. He's going much farther away . . . Lower Argentina.
MARTHE  *(Moved)* He is?
SAINT-LOUP  He is. He claims he needs a healthier life than the one we lead, and he prefers to court danger rather than stay in Paris where he suffers . . . in vain.
MARTHE  Ah! . . . It's a very recent decision.
SAINT-LOUP  He made it just yesterday, he says. But I imagine it's been simmering for a few days. . . . Anyway, you'll have a chance to interrogate him, I think he'll be coming here today as usual; if only to say good-bye.
MARTHE  He's leaving so soon?
BERGE  He told me he's embarking at Bordeaux in a fortnight, when he's finished his preparations. . . . He's got energy. *(He goes upstage.)*
SAINT-LOUP  The energy of despair.
MARTHE  Is it true, he's going so far away?
SAINT-LOUP  He'll tell you himself. *(Taking her aside)* What he might not tell you is that, to undertake this journey and start

147

the business he's planned over there, he needs the money I borrowed from him.

MARTHE *(Startled)* Ah! yes.

SAINT-LOUP We've got to find a way to pay it back to him . . . do you understand?

MARTHE Certainly . . . that's perfectly natural.

SAINT-LOUP Anyway there's time to discuss it again, since he won't be sailing for a fortnight.

MARTHE *(Troubled)* That's right . . . that's right, we'll discuss it later.

SAINT-LOUP *(To BERGE who is crossing left)* Are you going?

BERGE *(Exiting right)* I'll just pop into the study and write a letter. I'll see you again shortly.

SAINT-LOUP Never mind. I'm heading upstairs as well. *(To MARTHE)* Will you be here?

MARTHE No, I'm going to my room.

SAINT-LOUP See you soon then.

*(MARTHE exits left. SAINT-LOUP watches her leave . . . then, after a moment's hesitation, he exits right.)*

*(A pause)*

## Scene 2

GILL, LANTIGNY

GILL NORVÈGE *heavily pomaded, yellow chrysanthemum in his buttonhole, and* LANTIGNY, *tightly buttoned up in a frockcoat, enter upstage. They look to the left and right . . . then step forward.*

GILL What's this. No one here? Oof!

LANTIGNY *(Heading right)* I heard someone talking in here just now. I'll call a servant.

GILL No, don't bother. *(He stretches out in an armchair.)* Now tell me, the day you walked out with Jacques Romagne, what did he say?

LANTIGNY Nothing. He barely noticed me, he seemed quite despondent.

GILL He detests me! *(Laughing)* Ha! ha!

LANTIGNY The truth is he's not very fond of you!

GILL My dear fellow, I was smitten the moment I saw him. It's a funny thing, but ever since then I can't get him out of my mind. . . . You remember that head of St George of the Tuscan school that got me so

excited in Florence? He's it all over again. . . . What a lovely rage ignited in his eyes! *(Taking LANTIGNY's arm)* It wasn't fear that was making me quiver! . . .

LANTIGNY Don't trust him.

GILL Yes . . . yes. . . . Well, I can't help it, I have to see him again, I have to at any cost! Do you think I would have come back here otherwise? *(Dreamily)* Romagne, Jacques Romagne: the boy's got breeding. . . . He's precisely the type I was dreaming of for the young condottiere in my novel. I'll never find a more perfect model. These days when one meets creatures so like fiction in real life, do you think one can blithely ignore them?

LANTIGNY You also thought you saw a hero of the Renaissance in that boy Georges we picked up outside the Opera. And where did that get you? A Venetian nobleman, you called him . . . a Negro postman, I should call him! . . . since he's expert at blackmail.

GILL But we're not talking about hustlers now, Jacques's an artist, a remarkable poet, a being who shares my feelings.

LANTIGNY Your feelings? The boy is madly in love with that woman, and he actually considers you his rival.

GILL Oh! God! That woman stands between us! An amusing affair! A paradox of Parisian life. . . . Tell me, Lantigny, do you ever think of settling down with a wealthy bride?

LANTIGNY Who? Me? . . . *(Laughing)* Ho, ho, ho! . . .

GILL Do it, to amuse me. *(Watching the doors)* Still no one. *(Leaning over, in an undertone to LANTIGNY.)* He's the one who got rid of Durch for me.

LANTIGNY Who did?

GILL Romagne. Indirectly . . . I almost take pleasure in thinking about it. How I would reward him today, if he stopped resenting me on account of a woman, came to me and by his presence alone collaborated in my book. I would produce a masterpiece, I'm sure of it, my dear. Can you picture him, this Romagne, tricked out in a golden tunic, neck and arms bare, cruising the streets of Verona on horseback, protected by a gang of his henchmen, drunk with glory, against a background of an enthusiastic crowd pelting him with flowers. . . . His face impassive, his eyes aloof, pale with emotion, he has placed beneath his helmet two red roses which bleed on to his temples through his raven locks. And even the men greet him with offers of love, applaud him, aroused, yes, aroused by this apotheosis!

LANTIGNY  *(Admiringly)* What an artist you are!

GILL  Yes. Those were the epic days in which we could explore our emotions, poor over-civilized creatures that we are! Ever since then our era has been trying to impose laws on Beauty and prescribe what gender it's to be. Ah! it's ridiculous, really! As if we weren't to live by our aesthetics, by making our works come to life! . . . That's what Leonardo did and the exquisite Sodoma, that painter of graceful creations, so infatuated with beauty that it won him his nickname. I often dream of a heaven where we shall meet those charming persons again. A heaven which will be a bit like ancient Greece beneath a blue sky, governed by liberal laws that respect Art. . . . And to think that we shall never ever know such a heaven, we who are reviled, persecuted, condemned, we who plod with measured steps in this vale of whores and horrors, unable to slake our thirst or spread our wings without their being torn. . . .

LANTIGNY  Aren't you getting a bit elevated?

GILL  I am, but I come down to the earth often enough. After all: disgust, humiliation, frustration . . . a cramped, stupid life. . . . What's in store for me today? *(A pause. He rises abruptly.)* Just now, I was afraid *(Putting his hand to his heart)*, I was afraid of running into him on the stairs.

LANTIGNY  *(Getting up)* Here he comes!

*(They both turn upstage where* ROMAGNE *enters.)*

## Scene 3

GILL, LANTIGNY, ROMAGNE

ROMAGNE  Oh! I didn't expect to meet you here, gentlemen. . . . Are you going? Please don't let me stand in your way. . . .

LANTIGNY  *(Extending a hand)* Are you well, Monsieur?

ROMAGNE  Better, thank you. . . .

GILL  Please don't stand aside to make way for me, Monsieur Romagne. . . .

ROMAGNE  All right. Is it true, Monsieur, that you personally left your calling card with my concierge?

GILL  Are you surprised? Don't I owe you a visit, after all?

ROMAGNE  Oh! a visit from a celebrity such as yourself would do me too much honour!

GILL  Myself? In essence I'm nothing but a dilettante, I write to distract myself – when I'm too happy or too sad – and I only publish because I must. Paris is cruel.

ROMAGNE  And you are part of it, I know. Permit me in my modesty not to envy the lot of a great artist, and so take leave of him. . . . *(Bowing)* Gentlemen.

GILL  One word more, Monsieur Romagne. Where are you off to? I venture to insist.

ROMAGNE  *(Firmly)* Nowhere. I am leaving because you are staying.

GILL  You are jealous of me. . . . Yes you are . . . confess it.

ROMAGNE  I was in love with Marthe Bourdon . . . why should I hide it?

GILL  But who is stopping you from being in love with her?

ROMAGNE  You are.

GILL  How so?

ROMAGNE  *(With effort)* She loves you.

GILL  But do I love her? What about that?

ROMAGNE  But . . .

GILL  Do I strike you as someone addicted to the caprices of a woman? When I love, my dear, I love in other ways. I love more liberally.

ROMAGNE  Ah! ah!

GILL  You fail to understand me? You, a poet! You, a sensitive nature, you whose wild and red-blooded looks have better things to do than probe female neuroses. Come, come! Have you never looked in your mirror? Don't you constantly wish to be beautiful?

ROMAGNE  Good lord . . .

LANTIGNY  *(Squealing)* I do, dead on my feet today.

GILL  *(To* ROMAGNE*)* The recipe is an easy one. I shall give it to you.

ROMAGNE  I've no need of it.

GILL  Our looks don't matter, if our expression transmits our private sense of beauty. If we love what is perfect, what is great . . . Well, you are listening! . . .

ROMAGNE  *(Very nervous)* I can't help being a bit curious, for I don't see the point of this beauty lesson.

GILL  *(Taking a step towards him)* The point? . . .

ROMAGNE *(Recoiling and looking to the right and left)* Besides I'm rather surprised to find you and this gentleman here alone . . . *(to* LANTIGNY*)* excuse me, Monsieur, I don't recall your name. . . .

LANTIGNY  Lantigny.

ROMAGNE  I came to see my friends.

GILL  *(Amiably, approaching* ROMAGNE*)* Yes . . . but . . .

ROMAGNE  *(Recoiling and reaching the door)* Well, they aren't here. I'll come back later. *(He exits abruptly.)*

LANTIGNY  He's a real savage.

GILL  *(Dreamily, heading towards the exit)* I adore such savagery.

LANTIGNY  Ah!

GILL  *(Leaning on the piano)* He'll be back! But my nerves are in tatters, Lantigny, sit down at the piano: play me the death of Isolde and then that tune you composed, you know the one . . .

LANTIGNY  *(Approaching the piano)* "Weeping roses"?

GILL  Yes, "weeping roses."

*(*LANTIGNY *sits down to play.* GILL *slowly detaches himself from the piano and crosses down to drop into an armchair. A pause)*

## Scene 5

GILL, LANTIGNY, SAINT-LOUP, *entering right*

SAINT-LOUP  *(Surprised)* Norvège!

GILL  *(Calmly)* In person!

LANTIGNY  *(Leaving the piano)* Good afternoon.

SAINT-LOUP  And you're alone?

GILL  So it would seem.

LANTIGNY  I must say you have a funny way of being at home for your at-homes!

SAINT-LOUP  I'm sorry. I was just in here. I'll call my sister-in-law.

GILL  Don't bother. I'm not staying.

SAINT-LOUP  Our disgrace is complete! You're leaving without seeing her?

GILL  I am leaving without seeing her.

SAINT-LOUP  The caprice of your visit will have been of short duration.

GILL  Your welcome was too tardy.

SAINT-LOUP  The servant didn't know I was upstairs and I didn't hear you come in.

GILL  Next time I'll come equipped with a hunting horn.

SAINT-LOUP  Ho, ho! . . . What about you, Lantigny?

LANTIGNY  I . . . why . . . I..

GILL  I brought him.

LANTIGNY  Ah!

GILL  Yes . . . he has other visits to make.

LANTIGNY  Ah!

SAINT-LOUP  *(Sarcastic)* I'm ever so sorry.

LANTIGNY  So am I, I . . .

SAINT-LOUP  Particularly since Marthe Bourdon is here.

## Scene 6

THE SAME, MARTHE

MARTHE  Norvège! Are you leaving?

GILL  Dear madam, having a great deal to do, and having waited for quite a long time . . .

MARTHE  No one informed me. . . . But you can't go into eclipse like that; stay just a little . . . a tiny little bit.

GILL  *(Wearily)* So be it, a tiny little bit. *(He puts down his hat.* LANTIGNY *imitates him.)*

SAINT-LOUP  What about your visits, Lantigny?

LANTIGNY  Ah! that's true, my visits . . .

GILL  Why, go and pay them, my dear. . . .

LANTIGNY  That's right . . . that's right.

*(Comical hesitation; he puts his hat back on and exits.)*

SAINT-LOUP  I'll escort you to the door and then go and get Berge whom I left in my room; *(to* GILL*)* if you don't mind?

GILL  By all means . . .

*(*SAINT-LOUP *exits.)*

## Scene 7

GILL, MARTHE

MARTHE  So you were leaving without having seen me?

GILL  I waited for you.

MARTHE  I wasn't expecting such a surprise, I'd given up hope. You answer my letters so seldom nowadays. . . . You have deprived me of the prose I found all the more beautiful because it was meant for me alone.

GILL  I spoiled you too much.

MARTHE  Spoiled me! But if you deprive me even of that, what will I have left?

GILL  My friendship . . . my entire friendship.

MARTHE  Sometimes it is exquisite. . . . But it isn't enough. I gave myself with all my heart, all my mind. I came to you, attracted by your fame, it's true. . . . Your talent, your art, at first that was what seduced me. But there was also you yourself, the singularity of your personality, the refinement of your existence. . . . So I wasn't afraid of showing myself off with you in those days. If I was proud of feeling envied, I was also proud to incur the unspoken reproach of some, the scandal-mongering mockery of others . . . I was entirely devoted to you. . . . Today, to see you, I had to write to you, to implore you to come here or meet me at your home.

GILL  Didn't I come?

MARTHE  True, you are here. . . . Yet I feel you are far away . . . far, far away. . . . You haven't even kissed my hand . . .

GILL  *(Taking her fingers and kissing them casually)* Sorry, a slip.

MARTHE  *(In a moment of abandon)* Gill . . . Oh, Gill! . . . I wanted so much to love you!

GILL  *(Coldly)* Past tense Aha! So it's over now?

MARTHE  I don't know any more. . . . To love a Gill Norvège!

GILL  *(Sneering)* What a horror! isn't it?

MARTHE  You mean: what an error.

GILL  Now you've become like all other women.

MARTHE  Oh! I 've stopped having illusions.

GILL  You love someone else?

MARTHE  It would be too late, in any case.

GILL  Really? . . . How's that?

MARTHE  Actually, this is all beside the point. . . . What I have to say to you is more . . . more . . . *(With a sad smile)* serious.

GILL  Oho!

MARTHE  Yes . . .

GILL  Well?

MARTHE  Well . . . it's rather delicate . . .

GILL  *(Encouraging her)* You can tell me anything, can't you!

MARTHE  All right, here goes! Jacques Romagne is leaving *(movement from* GILL*)*; and my brother-in-law naturally insists that we pay him back . . . you understand?

GILL  *(Back in control)* Not at all.

MARTHE  You know perfectly well that Saint-Loup borrowed that money from him.

GILL  What money?

MARTHE  *(Astonished, with a mild laugh)* Why . . . that sum of money . . . I have to pay it back to him in a fortnight . . . I can count on you, can't I?

GILL  No, really . . . I don't understand at all. . . . You were in such a hurry to see me so you could talk business?

MARTHE  *(Intensely)* Oh no . . . not that, Gill. When I wrote to you, I wasn't thinking about that, I swear it. My brother-in-law mentioned it to me only now.

GILL  So?

MARTHE  *(More intensely)* You do believe me, I hope!

GILL  Such indignation! You who gave yourself so prettily. . . . And now the way you take yourself back!

MARTHE  I'm taking myself back?

GILL  Of course . . .

MARTHE  But hasn't your lack of affection granted me my freedom? . . . Confess it, I don't mean anything to you any more.

GILL  You exaggerate.

MARTHE  Nothing, I can feel it. . . . But that's not the reason I'm asking you to return what I lent you . . . and it pains me to offer you so easy an opportunity to be quits with me.

GILL  And aren't we quits already?

MARTHE  What do you mean?

GILL  I don't know of any further obligations I have to you . . .

MARTHE  We're not talking about 'obligations' to me.

GILL  I accept no constraints, as you well know, my pretty. . . . I did not take you by force, after all. I appreciated the charming gift of your affection for what is was worth; I would like, in exchange, to preserve my affection for you. Don't treat it roughly and it may yet turn to love every once in a while. Your hand? . . . *(She gives him her hand, distrustfully.)*

MARTHE  *(After a pause)* So, you'll send me the money?

GILL  *(Dropping her hand)* A one-track mind!

MARTHE  *(Aghast)* But . . .

GILL  Yes . . . yes . . . you love another, I can see it. Go ahead. If you want my money for the other fellow . . .

MARTHE  Not your money, his.

GILL  *(Pretending not to understand)* His? You owe him something, is that it?

MARTHE  What you owe me yourself.

GILL  Ah! excuse me. . . . At any rate, it's not that I refuse to do you a favour . . . but it offends me in these circumstances. . . .

MARTHE  These circumstances? . . . *(Throwing herself at him)* So I can't count on you?

GILL  *(Making a retreat, bored)* What I mean is . . .

MARTHE  No! I've misunderstood . . . or maybe I didn't make myself clear: Jacques Romagne is leaving . . .

GILL  And he needs what you borrowed from him. Of course . . . *(Stopping)* I have an idea: wouldn't it be preferable if this Jacques Romagne came to me himself?

MARTHE  *(Who has stared at him for a moment, her eyes out of their sockets; understanding and exploding)* Oh! . . . Oh! No! I'm dreaming. . . . And you say such a thing to me . . . me! You suggest that I . . . Why, then it must be true! . . . Can it be possible?

GILL  *(Laughing)* Calm down . . .

MARTHE  Calm down . . . calm . . . *(Swerving)* Oh! the shame of it! the shame! So that's why you've became so chary of your visits; that's why you desert me: your bargain with the sucker was over, I wasn't any more use to your ambition. So that was your ambition!

GILL  *(Approaching her)* See here . . .

MARTHE  *(Recoiling with a bound)* Don't come near me . . . don't touch me. You horrify me. . . . So that's the Gentleman of the Chrysanthemums, the monster Gill Norvège I refused to believe in. Because I didn't want to believe, I couldn't believe, because I never imagined that your lips were lying . . . yes, yes, lying, when they crushed themselves on mine . . . when they smothered me with kisses. I believed, when you took me, that your hesitation was meant to make you more desirable. Didn't you swear to me that it wasn't true, that I mustn't listen to the slander, that I could yield freely to your embraces. And I did yield freely and I surrendered to them, I swooned in your arms, I let myself go so far as to taste the hideous delights of your affections. Yes . . . yes . . . I didn't know . . . coward . . . that it was all calculation on your part.

GILL  *(Gesture of boredom)* Ah! if you don't mind . . .

MARTHE  *(With a nervous laugh)* Now I see it. Now I see it all. . . . Ah! now I can make sense of your secretary, the 'dear boy' as you call him, and the sordid fussing of your chaperone and all the rest of it . . . all of it.

GILL  Are you through?

MARTHE  *(Not listening)* You're even more monstrous than people say. . . . And they admire you! They adulate you, instead of giving you the thrashing you deserve, instead of spitting in your face. . . . You laugh!

GILL  All I can do is laugh . . .

MARTHE  Yes, it's true . . . I never expected. . . . You own Paris, the way the Linon de Londines do. . . . You reign over it together . . . You are our king! . . . That's why you put up with Tournay's articles and don't bother to rebut them. Ha! ha! *(Reciting)* 'Gill Norvège, the he–she, atrocious in his beflowered beauty, whose fickle mental moods, which he changes according to the weather, are venerated by Paris *(Emphasizing with a sneer)* and who – will – one day – open – his veins in a fit of pique – to die like his illustrious ancestor Petronius'. *(Gesture of GILL)* . . . Oh no! You will always be content to react with your 'girlish' vapours. All you need is your ghastly Mme Armide to appear in fashionable drawing-rooms and announce that you are downstairs in your carriage with a fit of nerves for people to run and coddle you. Ah! a puppet. Why, you're nothing but a puppet. Never let it be said that a woman of my sort never threw your real name in your face . . . puppet! . . . You dare stand there and hear me out?

GILL  I was waiting. Are you through?

MARTHE  Oh! don't come near me, I tell you . . . you smile, delighted to be a disgrace . . . pleased to have fooled me ignobly, because I let myself be taken in by your morbid charm . . . because I drank your poison . . . *(She stares at him from a distance.)* And that's the creature I loved, the one to whom I sacrificed all modesty, for whom I abandoned all pride . . . and got my reward, yes, for now I understand. You'd say I gave myself to you . . . but no, I bought you . . . you sold yourself . . . tainted goods!..

GILL  That'll do.

MARTHE  And you refuse to return the money, hoping to force me to follow you even farther, to be the accomplice of your baseness.

GILL  I do not ask you to follow me . . . quite the contrary. Yes, you are the one who attacks my affections, who, without understanding the quantum of nobility in them, destroys them with your female treachery . . . stupidly. . . . Insult me . . . it doesn't get to me. . . . But that boy . . . that charming boy is leaving, that's what makes me grieve. . . . *(He leans on a piece of furniture.)*

MARTHE   Again! you dare! Ah! no, the farce is over. Get out of here.

GILL   What?

MARTHE   Get out, get out, I can't take any more of this. . . .

GILL   Very good, very good, my dear. Gently, pray . . . I'm going . . . I shall leave you. You're a bit touchy today. . . .

*(He walks backwards to the door, inspecting things right and left. Once upstage, he stops, hesitating.)*

MARTHE   *(Marching on him)* Get out . . . get out . . .

*(GILL shrugs and exits.)*

## Scene 8

MARTHE, ROMAGNE, SAINT-LOUP

MARTHE   *goes to the door, stays there an instant, then vacillating, comes back downstage. . . . Choking, she rushes to the window and opens it abruptly. – The muffled sound of Paris and the hoarse cries of hawkers. – Then, exhausted by her effort, she collapses, sobbing, on the sofa. . . . JACQUES ROMAGNE and SAINT-LOUP enter right and stand in amazement. In the street we can hear a squad of newsboys shouting by turns and coming gradually closer: 'Read* THE CAPITAL, *new article by Gill Norvège . . .* THE CAPITAL, *sensational issue, article by Gill Norvège. . . .'*
MARTHE *raises her head, jerks away in disgust and collapses again.*
SAINT-LOUP *make a gesture to* ROMAGNE *meaning 'Now you can go to her'.*

*Curtain*

END

153

# Documents ─────────────────────

*Armory,*[1] 50 ans de vie parisienne (Souvenirs et figures). *Paris: Jean-Renard, n.d., pp. 96, 185–88*

People have said that I wrote *The Gentleman of the Chrysanthemums* out of spite. Mme Duval, Jean Lorrain's mother, had Georges Normandy[2] tell me of her anxiety concerning this play, performed after her son had died. Now, my play had been written in his lifetime, inspired by a phrase of his in one of his "Raitifs." When someone reproached him for not publicizing himself even more than he did, for not being the Petrarch of his times, he responded, "What next? The Gentleman of the Camelias?" There was my play! It is true that at a daytime vernissage, I did remark to Willy and Polaire in front of his portrait by La Gandara,[3] "Naturally! La Gandara only paints women," just as the original, a white flower in his buttonhole, pomaded, precious, walked up to us. Nevertheless, I had no intention of later caricaturing a man I admired, who had noted my beginnings in one of his "pall-malls." *The Gentleman of the Chrysanthemums* is no more Jean Lorrain than he is Oscar Wilde or Edouard de Max[4] (who almost performed my hero). He is a person invented for a satire aimed less at the vice itself than at its ridiculous display, and the complaisance with which Parisian society treats it.

[. . .] *The Gentleman of the Chrysanthemums*, a satire, as I've said, of private morals too boldly advertised, was meant to be played by Edouard de Max. A mutual friend, dear Achille Richard,[5] acted as go-between. De Max eventually got scared of the role. I read the play to Henry Krauss, but Sarah Bernhardt, in whose company he was a member, wouldn't release him . . . I almost got Pierre Ramiel, an actor who became a deputy and under-secretary of State, then Pierre Juvenet. Another person, since

become very famous but who cannot be named today, took such an interest in my play that he accompanied me home after the show he was in, and sat waiting on the curbstone until I brought down the manuscript. But Gémier would not let him out of his role in *L'homme qui assassina*. I saw Paul Clerget. . . . I saw heaps of others. . . . My colleagues at the N.T.A.[6] urged me to come to a decision. I had put together a brilliant cast. All I needed was a leading man. Finally I found him in the person of René Cresté,[7] who played Fantômas on the screen, and whose face was on every wall. He was crazy about the role and the play. In the halls of the Press Club over the Café Americain, where I was rehearsing, he became my spokesman, championing my cause. The production was announced in the papers, the date was set, and then, one day, Cresté did not show up for rehearsal. Worried, I went that night to see him at Parisiana where he was playing Renaud in *Claudine à Paris*. Mme Colette,[8] who was playing Claudine, informed me that the night before Cresté had had to be carried out, spitting blood. My play was down the tubes. I left, death in my soul. As I was walking down the boulevard, I was accosted by a young man of dubious morals, I mean he was pretty obvious. Naturally he questioned me about my play which was being talked of all over Paris. I told him my dilemma.

"I'll find you someone," he said confidently.

He walked with me, chatting away.

He did indeed find me someone. Someone who, in fact, he hadn't thought of but who, crossing our path, said "Good evening" in a tone that made me jump.

"Is he an actor?"

"Yes, but of no reputation."

"Introduce us."

He ran after the "Good evening" man, who agreed to leave the friend he was chatting with and have a beer at a café on the corner of Châteaudeue, where I offered him Cresté's role.

"It's tempting," he said. "It could make my reputation. But I'm hesitant."

All I could do was present him my card. The next day a lady friend of his encouraged him to accept. The day after that, he rehearsed the main scenes with Jeanine Zorelli.[9] Twelve days later, on the advertised date, Jean Ayme[10] won applause for my play, with his way of wearing a red-lined cape over evening dress which set off a natural elegance few actors could achieve. I may say that All Paris was squeezed into the auditorium of the Palais-Royal. Among others, one could see in the boxes Mme Camille du Gast, the Marquise de Morny, the mayor of the 11th arrondissement, Mmes Colette, Gérard d'Houville, all the critics in full fig and interested parties, avidly watching the performance of the leading role. I was put into the fireman's box. In the first intermission, Séché[11] headed my way.

"Well, old boy, it's all right!"

In the intermission after "two," while the curtain call for Jean Ayme and Zorelli was going on, he came back:

"It's a success."

After "three," I was dragged on stage, where I didn't want to appear, not even having the time to get rid of a cigarette butt in the corner of my mouth.

Paul Léautaud, writing as Fernand [sic] Boissard, described in the Mercure de France the astonishment of an audience, which, he reported, did not expect such a success. Two days later, Jean Richepain published in Comœdia a veritable dithyramb. Nozière, Camille de Sainte-Croix, Henri de Régnier, Adolphe Bresson, Catulle Mendès were no less laudatory. It was recognized that, while making my own debut, I had not hesitated in introducing a wholly unknown and very adroit actor, the very type of the role, in what was perhaps the riskiest play on the stage of the time.

All this from a "Good evening" heard at night on the corner of Rue Drouet and Rue La Fayette!

*Review by Louis Schneider in* Comœdia, *262, 18 June 1908, pp. 1–2*

The play has no obvious denouement, nor is it one of those that needs a complicated plot. Scabrous as its bizarre subject may be, it can be easily classified as a so-called comedy of character. And that alone is how it ought to be judged.

Very well! it must be admitted, without a shadow of false modesty, the character of the person studied has been studied very well, boldly and clearly, with broad strokes as well as nuances, and the sharply etched features do not prevent the nuances from being fine and delicate.

One may condemn, if one wishes, the singular choice of such a hero! But once this choice is granted, one can only praise the care and tact brought to it by the author in establishing this portrait, presenting it in all its life, and giving the whole a physical and moral substance.

It is also fair to note that this portrait never turns to caricature or even to violent satire. Certainly, the gentleman of the chrysanthemums often raises a laugh, but only for the truly ridiculous aspects his vice takes, abnormal and grotesque as it is for those who don't share it. And, besides, if the vice is stigmatised as odious by Marthe who is indirectly its victim, the aesthete of homosexuality is given plenty of time to present and defend his theories.

One may therefore say that the author has been neither systemically indulgent or hostile to him and has behaved as any good playwright should behave to his characters, in strict impartiality.

Finally, certain scenes, notably that ending Act Two, in which the homosexual seduces a woman, are well constructed, bearing the mark of special talent revealing a true man of the theatre.

It would be absolutely iniquitous to forget the actor who personifies the gentleman of the chrysanthemums, and who was, under the circumstances, a valuable collaborator of the playwright. There was a certain courage in daring to appear as the character of Gill Norvège. A complete victory rewarded this courage.

In appearance, expression, distinction, ambiguous good looks and also in cool and cynical pluck, the achievement was quite remarkable. Nothing in excess! Nothing dissmulated either! It was living, monstrous, elegant, amoral and graceful.

In the audience, women smiled, real men watched the women smile, and the stage hero's colleagues were obviously having a good time.

As to whether such a performance *castigat ridendo mores* [corrects manners through laughter], that's none of my business, I think, since I'm not tasked with being a watchdog over my fellow-creatures' virtues, but simply a retriever sniffing out the quarry of art.

*Review of Paul Léautaud, under pseudonym of Maurice Boissard, Mercure de France, 16 August 1908, p. 717*

The Nouveau Théâtre presented a really odd play to close out its season. *The Gentleman of the Chrysanthemums* is a character who derives both from a recently deceased boulevard writer and an English poet famous for his misfortunes as well as from M. de Phocas and Vicomte de Courpière, heroes of Jean Lorrain and M. Abel Hermant.[12] In M. Armory's play, his name is Gill Norvège, and he is an influential and feared journalist. His elegance, his artistic taste are famous, his "tattle" is the talk of Paris, and every young writer is ambitious to read his name in one of his columns. Delicate, subtle, precious, effeminate, cold, singular, abnormal, arid and jaded in appearance with perhaps a soft centre, he is attractive and off-putting, he interests and he repels. Many people – they amused me greatly – seeing him thus put on stage pursed their lips and huffed indignantly. When he was alive, they paid court to him. I don't know if you have caught on that this gentleman – and it didn't shock me – professes only a mild taste for the ladies. Young men have more appeal for him, indeed are the only ones with appeal for him, and he has a whole little court of them – a little harem, dare one say. However, short of money, teetering on the brink of collapse, and knowing he is loved by a beautiful and rich young woman, he forces himself to pretend to be smitten with her, to be a veritable lover, in hopes of repairing his finances. How awkward he is, both in words and gestures! His heart isn't in it, and we can see that he is not used to this sort of wooing and that women are not his usual sphere. Finally, he has to give it up, the game being beyond his powers. M. Armory has limned this individual marvelously. The whole play, besides, full of hints, allusions, merely indicated details, – in dealing with such a

subject, one must not lapse into crudeness, – is executed with remarkable tact and skill. To tell the truth, no one expected such a thing from M. Armory. In my experience, strolling in the corridors during the intermissions, I listened to the talk and the comments were always the same: "Eh, my dear fellow. This Armory, really. You must agree no one would have thought it of him. This play is really quite well done." I don't know if M. Armory has had a good press. Probably some idiocies from our usual highly respectable critics? But I can assure him on this point: he had a good audience.

The role of Gill Norvège is played by M. Jean Ayme, a young actor entirely unknown in Paris, but very professional.

*Review of the published play by "Numa Prætorius," Jahrbuch für sexuelle Zwischenstufen, 1910, vol. 11, pp. 69–71*

This play which had its premiere on 17 June 1908 at the Palais Royal, sponsored by the "Nouveau Théâtre d'Art," is the very first time a homosexual hero has been put on the French stage and in particular has for the first time made good use of the inner psychological aspects of homosexuality, whereas the few dramatic treatments in German concern only the more external conflicts caused by the criminal code and social pressures on homosexuals *(e.g., Moldau's* Truth *and Hirschfeld's "Mistakes").*

[*A plot summary follows.*]

The play is a mordant, indeed lampoon-like satire of a recently deceased, very well-known French writer (Jean Lorrain), whose person is rather crudely recognizable in the figure of Gill Norvège.

Truly amusing is the depiction of Gill Norvège as effeminate, affected, despite his renown and especially his renown as a homosexual adored by women, while in the great final scene his unbounded cynicism is displayed.

His aesthetic ideals, influenced by his disposition, are made fun of as well, although they are introduced in a poetic tirade in which Norvège envisages a new Greece. [. . .]

The whole play is couched in a sophisticated, piquant Parisian tone, its witty dialogue hinting at the main point, leaving it to be delicately guessed at between the lines. In short a play for connoisseurs.

## Notes

1  Armory, pseudonym of Carle Lionel Dauriac, b.1877 at Brest; came to Paris to study painting. In 1898 he published a collection of musical sensations, *Les Orgues de Fribourg*; staged various one-acts at open university theatres; and then wrote a series of novels and poems. His first professionally produced play, co-written with A. Achaume, was *Nuit d'alerte*. He was a member of the Montmartre artists' colony, collaborating in comic journals, revues and magazines.

2  Georges Normandy (b.1882), wrote several books about Jean Lorrain, including the first biography (1907)

3  Willy was the pen-name of Henry Gauthier-Villard, Colette's husband and collaborator. Polaire (Émilie-Marie Bouchard, 1877–1939), actress, created the title role in Colette's dramatization of her novel *Claudine à Paris* (1906). Antonio de la Gandara (1862–1917), fashionable French portraitist of Mexican ancestry.

4  For Lorrain and De Max, see the Introduction.

5  Achille Richard (d.1923), French poet, born in Milan.

6  The *Nouveau Théâtre d'Art* had opened on 11 Mars 1907, and had previously staged ten plays, full length and one-acts: up to then its most illustrious author had been H.-R. Lenormand.

7  Armory names most of the younger leading men working in the Paris theatre at the time. Henry Krauss had played Hamlet. Paul Clerget (1868–1935) became an aide of André Antoine. René Cresté (1880–1923) made his stage debut 1901; known mainly as a film actor, especially in Feuillade's mystery serials.

8  Sidonie Gabrielle Claudine Colette (1873–1954) was enjoying a particularly successful period in the Paris theatre with her dramatizations of her Claudine novels about a young girl's sentimental education.

9  Jeanine Zorelli, an experienced actress from the Théâtre Antoine and the Grand Guignol, had played both Pierrot and Herodias in Wilde's *Salomé*.

10  Jean Ayme was born in Lyon and studied painting; his acting experience has been in Brussels, Marseille and Lyon.

11  Léon Séché (1848–1914), French writer, one of the founders of the Nouveau Théâtre d'Art.

12  Lorrain's *Monsieur de Phocas* (1901) and *Monsieur de Courpière* (1907) by Abel Hermant (1862–1950) are novels about aesthetes, lesser variants on Des Esseintes in Huysmans *À Rebours*.

# Ania and Esther

*A romantic play in seven tableaux*
*by Klaus Mann*

(1925)

Translated from the German by Laurence Senelick

*Ania and Esther* is translated from the second edition of Klaus Mann, *Anja und Esther. Ein romantisches Stück in sieben Bildern*, Berlin, Oesterheld & Co., 1925

# Introduction

In 1925, when 19-year-old Klaus Mann (1906–1949) had gained a measure of notoriety as the author of a scandalous work, the play *Ania and Esther*, a cartoon by Theodor Heine appeared in the Munich satirical magazine *Simplicissimus*. It showed an ephebic Klaus in short pants standing behind his illustrious father Thomas. One of the youth's hands holds a sheaf of manuscript, the other is laid daintily on the shoulder of his sour-looking sire who is swotting away at a page full of crossed-out lines. The caption: "But you know, Papa, that geniuses never have geniuses for sons, so you must not be a genius."[1]

The joke was picked up by Bertolt Brecht, who remarked, "The whole world knows Klaus Mann, the son of Thomas Mann. By the way, who is Thomas Mann?" Such satire might suggest that in Weimar Germany, Thomas, for all his celebrity, was seen as the relic of an obsolete era, the Age of the Bourgeoisie, while Klaus was accepted as the representative of Youth, the enigmatic, perverse and unnerving rising generation. It was likelier, however, that the real laughing stock was Klaus who, from the start of his literary career, was disliked and distrusted by the Press, which ridiculed him as a *Dichterkind*, the aspiring offspring of a great writer incapable of emulating his father's achievements.

Klaus Heinrich Thomas Mann was Thomas's first son, born in Munich in 1906, a year after his beloved sister Erika. Some of his artistic temperament was inherited from

*Plate 11* Tableau 3 in the Hamburg Kammerspiele production, 1925. Major characters left to right: Gimietto, Esther (Pamela Wedekind), the Old Man with Eliza on his lap, Ania (Erika Wedekind), Erik, Kaspar (Klaus Mann) and Jakob (Gustaf Gründgens). The set resembles the cellar vaults of "Plato House" at Klaus Mann's Odenwald school. (Klaus Mann Archive, Munich.)

161

*Plate 12* The photographs which caused the quarrel between Gustaf Gründgens and the Manns, described in the documents to *Ania and Esther*. To the left, the snapshot of Gründgens as Jakob, Erika Mann as Ania, Pamela Wedekind as Esther and Klaus Mann as Kaspar. To the right is the photo as it appeared on the front page of the *Berliner Illustrirte Zeitung*, 31 October 1925, with Gründgens cut out and a picture of the "Dichterkinder" in street clothes stuck in the corner. (From Eberhard Spangenberg, *Karriere eines Romans*.)

his mother Katja Pringsheim, who, as the Nazis were later quick to emphasize, had Jewish blood coursing through her veins. Her father Alfred Pringsheim was a wealthy scholar and professor of mathematics at the University of Munich; he was also, paradoxically, a fervent proponent of Wagner. He had married Hedwig Dohm, an actress, whose father had founded the Berlin humour magazine *Kladderadatsch*, and whose mother was a pioneer of female emancipation. Katja Pringsheim was one of the first women in Germany to be granted a higher education.

Growing up in Munich under the influence of their art-loving grandparents, aloof father and nurturing mother, the Mann children were soon singled out for their extraordinary appearance and behavior. Klaus and Erika, along with their younger siblings Golo and Monika, were decked out in *art nouveau* or arts-and-crafts linen smocks and Russian blouses, garb that attracted the gibes of street urchins. They were reared by a succession of nannies and maids and regarded their household as a protected world, ruled by the benevolent despotism of the family and its attendant vassals. Most children begin with a similar vision of their environment, but it is soon dispelled on contact with public schools and other children. The junior Manns seem to have preserved the ideal longer and

consequently when it was shattered, the effect was all the more traumatic.

Klaus's idyllic childhood was first interrupted in 1915 when acute appendicitis brought him close to death; his convalescence testified to a desperate attachment to life, revealed in a reckless flurry of activities. In 1916 he and friends initiated the amateur theatricals that fed his love of dressing-up and pretending to be someone else. The uncertain postwar period allowed Klaus and Erika and their adolescent circle to cut classes and mingle with Munich Bohemia. In 1922, when their ventures into shoplifting ended in arrest and their parents discovered their clandestine friendship with the actor Bert Fischel, they were packed off to the Bergschule Hochwaldhausen in central Germany. This removal from the parental hearth introduced Klaus to the Youth Movement sweeping the country; progressive, with undertones both homoerotic and fascistic, it preached the salvation of Germany by fostering youth groups within natural surroundings.

In Thomas Mann's novel *Doktor Faustus*, the student Konrad Deutschlin declares:

The concept of youth is a prerogative and a priority of our people, the Germans; the others hardly know it. German youth represents, precisely as youth, the

Volksgeist itself, the German spirit, which is young and full of the future – immature if you will, but what does that mean! German deeds always come from a certain violent immaturity, and it is not for nothing that we are the people of the Reformation.[2]

Klaus's own opinion of youth was less uplifting: *"Every child is an anarchist and an opponent of society,"* he was to write. "Each one contains an atavistic primal urge to destroy; and the most gifted have it worst of all."[3] He regarded the youth who grew up during the First World War a lost generation, whose normal frivolity, restlessness and dissoluteness were exacerbated by an absence of viable values.

Later in 1922 Klaus was transferred to the Odenwaldschule, a co-educational school for talented problem children in the mountains near Heidelberg. This institution, founded in 1910 by Paulus Geheeb, had the hoped-for therapeutic effect: Klaus read voraciously and formed a respectful and lasting relationhip with Geheeb, a new kind of adult, trustworthy and unfettered by social convention, living according to his own code of ethics. Young Klaus's immersion in the school's natural surroundings coincided with the onset of puberty, and had the unexpected effect of eroticizing his environment. He later wrote, "My relationship to the landscape and to nature in general was determined by the mystico-erotic frame of mind in which I found myself. I embraced trees, I pressed my face against their bark, and I felt the soft cushion of moss as a caress beneath the thin soles of my sandals."[4]

Here too Mann formed sentimental attachments to other boys. He had already indulged this penchant at the Wilhelmsgymnasium in Munich, where the chief object of his affections had been a dark-haired, smooth-faced athlete named Elmar to whom he sent an anonymous, typewritten poem. In the mountains the new beloved was again an athlete, but this time a blond, Uto. In his autobiography, *Das Wendepunkt* (*The Turning Point*), Mann admits that strong, agile Uto was no Adonis, but possessed the kind of face he loved: high Slavic cheekbones, narrow eyes, fair Nordic hair that paled to tow in the sunshine, dry chapped lips, and ice-colored eyes mixed with silvery green

lights, full of a "sweet and terrifying innocence."

"I wrote him poetry," he recalled of Uto, "which he never managed to read. I addressed him with names which he thought funny: Ganymede, Narcissus, Phaedrus, Antinous. . . . He was a good lad, modest and gentle, devoid of malice; vain enough to delight in my homage but too naïf to recognize the true nature of my passion." Lists of Mann's favorite reading at the time enumerate Socrates, Novalis, Whitman, Poe, Büchner, Nietzsche, Strindberg, Wilde, Herman Bang, Verlaine, Rimbaud, Stefan George, Radiguet, Cocteau and Chaikovsky, all thinkers and artists distinguished for ideological and sexual unorthodoxy. "My Olympus is full of sick men and sinners," he would later remark.[5] "The intellectuals delved too audaciously into the secrets of the human soul, of society, of nature. What they brought to light from the depths was as dreadful as that Gorgon face whose glance is said to turn the beholder to stone."[6] In an essay of 1949 that appeared shortly before his own self-destruction, Mann called for a concerted mass suicide of European intellectuals, to create a shock effect equal to that provided by these forefathers.

On an impulse that was both self-punishing and self-indulgent, Klaus Mann decided to abandon school without parental permission. With Erika he threw himself back into the Bohemian atmosphere they so cherished. He paid his first visit to Berlin in 1923, and, fascinated by the metropolis, sought a way to return and settle there. His circle of friends expanded to include Pamela Wedekind, daughter of the late poet and playwright Frank Wedekind, who became a permanent companion in their adventures. The next year Mann announced that he and Pamela were engaged. "How will you support her?" asked his dismayed parents. To no diminution of their dismay, he replied that he would become a dancer.

Mann made some money by publishing three short studies of Rimbaud, Huysmans and Georg Trakl ("three decadent writers," the conservatives might say) in the liberal newspaper *Die Weltbühne*. This success brought him back to Berlin, where he settled into a boarding house, determined to make a living. Barely 17, he arrived in the capital at the nadir of the inflation period, when both German economy and German morale were at their lowest ebb. In this dog-eat-dog atmosphere, anything went, and prostitution, both male and female, was highly conspicuous. As he recalled in *The Turning Point*:

> The city seemed both pitiful and enticing: grey, shabby, demoralized, but still vibrating with nervous vitality, glistening, gleaming, phosphorescent, hectically animated, full of tensions and promise.
>
> I was in seventh heaven. To be in Berlin meant an exciting adventure all by itself!! . . . The romanticism of the underworld was irresistible . . . Berlin was my city! I wanted to stay. But how? The stupid money problem!
>
> Work? Why not . . . But washing dishes or playing elevator boy was out of the question. The position I sought had to be not only lucrative but amusing.
>
> (pp. 126–28)

The solution was to perform in a cabaret. Back in Munich, Mann had written a number of risqué songs for homespun theatricals. As he describes one of these parlour cabarets:

> The centrepiece of the programme was a charming little medley of a revue, which W. E. Süskind had written for us. A weary count with a long cigarette holder parodied Oscar Wilde's aphoristic style; a valet suddenly declared that his name was Dr Josef Ponten. Erika gossiped in her shop-girl dialect, and the dialogue was sprinkled with certain insidious, pseudo-profund "buzz words." A trenchant music-hall song was sung with the chorus:
>
>> "Perversion's really swell, my boy,
>> Perversion keeps you well, my boy,
>> Perversion beats the standard brand,
>> Perversion isn't hard to stand.
>> Perversion is beyond compare" –
>
> Whereupon a big metal sign swung down, with Perversion written in gaudy letters.
>
> That was the way seventeen-year-olds played.[7]

What more natural than that these precocious talents be transferred to the stage of a sophisticated metropolitan cabaret? Settled in Berlin, Mann paid a call on the elegant cabaret artiste Paul Schneider-Duncker and asked him for a position. Schneider-Duncker

phoned Else Wardt, the proprietor of "Tü-Tü," a cabaret with a reputation for "lavender" humor.

> He described me in the most flattering terms, while I sat beside him: "He's a real attraction for the modern German cabaret stage, something very original, which should be shown as soon as possible." – That very evening I was to go on. From a young actor who lived in the next room at the Wittenberg Square boarding house, I borrowed a tuxedo, a dickey and patent leather shoes. Trembling with excitement, I hurried to Kantstrasse. How astonished I must have been when the "Tü-Tü" crowd greeted me coolly. They sized me up with their eyes, which revealed an effort to conceal their contempt. The hall was still perfectly empty when I came on stage, pale in my tuxedo. Directly before me at a table sat several "colleagues"; I heard them laugh, while the footlights blinded me. My voice was gone, gone, gone. Not until I was on the stage did I consider which pieces I should select from my little lyric store. After a short pause I made up my mind and in a very shaky little voice began:
>
>> Perversion's really swell, my boy –
>> Perversion keeps you well, my boy –
>
> Not a hand stirred. Then in an even more wretched noise I warbled to the sneering cabaret crowd idling over their mochas, waiting for the real customers, that "We are so fond of makeup, 'Cause it makes us smell so sweet." – It was the most embarrassing situation of my life.
>
> Later I learned that Schneider-Duncker – highly talented both in his cabaret singing and his mode of teaching – had, after the dialogue which had sounded so encouraging in my presence, called the manageress of the "Tü-Tü" and said, "Listen, old girl, this raw youth is coming by tonight – a Dichterkind and so on – with the meshugener idea he has to do music-hall. Treat him so that he loses the taste for it." – I lost the taste.[8]

Erika had moved in and played small parts for Max Reinhardt; Pamela, who was in the acting troupe of a Cologne theatre, paid flying visits. Klaus had gainful employment as a theatre critic, which gave him both financial security and entry to the Berlin art world. But his "decadence" remained cerebral. "A little orgy" at a friend's apartment in Berlin, described years later, consisted harmlessly of staying up all night in colored pajamas, singing, declaiming, guzzling, dancing, painting each other's faces, and driving to Grünewald at dawn. He also experimented with drugs, since cocaine was as common as champagne in Berlin, although more expensive.

Distinctive homosexual activity in Berlin had been recorded since the eighteenth century, but the new licence that followed the 1918 revolution made it more conspicuous. Magnus Hirschfeld's Institute for Sexual Research virtually propagandized for a "third sex" and made open discussion of pederasty, transvestitism and hermaphrodites respectable, though the infamous §175 was still on the books. The numerous equivocal youth groups and male-bonding societies were amplified by less ambiguous gatherings. Gay bars, clubs and drag balls, all tolerated under the benevolent protection of the police, proliferated to such a degree that they were listed in guidebooks and a tour through the "queer circuit" became a feature of Berlin nightlife. The depressed state of the economy promoted widespread male prostitution, ranging from perfumed professional streetwalkers to unemployed proles who had no qualms about renting themselves for an hour or so. For all the blatancy of same-sex behavior during the Weimar Republic, in the popular imagination, homosexuals remained painted, lisping hustlers or monsters like the Hamburg butcher Franz Haarmann, who picked up homeless boys at the railway station, took them home and, after a bout of sex, murdered them and sold their flesh as pork.

Mann's advertisement of his homosexuality first appeared as a provocative pose of decadence which concealed profound and genuine feeling. He enjoyed intense male friendships, particularly with his Munich school-chum Ricki Hallgarten and the Parisian surrealist René Crevel. (His engagement with Pamela Wedekind broke off in 1927, when she became attached to the aging playwright Carl Sternheim.) His later diaries also record a series of transitory pickups who assuaged his immediate sexual needs, in contrast to his deeply-felt emotional attachments. However, Mann never wrote a theoretical apologia for homosexuality, in the manner of André Gide's *Corydon*.[9] In the writings of his youth, it is presented as a Bohemian alternative and challenge to conformist society, a prerogative of the lost generation. His own homosexuality affirmed his status as outsider, disenabling him for participation in political parties or ideological factions. In the "all the sad young men" mode of the pre-War homosexual, he saw his passional nature as setting him apart from the chance of ordinary pleasure as well. Significantly, both Hallgarten and Crével, among others in Mann's intimate circle, were to commit suicide. Mann himself was to make five attempts on his own life, before succeeding at last in 1949.[10]

1925 was to prove Mann's *annus mirabilis*: he first published a collection of short stories, wrote and acted in the play *Ania and Esther* (*Anja und Esther*), and spent the summer composing his novel *The Pious Dance* (*Der fromme Tanz*) which appeared the following year. Although the novel was a serious and lyric treatment of a young man's self-discovery as a homosexual artist in Berlin and Paris, *Ania and Esther* was a more light-hearted production.

Essentially the theme of the play is the collision of adolescent fantasies and ideals with the seductive call of the real world. In the 1923 Hamburg production, 18-year-old Klaus, Erika and Pamela played the lead roles along with 25-year-old Gustaf Gründgens, who directed the play as well. At this period, the ambitious homosexual actor was one of Mann's closest friends and was later briefly married to Erika. But already a worm of jealousy was burrowing into the relationship; newspaper stories about *Ania and Esther* regularly featured the *Dichterkinder* and their "descent" to the boards. Gründgens, with his lower middle-class background and stagey ways, often seemed out-of-place in the essentially upper-bourgeois ambience of the Mann and Wedekind households. Later, the tension between the Manns' literary ambitions and liberal politics and Gründgens' expedient careerism would culminate in a rupture. Once Klaus and Erika were exiles from Hitler's Germany and Gründgens a leading figure in the Nazi-dominated theatre, these bygone differences would be expanded into Mann's novel *Mephisto* (1936), whose actor-protagonist stands for all those artists who made their peace with the Fascist masters. The only damning characteristic Mann left out of his portrayal of "Heinrich Höfgen" was Gründgens' homosexuality, perhaps because he shared it.

*Ania and Esther* is set in a parodic version of the Odenwaldschule, a "convalescent home for fallen children," whose absent-minded director is modelled on Paulus Geheeb. With his full beard and short pants and his unabashed pedophilia, he is also a cartoon version of God the Father. A close-knit but spiritually complex relationship among four of the school's charges, Ania, Esther, Kaspar and Jakob, is thrown into confusion by the intrusion of handsome Erik. In contrast with the sensual, experienced, worldly Erik, a circus and cabaret performer who has been kept by both men and women, the children suddenly strike each other as insipid and affected. When Esther decides to leave the school with him, the other three are cast into impotent despair.

Not uncommonly, Klaus Mann's works of this period take place in enclosed worlds; the "home for fallen children" of the play seemed, in the words of one critic, a "dangerous mixture . . . of cloister and bordello." Like Henry Blake Fuller, Mann has recourse to Maeterlinck. The incantatory repetitiousness of the dialogue and the enigmatic statements and conduct recall Maeterlinck's claustrophobic world. The isolated hospice itself, with its folding doors and French windows, remind us that in Maeterlinck windows and doors are outlets to the supernatural beyond, to a world where Death holds sway. The outside world, in Mann, is equally deadly, but is all too real, in contrast to the protective environment of the hospice.

The Old Man, head of the institution, is an embodiment of uncontrolled sexual rapacity, who forces himself on 7-year-old girls; in the absence of mothers (who are characterized as abusive, weak-willed or uncaring), his fatherliness offers an affection which is, in Esther's words, "artificial and excessive." His strange combination of stilted deportment and emotional instability have been read by some literary critics as a token of Klaus Mann's inward psychological conflict with his father.

One of the last scenes in the play makes the body itself, in the person of the seducer Erik, responsible for "all the vulgar instincts" which Kaspar "has inherited from a disreputable father in his oddly mixed blood." Jakob proclaims Erik's flesh guilty for all the unwholesomeness, its powers of attraction the catalyst for the latent sexual conflicts of the pubescent; he screams at him, "Your flesh – your seven times damned flesh! . . . I feel a desire to punish your flesh! I feel an insane desire to chastise your flesh!" While Jakob chides the flesh of the young, Esther damns "the morality of the fathers" which "turns away in shock from the questionable sex which they are guilty of." The children may have perverse instincts, but they were inherited from the fathers.

One German critic has suggested that, except for the Old Man, who observes the carryings-on but does not get involved in the entanglements, all five leading characters are bisexual and that bisexuality is the norm. This is not really borne out by the play: Kaspar, Klaus's *alter ego*, seems exclusively homosexual; Jakob, with his fixation on Ania, seems to be heterosexual, although his vehemence towards Erik suggests a homosexual panic stirring amid his other neuroses. Esther, who transfers her affections from Ania to Erik, is the only member of the little group to carry out bisexuality in practice. As for Ania, her love for Esther is so strong than no other person, man or woman, can awaken similar feelings in her. She lets the two persons she loves, Esther and her brother Kaspar, leave without fighting for them. Through this behavior, she consummates "the ethos of the non-possessive." This is, for Klaus Mann, the distinguishing mark of true love – not to possess the beloved's body, even to know one will never possess it, but at every moment to be thankful that it exists and breathes.

Erik, the cynosure of so much desire, is presented by Mann as polymorphously perverse, with hints of incest, sado-masochism and prostitution in its portrait of his total sexual availability. Erik's resemblance to a sailor suggests the myth of the mariner as a loose liver, never averse to a bout of buggery at sea or a blowjob on land. Erik's role as the seemingly passive instigator of others' lusts also connects him with Lulu, that ingenuous siren of the plays *The Earth Spirit* and *Pandora's Box*, by Pamela Wedekind's father. He is similarly a forecast of the ambiguously attractive outsider who stirs a family's libidos in Peter Schaffer's play *Five Finger Exercise* and in the films *Teorema* by Paolo Pasolini and *Something for Everyone* by Hal Prince.

Stage plays are public events and therefore *Ania and Esther* was attacked vehemently for its homophilic sentiments and displays; Klaus Mann was even called "a felon against the German people" by one right-wing newpaper. Before the Vienna production, a rumor ran that Thomas Mann had refused to read the play because it was "too obscene." But he publicly denied such nonsense, saying "I am no boarding-school miss." In general, the elder Mann regarded the more outrageous antics of his children with a deliberately bemused air, rarely commenting, never condemning.[11]

## Notes

1  E. Spangenberg, *Karriere eines Romans. Mephisto, Klaus Mann und Gustaf Gründgens. Ein dokumentarischer Bericht aus Deutschland und dem Exil 1925–1981,* Munich, Ellermann Verlag, 1984, p. 32.

2  T. Mann, *Doktor Faustus: Das Leben des deutschen Tonsetzers Adrian Leverkühn, erzählt von einem Freunde,* Stockholm, Bermann-Fischer Verlag, 1947, p. 184.

3  K. Mann, *Kind dieser Zeit,* Reinbek bei Hamburg, Rowohlt, 1983, p. 101.

4  K. Mann, *Der Wendepunkt. Ein Lebensbericht,* Reinbek bei Hamburg, Rowohlt, 1984, p. 104.

5  K. Mann, *Das Wendepunkt,* pp. 111, 121–2.

6  K. Mann, "Europe's search for a new credo," *Tomorrow,* June 1949, vol. 8, p. 11. Also see H. Mayer, 'The alternatives of Klaus Mann and Maurice Sachs," *Outsiders. A Study in Life and Letters,* trans. D. M. Sweet, Cambridge, Mass., MIT Press, 1984, pp. 245–7.

7  K. Mann, *Kind dieser Zeit,* p. 170.

8  K. Mann, *Das Wendepunkt,* pp. 129–30.

9  Mann deeply distrusted Gide's facility in reconciling his pederasty with his Communism. In his essay, "The Controversy over André Gide," in the German emigré periodical *Die Weltbühne* in Prague in 1937, he suggested treating Gide "not only as a traitor, but as a mentally incompetent, pleasure-seeking old sinner, whose sell-out is abominable, but scarcely of intellectual consequence." "Der Streit um André Gide," in K. Mann, *Die Heimsuchung des europäischen Geistes,* Munich, Deutscher Taschenbuchverlag, 1973. p. 47.

10  Questions of the effect of Mann's homosexuality on his writing are dealt with, perhaps a bit too ponderously, by S. Zynda, *Sexualität bei Klaus Mann,* Bonn, Bouvier Verlag Herbert Grundmann, 1986; G. Härle, *Männerweiblichkeit. Zur Homosexualität bei Klaus und Thomas Mann,* Frankfurt am Main, Athenäum, 1988; and H. Neumann, *Klaus Mann. Eine Psychobiografie,* Stuttgart, W. Kohlhammer, 1995.

11  *Der Querschnitt,* December 1925, vol. 5, p. 1075; *Neues Wiener Journal,* 19 Feb. 1926. The only revival of the play I have been able to trace is a Dutch translation, directed by Teuntje Klinkenberg for the Project F Act.Op. 7, and performed in the major cities of the Netherlands in January and February 1984. See G. Bleijenberg, "Anja en Esther. Een toneelstuk van Klaus Mann," *Homologie,* Jan.–Feb. 1984, vol. 6, pp. 7–9.

# Ania and Esther

A romantic play in seven tableaux

## Klaus Mann

(1925)

## Characters

THE OLD MAN

ANIA  
KASPAR } his grandchildren

ESTHER

JAKOB

SIX BOYS

SIX GIRLS

TWO FEMALE ATTENDANTS

ERIK

*The play takes place in the present [1923], at summer's end.*
*The setting is an old hospice.*

## First Tableau

*The scene is a big, hall-like room in the hospice. Upstage a wide folding door, which opens into a back room. Left a glass door, with steps leading to the park. Right a small door to the outside. The room itself, very spacious and sparsely furnished, is panelled in dark wainscotting. Downstage right, a heavy, carved armchair. Over the big door upstage a crucifix set into the wall; left of the folding door stand two candelabrums.*
*Evening is drawing in and soon it will be dark, but when the curtain rises the stage is completely bright.*
*In the downstage armchair sits ANIA. She is wearing a plain, dark dress with a narrow white turned-down collar. Her hair is dark. . . . The six little girls stand in a row in dark tights in the middle of the room. They are in training. As the curtain goes up, they have each raised a white leg and spread their arms. ESTHER is standing, as teacher, in front of them, so that her back is turned to the audience. She flicks a long switch through the air so sharply that it whirrs. She is wearing a grey dress buttoned to the top, belted with a leather strap. – In the background, flanking the folding door, sit the two old FEMALE ATTENDANTS, hunched on two low stools. They play a kind of accompaniment to the children's exercises, one on a decrepit flute, the other on an out-of-tune zither. They sit bent over their work.*

ESTHER  *(Counting sharply)* One . . . two . . . and three!

*(The switch flicks back, the children bend their legs, then stand still in a straight line. Nevertheless the ATTENDANTS carry on their accompaniment. A screechy and yet sharply rhythmical dirge.)*

ESTHER  *(Turns around)* Now you can take a break. Next we'll practise the 'Dance in Black' again, at least the last position.

*(The row of children quietly breaks up. They simply sit on the ground or lean against the wall, as if exhausted. They all look rather pale. – Meanwhile the music drones on.)*

ESTHER  *(Lights up a cigarette)* I'm really worried about how it's going to come off tomorrow. It would make a difference. . . .
ANIA  *(Turns smiling to the ATTENDANTS)* If you don't get any special amusement out of playing, you may stop. We've been done for quite some time now.
THE ATTENDANTS  *(Both raise their heads simultaneously)* Done? . . . We didn't notice. . . . *(They stand up, put their instruments under their arms and hobble to the exit right.)*
ESTHER  *(To them)* We'll call you if we have another rehearsal.
THE ATTENDANTS  *(Hobbling out)* Thank you, meanwhile we'll set the table for supper.

169

ESTHER   *(To Ania)* Incidentally you can't possibly form an opinion of the potential effect of the dances with that ghastly music. Tomorrow morning, at the dress rehearsal, you'll be surprised when you hear the orchestra from town.

ANIA   I really enjoy the Attendants' music. . . . It sounds like the Old Man's beasts roaring on a hot stormy night.

ESTHER   *(Looks at her)* Yes . . . you're right. . . . But as accompaniment to a dance ensemble it leaves a lot to be desired.

*(One of the little girls has silently lit a cigarette.)*

ANIA   Ruth has a cigarette in her mouth again.

ESTHER   She can't quit so the Old Man lets her have five a day. . . . I consider the success or failure of tomorrow's premiere to be crucial, because it's been over a year since we've produced anything for the so-called public.

ANIA   That's because the children have to learn everything from scratch. We're the only ones left of the previous "generation" . . . along with Jakob and Kaspar . . .

ESTHER   Yes, that's true – . They've all gone away. . . . Where are they all now . . . ?

ANIA   *(Interrupting)* If you really want to rehearse 'Dance in Black' some more, you'd better start soon. They might ring for supper at any moment.

ESTHER   *(Throws away her cigarette)* All right . . . get up! *(She seizes the switch, takes a position. The girls quickly stand up and form a row again.)*

ESTHER   Somebody run and fetch the music ladies. You're standing as stiff as blocks of wood. . . . Run, Eliza, run! *(A little girl runs out.)*

*(From the park* THE OLD MAN *enters. The* SIX BOYS *follow him.* THE OLD MAN *presents a curious appearance. He has a long, white beard and his legs, hairy as an ape's, are bare from the knees down. His manner is one of rigid and decrepit cordiality. . . . The boys wear short white smocks with brown belts and bright red borders at the low-cut necks; bare legs in white shorts. They are between 12 and 14.)*

THE OLD MAN   Do you intend to go on rehearsing the children, Esther . . . my dear? *(He strokes her hair.)* Yes, yes, yes . . . you are indefatigable. But unfortunately I

have to kidnap them. I want to go over their finale song at least once before supper, the last part didn't work right. Tomorrow, though, I'd rather they didn't do anything before the dress rehearsal, and after supper tonight they must hop into bed at once.

ESTHER   What a shame. . . .

ANIA   *(To* THE OLD MAN*)* Take them with you. I can't imagine that the 'Dance in Black' can be made any better.

*(Little* ELIZA *comes running back in.)*

ELIZA   Here come the music ladies. – *(The* ATTENDANTS *hobble in behind her.)*

THE FEMALE ATTENDANTS   Here we are again . . . here we are again . . . don't be in such a hurry . . .

THE OLD MAN   *(To the little girl)* Come over here, Eliza. Take it easy . . . you're all out of breath. . . . How your little heart beats! . . . There, there, there . . .

ESTHER   *(To the* ATTENDANTS*)* No . . . you may go again. Unfortunately I can't use you. *(The Women hobble off muttering.)*

THE OLD MAN   *(To* ELIZA*)* We'll sing our rose song just once before supper. Now your heart is calm again. . . . We'll all go into my study. *(Near* ESTHER*)* Esther . . . is my little child sad, because she can't go on working any more today? Ey, ey, ey . . . who would have thought it a couple of years ago?

ESTHER   Oh please . . . I'm only a little nervous, tomorrow's so soon upon us.

THE OLD MAN   Why should you be, my dear? The little children will do their best with charm and finesse. Eliza and Gimietto are precision itself, and they're the leads. . . . Now come with the Old Man! *(He exits, holding* ELIZA *by the hand. The other girls and boys follow.)*

ESTHER   I am sure that the rose chorus is perfect as it is. The Old Man only wants to be with Eliza, that's all he cares about.

ANIA   Let him have his pleasure. It does no one any harm, Eliza least of all. Come, sit by me on the back of the chair. . . . Now the children are singing.

*(The song filters in, muffled.)*

THE CHILDREN SING:

'Let us sing and merry be

Amongst the roses,
With Jesus and our friends are we!
Who knows how long a life we'll see
Amongst the roses!'

*(During the song* KASPAR *and* JAKOB *appear at the door to the park.* KASPAR *is wearing a buttoned-up suit of dark, but not black material.* JAKOB *is dressed similarly but more unconventionally – with long cuffs and remarkably pointed, maybe red, shoes.)*

JAKOB   They sing beautifully.
ANIA   . . . The second verse. . . .
THE CHILDREN SING:
'Now we uncork Jesus' wine
Amongst the roses.
Then may we all in love entwine,
Our hearts' delight be yours and mine
Amongst the roses.

Cyprus wine for us he'll pour
Amongst the roses,
We shall all be drunk for sure,
Drunk with sweet love ever more
Amongst the roses.'

*(*JAKOB *and* KASPAR *come farther downstage.)*

KASPAR   I really wanted to do a little more work with the boys on that last dance, the one I lead them in. But the Old Man took them away.
ESTHER   The same thing happened to us. So it'll have to be all right as is.
KASPAR   Esther, I expect the dance you've been working on with the children to make the strongest impression of the whole programme. It has a most sublime and heartfelt elegance . . . I may be wrong, but I think that grace can get to the point where it turns back into the grief it once was.
ESTHER   I want it to do honour to the Old Man and the hospice. . . . Ania thinks it's good too.
ANIA   If people aren't moved by it, then they're callous brutes. I think it must break down the most ingrained prejudices. In comparison our dance of the "grey angel" almost seems prim and repellent. . . . I confess whenever I hear the Old Man rehearsing the children, I feel as if this song must move everyone to his heart of hearts.
JAKOB   I can never make up my mind which of my cabaret songs I want to sing. The

cosmetics song might seem too frivolous and too trivial. After all, people don't have a very high opinion of us. Superficial minds might consider these ditties not much different from ordinary cabaret material. . . . What do you think, Ania?
ANIA   It's so hard to give advice. I tend to think you sing that song with such intensity it ought to cancel out the accusation of frivolity at least.
JAKOB   Anyway I've decided not to recite the ballad of the dead youth and the perverted little girl.
ESTHER   I agree, I think that story of an ice-cold love affair with a corpse sets somewhat too high a standard for the audience's comprehension.
KASPAR   Anyone incapable of appreciating the ineffable sadness of the corpse song would be highly likely to call it immoral.
JAKOB   And yet I love that ballad best of all my pieces.
ESTHER   We still have a problem with how the first long pantomime will be received. Isn't it too tedious, but then again, isn't it too risqué in its erotic entanglements? . . . We mustn't forget that it takes up almost the whole first part of the programme.
ANIA   I think you're worrying needlessly. Even the most uncouth spectator should enjoy its glamour.
KASPAR   How pretty the costumes will be! . . .
ESTHER   I really took a lot of trouble in designing them.
KASPAR   And, believe me, it wasn't so easy for me to come up with the 'erotic entanglements' you refer to. I've put more of myself into this play than you'd imagine.
ESTHER   I'm sure no one will doubt the *sincerity* of our work. I was only thinking about its purely superficial effect.
THE CHILDREN SING:
"Let the glasses go around
Amongst the roses,
Then gaily we'll be homeward bound,
And joyful all forever found
Amongst the roses!"
ANIA   And joyful all forever found . . . that moves me so . . .
JAKOB   The Attendants told me that we're sold out.
ESTHER   Yes, despite the long ride from town.

*(A dinner bell rings.)*

ANIA   They're calling us to supper.

KASPAR   The old man and the children are coming back in. Gimietto is partnered with Ellis again. Did you hear how clear his voice was in the singing?

*(THE OLD MAN, holding ELIZA by the hand, comes from the park. Behind him the other children. The girls are now wearing white dresses.)*

THE OLD MAN   So, now the children have sung. Were you able to hear their voices? . . . But Ania doesn't look too well. Is anything wrong, Ania?

ESTHER   Yes, I was thinking the same thing. You must tell me if you need anything.

ANIA   No . . . I am all right. No, I don't need anything. It's only the effect of the light . . . and I may be tired.

*(From within, the ATTENDANTS open the folding door leading into the back room. Not all of the room which is almost as wide as the actual stage can be seen, only a long section of it. In contrast to the half-darkness of the downstage room it is brightly lit. It is painted grey. Across the whole room runs a wooden table, laid for supper. Backless stools stand around the table. THE OLD MAN's chair is raised alone in the middle patriarchally.)*

THE ATTENDANTS   *(Curtseying by the door)* Dinner is served . . . please . . . dinner is served.

*(THE OLD MAN, KASPAR, JAKOB, the boys and the girls go in. But ANIA, who starts to get up, is pulled back into the chair by ESTHER.)*

ESTHER   *(To those going out)* Right away . . . just a moment . . . we'll be right in. . . .

THE OLD MAN   *(Sitting in his armchair right at the table)* All right . . . we'll start in the meantime. *(He begins to eat supper.)*

JAKOB   *(already at the door)* Isn't Ania feeling well?

ESTHER   She's all right . . . we'll be in in a minute. . . .

*(When they are all sitting – the boys with their backs to the audience, the girls facing it – the attendants close the folding door from within. JAKOB and KASPAR sit among the boys. The*

*chairs for ANIA and ESTHER remain empty among the girls.)*

ESTHER   *(By ANIA, on the chairback)* Ania . . . is there anything wrong with you?

ANIA   No, no . . . what makes you think that? I'm quite well.

ESTHER   Sometimes suddenly I get so worried about you . . . that you might die all of a sudden . . .

ANIA   You mustn't worry. . . . You shouldn't worry about anything . . .

ESTHER   But if you were dead, what would I do then? I think I could commit the most monstrous crimes and go away from here and throw myself into all sorts of things . . . if you were dead.

ANIA   We must go inside with the others. Can you hear, they've started eating.

ESTHER   And how quickly it's got dark! . . . Listen!

*(Outside a voice is calling something like Hallo or Yoohoo – a kind of shout or cry for help.)*

ESTHER   *(Suddenly trembling)* What was that?

ANIA   A boy's voice. . . .

ESTHER   But it was nobody from the hospice shouting. I know that much. . . .

ANIA   You're trembling.

ESTHER   Am I? . . . Yes, I don't know myself what's got me so upset. But it's over now. . . . Actually I wanted to tell you something; that's why I asked you to stay. It's nothing much . . . nothing important really. . . . Just a passage in an old book that I wanted to tell you about. I haven't told anyone about it until today . . . none of the others . . . or the old man either. . . . But I've been thinking about it for weeks. Like music, you know, it runs in my head. But I haven't told anyone. It comes from such an old book. . . . It's all about the stars.

ANIA   The stars . . . ?

ESTHER   It says that the stars sprinkled through the night are like shimmering tears. *(Suddenly ecstatic, almost crying out.)* What an infinite grief there must be in those eyes to make them weep . . . *(Quietly again, shrinking back into herself)* . . . says the old book. . . . Now that I've said it, I'm freezing. . . . But isn't it beautiful? . . . The dear stars as God's tears, the tears of a mournful God.

ANIA   *(Very slowly)* Don't you believe that

God is cheerful too, immensely cheerful . . . immeasurably cheerful . . . ?

ESTHER But we know nothing about it . . . we mortals know nothing. Or only very seldom; . . . or almost never. . . .

ANIA (Gets up, walks slowly to the door) But now we have to join the others.

ESTHER (Runs after her, stops her right in the middle of the room) Stop . . . wait just a moment. . . . I would like to tell you something else too, in haste, something I've been thinking about so much lately . . . something quite different. . . . I was wondering whether the two of us, you and I, will ever be made saints . . . saints, yes, by the church, by the Pope himself . . . the Old Man will certainly put in a recommendation, he's supposed to be a close friend of the Pope's. Then we shall be St Ania and St Esther. Then we shall stand silver over the farmhouse doors. Then old women in their hoods will pray to us and so will skinny fair-haired schoolgirls and the boys too. Then our faint voices will be much heeded by gentlemen. And when we die, there will be a great to-do among the angels . . . they will flap their stiff plumage to give their new comrades a festive welcome. . . . Then whatever we do will be holy . . . (Suddenly very quiet) . . . including the things we're always doing with one another. (Another, almost jubilant outburst) Because we'll be saints!

ANIA (Strokes her hair) Would you really like that so much?

ESTHER And you, I do believe, are one already. I truly believe that you are one already, you are so meek, so very full of meekness, much more than ordinary people can be. Sometimes you resist – but even your resistance is full of meekness. (Very quietly, close to her) For me you are like a saint. A dark saint. A dark silver saint. Saint Ania. My own Saint Ania. My Ania.

ANIA (In a sudden and deeply ardent passion clasps ESTHER's hand) I don't know . . . saint . . . saint . . . I don't understand the word any more. Now the words stop . . . now they sink . . . deep . . . (She kisses her hands.)

ESTHER Let's not join the others now. . . . Come . . . come with me now . . . into the garden . . . into the night . . . into the garden . . . come . . . come . . . (Their embracing figures disappear into the shadows.)

(For a brief moment the stage is empty. The sound of muffled talk from the dining-room, then the two old female ATTENDANTS hobble in right, carrying bowls of food across the stage.)

ONE ATTENDANT Fräulein Esther and Fräulein Ania didn't come to supper.

THE OTHER ATTENDANT Oh yeah, yeah . . . once again . . . once again. . . . (They go into the dining-room, opening the folding door no further than necessary to slip in. For a moment one can see THE OLD MAN, silently shoveling food into himself.)

(Now ANIA and ESTHER return from outside. With them is ERIK, whom they half lead. It is now so dark that at first one cannot make out his appearance, but his voice resonates clearly.)

ESTHER Yes, now at least tell us how you got in here? . . . Scaring people like that!

ERIK (Who can't quite stand up straight) I don't know . . . please excuse me . . . I must have got lost . . . please excuse me. Where am I exactly?

ESTHER That isn't so easy to explain. Besides it's none of your business. You scared me silly.

ANIA You are in an old hospice which houses a so-called 'Convalescent Home for Fallen Children.'

ERIK (With a slight laugh) A convalescent home? A convalescent home for fallen children? . . . Then I belong here. . . .

ANIA Are you sick?

ESTHER I got the impression you were drunk.

ERIK Sick? Drunk? . . . Maybe both.

ESTHER Are you the one who shouted so strangely in the garden before?

ERIK Did I shout in the garden? . . . That may well be.

ESTHER (Quietly) You got me so upset.

(The door to the dining-room opens. A boy comes out.)

THE BOY The Old Man wants to know if there is a stranger here . . . he heard voices.

ANIA Yes, there is someone here. The Old Man should come in. And light the candelabrums!

(The boy turns on the lights. Goes back into the dining-room.)

(ERIC *stands blinking in the sudden brightness. He is a lad of rather proletarian appearance, in a sort of seedy sailor suit with a matching cap.*)

ESTHER   (*Looks at him and smiles*) You did shout in the garden . . . Your voice has a clear ring to it . . . (*Suddenly subdued, charmed*) . . . but it was an impertinence.

(THE OLD MAN, KASPAR, JAKOB *and some of the children come in from the dining-room.*)

THE OLD MAN   (*In a very good humour*) Aye, aye . . . a new guest.

ERIK   (*Pulls off his cap*) Yes . . . excuse me . . . I got lost. . . .

THE OLD MAN   I imagine you've come from the town.

ERIK   Yes . . . from the town . . . that is, I'm sick. Not actually sick . . . but . . .

ESTHER   (*To* THE OLD MAN) He is quite simply drunk, of course.

KASPAR   (*Looks at him*) He'll have to spend the night here.

ESTHER   Yes, he'll have to spend the night in the hospice.

THE OLD MAN   What is your name?

ERIK   My name is Erik. (*He staggers, then laughs at it.*) May I sleep here? . . . If I could sleep here, I could even pay. I still have lots of money left. All right? I'm tired . . . and after all this is a convalescent home.

THE OLD MAN   (*With sudden energy*) Yes. This is a convalescent home.

KASPAR   He can bunk with me. I'll sleep on the sofa.

THE OLD MAN   The Attendants will prepare the guest room. There he'll sleep soundly. (*Suddenly walks over to him, smiles at him gently.*) Sleep safe and sound, young Erik, sleep safe and sound. . . .

ERIK   (*Closes his eyes*) Safe and sound . . . the sleep's bound to be good here. (*His hand makes an unconsciously vehement gesture, as if to ward off* THE OLD MAN) Safe and sound. . . .

ESTHER   (*Stammering*) He is afraid of him . . . look . . . he is afraid of the Old Man . . .

THE OLD MAN   (*Continues to smile*) Somebody should take him to bed now. (*He stares at him, smiling gently, as* JAKOB *and a little girl lead him out. When he is gone:*) Here he shall have a healing sleep – that *splendid* fellow. (*He first shakes* ANIA's *hand, then* ESTHER's *and* KASPAR's.) And so good

night. Now I'll put the little ones to bed. Won't you come up and say good night?

KASPAR   Yes . . . perhaps we'll come later. . . .

ALL THE CHILDREN   (*Bowing and curtseying to the three and saying in hollow, tinny voices*) Good night. (*They follow* THE OLD MAN *Indian file.*) KASPAR (*Hand on his brow*) What did his voice remind me of? I don't know . . . if only I knew. . . . I must have heard it somewhere before. – Is he a real sailor?

ESTHER   (*Laughs*) He could turn out to be anything at all of that sort.

KASPAR   But his voice was strangely clear . . . strangely clear. . . . Yes, sleep well. Good night, Ania.

ANIA   Are you going back to the children, Kaspar? . . . You forgot to say good night to Gimietto. He looks so sad.

KASPAR   Yes . . . I'll go straight to the children. . . . Good-bye! (*He goes out.*)

ANIA   (*After a pause, in a very tremulous voice*) Are you coming . . . are you coming to me tonight for a while?

ESTHER   No . . . unfortunately not . . . tomorrow we've got to dance, so we'd better get a good rest for once. (*She hesitates a moment, then curtly*): Good night. (*And goes out*)

(ANIA *stands motionless centre stage.* JAKOB *comes in.*)

JAKOB   The intruder fellow's fast asleep . . . dead to the world. . . .

ANIA   Yes.

JAKOB   Ania, my dear Ania . . . wouldn't you like to take a little walk in the park with me?

ANIA   (*Shrugs in mild resistance*) No . . . how can you ask me that? It's so cold.

JAKOB   But you always enjoy walking in the fallen leaves.

ANIA   Aren't you going to turn off the candelabrums?

JAKOB   Sure . . . only it'll be dark then.

(*He puts out the lights. Stands bent over in the background.* ANIA *stands erect.*)

## Second Tableau

ERIK's *bedroom. A small, almost cell-like space. Upstage a relatively high window. The room is on the ground floor, so one can look directly out the window into the garden. Right, against the wall a very plain bed with a chair next to it. Left, across from it, the door. – It is morning. The sun is shining into the room.* ERIK *is lying in bed, in the posture of a sleeping child. He is wearing a coarse linen nightshirt and is covered by a homely woollen blanket.*

*By the bed stand a little* GIRL *and a little* BOY – ELIZA *and* GIMIETTO –, *dressed in white as at the end of the first tableau. The girl is carefully carrying a tray with cup and saucer, breakfast dishes, the boy is carrying a teapot on a stand.*

THE GIRL   He's still asleep.
THE BOY   We have to wake him up.
THE GIRL   Will you do it?
THE BOY   What if he curses me out . . .

*(Erik moves in his sleep.)*

THE BOY   Is he awake now?
THE GIRL   No – I'll have to wake him up. *(Without putting down the tray, she tickles him very carefully.)*
ERIK   *(Wakes with a yawn, sees the children by the bedside)* Who are you . . . ?!
THE GIRL   The Old Man had us bring you breakfast.
ERIK   The Old Man . . . ?
THE BOY   Even sent you some of his own best marmalade.
ERIK   Right – just put it down . . . thanks a lot. . . .
THE CHILDREN   *(Put their things on a small table next to the bed. Immediately walk back to the door)* Do you need anything else?
THE GIRL   The Old Man says if there's anything you want, feel free to let us know.
THE BOY   For instance if you would like to take a bath.
ERIK   A bath? . . . Thanks. But maybe you could tell me where I am?
THE BOY AND THE GIRL   *(In perfect unison, in very high voices, reciting something they have learned but don't quite understand)* You are in the Convalescent Home for Fallen Children. *(They go out.)*
ERIK   *(Stares after them in shock)* Convalescent home? . . . Fallen children? . . . And how incredible the air is here . . . as if there were a caged animal nearby. But the children look pale. *(He lies back again, stares at the ceiling.)* And this room . . . I feel as if I'm lying in a monk's cell. . . .

*(Without knocking first,* ESTHER *enters. She is garishly made up and is already in her* pantomime costume. *She is wearing a tight, white silk dress, with brightly colored shoes and a bright red or green spun-glass wig. She has the long switch from the first scene in her hand.* ERIK *doesn't notice her at first, as he lies still, staring up at the ceiling.)*

ESTHER   *(At the door, sharply)* Good morning.
ERIK   *(Leaps up, stares at her in shock)* Good grief. . . .
ESTHER   *(Smiles)* You're startled by my costume. But there's no reason to be. This morning is our dress rehearsal, and naturally it's more convenient to don the motley as soon as we get up.
ERIK   *(Smiles too)* You look so colourful.
ESTHER   *(Sits on the chair next to his bed)* But it's pretty, isn't it, my costume? I designed it myself.
ERIK   *(As if dazzled)* Colourful – unnaturally colourful. . . .
ESTHER   *(Unusually serious and lady-like)* Actually I wanted to ask after your health and find out how you slept last night. Yesterday I had the impression you weren't feeling too well.
ERIK   No . . . definitely not. . . . To tell the truth, I can't exactly remember. But I'm here now.
ESTHER   *(Sprightly)* And maybe you'll stay another couple of weeks and be completely cured.
ERIK   I don't know. . . . Don't you think it smells like an animal cage around here?
ESTHER   There's good reason for that, the Old Man's animal cages start right under your window.
ERIK   The Old Man? Who is the Old Man? . . . Is he a lion tamer? . . . Everyone around here refers to him.
ESTHER   *(With a certain solemnity)* The Old Man: he runs this hospice.
ERIK   What about you? Are you a student or a teacher here? I mean: are you a fallen child or are you somebody who can reform them?
ESTHER   *(Quietly)* I have been here many, many years – I was brought to the hospice when I was 8 years old – by the way, no one is actually reformed here.
ERIK   But it's got be some kind of reformatory, from all I hear about it.
ESTHER   *(Suddenly stands up, shyly withdraws)* In the short time at my disposal I cannot enlighten you on that score. No, reformatory is definitely not the right word

. . . *(Suddenly smiling and takes a few steps towards him)* . . . but I will tell you this: today at the table you shall sit between me and the Old Man. Then I will take pains to enlighten you further . . . all right?

ERIK  All right. . . . *(Looks at her and suddenly laughs)*

ESTHER  What are you laughing at?

ERIK  You're so colourful . . . and so comical . . . awfully colourful . . .

ESTHER  Yes . . . I designed it myself. . . . One more thing . . . Erik: I would very much like you to be in the dressing-room tonight . . . we're opening our show today . . . You should be in the dressing-room with us. . . . I really would like it . . .

ERIK  Well, if you really would like it . . . and if 'the Old Man' has nothing against it . . .

ESTHER  Oh, he doesn't object to much. And besides *(Suddenly laughing very loudly)* people who live in glass houses . . . *(Breaks off: affectionately)*: But you are still tired. . . . Get some more sleep. . . . *(Her hand reaches out as if she wanted to stroke his hair, but she pulls it back and runs to the door.)* Good morning. *(She is gone.)*

ERIK  Now she's gone . . . am I dreaming or not, I'm not quite sure. If I close my eyes really tight: no more weird faces can show up like the one that just appeared. *(He closes his eyes.)*

*(Now* JAKOB, *similarly costumed, quietly enters. He is wearing a kind of Spanish outfit with a pointed sword and a blood-red ruff.)*

JAKOB  *(Quietly, but very sharply)* Are you still asleep?

ERIK  *(Leaps up, stares at him)* Now what is it?

JAKOB  You seem to have been dreaming. I just thought it might be more polite to look in on you this morning. You are still *very* foreign to this environment and that usually leads to depression and tedious melancholy.

ERIK  No . . . thanks. . . . I'm not depressed . . . thanks. Are you got up for the dress rehearsal too?

JAKOB  *(A touch of spite in his voice)* You've guessed it. . . . I find, by the way, that not only are you not sick, but you look downright *obviously* healthy.

ERIK  Why should I look sick? *(Laughs at the ceiling)* No, I'm healthy!

JAKOB  Then you don't need any more

coddling. I wish you more refreshing sleep. I don't suppose you're often enervated by nightmares. *(He bows himself out.)*

ERIK  His face was all stiff with makeup . . . stiff as a mask . . . and why did he speak in that artificial and hysterical way?

*(A cautious knock at the door.)*

ERIK  Another visitor. Please, come in!

*(*KASPAR *comes in wearing a buttoned-up costume of heavy black silk, and also with coloured hair.)*

KASPAR  Excuse me for disturbing you. . . .

ERIK  Don't mention it.

KASPAR  I just wanted to look in on you, before I have to go down to the stage, to find out how you are, of course . . . and also . . . do you mind if I sit down for a second? I am still so tired.

ERIK  Sit yourself down, you and I share the feeling.

KASPAR  Oh, do you feel the same way? . . . When you first awake from sleep you can't walk? . . . You can't break free from it, perhaps because it's got you deeply entangled in it? . . . I always spend the first hour of the day half asleep.

ERIK  Yes . . . sleep is a beautiful thing. . . .

KASPAR  Sleep is the only beautiful thing . . . with one exception . . .

ERIK  I don't agree with you there.

KASPAR  But actually I wanted to give you something . . . which as a matter of fact has to do with sleep. Last night I was up very late, writing late, because my mind was a bit muddled. Here . . . *(He gives it to him with his face turned away.)*

ERIK  *(Looks at it, almost with respect)* It's a poem. . . . Is it for me?

KASPAR  Just read it. . . . *(Suddenly stands up.)* But I'd rather not be here when you read it. . . . I'd rather not see it. And if you'd rather sleep, then, please, go to sleep. Sleep is more beautiful . . . although this has something to do with it. . . . *(He is already at the door.)*

ERIK  *(Looks at the paper)* Are you dancing now?

KASPAR  Yes . . . I'm dancing in my pantomime. With Ania and Esther.

ERIC  *(Looks at him)* Is there anything you can't do: dance and write poetry. How much you must have to get rid of. . . . What are your experiences like here?

KASPAR   There's only one experience to be had here, and you couldn't understand that. But I almost feel. . . . *(He turns around.)*

ERIC   Come here! Give me your hand! Why are you in such a hurry to run away?

KASPAR   *(Almost in fear)* Yes . . . I have to dance now. . . . But maybe I can sit next to you at lunch?

ERIC   No, unfortunately that won't work. Somebody else asked me ahead of you.

KASPAR   Yes . . . yes, I should have realized that. Excuse me for asking. . . . Good-bye. *(He is gone.)*

*(ERIK gazes earnestly after him. Then he sinks back in thought. He reads with childishly earnest attention. During the reading a smile comes to his face. – Then there is a gentle knock.)*

ERIK   *(Speaks, without looking up from the paper)* Please come in. . . .

*(ANIA enters. She is wearing a black silk dress with a wide farthingale that makes her look half a horsewoman, half a Spanish court lady.)*

ANIA   *(At the door)* I'm disturbing you . . . you're reading, as I can see. . . .

ERIK   *(Looks at her with eyes clouded by reading)* Yes . . . a poem. But I saw you before, yesterday . . . in the garden . . . at night. . . .

ANIA   Along with Esther.

ERIK   I thought you were alone. . . . Come over here! Would you also like to ask about my health?

ANIA   I'd like to say good morning to you.

ERIK   Of all the people who came here this morning, you have the most understated costume.

ANIA   It depends on how the roles are cast in our pantomime. . . . Were there a lot of people here this morning?

ERIK   Yes . . . I don't know any more . . . I'm not really awake yet. Just now I've been reading this poem that Kaspar wrote for me, when he was half asleep.

ANIA   Did Kaspar write you a poem? . . . Do you know that he's my brother?

ERIK   Is he really your brother? . . . Maybe he resembles you in lots of ways.

ANIA   My half-brother to be more precise. We have different fathers.

ERIK   Your half-brother . . . may I kiss your hand?

ANIA   *(Alarmed)* No – why do you want to?

ERIK   *(Urgently imploring)* I'd like to . . . I would like to! You really can't object to that!

ANIA   *(Half-smiling, offers him her hand)* I don't object to it much.

ERIK   *(Presses his mouth tightly and fervently to her hand)* How cool your hand is . . . oh . . . how cool. I would like to warm it up . . . and your arm, you have such thin arms, the kind little boys have.

ANIA   *(Her eyes closed)* Don't. – What are you doing . . . don't . . .

ERIK   Of all the people I may have seen last night, you're the only one I can remember . . . you were standing in the garden . . .

ANIA   *(Pulls away, runs to the door)* Don't . . . you mustn't! Why did you hold on to me? *(She feels up and down her arm as if it hurt.)* Why did I let myself let this happen? Did you act this way with the others? *(Suddenly looks down at the floor.)* Did you . . . did you stroke Esther like that?

ERIK   *(Protesting vigorously)* Not Esther . . . no, I did not stroke the others like that! Come back, please: come back again!

ANIA   You mustn't plead with me this way. I don't want to be unfriendly to you – *(Music strikes up in the distance)* Oh, the overture is beginning. I have to go now. . . . Good-bye. . . . *(She is already out.)*

ERIK   *(Calls after her)* If you can't stay with me, at least tell me your name . . . what's your name, so I can think about you.

ANIA   *(Already at a distance)* My name is Ania . . . Ania. . . .

ERIK   Ania . . . Ania . . . a gloomy name. Ania and Esther. Ania and Esther . . .

*(Outside the window THE OLD MAN walks past, he can be seen from the chest up.)*

THE OLD MAN   *(Peeps smiling in the window)* Oho, the slugabed! We've long been hard at work. Now sleep out your sleep! *(He has gone by smiling.)*

*(He is followed by the Indian file of children, who are tall enough for their heads to be seen in the window. The heads go by the window like puppets in a puppet show.)*

ERIK   *(Has half sat up in bed to see them. Then*

*he falls back into the pillows.)* But now . . . I really don't know where I am. . . . Not on earth, surely not on our ordinary old earth. . . . And that music. . . . And that smell of cages . . . and the Old Man's laughter . . . and lovely Ania . . . and that Esther. . . .

*(The music swells; ERIK closes his eyes.)*

## Third Tableau

### The night of the show

*Big company dressing-room or rather green-room. The room is wide, but not very deep. Upstage along the wall a row of twelve little chairs; in the middle a thirteenth, bigger, heavier. – Far upstage right, a low door, covered by a grey curtain, which, when the curtain is lifted, reveals a long, narrow, low gangway leading to the stage. – Downstage chaos and confusion. A couple of chairs, a pair of small tables. Far down left, against the wall, a dressing table, strewn with a hodge-podge of make-up materials. – The whole room is steeped in grey, it is tawdry and full of cigarette smoke. Present are: ANIA, ESTHER, KASPAR and ERIK. The first three are made-up and in their dance costumes. ANIA and ESTHER are all muffled up, enswathed in grey fabric, and their faces are also framed and draped. Their faces are made up in bright colours. KASPAR is wearing a big silver costume, closed to the top like a suit of armour, and he also has a grey cloak thrown over the armour. ERIK is dressed as he was in the first tableau. – They are smoking cigarettes.*

KASPAR   Jakob's coming back now.

*(He goes to the little door and pulls back the curtain. JAKOB comes down the gangway. He is grotesquely dressed in a green tousled wig with lots of gaudy ribbons on a motley jacket. He is carrying a lute. He is completely drained and, staggering a bit, goes to sit downstage. – The curtain to the gangway remains drawn back.)*

JAKOB   *(Hand on his brow)* It was revolting. . . . I feel I couldn't hit the right note. Did you think it was awful too?
ANIA   We couldn't hear you back here.
KASPAR   Was there applause?
JAKOB   Yes . . . sure. . . . But the audience is dreadful. They're always half amused, half

disgusted. While I was singing I couldn't get over the feeling that they didn't understand a word . . . they always think we're making decadent little jokes. Jokes . . . Jokes. . . . My head aches. But a person could throw his heart to them. Just talking about how blasé those ladies and gentlemen were makes my throat close up.
KASPAR   You mustn't think about them.
ANIA   Would you like something, Jakob? Do you want anything? . . . If you like, I'll rub your forehead with cologne.
JAKOB   Thanks . . . you're sweet. *(His hand feels for her, but she moves it away.)*
ESTHER   *(Suddenly and unexpectedly in a slight pause)* Sometimes I wonder what our mothers would say if they could see us like this. Would they understand us? Or would they bawl us out for being so mixed up?
ERIK   My mother almost never scolded me.
ESTHER   My mother was ill. She was depressed. Blond and quiet and beautiful . . . very psychotic. She and my father would quarrel in the cruellest way, even though they loved one another. Then each of them would try to get me on their side.
ERIK   Anyway I rarely saw my mother. She worked in a circus.
ESTHER   My father was once a Catholic priest, but he broke the bonds of the church because of a scandal. Nevertheless he always wore a frockcoat and punished us as if he were the Cardinal Grand Inquisitor.
ERIK   But whenever my mother saw me, she'd kiss me.
KASPAR   Is your mother dead?
ERIK   I don't know . . . yes . . . she is dead now. Why do you ask?
ESTHER   *(Laughs harshly)* He'd like to see how she kissed you. *(Suddenly leans close to him)* What did she call you! What did your late mother use for a nickname?
ERIK   She called me . . . I can't tell you.
ANIA   Kaspar and I . . . we barely knew our mother. She died soon after Kaspar was born, when Kaspar's father deserted her.
ERIK   Who was Kaspar's father?
ANIA   Nobody knows. He came from some-where, and he left . . . at that time mother had long been separated from *my* father.
ERIK   But your mother was the Old Man's daughter. He is your grandfather. You are his grandchildren. . . . It strikes me as almost . . . uncanny. . . . What was your father like, Ania?

ANIA   He was a high-ranking officer, at least at the time of his marriage to my mother. All I remember of him very dimly: a light grey uniform. . . . A strict gentleman. . . . My mother really didn't love him very much . . .

JAKOB   *(Very quietly from upstage)* Even when she talks about this father, who today wouldn't hesitate a moment to deny she's his daughter, there's something like pity in her voice.

ESTHER   We mustn't feel sorry for him. If anyone is our enemy, he is. The fact that he represents the highest, perhaps the most perfect type of the species worthy of our hate makes him only that much more dangerous, that much more detestable. I don't care if he is Ania's father, she has *nearly* nothing in common with him. . . . Oh, I can hear the clever and well-chosen words he'd use to keep us apart, to proclaim that our passion, our pleasure is immoral, improper, undisciplined. I can hear his words. . . . They don't apply to us. But the demeanour, the cleverness behind them, make them wound like well-aimed darts.

KASPAR   Besides, that estimable individual hardly needs our sympathy. He lives well respected and well-to-do in the big city. Able is he and serves the state.

ANIA   I believe, Kaspar, that your opinion is too harsh. When all's said and done, he is alone with his general's uniform.

ESTHER   *(In a voice distorted by mockery)* He has retired, I regret to say, from military service and taken up the useful occupation of humanitarian, pedagogic writing.

JAKOB   He is the only person the Old Man considers to be his enemy. . . . But then the Old Man was the one who persuaded Ania's mother to get a divorce.

ERIK   And then came the other man, Kaspar's father. What did he look like? Kaspar, what you do think your father looked like?

KASPAR   He must have been young . . . probably good-looking. . . . He certainly had a clear voice. . . . Maybe he looked like you.

ERIK   Why should he have looked like me? He was definitely different. . . . Your mother died because of him.

ANIA   But the Old Man says I remind him of my mother in almost everything. Kaspar must get a great deal from her too, but naturally he inherits traits from his father as well.

ERIK   It certainly wasn't easy for your mother, not loving the one and dying on account of the other.

ESTHER   If our mothers could see us, maybe they'd burst into tears.

KASPAR   But maybe it's all crystal-clear to them. They have only to look at us and know that things are all right as they are.

ESTHER   I don't believe that, they must have guilty consciences. *Because they are guilty.*

ANIA   We're not the ones to assign guilt, we mustn't blame anyone. They couldn't suspect how oddly things would work out.

ESTHER   I say the parents are to blame!! It was easier for them! Parents have it easier!! . . . That is my sacred belief!

KASPAR   Maybe that's why things aren't so wonderful for them.

ESTHER   Should we feel sorry for them because they, aggravating breed that they are, have to do without things being wonderful for them? That's precisely why they may have it a thousand times more comfortable, a thousand times easier. With their unforgiveable lack of scruples, they brought us into the world. They had a firm foundation beneath their feet, which we had to lose. *They* had their little griefs to curl up in, their little foibles that were warm and cosy. But we have to feel jeopardized at every moment as no generation ever felt jeopardized before. We are set down helpless between the greatest extremities, and there's no one to lead us. Now the morality of these fathers turns away in terror from the dubious generation they have wronged.

ANIA   *(Standing up, after a brief pause)* Now the children have finished their dance.

KASPAR   I have to go out for the next number. It's the one in which I lead the children.

ANIA   And then we dance, Esther. *(She stands beside her.)*

ERIK   *(Smiling at the names)* Ania and Esther. . . . The dance of the grey angel. . . .

ESTHER   I don't know what's wrong with me today. I feel wiped out.

ANIA   *(Gently caresses her hair)* You are over-excited . . . calm, calm . . .

ESTHER   Your hand is so heavy.

ANIA   Yes. *(She lets it fall.)*

ESTHER   *(Suddenly wheels round on* ERIK, *flaring up intensely)* But now Erik must tell us some more about *his* mother.

ERIK   I've got nothing to tell.

ESTHER   Oh, sure you do, you just have to
say where you lived, what you ate. . . .

ERIK   We had a little room off a courtyard.

ESTHER   And in the courtyard did you play
ball with the other boys? Did you laugh as
you ran across the paving?

ERIK   When my mother came home at night,
she'd be wearing high heels. She performed
in the circus in a garish red wig. She
worked with my father in the ring, but they
weren't married.

ESTHER   And whenever you came home,
you'd crawl in bed and go to sleep. You
would put on your nightshirt. You were 13,
14, 15 years old . . . a regular big boy. . . .
But you slept in the same room with her.
And days you tussled with your chums. . . .
How old are you now?

ERIK   I'm 18. . . . Sometimes she'd hit me
too, but not too often, and it didn't hurt.
She would take the whip she used for her
act in the circus. She'd strip me naked and
fling me across the table. She never hit me
when I had angered her, but only like that.
. . . I'd yell, but I didn't yell because it hurt.

ESTHER   No, whips don't hurt. . . . You're
more than a year younger than I. Did your
mother meet with an accident?

ERIK   Yes . . . she had a fall in the circus. But
by then I had stopped living with her.

JAKOB   Here come the children. I can hear
the audience applaud.

(A very distant sound of hands clapping. Down
the narrow gangway come the SIX GIRLS and
SIX BOYS. They walk, without speaking, slightly
panting and mildly trembling. They are dressed
in black and also very heavily made-up. The
girls wear short black frocks and their legs are
bare and white. The boys wear very short, black
trousers with long black stockings and belted
black jackets with white frills. They all sit in a
row on the chairs along the wall.)

KASPAR   (Calls out of the boys) Come here,
Gimietto, your hair's in a tangle again.
Come here, I'll smooth it down for you.

(GIMIETTO walks over to him, somewhat
unsteadily, and KASPAR smoothes the boy's
hair.)

ANIA   Now you have to have a drink. Wait,
I'll ring for the Attendants. (She rings.)

KASPAR   (To GIMIETTO) Did it go well? Did
the people like it?

THE BOY   I don't know, they did applaud.
But lots of them laughed and lots of them
hissed. . . . I don't think they liked us at all.

KASPAR   (Turns his face) But now we'll
dance together. And they may be tired of
sitting . . . we'll do it beautifully. And then
comes the grey angel and then your final
chorus.

THE BOY   (As if dazed by fatigue) Is the last
number on so soon? The rose chorus?

KASPAR   Yes, we'll soon be done. Here come
the drinks.

(THE FEMALE ATTENDANTS slowly come
down the gangway, each carrying a tray of
glasses. They walk along the row of children.
Each one takes a glass, saying "thank you"
quietly and shrilly. Then they gulp down the
drinks in silence.)

KASPAR   (To GIMIETTO, who is drinking
hastily) Did Ellis dance out of the line
again?

GIMIETTO   No, I don't think so . . .

A GIRL   (Bent over her glass) I tripped.

ANIA   Did anybody see?

THE GIRL   No, but my foot hurts.

(Pause. The children sit with half-closed eyes.
GIMIETTO too, standing by KASPAR, seems to
fall asleep.)

ERIK   (Quietly, almost in fear) Why don't they
talk?

ANIA   They're tired.

KASPAR   (Stares at ERIK, while he strokes
GIMIETTO) They are so tired. . . . The
"Dance in Black" is their most strenuous
number.

(The OLD MAN can be seen lumbering down the
gangway.)

ESTHER   (Looking towards him) When he
comes down the gangway, he looks as if he
were climbing a rugged mountain path.
How his beard wags before him. . . .

THE OLD MAN   (Enters, without at first taking
notice of anyone else turns with his stiffly
formal courtesy to ERIK, as the only stranger)
Oh, you are here with the artistes, Herr
Erik. I'm delighted that you have made
yourself at home already. I very much
hope that you have fully recovered in the
meantime. (Smiling into his beard, he shakes
his hand.)

ERIK    (Bows, extremely embarrassed) Thanks
  . . . oh, thanks a lot. . . .
THE OLD MAN    (Turns away from him, to the
  children) The first bell has rung. Didn't you
  hear it?
KASPAR    They are so tired.
THE OLD MAN    You should be getting ready
  yourself. You have to go on with them.
KASPAR    I will. (He sits at the dressing-table.)
THE OLD MAN    (Sits in the centre chair,
  among the children) I'll sit with you for a
  moment. Give me your hand, ELIZA, you
  tripped. (He lovingly takes the hand of the
  little girl sitting next to him.)
ESTHER    (Sitting lost in thought, suddenly with
  a certain sharpness) The children's make-up
  has to be touched up. Their lips are much
  too pale.

(Each of the children pulls a little compact
mirror out of a pocket. They work on their
bowed faces diligently.)

KASPAR    (Rises, freshly got up, pulls off the
  cloak, stands in silver slenderness before the
  children) There goes the second bell. We're
  ready!

(The children stand in a row.)

KASPAR    Come on, Gimietto, we go on first.
  (They go out Indian file, KASPAR and
  GIMIETTO in front, then the boys, lastly the
  girls – up the gangway.)
THE OLD MAN , ESTHER, ANIA and JAKOB
  (In muted unison) Lots of luck.
ERIK    (Somewhat behind them, very clearly)
  Luck . . . lots of luck!

(The Indian file disappears. Music strikes up in
the distance.)

ERIK    Now they're dancing. . . .
ESTHER    It's really amazing that he can
  dance. He's so clumsy.
ANIA    (Quietly) But maybe the grace born of
  clumsiness and strain is the most sublime.
THE OLD MAN    (Pawkily, from the
  background) Ania is right there.
ESTHER    (Winking at ERIK) And then he
  writes poetry as well. The over-abundance
  of his experiences does take so many
  forms.
THE OLD MAN    (Suddenly turns, in an
  uncanny way, to ERIK) I would like it, since
  we're together here, if you briefly

described some of your impressions of life
  in the hospice.
ERIK    I honestly don't know . . .
THE OLD MAN    Whether they're to your
  satisfaction, generally speaking, that's all I
  mean. Many strangers feel at first
  instinctively repelled. Many, I admit,
  become aware over a long stay of an almost
  irresistible desire to remain here. (Half
  joking) Who knows, who knows, perhaps
  something similar is going on in you.
ERIK    No, no, I can't expect you to. . . .
THE OLD MAN    (With sudden, profound
  earnestness) You remind me of someone
  else, by the way.
ERIK    Do you mean your daughter's second
  husband? . . . Kaspar was just talking about
  that earlier. . . .
THE OLD MAN    (Sunk in contemplation,
  strokes his beard) Then you will remain no
  longer one of us . . . some do, some don't.
  . . . Perhaps you even . . . (Suddenly aloud):
  But if anywhere in the world you meet
  someone who needs it: send him to me.
  (He raises both arms in a surprisingly
  ungainly burst of emotion as in a gesture of
  embrace.) The confusion of all young
  people has a place in these precincts . . .
  the most tormented and most restless
  children of good families may carry on
  here in peace. (They have all turned their
  faces to him. His eyes are closed, his face is a
  big, white mask, then he stands up, moves
  laboriously to the door, where
  he turns around once more.) I want to
  watch the children dance. (Smiling and
  muttering he trudges up the gangway
  and out.)
ERIK    (Quietly) He's gone now. . . .
ANIA    Does he frighten you?
ERIK    I don't know. . . . He has the face of a
  dead man. And yet he gives off a glow, a
  dead glow. . . . But you are his
  granddaughter.
ESTHER    Yes, Ania, in so many ways you
  remind me of him.
ERIK    (Breathes heavily) Ah, how thick the air
  is here. . . . It must be the cigarette smoke.
JAKOB    (Stands upstage) My mother too was,
  unfortunately, mentally ill. Small and
  hunchbacked as well. But one thing I'm
  absolutely sure of: whenever she looked at
  me, she laughed. Her twisted face
  jammed between the bars of the asylum
  window . . . she would laugh and laugh. . . .
  (He lays hands on his green wig.) I'm

ashamed of this motley costume I've sewed
myself.

ERIK  Now I certainly won't be staying.

*(ESTHER turns her head and stares at him.
ANIA sits, somewhat bent over at the dressing-
table, looking in the mirror. JAKOB, in front of
the grey wall, is like a garish mask.)*

## Fourth Tableau

*Same set as the first tableau. It is rather dark.
The candelabrums are not lit. Only an isolated
lamp is burning over the folding-door.
ANIA and ESTHER stand at a considerable
distance from one another. Downstage in the
armchair sits KASPAR. KASPAR is wearing
the grey suit from the first tableau. ANIA and
ESTHER are wrapped up in long capes for they
are freezing. – It is late evening, after the
show.*

KASPAR  Today, all through the show I
thought how nice it would be if we were
old.

ANIA  I go on believing we will never grow
old.

KASPAR  It's not that we're weak. Our
parents, who were young at the end of the
last century, were much weaker.

ESTHER  I also believe we won't grow old.

ANIA  Anyway I feel as if no previous
younger generation ever had so much to do
with death or so intimately. We don't often
talk about it. But the thought of it is in
everything we do.

KASPAR  That's because . . . the air has never
before been so densely permeated
with something else. You know what I
mean. . . .

ANIA and ESTHER *(Together, but their faces
turned away from one another)* Yes.

KASPAR  But something has to come from it
all . . . some sort of creativity . . . some
work of art. . . . One of us *has* to sing a
song, *our* song. . . . What will it be like?

*(ANIA turns her head suddenly and looks at
ESTHER.)*

KASPAR  And one of us has to *paint* the
picture, our picture. It's bound to be a
peculiar picture . . . And one of us has to
tell the story. What will it be like. Perhaps
we'll be the only ones able to understand it,
for we are living every bit of it.

ANIA  *(Averts her glance from ESTHER again)*
Yes. We are living every bit of it.

*(ESTHER says nothing. But as if suddenly
struck by far too sweet a thought, she stretches
out her arms with a smile.)*

KASPAR  *(Sits sunk entirely into himself)* I've
been thinking it over all night long.
Thinking about the works we have to
produce, and what they will be like. . . . But
now I have to go looking for someone.

ESTHER  *(Suddenly cries out)* Why don't you
*say* that you want to go and look for Erik?

KASPAR  Why should I tell you?

ESTHER  Incidentally you're not likely to
find him. He has gone out.

KASPAR  *(Remains in the chair)* I don't know
. . . really I don't . . . why you are so upset.
There's nothing for you to worry about. I
only want to see Erik again to say good
night.

ESTHER  Your lying makes me nervous. As if
I didn't know perfectly well what you
mean with your story and how we're living
every bit of it. Just let me tell you: if you
make me . . . *(She suddenly turns away.)*

KASPAR  *(Makes a move to go to her, but goes
angrily to the door to the park)* Good night
then.

ESTHER  *(Turned away)* You may find him in
the park. I believe he is in the park.

KASPAR  Yes . . . then I'll look for him. *(He
goes out.)*

*(ANIA and ESTHER are alone. They stand erect,
each in her place.)*

ESTHER  *(Speaks so that the silence won't
become worse)* Now they're all asleep. . . .
And how loudly today The Old Man's
beasts roared. . . . These nights following
an opening are ghastly. Besides, when you
come down to it, it was a fiasco.

ANIA  *(Motionless)* Was it a fiasco?

ESTHER  *(Very nervous, has an object between
her fingers with which she plays)* At least
that's how it seemed. . . . We should be
performing in big cities, in smoke-filled
night clubs. . . .

ANIA  Yes . . . if a person could . . .

ESTHER  *(Abruptly)* By the way it was very
strange what Kaspar was saying before . . .
about the story. . . .

ANIA  That we're living every bit of it . . . He
was quite right.

ESTHER   And that it would be sad.

ANIA   Did he say that it has to be sad?

ESTHER   It was in his voice.

ANIA   Everything beautiful is sad.

ESTHER   *(Almost breaks the object in her hand)* Is every sad experience, my dear Ania, a beautiful one for you? *(Suddenly uttering a brief laugh, hurrying on, almost crazed)* I've never had anywhere near as much fun dancing as I had tonight. Never has it made me so happy . . . the dance of the grey angel. . . . *(Without looking at her, she takes a step closer to* ANIA*.)* Were you ever as beautiful as you were today – Ania!

ANIA   *(Still motionless)* You barely looked at me while we were dancing.

ESTHER   *(Only a step away from her, still playing with the object)* I felt as if you were dancing the story today . . . our story. . . .

ANIA   Maybe I was dancing *my own* story.

ESTHER   But we share it in common . . . the story.

*(*ANIA *doesn't reply.)*

ESTHER   But we always shared it in common. . . .

*(With halting steps* ANIA *moves away from her, farther upstage.)*

ESTHER   What I was saying to your brother earlier . . . that I knew perfectly well which story he was referring to . . . of course I only meant by that . . . that I knew perfectly well he was referring to *our* story . . . and that he only wanted to tease us a bit with it. . . .

*(*ANIA *motionless)*

ESTHER   Oh . . . oh, how gruesome these opening nights are! *(She bows her head, she stands bashfully hunched over.)* Yes, do you really think I'm lying, Ania?? *(Straightens herself up explosively, cries)* But you are driving me to lie! You're the only one to blame!! Your erratic behavior is a constant accusation to me, a perpetual reproach! Your silence tortures me! Your beauty tortures me! You are to blame for my lies! You drive me to say that we are close! . . . But we are not close! Nothing connects us any more! . . . Oh, how your meekness has martyred me . . . always . . . always you have tortured me. You are to blame, you

alone are to blame!! . . . But I *love* him! You *knew* I loved him before I knew it, from the very first instant! *Why* didn't you say something? Why were you so silent? You danced the grey angel to my face. . . . Your beauty accused me – you are to blame that I lied. . . . I love him more than I can say. . . . *(She stands weeping, she hides her face in her hands.)*

*(*ANIA *stands in the dark, she can be made out in the background as only a narrow outline. After the outburst* ESTHER*'s crooked hands drop. She stands still again. – Then* ERIK *hurries into the room from the park, an almost ecstatic smile breaks out on her face.)*

ERIK   *(Still panting, as from a run in the park. When he sees* ANIA *and* ESTHER*, he stops at the door. After a pause he begins to speak shyly)* You stand so strangely in the dark.

*(Pause, no one moves.)*

ERIK   You look like two black madonnas. And yet you have no child.

ESTHER   *(In a sing-song, cooing voice, without looking at him or turning her head)* Maybe the Holy Ghost will bestow one on us.

ERIK   *(With a bit of a laugh)* I can't imagine it. Besides, you look so *frail* next to one another.

ESTHER   *(In the cooing voice, still not turning her head)* If the frailest body receive the seed, it may perhaps bear the most precious fruit.

ERIK   I . . . just can't imagine it. . . . I actually came in to say goodbye. Very early tomorrow morning I'm leaving, when you'll still be asleep. . . .

*(*ESTHER *turns her face to him now, without leaving her place and looks at him)*
*(*ERIK *closes his eyes, feeling her gaze on him, with closed eyes smiles beneath her gaze in the middle of the room.)*
*(*ANIA *stands with face downcast.)*

ERIK   *(Very quietly, like a child speaking in a dream)* You look at me so . . . Esther! Why do you look at me that way?

*(*ESTHER *also closes her eyes, a smile like his on her features. Moves to him as if sleepwalking)*

ERIK   *(In a dream)* Now you're wandering . . .

up to me. . . . *(They stand next to one another with closed eyes.* ANIA *still stands with deeply bowed face.)*

ESTHER    *(Singing)* When we are alone, you must tell me even more about the big city where you live. The smell of this big city and its human turmoil envelopes your body more powerfully, more coolly than ever the smell of woods and vales enveloped a young warrior.

*(*ERIK *lifts his hands to embrace her, but lets them fall again)*

ESTHER    *(Has entwined her hands in his hair)* Your hair . . . how warm, how young, how boyish your hair is. *(Her hands slide farther over his face.)* I feel your face . . . your *living* face . . . your voice, your eyelids, your dear mouth, your dear, dear mouth . . . ! *(She slides down him, sinking, strokes his whole body.)* I feel your body . . . your body . . . your dear, dear body . . . your knees, your warm hands . . . your chest . . . your shoulders . . . let me feel the boyish hair on your body . . . your living face, your body. . . . *(She half crouches at his feet. She fondles his hands with her loosened hair.)*

ERIK    What are you doing? What have you plunged my hands into?

ESTHER    I am washing your hands with my hair – that's my way of honouring you. . . .

ERIK    It is as if you were pouring a thick, sweet liquid over my hands. It feels good. You're pouring a wonderful drink over me. . . .

ESTHER    *(To his feet)* I love you so.

ERIK    My hands have never plunged into such wetness. They are not used to it.

ESTHER    Oh, over your living face . . . your dear mouth . . . your body. . . .

KASPAR 's voice *(From the park)* Erik . . . Erik, I'm looking for you.

ANIA    *(Replies in a very clear voice, without changing position)* Erik is not here.

KASPAR's voice    *(Nearer)* Ania . . . is that you? Haven't you seen Esther either?

ANIA    Esther was with me a little while ago.

KASPAR's voice    Then come to me, my dear, in the park. I'm feeding the Old Man's beasts.

ANIA    All right . . . yes . . . I can come at once . . .

*(She goes slowly to* ESTHER *and* ERIK, *who still compose an unchanged group.)*

ANIA    Esther . . . I'm going now . . .

ERIK    *(Eyes closed)* Good-bye, Fräulein Ania.

ESTHER    *(Her face pressed to Erik)* Yes . . . good-bye then.

ANIA    *(Still standing there, cannot leave)* I'm going to the park.

ERIK    Say hello to Kaspar for me.

ANIA    Yes, I'll give him your regards.

ESTHER    *(Lifts her face, her eyes are still cloudy and as if drunk with sleep)* Are you going to the park now? . . . Good-bye. Yes, I already said that: Good-bye. . . . You mustn't stand there so stiffly. . . . Isn't he beautiful? *(Her face falls against* ERIK *again.)* . . . He is really beautiful. . . . Beautiful is my love. . . . You mustn't stand there so stiffly. . . . His hair, his dear mouth, his living face. . . .

*(*KASPAR *appears in the door-way.)*

KASPAR    *(Sees* ERIK *and* ESTHER. *Seething with rage he raises his fists. His voice is all choked up.)* Esther . . . Esther, you must let go of his hands . . . you don't know what you're doing . . . Esther! *(She does not hear him.)*

ANIA    *(Turns serenely towards him)* I'm coming now, Kaspar. We also have to see the children. Did you say good night to GIMIETTO yet? *(She gently takes him by the shoulders.)*

KASPAR    *(Almost collapses on to her)* Yes, Ania, we'll go now . . . to the children . . . Ania and I are going now . . .

*(Leaning on one another, as if neither could move without the other, they disappear into the park.)*

ESTHER    *(When Ania is gone, turns her head once more to the door)* Ania, is Ania gone? Didn't Ania say something else to us?

ERIK    *(Not listening to her)* May I come down to you, Esther? . . . My body is aching for you now.

ESTHER    Yes – now you may come. . . .

*(He embraces the crouching woman. They lie entwined.)*

## Fifth Tableau

ERIK's *bedroom, as in the second tableau*

ESTHER *is lying in bed. She has on a white silk*

*nightshirt, her hair is loose. She is covered up to the chin with* ERIK*'s woollen blanket. –* ERIK *is sitting beside her on the bed. He has removed his jacket, is wearing only his blue trousers and an open shirt.*
*It is 2 or 3 o'clock in the morning. On the wall a candle flickers in a sconce.*

ESTHER  *(Her eyes closed)* You have to tell it to me all over again. You must tell it over again and again and again. . . . Your words make me happier than I've been in years.

ERIK  The people who were my employers at the time soon threw me out of their house, of course. They said I had every vice in my blood. But that was only because both their teenaged daughters behaved in a very funny way with me. At night when I went to bed, one of them would suddenly crouch quivering outside my bedroom door. Naturally that bothered her parents. The other girl I kissed once . . . mainly because she asked me to. . . . The parents wouldn't forgive me that. And yet basically they were fond of me. Everyone cried when I left. Later at frequent intervals I'd get love letters from the girls, on bright green paper.

ESTHER  And then . . . what did you do then?

ERIK  Then I became a waiter, but only for a short time. I worked in a big hotel. That's where I met Lolo.

ESTHER  Lolo? Which one's that? Tell me all about Lolo!

ERIK  She told me that she loved me. . . .

ESTHER  She loved you. . . .

ERIK  We travelled together. She wanted it so badly, although she was really too old for me. She was a star in musical comedy and rich.

ESTHER  Why did you break it off with her?

ERIK  I didn't break it off. She died. Or rather: actually she took her own life – she did it because I'd become friendly with Freddy . . .

ESTHER  Who is Freddy?

ERIK  Freddy was a tap dancer. He introduced me to cabaret.

ESTHER  You were in cabaret too?

ERIK  Yes, I danced with Freddy. But it was too strenuous for me, in the long run. Then Freddy started to take a drug, which I quickly got addicted to. Only naturally I immediately overdid things. That brought me down a bit.

ESTHER  And now Freddy is dancing without you?

ERIK  Yes, now Freddy is dancing alone again.

ESTHER  So actually you've been with no one for a long time. . . .

ERIK  No . . . I don't know why myself. *(He smiles at her.)* But we'll stay together a long time . . . right? . . . We'll stay together a long, long time.

ESTHER  Yes . . . a long time. . . . Would you really like that? Would you really like to stay with me?

ERIK  Yes . . . sure. . . . We get on so well together. Sure, it'd be real nice. . . . Quiet, did you hear something?

*(*ANIA*'s figure briefly appears at the window from the breast up. She walks out of the darkness up to the window and utters a little sound, a short word, half* ESTHER*'s name, half a lamentation. Then she disappears again.)*

ERIK  *(Trembling)* What was that?

ESTHER  *(Has thrown herself on him, so that he cannot turn around)* I don't know . . . an animal howling in the woods.

ERIK  The voice sounded human.

ESTHER  It was an owl . . . a night bird . . . some kind of dark beast from the woods. Don't tremble, Erik. You mustn't tremble, my dear; give me your mouth . . . *(They kiss.)*

ESTHER  Erik . . . Last night I said a bad thing in the dressing-room . . . about life, that we shouldn't have been born. You must forgive me for that, Erik. I won't upbraid our parents any more. I thank them now; for I have found you, I've discovered a sense of meaning . . .

ERIK  But now you have to tell me about the Old Man, about the hospice. Everything here is so peculiar. . . .

ESTHER  Yes, it is . . . a really weird place to be living in, it certainly is.

ERIK  From the first moment I came to the hospice, it was as if I couldn't breathe freely any more. The air is so packed with . . . I don't know what . . . electricity . . . and this constant smell of the Old Man's beasts. Is it true that the Old Man loves nothing in this world except his beasts.

ESTHER  Yes . . . and his little girls. . . .

ERIK  That's what everyone told me, but I couldn't believe it. Anyhow I've never heard a man laugh so strangely . . . and Jakob, what's up with Jakob?

ESTHER   You're asking too many questions. Just the home lives of all these people . . . you heard about it today in the dressing-room.

ERIK   The children move me so. Why are they all so pale? Why are they . . . fallen?

ESTHER   Each of them has his own fate. For the most part their parents are sick or totally degenerate. The children are mostly found in low dives or on the street. Eliza and Gimietto for example were turned up in an establishment of a highly peculiar nature.

ERIK   And Kaspar? I have to learn something about him at least. His place in all of this is so unclear, so blurry . . .

ESTHER   Yet he wrote you a poem.

ERIK   Yes, that was lovely. I almost understood it. . . . Sometimes I think there's a power in him. When he threw off the cloak last night, for instance, before he was to dance, and then stood before the row of children . . . slender in front of them. . . .

ESTHER   I was a good friend of his. We were *all three of us* close friends. . . .

ERIK   I like him a lot, and sometimes I think . . .

ESTHER   *(Half to herself)* It's almost as if, now that I have possessed you, I could think of him again for the first time without anger. He's bound to be miserable now. And it's a lovely thing that he should be fond of you too, really it is lovely. . . .

ERIK   I like all of them. But they carry on so strangely. And the whole thing is strange, the hospice itself. I can't figure it out . . . whether it's a reformatory or a cabaret or a kind of nunnery or . . . or the opposite . . . it's driving me crazy. But I'll be leaving now.

ESTHER   Yes, we'll be leaving now . . . tomorrow. . . .

ERIK   *(Deeply surprised)* We? . . . Yes, that sounds almost . . . ?!

ESTHER   But what did you think?

ERIK   *(Comprehending and with childlike joy)* Yes, that sounds almost as if you wanted to go *with* me!!

ESTHER   *(With closed eyes, very quietly)* Yes . . . did you think I would stay here?

ERIK   *(Rejoicing)* And that means it's true that we'll be together a long time . . . not just let's-pretend . . . but true!!

ESTHER   And he was thinking . . .

ERIK   *(Embraces her)* I don't know what I was thinking. . . . But now you're going with me. . . . I'll teach you to tap dance. . . . We'll live together in the big city . . . a long long time. . . .

ESTHER   *(Yielding utterly to his embrace)* We'll live together . . . we'll live . . . we'll live. . . . I don't belong to them any more now . . . never again. . . . They carry on strangely . . . but we are alive . . . we are alive. . . .

ERIK   We ought to get married, the managers prefer it. Got any money?

ESTHER   Yes . . . Mama left me some, I think . . . sure, she must have left me some.

ERIK   And then we'll earn some too. We'll earn lots of money. You've got to have an outfit made for you . . . lots of outfits, it's a must. Red outfits, green outfits, like Lolo had. . . .

ESTHER   Like Lolo had . . . we're living . . . we're living . . . we're living together . . .

ERIK   *(Kisses her)* I never considered it . . . not even when you were stroking my hands with your hair. I never dared to think of it, Lolo was middle-aged and came from musical comedy and Freddy was only a tap dancer. But you were the grey angel, even if at times you looked so colourful. Last night I thought you were a black madonna when I walked into the dark room . . . a frail one, a sterile one . . .

ESTHER   And would you have left here without me?

ERIK   I hadn't given that my full consideration yet. Yes, maybe I would have left without you.

ESTHER   *(Embraces him more ardently)* But I would not have let you go without me . . . I would not have let you go alone . . . that would I not have done – never would I have done that. . . . After I stroked your hands with my hair, after I had felt the beauty of your body . . . your warm kisses . . . your mouth . . . I could never stay here without you. Was I a grey angel? . . . But now we'll learn to tap dance together. . . . Now I'll buy myself lots of outfits, like Fräulein Lolo's . . . red and green and yellow . . . now we'll live together . . . we'll live . . . we'll live . . .

ERIK   *(With a sudden thought)* What about the Old Man?

ESTHER   The Old Man? What do I care about the Old Man?

ERIK   And Kaspar?

ESTHER   Kaspar? . . . Oh, Kaspar won't be sad. . . . He's fond of you: why should he be sad? We'll take him with, we'll take Kaspar with us. We'll go together all three, it'll be better for him . . .

ERIK   Yes, if Kaspar agrees, he can come with us. I don't exclude anybody. . . . What about the pale children you've been training?

ESTHER   Somebody else will train them. We'll send them picture postcards from the big cities . . . we 'll send picture postcards to everyone we know . . . I'll buy myself garish outfits . . .

*(Brief pause)*

ERIK   *(Very quietly)* Do you know, Esther, what that screaming was in the woods earlier?

ESTHER   Screaming in the woods? . . . The nights here are so eerie . . . no one ever knows what the voices are yammering about. . . . But it will soon be day. First the countryside will turn bright grey . . . then the sun will break through . . . then we'll go to the city by the fastest express . . . there I'll buy myself garish outfits . . . be still! There are so many owls around here. . . . Wasn't it a gloomy little night owl? . . . Give me your mouth. . . .

## Sixth Tableau

*The scene is the main entrance to the hospice. It is grey and gothic. At the right* ANIA *sits on a stone bench, and, bent over a dish, stems some sort of berry. – On the left side doors with gratings lead to* THE OLD MAN's *animal cages. – Next to* ANIA *stands* JAKOB. *It is early morning.*

JAKOB   The children will soon be coming back from their walk.

ANIA   And the Old Man is feeding the animals. It must be ten o'clock.

JAKOB   Something in your face has changed since yesterday.

ANIA   *(Over the dish)* You think so?

JAKOB   But you refuse to tell me about it.

ANIA   I didn't sleep well.

JAKOB   I would have liked to have seen you last night. But I couldn't find you anywhere. I had the feeling yesterday that you might have needed someone.

ANIA   No . . . I needed no one yesterday.

JAKOB   You're stemming berries?

ANIA   Yes. For the children, for dessert.

JAKOB   Last night you were so sweet to me. You asked me whether I needed lavender water.

ANIA   It was only natural, after you'd been singing. I didn't mean anything in particular.

JAKOB   No – I didn't suppose it meant anything more. Shall I go now?

ANIA   You'd be bothering me if you stayed.

JAKOB   I'll go and meet up with the children.

*(He exits right.)*

(ANIA *sits and works silently at her berries. Once, as in sudden frailty, she lets her head sink heavily on the dish. At that moment, however,* THE OLD MAN *walks out the main entrance. He is carrying a bucket of fodder for the animals. –* ANIA *straightens up.)*

THE OLD MAN   *(Greets her heartily)* Good morning, Ania. Are you sitting here basking in the sun?

ANIA   Yes . . . and autumn is so early this year.

THE OLD MAN   Yes, yes . . . splendid autumn. . . . *(He passes her on his way to the animal cages. He feeds birds, which are not visible, only their croaking can be heard through the bars. He half turns his head to* ANIA, *while he goes on feeding them.)* Have you seen Esther today?

ANIA   *(Over the dish)* No, I have not seen Esther today.

THE OLD MAN   That's no reason for you to be sad. She'll come . . . she'll come back . . .

ANIA   Do you think I'm sad? . . . I'm only sitting here in the sun . . .

*(Meanwhile, to feed the birds,* THE OLD MAN *has gone to the cage off-stage.* KASPAR *walks out of the house.)*

KASPAR   Glad I ran into you. . . . Good morning, Ania!

ANIA   Good morning.

KASPAR   I was looking for you in particular last night. Where did you get to? Half the night I was looking for you.

ANIA   But you always sleep so soundly.

KASPAR   Last night I couldn't. . . . Did you sleep? You weren't in your room.

ANIA   No, I was in the woods . . . and in the park . . . and also in the dark lanes . . .

KASPAR   But you weren't in the church.

ANIA   *(With a surprisingly vehement gesture of pride)* No, there was no reason for me to look in the church.

KASPAR   I know . . . you don't need that. . . . But I was in the church last night, for the first time in a long time. And perhaps that's why it's good that we didn't meet up last night. I've been thinking a lot of things over.

ANIA   What have you been thinking over . . . last *night*?

KASPAR   I've been poring over my life. . . . But that's nothing to do with you. It had a lot to do with me though. That's why I had to give it so much thought.

ANIA   *(Suddenly lifts her head)* You want to go with them too?

KASPAR   *(Suddenly ashamed and as if he didn't understand)* Go with whom?

ANIA   *(Stares fixedly at him)* Are you up to it?!

KASPAR   I'm *delighted* by it. . . . I'm actually *delighted* by it. . . .

ANIA   But have you forgotten how *loathsome* it is out there? We had to spend our childhoods there of course. Don't you *know* any more how bad it is . . . those people who thought of nothing but how to exploit us, whose loving-kindness poisoned the air. . . . Those women with their tasteless vanity, their trivial vices. . . . Those clever, moral men, with their smug hypocrisy . . . don't you *know* that any more? . . . And that money, that money, which violently condenses all lesser things, so that it turns into the greatest symbol of that life, that ghastly money that they need out there, need *urgently* . . . yes, have you forgot all of that?

KASPAR   *(Quietly)* You're trying to scare me. . . .

ANIA   Well, if you aren't scared, then I have to scare you. I know you, Kaspar, you'll suffocate out there . . . I know you . . . you won't be able to stand it . . . you can't tolerate what's loathsome. . . . And how do you know that they want to take you with them, Erik and she? . . . Will she let you?

KASPAR   She asked me to.

ANIA   They did it so they'd have some kind of connection with us, with the hospice to support them. Otherwise they'd go under much too quickly. . . . Of course you won't be able to support her very long.

KASPAR   *(Very quietly)* And what if, Ania, what if I am scared now . . . ? *(He turns, then)* How beautiful . . . beautiful, you know, it must be out there! And we are the very ones, we who are fundamentally alien to all that, we, it occurred to me, should be able to appreciate that enchantment and pleasure far differently than the natives can. Think about it: . . . when night falls in the big city . . . and the electric signs are glowing . . . and music pours out of all the bars . . . and the whores wear red boots. . . . If only I were right in the middle of it and thinking of you, my sister Ania. . . . We must be able to enjoy it in a totally different way. *(His voice suddenly finds itself, he speaks more slowly and much more earnestly.)* And then I also thought of being out there in the cities, you know: surrendering wholly to the cities but still with longing for home in my heart . . . I thought . . . I thought to myself that out there I might be able to create the *work* . . . sing the song . . . or dance the dance . . . or tell the story: *our* story.

ANIA   Yes, in that case you have to go. In that case it wouldn't be right for me to dissuade you. Go on then. *(A short pause. She silently stems berries. Then she begins again, great affection in her voice.)* And she . . . do you believe that she, that Esther will also be able to endure it? She has nothing to do with the work. . . . She doesn't really want to create, she has nothing to accomplish . . . she is only a woman . . .

KASPAR   *(His face turned away)* But . . . she has *him* . . . and together with him . . .

ANIA   *(Shakes her head)* They won't stay together long.

KASPAR   That's true. They won't stay together long. It's not in his nature . . . probably not in hers either.

ANIA   She is like a child, like a nasty, deceitful . . . angelic child. . . . If they split up, what will she . . . what will Esther do then?

KASPAR   She'll find someone else. So long as she isn't stuck-up about it. So long as she takes, . . . takes a little trouble to make contacts.

ANIA   *(As if in acute, momentary fear)* And then . . . and then? When that's over? For even you can't believe that she will be able to stay with him or the next one or the one after that. – What then? *In the name of God's compassion, tell me, what will she have left?*

KASPAR   Then she'll come home.

ANIA   *(Lets her hands drop as if released)* Now I know . . . thank you. Then she'll come home . . . to the hospice . . . to the Old Man . . . to the children . . .

KASPAR   Why don't you say it, Ania, that she'll come home to *you?*

ANIA   *(Sits still again)* Homecoming . . . coming home to me. Then she'll be weary . . .

KASPAR   Maybe even dead.

ANIA   Yes, maybe dead. But quiet in any case. Then you'll come back too . . . a bit worn out, no doubt, not quite so many thoughts in your head and almost no longings . . . quiet, quiet . . . , it'll be a cheerful homecoming, a sweet-tempered homecoming. And where young Erik may be, not one of us will ever know again.

KASPAR   No . . . what would this Erik mean to us then?

ANIA   *(looks at him with a smile, almost mischievously)* But he is beautiful . . . isn't he? Isn't he beautiful?

KASPAR   *(Looking into her eyes)* Beautiful he is.

ANIA   *(Humming a kind of tune, over the berries)* Fewer clever thoughts . . . almost no longings . . . a cheerful homecoming . . . quiet, quiet . . . a sweet-tempered homecoming. . . .

*(*THE OLD MAN, *his bucket now empty of fodder, enters cheerfully from the cages.)*

THE OLD MAN   Now they have enough, the sweet-toothed little maws, enough for an hour. . . . What have you been talking about?

ANIA   About what will happen next.

THE OLD MAN   You're all so avidly interested in that. Well, it's only natural.

KASPAR   *(Suddenly goes to him and gives him his hand)* Good morning, grandfather!

THE OLD MAN   *(Flattered, laughs in his beard)* Grandfather? . . . Such politeness I am not used to. Is it only because you plan to abandon me now?

KASPAR   *(Recoils)* How do you know that?

THE OLD MAN   *(Still laughing and waggish)* I know everything. *(Once again in his suddenly stiff burst of feeling, the face petrified into a white mask, the arms ponderously uplifted.)* I know everything!! *(*KASPAR, *as if gripped with panic, simply runs off right.* THE OLD MAN *repeats, almost*

*whimpering, with drooping head)* Must . . . know everything. . . .

*(*ERIK *hurries out of the house, the sailor's cap on his head. He stops dead, for he sees those present and doffs his cap.)*

THE OLD MAN   *(Unusually amiable)* There is our Herr Erik as well! Slept well, Herr Erik? Pleasant dreams? Gradually getting used to the new surroundings? It would displease me if anyone were to want for anything.

ERIK   *(Bows to him)* Thanks . . . no . . . thanks. *(He goes up to* ANIA *and kisses her hand.)* Good morning, Fräulein Ania. You're stemming berries, but Esther will be coming soon. . . . Good morning, I'd very much like to pluck some flowers and also say good-bye to the animals. *(He goes away, turns his head once, to throw* ANIA *a smile.)*

*(Almost without moving* ANIA *goes back to work on the berries.* THE OLD MAN *stands ponderously centre stage and strokes his beard. Short pause.* ESTHER *walks out of the house.)*

ESTHER   *(Stands on the steps)* Is the Old Man here? *(She spots him.)* I'd like to talk to you alone for a minute.

THE OLD MAN   Is it something important?

ESTHER   It's important to me.

THE OLD MAN   I have no secrets from my granddaughter . . . at least none that you could share with me.

ESTHER   Well, as far as I'm concerned, Ania may listen. . . . All I have to say is that I am leaving the hospice today.

THE OLD MAN   Yes.

ESTHER   What does 'yes' mean? What do you mean again with that 'yes'?! Did you understand me: I am leaving you . . . forever . . . going away . . . and Kaspar is going with me!

THE OLD MAN   And Kaspar is going with you.

ESTHER   Thank God it seems to make no special impression on you. Now, I have the peculiar love declarations which you made me almost daily since I was 7 years old, and which, to be frank, I never took too seriously.

THE OLD MAN   That was wrong of you.

ESTHER   You're letting me leave like some ordinary guest.

THE OLD MAN   The only question is how we

can most appropriately fill the gaps left in our program by your and Kaspar's going away. Perhaps Gimietto and Eliza are talented enough to help us out with a solo.

ESTHER   So those are the only thoughts that move you at this moment?! . . . Oh, I never overestimated your capacity for being hurt! That's how you are: stiff, dead, terminally unkind! How deficient your love is in the warmth of life, how artificial and stilted your passion is! This is how he lets me go! And still *dares* to maintain his shameless assertion that he once loved me!

THE OLD MAN   (*Very ponderously, very slowly*) Esther, what do you think I have experienced with all the children I have raised? What do you think that I have yet to experience with all the dear children who are now with me? . . . Already so many are gone from me: I could not stop them. . . . But perhaps you will come back.

ESTHER   (*Convulsively*) No . . . I will not come back! Once I'm out of here . . . no, no . . . no coming back . . . no, no, no, no. . . . And now I have to pack. I don't own much; but what I do own I have to pack it all. For I am not coming back. I must certainly buy lots of new things in town at once, lots of outfits which I'll need there. There of course I can't go out in the black and grey smocks everybody wears around here. Red outfits . . . red and green and yellow outfits. (*She turns around, goes up the steps, to the door. At the door she turns to* ANIA, *for the first time since her entrance. Now her voice becomes more gentle.*) Ania . . . if you could perhaps help me with my packing . . . ?

ANIA   (*Preparing to get up*) Gladly. . . .

ESTHER   (*Suddenly impetuous and shrill again*) I mean . . . actually it's not a lot of work. But it makes me nervous when there's somebody else around. Stay, stay and sit. (*She goes into the house, without looking back.*)

THE OLD MAN   (*Walks to* ANIA, *looks at the now bowed seated figure*) Now I will leave Ania alone. Now no one should talk to her. If you can weep, Ania, then weep. Now no one is looking at you. (*He goes.*)

(*A short while* ANIA *sits, without moving. Then a distant sound of distant steps. The children come back from their walk. They have little grey capes over their suits and dresses.* JAKOB *is leading the first of the girls. When he sees* ANIA *sitting, he runs over to her, leaving the little girl*

standing centre stage. Meanwhile the rest of the Indian file goes, chattering and laughing, up the steps and into the house.*)

JAKOB   You look so odd sitting like that. . . . Shall I bring you a cushion?

ANIA   No, thanks.

JAKOB   You're freezing and trembling for real. I'll bring you warm blankets.

ANIA   No, just go. Little Eliza is waiting for you. You have to give the children their singing lesson.

JAKOB   (*Goes up to the little girl, takes her by the hand and leads her up the steps, behind the others. But at the door he turns once more.*) But if I can be of any help. . . .

ANIA   No . . . no . . . thank you. . . .

(JAKOB *disappears into the house*)

ANIA   (*Sits still, stares in space. She evens out the berries in the dish with both hands*) And one – asks the other – whether he might – help *in any way.* – And he cannot. – (*She slowly stands up; slowly goes step by step to the main entrance. At the door she staggers, as if attacked by a sudden weakness. The dish falls from her hand, shatters on the flagstones. She sinks, weeping loudly, as if shaken by physical pain, against the pillars. – The two old* ATTENDANTS *run in a hurry out of the house, drawn by the noise.*)

THE ATTENDANTS   O dear, o dear . . . the lovely berries on the ground . . . and shards all over and the dish kaput. . . . What will the dear children have for dessert now? (*They bend over to collect the berries.*)

## Seventh Tableau

*The scene of the first and fourth tableaux*

Amid lots of suitcases stacked up center stage stands ESTHER in travelling clothes. She is dressed with a forceful vigour that has a grotesque charm, with long leather gloves, a belted overcoat, a man's hat and a walking-stick. – ANIA, dressed as ever, stands to the side.*

ESTHER   At first you'll feel rather hard done by when you miss your brother Kaspar. You were, after all, more closely bound to him than you knew yourself. In so many things you are alike, and your differences cancel each other out in so happy a manner than one can hardly imagine one of you without the other. *(Her voice is a monotone, her eyes fixed.)*

ANIA   Yes . . . it will be hard.

ESTHER   *(Suddenly sits on a suitcase, as if she can no longer stand because of fatigue)* Now that I have to go, so many things suddenly come to my mind . . . quite insignificant little experiences we shared . . . years ago perhaps. They crowd in upon me for real.

ANIA   I've been thinking about it too: we were still little girls. . . .

ESTHER   And you looked like a boy, with your short black hair . . . like a serious boy. . . .

ANIA   How we dared to feed the animals the first time with the Old Man. . . .

ESTHER   And the big eagle bit me in the finger.

ANIA   It bled.

ESTHER   Yes, it bled. But then you stood behind me and prepared white cotton and took care of me. And it was a serious boy caring for his bride.

ANIA   In the first years you couldn't leave off making up your face.

ESTHER   Yes . . . how often you hid my lipstick. . . .

ANIA   You had been used to it at home.

ESTHER   Mama liked to see it, but when Papa came home, he'd howl with rage.

ANIA   Red lipstick over your eyes and blue streaks under them: that's how you danced.

ESTHER   We practised together, in those days it was Wolf who wielded the switch!

ANIA   And you wielded it next. . . .

*(Short pause.)*

ESTHER   What ever became of Wolf?

ANIA   Maybe you'll run into him somewhere. He'll be dancing . . . tap . . . dancing. . . .

ESTHER   Marie Thérèse was here too in those days. She had such a white little face. . . .

ANIA   How she loved you. . . . Whenever you came into the room, she'd make a really evil, mean face, out of sheer love.

ESTHER   Then she died young.

ANIA   In those days your psychotic mother would come on a visit every so often. In her grey carriage she would drive up. . . .

ESTHER   And the milky pearls clicked on her neck.

ANIA   The Old Man was exquisitely polite to her.

ESTHER   He'd plod down to the carriage door, help her out and laugh at her in his beard.

ANIA   Mama would stroke your hair, staring at it with very clouded eyes. Her eyes didn't want to see anything any more.

ESTHER   When she was away, the Old Man kneeled down to us and spoke ploddingly about his love. I was alarmed by all the endearments, whenever that big red mouth in the beard would come close to me.

ANIA   Your poor mother was soon put in a madhouse.

ESTHER   But in those days, I think, you had long hair. Right from the start you had it braided just like now . . . so thick at the nape. I can barely imagine you with a different hair style.

ANIA   That's the way I always wore it.

ESTHER   When the three of us would go for a walk, Kaspar and you and I! We were like crazy and angered all the farmers and danced all our dances in the meadows and even on the highways.

ANIA   All our dances – we had so many. We'd think up new ones every day. Everything we experienced we could express through them. But basically we always experienced the same thing in colorful variations.

ESTHER   When we and Gert worked on the jumping-jack pantomime, we'd dance it in the little front gardens of the farmhouses. And Kaspar would shout his poems and accompaniment. . . . We shouted all his poems. . . .

ANIA   And when the farmers tried to thrash us, I had only to throw them a serious look. . . .

ESTHER   And because you had such proper manners . . .

ANIA   They let us go!

*(They both laugh. –* THE FEMALE ATTENDANTS *come from the park.)*

ONE ATTENDANT   Fräulein Esther's carriage is waiting. We'll carry the bags.

*(Each one picks up one of the many suitcases and hobbles to the door with it.)*

ESTHER   *(Panicked, as if shocked)* The carriage . . . the carriage . . . ?

THE ATTENDANTS  *(Already at the door)* Yes, yes, yes, the carriage to ride in, little Fräulein, the carriage *to ride in! (They disappear into the park.)*

ESTHER  *(Hand on brow)* The carriage to ride in . . . the carriage to ride in . . .

ANIA  *(Goes slowly to the door, turns around at the door, looks at* ESTHER*)* Esther . . . I want to ask you something else: if you . . . out there . . . should have a child . . . please send it to the Old Man in the hospice.

ESTHER  *(Laughs much too loudly)* But where did you get such an idea? What makes you think I might have a child?

ANIA  For it's just as dangerous for the child, I've been thinking about this, as it is for the work of art . . . that Kaspar wants to create out there, our work of art, born of passionate surrender to life, but always with a longing for home. *(In an uninhibited, but broader and purer rapture)*: And your child, who knows what it will be like. *If the frailest body receive the seed, it may perhaps bear the most precious fruit.*

ESTHER  *(Confused amid the suitcases)* But a child . . . but what makes you think I 'd have a child??

ANIA  And you will long for home, I know that too *(Very quietly, before making her exit)*: that I know. . . .

ESTHER  *(Stands, her eyes blinded by tears. When* ANIA *is gone, she suddenly realizes she is alone, turns in shock to the door)*: Ania . . . Ania, where are you? *(She strikes her hands before her face.)* But I can't go away from here . . . I *can* not . . . what should I do out there? What *am I supposed* to do? . . . Ania, come back, my dear Ania! Did I ever insult you? . . . You know how I meant it. Did I ever cry out it is your fault? . . . You know whose fault it is! . . . Come, come, come, come. . . . What am I going to do without you? I can't go tap-dancing. . . . And a child? What did you say about a child? . . . I'm only a dancer . . . I can't have children . . . Ania! My dear Ania!

*(*THE ATTENDANTS *come back to pick up another suitcase.)*

ESTHER  Don't . . . don't take down any more bags! Don't . . . no . . . I won't be going away . . .

ATTENDANT  Yes, should we bring back the other two suitcases?

ESTHER  No . . . yes, I don't know . . . I don't know. . . . A big eagle bit me in the hand . . . Ania had prepared white cotton . . . and was a serious boy . . . and took care of me . . . What shall I do? God in Heaven: what shall I do?!

*(*ERIK *comes in from the park. He is carrying a bouquet of colourful autumn flowers. He is dressed the same as ever.)*

ESTHER  *(Relieved to see him)* Erik!! Erik, there you are! *(She runs to him, throws herself round his neck, nestles close to him.)* I had forgotten you . . . I had forgotten your body . . . your voice, your face, your flesh. . . . Oh, that you're here! Oh, that you're alive . . . alive, you breathe, you laugh. . . . You've brought me flowers . . . colourful flowers . . . thank you. . . . *(She lets the flowers fall to the floor.)*

ERIK  You're out of breath. We must be off, we'll miss our connection. . . .

ESTHER  Don't talk – give me your mouth . . . give me your hands. . . . I thought I couldn't go away from here . . . I'd forgot what will bind me to life . . . your voice, your face, your living flesh. . . .

THE ATTENDANTS  *(Hobbling and giggling they take the suitcases out)* Na, now it's all as it was . . . you see, little Fräulein . . . all right again. . . .

ERIK  *(Caresses the shuddering woman)* I'll kiss you all during the ride . . . during the ride in a jolting car I'll kiss you . . . Kaspar will sit across from us and look a little dismayed at that. The Old Man will sit across from us. . . . He'll accompany us part of the way . . . but he'll laugh. So, now you have to say your goodbyes to the children, to Jakob, to the beasts. . . . So . . . I'll kiss you all during the journey. . . .

ESTHER  *(Pulls back her head, laughs in his face, her arms still slung about his neck)* You will kiss me all during the ride . . . all during the ride . . . and out there . . . and when we tap-dance. . . . *(Suddenly lays her head on his breast, very quietly)* Erik, my love, do you really believe that I will have a child? *(She laughs, pulls away from him)* Now I want to say good-bye to the kids. Wait . . . I bought them some chocolate! *(She runs out.* ERIK *looks after her, laughing.)*

*(*KASPAR *comes in from the park. He is also in travelling clothes, which must not be too loud.)*

KASPAR  Isn't Esther here? . . . I thought I heard her voice . . . and she was laughing too. . . .

ERIK  Yes, she laughed at the end. . . .

KASPAR  *(Very labouriously)* Erik . . . Erik . . . she told you things that others might want to tell you . . . she says it all, she laughs and she cries over you . . . and all others can do is thank you. But maybe words unspoken are the darkest and most passionate.

ERIK  To me . . . Kaspar . . . to me anyone may say . . . whatever he likes . . . and I understand the unspoken words as well as the spoken ones . . . I mean, I don't understand any of them. That's how things are with me . . . and sometimes I think, nothing people say gets through to me, *right* through to me, you know. And yet it fills me up, sometimes I'm totally drunk on all they have given me. . . . Without understanding any of it. . . .

KASPAR  If I can manage to create something out in the world, something I could *not* create here . . . then at least you'll know that you gave me the strength to do it. If I accomplish anything, Erik, you should always know that I have you to thank for it.

ERIK  Yes . . . you've got something . . . you will achieve something. . . . But sometimes I wonder, not very often, but sometimes, what have *I really got?* *(He suddenly laughs.)* But what am I talking about? . . . We have to leave. *(He is about to go out, while* KASPAR *stands silently in place. But* JAKOB *runs into him in the doorway.)*

JAKOB  *(In his gruffest and most distorted voice)* I'd like to talk to you.

ERIK  Yes, I wanted to say goodbye to you too. But you know, I've got only a little time left.

JAKOB  *(Sharply to* KASPAR*)* Kaspar, will you please leave? . . . You can see that I have something to say to Herr Erik.

KASPAR  Yes . . . excuse me . . . *(Rapt in thought, he goes into the park.)*

ERIK  So formal . . . ?

JAKOB  I assume you know that from my earliest youth, which means, since she and I met here in the hospice, I have been on the most intimate terms of friendship with Ania.

ERIK  Yes . . . I know . . . I mean: if you say so, then it must be so. . . .

JAKOB  You have seen Ania. Anyone who sees her must guess who she is. Anyone who has once seen those eyes must guess *what* she is.

ERIK  I've seen her . . . sure, right from the start in the park. . . . She was standing in the dark shrubbery like a holy image. . . .

JAKOB  Needless to say, you could not make even a rough estimate of what I owe her. If it weren't for Ania I'd be dead or insane today, but that's got nothing to do with you. I'm telling you just so you'll recognize I have the right to reprimand you for your behaviour to Ania.

ERIK  I'm trying as hard as I can but I don't catch your drift.

JAKOB  I don't know who you are. I don't know how you managed to get here. But I do know that here, here in this place, whose air you are not worthy to breathe, here among these people, whose fate you cannot even imagine . . . you have planted doubt, distress, detestable confusion. It's ridiculous, but can things come to pass that the purest, yea, the holiest among us must become the victim of your crass power-play!

ERIK  If I get your drift . . .

JAKOB  The way you play the innocent dreamer offends me. You know that you have maliciously robbed Ania of the only human being to whom she was truly, deeply bound: the girl you took pleasure in seducing: Esther.

ERIK  But I didn't seduce Esther. . . . But I don't want to hurt Ania. . . .

JAKOB  Since God endowed you with attractions of a crude sort you didn't have to call on your modicum of intelligence to attract this girl. The fluid which simply emanates from your body was quite sufficient to draw Esther into your arms. On your suggestion, I assume, she turned away from Ania like a brutal child. . . . Then, as if this act of cruelty *still* hadn't slaked your capricious thirst for power, you casually took from Ania . . . from Ania you casually took the only other person who is not alien to her on this earth, you took her brother. All the base instincts in the strangely blended blood he inherited from an infamous father, you stirred up in him. You made yourself his master . . . casually . . . casually as if the girl weren't enough for you, you robbed Ania of the other person for whom she had feelings . . . like flies they both succumbed to your stupid power. And now she is alone!! *(He shouts shrilly in deep despair.)* And now Ania is *entirely* alone!!

ERIK   *(Not to him, but quietly to himself)* His view of these things is incredible. But that's not really how things are. In the very beginning it was Ania's hand I kissed. What about Esther? And Kaspar? . . . I had nothing to do with it. . . . I don't understand him.

JAKOB   *(Shouts)* That's why I call you to account: because you, an audacious intruder, has robbed this saint of the only persons who bound her to our earth!

ERIK   But . . . but she still has you . . . you, Jakob . . .

JAKOB   *(His head droops, very quietly)* Me? . . . No . . . she has nothing to do with me. . . . Maybe she feels sorry for my torments . . . not me, no, not me. . . . *(He stands suddenly disconcerted, his head bowed.)*

ERIK   *(Lifts his hand as if to caress him)* You shouldn't say any more.

JAKOB   *(Recoils, shouts again)* Don't touch me! For God's sake, don't you touch me! I am afraid of your flesh! Your flesh is to blame for it all! Your flesh . . . Your seven-times damned flesh has made Ania unhappy! I would enjoy punishing your flesh! I would take wrathful pleasure in chastizing your flesh! Maybe everything will be all right again after I've taken your life! *(He pulls a long, dangerously tapering revolver out of his pocket, and aims it at* ERIK.*)*

ERIK   *(In the most primal, intense fear of death, staggering back, his arms before his face)* Don't shoot! For God's sake, don't shoot! Please, please, don't shoot! What have I done wrong? . . . Don't . . . don't. . . .

JAKOB   *(Stops, gloating over his fear, then points the revolver at him again)* What have you done? . . . You have lured the girl that Ania loved, probably so you could pocket Esther's fortune. It's just occurred to me: it's *highly* likely you did it for the money! . . . That's why I take pleasure in punishing your flesh . . . that's why I pull the trigger!!!

ERIK   *(Screams)* Help! Help me! Murder! I haven't done anything wrong! He's trying to kill me!

*(At this moment* THE OLD MAN, ESTHER *and* ANIA *enter through the door left.* THE OLD MAN *also wears a sort of travelling outfit, a big hat and over his usual clothes an old, black, coarse woollen water-proof overcoat. He is leading little* ELIZA *by the hand.)*

THE OLD MAN   *(Laughing)* Oh . . . what sort of rumpus and noisy farce is this? What's the cause of all the disturbance?

ERIK   *(Still gasping)* Thank you for coming. . . . He's behaving so funny. . . . I really don't know what he's after . . . and I'm still so on edge. . . .

JAKOB   *(His revolver down, looks very startled at* THE OLD MAN*)* Yes, . . . yes, you're going away too?

THE OLD MAN   *(Still laughing)* Going away? Why should I be going away? . . . I'm escorting the young couple and my dear grandson as far as the next station. It's the proper thing for a good grandfather to do. And Eliza will take part in this pleasure trip.

ANIA   *(To* JAKOB*)* Won't you come down to the carriage?

JAKOB   *(Frantic)* No . . . no, unfortunately, I positively cannot. I *have* to call the children together now. It's just time for their singing lesson. *(He holds out his hand to* ESTHER.*)* Unfortunately . . . I . . . positively . . . cannot. . . . Adieu, Esther!

ESTHER   *(Already at the door, ignores the extended hand)* Adieu . . . yes . . . adieu, Jakob.

*(With a cloak over her arm and carrying many little packages, she goes into the park.* THE OLD MAN *follows, holding* ELIZA *by the hand.)*

ERIK   But you might give *me* your hand, Jakob. What you were getting at before, I don't quite understand. I think you were talking total rubbish. But I don't want to leave on bad terms with anyone here, so you may as well give me your hand.

JAKOB   *(Beats a rapid retreat to the door)* Your hand . . . no . . . not your hand. . . . I told you before: I am afraid . . . I am very much afraid of your flesh. . . . But I can still wish you the very best of luck. I hope things go well with you, most of the time anyway. . . . Adieu. *(He is gone.)*

ANIA   Was he insulting you, Erik?

ERIK   To tell the truth, I think he's sick. He accused me of all sorts of things I never dreamt of.

ANIA   He was probably talking about me. You mustn't hold it against him.

ERIK   No – no, I don't hold it against him. But he said that I intended to hurt you and offend you horribly. That was not my intention. You know better than I that it wasn't. And the way things have worked out with Esther and with Kaspar too: God is my witness, it was none of my doing. To put the blame on me means you don't believe in fate. The very first morning it was your hand I kissed . . .

ANIA   *(Hastily)* Let's not talk about that now . . . for Esther's sake don't . . .

ESTHER's voice   *(From the park)* Ania . . . Erik! Why aren't you coming?

ANIA   We have only a very little time left . . . listen: the horses are pawing the ground, the whip cracks, the coachman on the box is clearing his throat. . . . I feel as if I had a lot to say to you. . . . But maybe it's only this: . . . We have so little time . . . Maybe all I had to say to you is *that you should love Esther as deeply as you can . . . you should stay with her as long as you can. . . .*

ERIK   Yes, because you ask it . . . thanks, I'll try. . . . *(Suddenly bends and picks up the flowers which* ESTHER *had dropped.)* Here are some flowers I picked for you. For you, Ania. Esther thought they were meant for her. But I picked them for you . . . take them. . . .

ANIA   *(Strokes the flowers)* Thank you . . . I'll keep them by me. . . .

ERIK   *(Kisses her hand)* I've been so struck by what Jakob was saying before . . . for, if ever I . . . loved a woman. . . .

ANIA   *(Starts to go)* Now . . . now I still have to say goodbye to Esther.

*(She leaves the flowers lying on the chair. She runs out.* ERIK *follows her.)*
*(After a short while the two* FEMALE ATTENDANTS *run in at right, waving red handkerchiefs.)*

THE ATTENDANTS   *(Running across the stage)* Now the carriage is driving away . . . Fräulein Esther and Herr Kaspar are driving away in the carriage! *(They stand and wave.)*

JAKOB   *(Comes through the door the same way, walks over to them)* Are they gone yet?

THE ATTENDANTS   *(Hobbling back across the room, the handkerchiefs now before their* faces*)* They're gone now. And Fräulein Ania is standing by the side of the road waving and waving. . . . *(They have hobbled out.)*

JAKOB   *(Repeats almost mechanically)* Waving . . . and waving. . . . The Old Man was as calm as if he were carved out of stone. He even laughed. Fate runs past his eyes . . . and runs – and goes on running forever. But his eyes know everything. That's why they gaze so strangely. . . . And I pulled a revolver. And still don't know anything . . . and I am the fool who reared up on his hind legs. And he is as impassive as if carved out of stone. And I am the fool who stands outside and shouts.

*(ANIA enters slowly.)*

JAKOB   Are they out of sight?

ANIA   Yes, they're gone now. . . . The children are already waiting for us.

JAKOB   They're sitting in the dining room.

ANIA   Eliza won't be there. She's gone with the Old Man. *(They have gone into the back room.)*

*(The song of the children begins clearly backstage.)*

'Merry-making in the village,
The gardener the grass will mow,
An organ peals in tones so low,
Sound blends into gold sunshine,
Sound and shine.
Love sets its seal on bread and wine.'

*(Suddenly* ESTHER *comes running from the park, out of breath. She seems to be looking for something in the room, finds the bouquet of flowers on the chair, grabs it and rushes out the door into the back room. The boys and girls are sitting at the table – grouped as at the meal in the first tableau: the boys their backs to the audience, the girls facing it. – They are wearing their white smocks and attentively turn their eyes to the notebooks lying in front of them on the table. On the throne in their midst sits* ANIA, JAKOB *stands behind her. – Everyone gazes in astonishment at* ESTHER *who hastens to* ANIA.*)*

ESTHER   *(Completely out of breath, to* ANIA*)* Yes – I made them stop the carriage . . . something occurred to me. Erik made me a gift of these flowers, and I'd left them here. Then I suddenly thought that I ought to give them to *you* . . . you . . . Erik's flowers. *(She lays them before* ANIA, *on top of the table.)*

ANIA   *(Grinning broadly)* Thank you . . . yes . . . thank you.

ESTHER   *(Turns, with nothing else to say. Goes, trudging now and with head bowed, to the door. She stops once again.)* Yes . . . this is how I'll preserve you in my memory. . . . I'll never forget this picture: you sitting like a saint amid the children and that misshapen archangel behind you . . . it'll live in my heart. *(Listening, very brightly)* Erik? . . . Yes, yes, Erik . . . I'm coming. . . . *(She runs out.)*

ANIA   Now let's go on singing. . . . Are you crying, Gimietto? Are you crying because Kaspar has gone away? . . . Sing, sing. . . .

THE CHILDREN SING   *(Attentively looking at their notebooks)*

'In a group of maidens sneaks,
And at the last the rooster crows.
A rusty grating gently creaks.
In crown and garlands twined of rose,
Garlands twined of rose,
Doth Mary, pale and thin, repose.'

*(Meanwhile* ANIA *caresses the flowers.)*

END

# Documents

*From Klaus Mann,* Der Wendepunkt. Ein Lebensbericht, *Reinbek bei Hamburg, Rowohlt, 1984, pp. 163–6*

Erika was very young and so were Pamela and Gustaf Gründgens. We were still half children, when we found ourselves together in Hamburg, to perform my play *Ania and Esther*. Gründgens[1] was the multi-faceted star of the Hamburg Kammerspiele, which, under the direction of Erich Ziegel,[2] had developed into a literary stage of the first rank. It glittered and sparkled with the talent of the charming, fanciful, delightful, flirtatious Gustaf! All Hamburg was responsive to his magic. What versatility! What virtuosity in dialogue, mimicry, bearing! His repertory embraced all genres and periods [. . . ] He was an actor *par excellence*.

In one of his mercurial, intense moods he fell in love with my play; he was particularly taken with the idea of putting on *Ania and Esther* with Erika and Pamela in the title roles. And I, the author, was to take part as well. Gustaf had got it into his head. His invitation, which reached me in the form of a tempestuous telegram, came as a complete surprise. I had never thought of trying my hand as an actor. But then why not? It would be a new adventure, a charming experiment . . . I agreed, speaking for Pamela and Erika as well.

The first meeting with Gustaf remains unforgettable. With the dash of a neurotic Hermes he burst into our hotel room. So light-footed were his steps that one could not help but glance mistrustfully at his somewhat worn-out but somehow very chic sandals. Were there tiny wings on them? No; it was no ancient garb of the gods that draped his shoulders with noble nonchalance, just a rather shabby leather overcoat.

He was handsome, with a straight, rather too fleshy nose, proud lips, jutting chin; everything was of pure and forceful form. The slight distortion of his expression was traceable to the monocle which he wore on account of extreme myopia. [ . . . ]

If his behaviour towards people, especially those in a position to judge him, was nervously spasmodic and obviously insecure, he acquired all the more self-control and equilibrium in his own sphere of life and work, on the stage. How helpless, how embarrassed I felt when I compared my own ungainly actor's movement with Gustaf's innate and, for all his youth, veteran bravura! I was to play Kaspar, while he was satisfied with the truly thankless role of the gloomily inhibited Jakob. But at the rehearsals he paid scant attention to his own lines, but was first of all the director, who guided and supervised us all with remarkable authority. With what tender care he rehearsed and encouraged Erika! How well he knew how to attract and subdue Pamela! But his hardest work was with me: he showed me how to do everything. "In this passage, Klaus, I'd be somewhat *nastier*. Understand what I mean? A little smile – enigmatic, treacherous . . . no, not that way! Nowhere near nasty enough . . . Try it again!"

The premiere took place in autumn 1925, simultaneously in Hamburg and Munich. In Munich, where Otto Falckenberg[3] had brought out the play at the Kammerspiele, the reaction was spiteful from press and audience alike. Our Hamburg production on the other hand might be called a breakthrough success – at least a rather tumultuous *succès de scandale*. From the shores of the North Sea to Vienna, Prague and Budapest a storm-wind rustled the forest of newspapers: "Authors' offspring indulge in play-acting!" Many of the articles were venomous, while others took a tone of gracious condescension; some critics even conveyed a certain understanding of the intentions and qualities of my play. But whether the commentary was mocking or enthusiastic, we welcomed its abundance for its publicity value. The "authors' offspring" played to full houses

*[This passage in the original manuscript was omitted in the published edition]*

[especially after our portrait appeared on the front page of the extremely popular *Berlin Illustrated*. Such an honour was bestowed only on boxers, generals and film stars; but now it was our made-up faces – mine next to Erika's and Pamela's – that stared back at the German public for a full week from every kiosk in town and country.

[And Gustaf? His picture had originally appeared in the group photo, but was removed by the Berlin editors – without our knowledge of course. He was not an "author's offspring" and therefore not interesting enough . . . What a moment of deadly embarrassment when he discovered the affront! He sat motionless, stiffly erect, his lips pressed together, his face frozen into a pale mask. Not a word, not a gesture – only the mute reproof of his gem-like eyes! He was almost unbearable . . . Did he ever forgive us the offense? Not likely – although there could be no doubt of our innocence. But such things are never forgotten. Incidentally, there were times when, as a refugee, my existence met by deadly silence in Germany, I would have the misfortune to run across a portrait of the great Gründgens on many a front page. Then I'd think, not without cheerful irony, of the painfully constrained deportment, the wondering gaze with which he had once, in the canteen of the Hamburg Kammerspiele, greeted our apologies and the malicious gibes of colleagues.][4]

I can still see Gustaf and me standing backstage, tense, both poised to spring while waiting for our cues. Gustaf looks really imposing in his monkishly stark, dark costume, his eyes a bit crossed with hysteria beneath the baroque adornment of a flame-red wig. He has put an arm around my shoulder; we eavesdrop on the on-stage dialogue, the lyrically moving, passionately pointed duologue between Ania and Esther. "Isn't she wonderful," breathes the man with flaming hair at my side. "Her voice . . . " And I know which of the two voices he means.

I had it good in Hamburg. Days with Erika, Pamela, Gustaf and a colourful assortment of new friends, evenings in the theatre, nights in low dives and sailors' dance-halls in the St Pauli district, just the thing to make me restlessly happy. How long? Six months or eight . . . My restlessness – or my fear of repetition, monotony and ennui – never let me linger in one place, with one circle of friends, one occupation. It moved me on.

*Gustaf Gründgens, "About Klaus Mann," in Der Freihafen (Hamburg), 1925/6, vol. 2, p. 16*

The younger generation has found its poet in Klaus Mann. Everyone accepts this as fact.

In his earlier collection of stories *Before Life Begins* (Hamburg: Enoch Brothers, 1925) there is [. . . ] a marvelous tale: *The Youths*, which, for the first time, illuminated the psychic complexity of our youth with painful objectivity, a youth whose existence, despite all paths to strength and beauty,[5] is not to be explained away. For everyone who has grown up with the younger generation, the astonishing mastery of form in these stories made a great promise which Klaus Mann has brilliantly kept in *Ania and Esther*. With inexorable love he shows his generation in all its knowing ignorance, its inhibited lack of inhibitions, its pure impurity. These children eat early of the Tree of Knowledge and suffer hard for their precocious wisdom; unprotected and open to the most shopworn sensations, they wage a fierce battle to find the right potentiality amidst a thousand options. One must love these persons who have so much love in them and go astray with painful awareness. And with a rueful smile one watches these nine-times-clever ones, their eyes wide open, wreck themselves on Erik, the still uncomplicated "male," the beautiful non-doer who simply exists. Above all, one must love the creator of these persons, who so animated his characters and sadly sent them through this exciting play and did not – like most prophets of today – leave them sitting in a mess, but with helping hand led them to clarity.

And that is the essential thing about this Klaus Mann: he is not only a depictor of the new youth, he should perhaps be called their signpost and guide.

## *Notes*

1 Gustaf Gründgens (1899–1963), one of the most important actors in the history of twentieth-century German theatre, came to the Hamburg Kammerspiele in 1923, and soon was its leading man. Compromising with the Nazis, he remained a prominent actor-manager under Hitler, earning him Klaus Mann's satirical portrait in *Mephisto*.

2 Erich Ziegel (1876–1950) opened the Hamburg Kammerspiele in 1918 with a Wedekind week and turned it into the most distinguished regional German theatre, with an Expressionist repertoire and a company made up of young actors.

3 Otto Falckenberg (1873–1947) who managed the Munich Kammerspiele 1917–1944 began as a specialist in Strindberg and symbolism, seeking "to convey the visionary through the medium of the real."

4 The suppressed passage appears in E. Spangenberg, *Karriere eines Romans. Mephisto, Klaus Mann und Gustaf Gründgens. Ein dokumentarischer Bericht aus Deutschland und dem Exil 1925–1981*, Munich, Ellermann Verlag, 1984, p. 21.

5 An allusion to *Wege zu Kraft und Schönheit*, a government-sponsored feature-length documentary film (1925) promoting calisthenics and gymnastics as the way to the "regeneration of the human race." With its kitschy scenes of naked youths in pseudo-Greek and Roman arenas, it had a certain homoerotic appeal but would have struck such romantics as Mann and Gründgens as absurdly tasteless.